Dancing Down the Barricades

Dancing Down the Barricades

SAMMY DAVIS JR. AND THE LONG CIVIL RIGHTS ERA

A Cultural History

Matthew Frye Jacobson

UNIVERSITY OF CALIFORNIA PRESS

University of California Press
Oakland, California

© 2023 by Matthew Frye Jacobson
First paperback printing 2024
Names: Jacobson, Matthew Frye, 1958- author.
Title: Dancing down the barricades : Sammy Davis Jr. and the long civil
  rights era : a cultural history / Matthew Frye Jacobson.
Description: Oakland, California : University of California Press, [2023] |
  Includes bibliographical references and index.
Identifiers: LCCN 2022028884 (print) | LCCN 2022028885 (ebook) |
  ISBN 9780520391802 (cloth) | ISBN 9780520391819 (ebook)
Subjects: LCSH: Davis, Sammy, Jr., 1925-1990. | African Americans—Civil
  rights—History—20th century. | Entertainers—United States—
  Biography.
Classification: LCC PN2287.D322 J33 2023 (print) | LCC PN2287.D322
  (ebook) | DDC 792.702/8092 [B]—dc23/eng/20220815
LC record available at https://lccn.loc.gov/2022028884
LC ebook record available at https://lccn.loc.gov/2022028885

32   31   30   29   28   27   26   25   24
10   9   8   7   6   5   4   3   2   1

To my many teachers,
including the ones who probably think they were my students

CONTENTS

ILLUSTRATIONS

ACKNOWLEDGMENTS

This has been a journey, as all book projects are, and I am lucky to have had so many fellow travelers. This one has been a longer journey than most, though. Its origins stretch back about twenty years to its conception as a chapter in a different volume that will never be written, as it turns out, languishing under contract for over fifteen years with University of California Press—hah! That book was to be a cultural history of the long Civil Rights era. Its table of contents included a chapter on the integration of baseball (now a documentary film), one on the folk singer Odetta (now a book in the 33 1/3 series), and a book on comedian/activist Dick Gregory (forthcoming). This will conclude my Civil Rights tetralogy, I think. When I went back to the original research folders I had assembled on Davis, I realized that I would have to take this moment to thank my then-research assistant, now a tenured professor at Wesleyan, Megan Glick. Time does get away, doesn't it?

The long gestation of this project has given me plenty of opportunity to take stock of the many influences, models, and important pieces of advice I have gathered over the years. I am grateful to Judy Smith, whose mentoring and friendship have sustained me for nearly forty years across the span of my career, and for the example of her own work, especially *Becoming Belafonte: Black Artist, Public Radical.* I haven't seen Judy nearly as much I would wish in recent years, but I was able to get her close, critical, lifesaving reading of this manuscript. My most systematic analysis of race in US political culture took shape under the tutelage of Bob Lee at Brown University; if I'm lucky, his influence still shows. Early mentors who were responsible for my catching whatever bug it is that leads one to do this kind of work in the first place include David Marr, David Powell, and Richard Jones (all at The Evergreen

State College), and Christopher Wilson and Carol Petillo (at Boston College). A middle-school English teacher named Evelyn Baird once told me that she thought I might one day write a book. I didn't know what to make of it at the time, but I will note that I never did forget it. (Mind what you say to kids.)

As ever, I am challenged, schooled, and energized every day by my ongoing conversations with colleagues at Yale in African American Studies, American Studies, History, and Ethnicity, Race & Migration. I came here in 1995, figuring it would be a good move for me intellectually. Still here, still learning. In the context of this project, special thanks to Jean-Christophe Agnew, Laura Barraclough, Alicia Schmidt Camacho, Hazel Carby, George Chauncey, Aimee Cox, Michael Denning, Kate Dudley, Rod Ferguson, Beverly Gage, Glenda Gilmore, Paul Gilroy, Jay Gitlin, Ron Gregg, Zareena Grewal, Jonathan Holloway, Greta LaFleur, Albert Laguna, Katie Lofton, Lisa Lowe, Mary Lui, Joanne Meyerowitz, Charlie Musser, Tavia Nyong'o, Gary Okihiro, Steve Pitti, Ana Ramos-Zayas, Joe Roach, Marc Robinson, Karin Roffman, Elihu Ruben, Michael Veal, Laura Wexler, and Bryan Wolf. Colleagues in the African American Studies Department hosted a works-in-progress talk and workshop, providing many important suggestions and corrections at an important juncture: thanks to Crystal Feimster, Elizabeth Hinton, Nick Forster, and Gerry Jaynes. My friend, colleague, and department chair, Jackie Goldbsy, is singularly responsible for my returning to this project after many years away. Jackie's interest and encouragement were crucial to my assessment that this little craft might be seaworthy after all. Gabrielle Niederhoffer generously spent time watching archival film with me and teaching me the nomenclature of tap-dance moves. Ella Starkman-Hynes chased down materials at the Schomberg Center for Research in Black Culture and the Billy Rose Division of the New York Public Library—as I thank her for this hard work, I also thank the staffs there as well. Melissa Barton and other staff members of the Beinecke Rare Book and Manuscript Library at Yale were tremendously helpful and generous in locating materials throughout the collection. The mighty Van Truong did an amazing job of scouting images and permissions for the book, and advising on various technical matters. Aaron Green at Easy Song Licensing assisted in locating rightsholders and obtaining permissions for quoted song lyrics; I am also grateful to Hal Leonard LLC for granting rights to reprint lyrics from "Puttin' on the Ritz," "There's a Boat Dat's Leavin' Soon for New York," "She's Got It," and "Why? (The King of Love Is Dead)." Nate Jung gave the manuscript a close read and provided some important framing comments down the home stretch.

This material has taken shape in conversation with students in "Race and American Studies," "Methods and Practices in US Cultural History," "The Politics and Culture of Race in America," and "The Formation of American Culture" over the past two decades and more. There have been scores of them, but I specifically remember instructive conversations on race, the culture industries, or the long Civil Rights era with Wendell Adjetay, Mary Barr, Amy Bass, Robin Bernstein, Lucy Caplan, Brian Distelberg, Anna Duensing, Joshua Feinzig, Francoise Hamlin, Brian Herrera, Micah Jones, Mark Krasovic, Adrian Lentz-Smith, Ben Looker, Lisa McGill, Justin Randolph, Theresa Runstedtler, Taiye Selasi, Eshe Sherley, Katy Stewart, Viet Trinh, and Azmar Williams. I apologize for overlooking anyone, as I surely am.

Josh Kun has been a valued interlocutor and model (his liner notes on Sammy Davis Jr. deserve your attention), and he offered important advice and corrections on this project. Over the years, it has been my luck to call him a good friend as well. If he alone were to find some value in this work, I couldn't ask for more. Gayle Wald, Tom Guglielmo, Melani McAlister, Dara Orenstein, and their students and colleagues in American Studies at George Washington University hosted me for a trial run of this work in 2019, offering helpful commentary, criticism, encouragement, and advice. I have also been fortunate beyond words to be in conversation with many scholars in the national network of the American Studies Association for the last twenty years and more. My thanks for great work, comradeship, and barstool conversations to Rachel Buff, Joel Dinerstein, Farah Jasmine Griffin, Matt Guterl, the late Amy Kaplan, Kara Keeling, Robin Kelley, Mark Naison, David Roediger, Carlo Rotella, Scott Saul, Nikhil Singh, and Jacqueline Stewart.

This project ran parallel to a second project I have been working on since 2018: *Historians Imagine* is a book devoted to the craft, based on interviews with scores of wildly creative practitioners. It has been an honor to work with Patty Limerick on the webinar version of this (and damn fun, too), and I have learned a lot from her along the way. She and our interviewees have surely left a mark on *Dancing Down the Barricades,* as my own practices became inflected by their collective wisdom. In addition to many people thanked above and below, inspiring direction came my way in this context from Laura Briggs, Vince Brown, Michael Cohen, Erin Cole, Phil Deloria, Jack Halberstam, Kelly Lytle Hernandez, Andy Horowitz, Karl Jacoby, Manu Karuka, Ari Kelman, Amitava Kumar, Seth Moglen, Natalia Molina, Dana

Nelson, Deborah Nelson, Franny Nudelman, Jeanie O'Brien, Jenny Price, Leigh Raiford, Andrew Ross, Stephanie Smallwood, and Sherrie Tucker. *That* is some high living.

I owe a huge debt to several scholars, writers, and documentarians whose work on Sammy Davis Jr. gave life to my own reflections and made my researches possible. I especially thank Gerald Early, Wil Haygood, Gary Fishgall, Sam Pollard, and Carole Langer, most of whom I have never met, though inside my own head I have been in silent dialogue with them for some time.

Thanks to Niels Hooper and the fabulous editorial staff and anonymous reviewers at the University of California Press. Very special thanks to Catherine Osborne for her expert handling of the final edits. Her attention to detail, her judgment, and her wordsmithing finesse all made this a much better book. The remaining shortcomings are all my own. Deep thanks to Victoria Baker for her magnificent and obsessive attention to detail on the index.

Thanks to my writing group—the Cocktail Writers—Dan HoSang, Leah Mirakhor, and Chandan Reddy, who got me in front of my computer every single morning, amid a Covid pandemic that knocked so much else off the rails. In defense of the Cocktail Writers, I should explain that there really wasn't all that much drinking. But there was always the *promise* of drinking, and sometimes that's just what you need. Cheers, you guys.

My father, Jerry Jacobson, has always given my work a refreshingly uncritical read, which is pretty great. More important have been his love, his boundless encouragement, and the model of his own intellectual curiosity. And his love of twentieth-century music and film. He brought the New York jazz scene of his youth into the Boulder, Colorado suburbs of my own, and it seems to have stuck. My late mother, Sarah Frye Jacobson, would have been deeply amused that I spun a serious book out of many of the "texts" she and I shared from the family room couch the year I was home from school with rheumatic fever in fourth grade—*The Mike Douglas Show, Rowan and Martin's Laugh-In, Hollywood Palace, The Patty Duke Show, I Dream of Jeannie*. But even amid the tinny annoyance of TV's canned laugh tracks, I learned a lot about patience, life, and contemplation from her that year, and every year. I cherish her example and her memory. My children, Nick and Tess—now grown, holy cow!—have always kept an appropriate distance from my work, but they've always been in my corner, too. As I have tried to be in theirs, with love. Something of their wry humor is probably in here.

Daphne Brooks has been an inspiration and a beautiful fellow traveler through these past years. Every year, for sure, but especially the pandemic years, when we shared a house and a level of isolation that I could not imagine enduring with anyone else in the world. True. Her brilliance, her depth of knowledge, her passion for music and performance culture, her joy in inquiry, and her lively sense of humor—including some serious shade—all deepened the pleasure of this project, and surely made it better, too. Every day with Dr. Brooks is a master class—I'll say that out loud every chance I get. Thanks for every bit of it. (Don't jinx it.)

AUTHOR'S NOTE

"Why do you get to be on the stage?" a famous African American singer once asked me in advance of an academic panel devoted to another very famous African American singer. It struck me as a fair question, and a good one: she was referencing my whiteness. The same might be asked of my work on Sammy Davis Jr. The simplest answer is, if I didn't believe that book learning could be productive, I never would have become a historian in the first place. Consider this a historian's studied meditation on a life very different from his own—which, after all, is what historians mostly do.

The more complicated answer would have to acknowledge the long and problematic history of white writers who have coopted or capitalized on African American subjects, and also of white readers who have fetishized black figures in burnishing their own liberal self-image. One enters a landscape that is already densely peopled, and not always by role models. It is incumbent upon the white writer of African American history ever to keep sight of her own social location, to recognize and resist appropriation in all its forms, to reckon in every moment with his participation in the structures of whiteness. When someone asks, "Why do you get to be on the stage?," in other words, to understand with some humility exactly what is being asked and to claim nothing beyond archival work and book learning. The trick is to recognize how and when to mobilize one's own humanity as a resource, and to recognize how and when the social location of whiteness will be an impediment—to know which are the things you cannot know, and to understand that you are entering a racialized field of power relations simply by virtue of writing *about* a racialized field of power relations.

At the end of the day, I find myself leaning heavily on Pat Parker's great, paradoxical intervention in "For the White Person Who Wants to Know How to Be My Friend":

The first thing you do is forget that i'm Black.
Second, you must never forget that i'm Black.[1]

When "writing while white," one must be vigilant about the ideological work performed by one's own words and formulations. I embark upon this book as a historian of a country forged in racism, convinced that Davis's life usefully and perhaps uniquely illuminates the workings of race in the twentieth-century culture industries. Like my previous books, *Dancing Down the Barricades* is about the United States' political culture writ large, and about the potent poisons that endure at its core.

I'd been marching since I was seventeen. Long before there was
a civil rights movement I was marching through the lobby of
the Waldorf-Astoria, of the Sands, the Fontainebleau, to a table
at the Copa. And I'd marched alone. Worse. Often to black
derision.

—SAMMY DAVIS JR.

A disturbing moment troubles the opening scenes of *Sergeants 3*, the Rat
Pack's 1962 western based on Rudyard Kipling's *Gunga Din*. Shortly after the
opening credits, Sammy Davis Jr., as an ex-slave named Jonah, stands atop the
bar in a western saloon, shuffling and playing a bugle to the mixed jeers and
encouragement of the white cowboys who fill the room. "Why don't you
dance?," a menacing mountain man type demands. Jonah responds with a
nifty time step before a second man shouts, "I'd rather hear him play!" The
room erupts in rivalling chants of "Play!" and "Dance!" "Gentlemen," Jonah
laughs nervously, "now I can either play, or I can dance. But I can't—" A gruff
voice interrupts: "Oh yeah you can. [Cocks his rifle.] You can play *and*
dance." Which Jonah does, amid riotous and derisive laughter. A gunshot
rings out; a puff of dust indicates a bullet hitting the bartop a few inches from
his feet. This effectively ends the scene, as the gunshot fetches the intervention of the titular sergeants—Davis's Rat Pack buddies Frank Sinatra, Dean
Martin, and Peter Lawford—from the bordello upstairs and attention rapidly shifts, ending the coerced bullet dance about one minute in.

Most discomfiting to today's viewer will be that this is all played for laughs,
mere "hijinks" or "antics" from the Rat Pack. The trope of the "bullet dance" in

comedic form has been common enough in popular culture, from Yosemite Sam and Bugs Bunny to *The Simpsons,* and so the comic sense alone is familiar here, though when added to the undercurrent of racial violence it rankles. But the scene becomes all the more unsettling if one knows, first, that the bullet dance was in fact lived history in the United States (predating even *Gunga Din*), and second, *that Sammy Davis Jr. himself had once endured it.* While in the army at Fort Francis E. Warren in Cheyenne, Wyoming, Davis was suspected by a group of white soldiers of paying "improper" attentions to a white WAC captain. "What you gotta learn," one of his tormenters told him, "is that black is black and it don't matter how white it looks or feels, it's still black. . . ." After assaulting Davis and writing "I'm a nigger" across his chest and "Coon" across his forehead in white paint, the ringleader pulled his weapon and instructed, "Dance, Sambo." Reports Davis, "I started moving my feet and tapping. . . ."[1]

One has to wonder exactly what Davis was experiencing as he played a similar scene for laughs a mere twenty years later. How to read the confluence of comedy and coercion in a text like this? From the historical reality of the bullet dance in antebellum North America, to its menacing replication in a racial skirmish on an Army base during World War II, to its putatively comic refrain in a lighthearted adventure film in the 1960s, the telescoping of historical time and the condensation of racialized meanings is what most interests me in *Dancing Down the Barricades.* "During slavery the master wanted to protect his investment," Southern Tenant Farmers' Union organizer John Handcox once said, reflecting on the limitations and false promises of emancipation. "When we was freed, they just let us loose, and didn't care what happened to us. Whites started hangin' and shootin' blacks. The way I see it, under slavery we used to be the master's slave, but after slavery we became everybody's slave."[2] The character of Jonah might surely have agreed, as he danced atop the bar. But as white supremacy persisted and evolved across a century and more after slavery, Davis, too, had to reckon with what "emancipation" might yet mean, and how performance itself could be an instrument of bare survival or of more complete liberation amid the perpetual enforcement of white supremacy—whether the frank and brutal version at Fort Warren or the subtler coercion on the soundstage of *Sergeants 3.*

It has been supremely challenging, in the face of the constant emergencies and the grotesque uncertainties of the twenty-first century, to address questions of race and justice by turning to a figure like Sammy Davis Jr. Any reader might be forgiven for asking, amid surging white nationalism and the urgency of the Black Lives Matter movement, *why Davis, why now?* The beginning of an answer lies in the arc of Davis's career. This means not only its span from the 1920s through the 1980s, but its continual evolution and transposition, from the vaudeville stage, to the nightclub and casino circuit, to the recording studio, to Hollywood and Broadway, to television, to publishing. Davis moved through practically every kind of space and genre that the culture industries provided, and so his career illuminates with unusual clarity the workings of race in these industries across a wide swath of the twentieth century. He became a kind of palimpsest of American culture writ large, a page upon which the traces of many varied and successive texts can still be read. His performance repertoire was a unique site where minstrel actors like Bert Williams, blackface jazz singers like Al Jolson, blues singers like Ethel Waters, Borscht Belt comedians like Eddie Cantor, pop singers like Frank Sinatra and Nat King Cole, and Chitlin' Circuit performers like Pigmeat Markham all met and mingled. He was associated in the public mind with outlaw lovers like Mildred and Richard Loving, he befriended social observers like James Baldwin, and was admired by political figures as diverse as Martin Luther King Jr. and Richard Nixon. Over the years he shared spaces with Bill "Bojangles" Robinson, Mickey Rooney, Eartha Kitt, Milton Berle, Otto Preminger, Marilyn Monroe, Muhammad Ali, Harry Belafonte, Ed Sullivan, Elvis Presley, Donald Rumsfeld, and Jimi Hendrix. Davis was both adored and despised in ways that themselves reward study. How race operated in this singular life generates a granular understanding of the twentieth-century color line more broadly.

Dancing Down the Barricades is neither a work of criticism nor a conventional biography. That work has been accomplished beautifully in books by writers like Gerald Early and Wil Haygood, and in liner notes by Josh Kun. Rather, I conceive this foray as one of those figure-and-ground puzzles that, depending on how you look at it, seems at once to be an ornate, sculpted vase and to be two faces in profile. The "figure" in this instance is Davis in particular aspects of his career: the minstrel, the actor, the entertainer, the celebrity. The "ground," meanwhile, is the social and cultural surround that gave shape to his life and work and that lent racialized meaning to his every move. These elements include the vaudeville circuit, Hollywood liberalism, contending racial narratives as "the American Creed" gave way to Black Power, and the Movement itself. The intent here is to shed light not only on Davis's singular life (figure) but on the textures of racialized cultural politics across the twentieth century (ground), and further, too, on the more general matter of how an individual *inhabits* an encompassing history that can run years, decades, and even centuries deep in its salience. The past is what the present is made of, and elements of Davis's twentieth-century present cannot be extracted from the deep histories that produced it: late-nineteenth-century entertainments, antebellum slavery, eighteenth-century citizenship law, seventeenth-century racialized marriage codes, and indeed the fugitivity that had characterized black life in the diaspora reaching back to 1619.

There was a time when the phrase "Civil Rights era" was taken to encompass the period between the *Brown v. Board of Education* decision in 1954 and the Voting Rights Act of 1965 (or perhaps the King assassination in 1968). We now know that this is far too narrow a frame. It occludes the continuities and struggles across a longer span of time; it misleads by foregrounding the South at the expense of a rich history of African American organizing around schools, housing, employment, and *de facto* segregation in the North; and it privileges clerical, mostly male leaders at the expense of the scores of radical women activists who organized in neighborhoods in Philadelphia, Detroit, or Chicago and who may have taken inspiration from Garveyism or the CIO. But more importantly, the shorter timeline promotes a politically charged lie that the move toward racial justice emanated magnanimously from the federal government, ignoring Frederick Douglass's famous dictum that power concedes nothing without a struggle.[3]

Though Sammy Davis Jr. was no Frederick Douglass when it came to theorizing the dispositions of power, still the path he cut through the twentieth century demonstrates the contested legacy of the emancipation for which Douglass fought. One important feature of Davis's arc has to do with the nature of his assimilationism, a tacit politics that endeared him to many white people but earned some skepticism or outright scorn among his fellow African Americans. "Sammy Davis is multitalented," offered James Brown in a typical barb, "*but he never did himself.*"[4] This is less significant as a matter of "personality" than as a window on the politics of race in the United States. We tend to think of "identity politics" as a creature of the post-Civil-Rights era and the decades of "multiculturalism" and culture wars that followed. But the founding premise of the Republic some two centuries ago and more, and in particular the patterns of inclusion and exclusion implied in the framers' understanding of who "We the People" *had* to be, established the foundations of a Republic shot through with "identity politics." When, in 1790, Congress established "free white persons" as the only comers eligible for citizenship in the nation's first naturalization law, this was "identity politics" *par excellence.* Along with other laws and policies of the new nation, it structured the vaunted "individual liberties" of the founding documents in an unforgiving framework of *group rights,* grounded in white supremacy from the start. African-descended peoples were enslaved as a group and emancipated as a group, only to be Jim Crowed and to struggle for emancipation yet again as a group; women were disenfranchised and then granted the vote as a group; Indigenous peoples were "removed," sent to reservations, "allotted," and granted citizenship as a group; Chinese immigrants were excluded as a group; Japanese immigrants and Japanese Americans were interned as a group; Hawaiians, Puerto Ricans, Cubans, Chamorros, and Samoans suffered versions of conquest as groups, and their second-class status in the political culture was articulated in group terms as well. All of this has occurred in a nation that prizes "individual liberties" above all else, and in fact reckons its own political genius as having devised such liberties.

But this framework of "We the People *and Others*" shaped the responses of the excluded as well. For those left to fight their way into the circle of "We the People" on equal terms—whether emancipated Africans, Asian "aliens ineligible for citizenship," or women in the suffrage era or again in the battle for the ERA—there has been only a *structured* choice available in the political culture. One option is to stake a claim for inclusion based upon "sameness." This is the assimilationist argument: admit us because we are just like you. Or, you can stake the claim on "difference," using the pluralist formulation: we are indeed different from you, *but not inferior.* In our very difference—in our inherent *gifts*—we will enrich the Republic. It is this choice that has structured "identity politics" for centuries, and its polarizing logic mapped the Booker T. Washington—W. E. B. Du Bois debate just as surely as it did the cultural politics of the Yiddish ghetto at the turn of the century or American feminism across generations. It has also structured social and aesthetic styles. (As a sort of shorthand, Sammy Davis: sameness; *Miles* Davis: gifts.) In purely artistic or aesthetic terms, such choices are closely related to Houston Baker's foundational distinction between "mastery of form" and "deformation of mastery." One adheres to traditional formal requirements in order to be heard by the reigning (racist) arbiters of taste, floating "like a trickster butterfly in order to sting like a bee," as in Claude McKay's incendiary sonnets. The other makes a frank proclamation of artistic independence and foregrounds its difference, "a go(uer)illa action in the face of acknowledged adversaries."[5]

But this matter is neither as narrowly artistic nor as specifically African American as Baker allows. These principles of sameness versus difference spill well beyond the purely aesthetic question of form, and in the present context ought to be understood as undergirding political economy and the structures of citizenship and politics in this settler democracy as well. As has been the case for so many other men in oppressed or excluded groups, further, Davis's version of the struggle for inclusion was embraided with a highly pronounced *masculinism*. This is not only the masculinism that was deeply written into the social contract and dominant notions of citizenship in the United States, but in Davis's case also the masculinism of the entertainment circuits, of a racial politics predicated upon patriarchal dreams, and of a wolfish, playboy culture where licentious sexuality could become a stand-in for freedom itself.[6] Being "one of the boys" in his Rat Pack years was perhaps the acme of Davis's version of assimilation, even if he was never quite on equal terms with Frank Sinatra and Dean Martin.

Davis keenly felt the politics of inclusion and exclusion, and his choice to plant his life squarely on the assimilationist philosophy defined his persona on both sides of the color line. So too did his conversion to Judaism, which itself generated acres of print on the question of identity. But if Davis's assimilationism, as both a philosophical principle and a cultural style, embodied centuries' worth of struggle over "We the People" in the United States, it also bore a very specific timestamp. Davis embraced a brand of assimilationism that was gasping its last breath by the dawn of the 1970s, when "black is beautiful" had become a commonplace and even network television was beginning to adopt a pluralist approach to "difference" among African Americans (*The Jeffersons, Good Times*) as well as white ethnics (*Bridget Loves Bernie, Kojak, Rhoda*). It was his assimilationism, indeed, that made Davis seem such a cultural throwback in the eyes of an upcoming generation, even as he began to wear an Afro and occasionally to don a dashiki.

But if that timestamp put Davis sure enough out of step with the new pluralism, it is also the case that the new pluralism has encouraged an important misreading of assimilationism of all kinds, whether Davis's, Jewish writer Mary Antin's, or Japanese petitioner for citizenship Takeo Ozawa's. The post-Civil Rights ethos tends to applaud the *argument from difference,* that is, in a manner that misreads an important thread of dissent within the argument from sameness. In a context where one is defamed as being so "inferior" that the very possibility of admittance is questioned, then the egalitarian presumption at the core of assimilationism does not necessarily denote "self-loathing," as is so often claimed, but might conceal an unexpected blade of radical principle. Davis's politics might not match the post-Civil Rights ethos, this era of pluralistic assertion, but they do illuminate

FIG. I. Davis in *Rufus Jones for President*, 1933.

something significant about the political culture's available choices and about the struggle around ongoing questions of inclusion and exclusion—the struggle for "We the People."

Set against the timetables of the long Civil Rights era, Davis's career looks something like this. He was born in Harlem amid the excitement of the Renaissance and began working as a child performer in a Jim Crow entertainment world, but at a time when phrases like "the New Negro" promised something different. He traveled the vaudeville circuits throughout the Great Depression, tap-dancing and working a brand of stage *schtick* that held to minstrelsy's norms of racial disparagement and self-deprecation, even as the Popular Front forged a robust left public around issues of racial justice. He came of age as a performer during the war, in a Special Services/USO environment that was still very much steeped in the minstrel tradition, right down to the burnt cork, even as the United States fought a "war for democracy." He rose to stardom in the late 1940s and the 1950s, when Cold War America was very much in need of symbols of its own racial "tolerance," even if the "deliberate speed" of the *Brown* decision, spectacles of violence like the Emmett Till murder, and the tightly-organized, state-supported, armed opposition to desegregation in places like Alabama and Mississippi had a different story to tell. By the time of the Civil Rights and Voting Rights Acts in the mid-1960s, Davis had become one of the most famous African American men in the world (second only to Martin Luther King Jr., before being edged into third place by Muhammad Ali). He was a fixture in Vegas, on network television, in Hollywood film, and on the Billboard charts. And by the time Black Power had crested and been met by Richard Nixon's "law and order," Davis was becoming a passé symbol of the *pre*-Civil Rights era for a nation that was still contesting what *post*-Civil Rights might mean.

As this whirlwind sketch begins to suggest, as important as the duration of Davis's career over the middle decades of the century was his participation in myriad genres and forms across the culture industries, from vaudeville, to recording, to the nightclub and casino circuit, to Broadway, to Hollywood, to network television, and even to publishing and photography. ("Nobody interrupts a man taking a picture to ask ... 'What's that nigger doin' here?'" he once told Burt Boyar.)[7] In his magisterial study of race, culture, and political economy, *Forging Memory and Meaning*, Cedric Robinson wrote of the astonishing longevity and the continuing immediacy of the historical "big bang" of European expansionism and the Atlantic slave trade in the making of our social world, as well as the significance of seemingly "innocent," even frivolous entertainments and cultural forms to "the relentless juggernaut of Black inferiorization."[8] Beginning several centuries ago, notes Robinson, "The Negro marked the boundary beyond which the heritage of English or 'white' fathers could not extend. The Negro even dissipated the promise of Christian redemption. No principle, no matter how ancient or sacred, could stand before the gathering onslaught of the industry of inventing the Negro."[9] Robinson sketched a skein of ideational tricks and traps, intellectual traditions, culture and information industries, and modes of "knowledge" that went into the making of "the Negro" in the service of racial capitalism across the early modern and Enlightenment periods, from Elizabethan drama to the treatises of natural philosophy to the minstrel stage and circus to, eventually, the cinema. This congeries of forms dispensed among white people in the United States— both before and after Emancipation—that "paltry dividend" of white supremacism Du Bois called the "wage of whiteness," in exchange for fealty to a corrupt and corrupting hierarchal system: "The scrap which was [whites'] reward was the installation of Black inferiority into their shared national culture."[10]

But in the United States one is never as far removed as one thinks from that early modern colonial project, the "industry of inventing the Negro."

Sammy Davis Jr. certainly was not. At age seven, in a film called *Rufus Jones for President,* he and his adult colleagues replicated on screen quite precisely the "pompous dress and inane dialect" by which, according to Robinson, early nineteenth-century lithographers had parodically "imagined black freemen and even foreign dignitaries (Haitian, Nicaraguan)" along with "Black ambitions for equality and the abolitionists' desire for slavery's end."[11] As a young man on the vaudeville circuit, Davis chafed at some of the stage conventions and norms that had been bequeathed directly from the minstrel stage. He was put off by the self-abnegating comic patter, the obsequiousness and deference before white audiences, the blunting of virtuosity by enforced clownishness, the imposed "Negro" dialect. As his star rose, around the time of his first Broadway play *Mr. Wonderful* (1956), Davis found himself hungering the "displays of bourgeois respectability" that, as Robinson argues, were the culture's false alternative to "a profound challenge or radical critique of racial capitalism."[12]

But then again, in *Mr. Wonderful* Davis also staged a tribute to Al Jolson, the single most influential figure in bringing blackface minstrelsy from the vaudeville stage to American film. Rooted in a deep history of conquest and slavery, "inventing the Negro" was an ongoing project in the American culture industries, even as Davis danced across various performance platforms in the mid-twentieth century. He had inherited both a set of entertainment practices and forms *and* a racial sensibility that dated back to the early twentieth century. These served him well, and indeed took him to the top, in the 1940s and 1950s, but did not age well as the Civil Rights struggle advanced after the sit-in era. The tap dancing, the vaudeville humor, the repertoire drawn from Frank Sinatra's American standards—all of this began quickly to wear thin for a rising generation reared on Chuck Berry, Charlie Parker, Nina Simone, James Brown, Aretha Franklin, and Dick Gregory. So too did Davis's fight against racism as an individual quest for *acceptance* rather than for *justice,* his fight against the forces, not of "institutional racism" (much less racial capitalism), but of mere "bigotry" or "intolerance."

Dancing Down the Barricades is a book about politics, then. This includes cultural forms that do political work. It includes the politics of representation, meaning both racialized hiring practices on stage and screen, *and* the articulation and dissemination of racial meanings through popular imagery and narratives. It examines the various ways that politics could repay or punish cultural workers, and the ways that "celebrity" might be bent toward projects of social justice. The book takes the Sammy Davis Jr. story out of the strictly show-biz realm of Bill "Bojangles" Robinson, Eddie Cantor, Frank Sinatra, and Gregory Hines, and sets it instead in conversation with A. Phillip Randolph, Gunnar Myrdal, Martin Luther King Jr., Diane Nash, Shirley Chisholm, and Stokely Carmichael. Beyond the biopic romance of the rags-to-riches showbiz story, Davis's trajectory has much to say about the economics and culture of segregated entertainment circuits; the patterns of racial deference in twentieth-century performance traditions; the street-level experience of Jim Crow, and the diverging generational outlooks by which African Americans met it; the postwar imperatives of desegregation, and the grain and pace of this political work; the social geography of race and the varying political moods of Civil Rights activism; the place of white allies (and white "allies") in the liberation movement; the public and private faces of racism and antiracism; the play of race politics in dance, song, and script; and various cultural forms as a *means* of expression and liberation, the culture industries themselves as sites of contestation.

"There is still opportunity in America for a black man," Davis insisted around the time of the Montgomery bus boycott; "he's got to fight for it maybe harder than a white man, he's got to fight for his stretch of dignity. Once he gets it—and if he utilizes it properly—*then* he makes it a little easier for the other guy."[13] The extent to which Davis's triumphs in the industry really did advance "the other guy" was a question that dogged him throughout his career. Many of his black colleagues were skeptical that the arts Davis had on offer ever did produce much in the way of liberation. Davis himself was often torn between the claims that certain battles he fought—desegregating the Sands Hotel, for instance—were for his people or for *himself.* Was he dancing the barricades down, or merely dancing down them? Davis "was exhausting to be with," Eartha Kitt once sighed, and this had everything to do with the ways that his personal, psychic hungers were fused with an impatience with Jim Crow's limits. "There was always that nervous tension surrounding him, of having some place to go and not knowing how to get there," Kitt said, describing both inner yearnings and external roadblocks. "I'm going to be bigger than you are one of these days," he told her, to mixed consternation and amusement.[14] But being "bigger" was Davis's best and only plan for quieting his demons and for overcoming Jim Crow. As Gerald Early writes, "few performers have reflected the glory of their times more fully or carried the burdens of their times with greater anxiety or gut-wrenching honesty than did Davis."[15] Which is just to note that there was a little bit of the bullet dance in everything Davis did.

ONE

Star Rising at Twilight

A CHILDHOOD IN VAUDEVILLE

I was raised on the tag end of vaudeville.

—SAMMY DAVIS JR.

Show business teaches you.

—ELVERA SANCHEZ

"I'M GOING TO SAY a line now that's going to probably cause a great deal of laughter and probably some consternation," Davis said in 1985 on *Late Night with David Letterman*. As a child star, "I appeared in blackface." He paused comically, gesturing toward his dark skin. "That means burnt cork."[1] Indeed, black performers as well as white blacked up in the era of stage minstrelsy. But in Davis's case, as he told it, the cork was doing double duty. Owing to 1930s child labor laws, his father and "uncle" Will Mastin used the burnt cork (and a fake cigar) to disguise the boy's age, passing him off as "a forty-four year old midget" for the sake of their vaudeville stage act. The ruse was made plausible by precedent—three-foot-tall "Princess Pee Wee" had traveled the vaudeville circuit with the Whitman Sisters throughout the 1920s—and in the ambit of most child welfare authorities, Davis probably did not come off as dancing "like a child," even to those familiar with Fayard and Harold Nicholas, the electric duo then lighting up the Cotton Club.

But behind the comic effect of this retrospective story as told in the 1980s lies a more significant truth about the Davis biography. In losing his childhood to the vaudeville circuit, Sammy Davis Jr. was reared *into* the sensibilities—both social and professional—of an era far preceding his own. The generational dynamics of his career would become increasingly important over time. He was mentored and stewarded into the limelight by Eddie Cantor, who was more than thirty years his senior; by the 1970s he was taking on the persona of Bill Robinson ("Mr. Bojangles"), almost fifty years older. Born in 1878, Robinson was Will Mastin's strict contemporary, and only ten

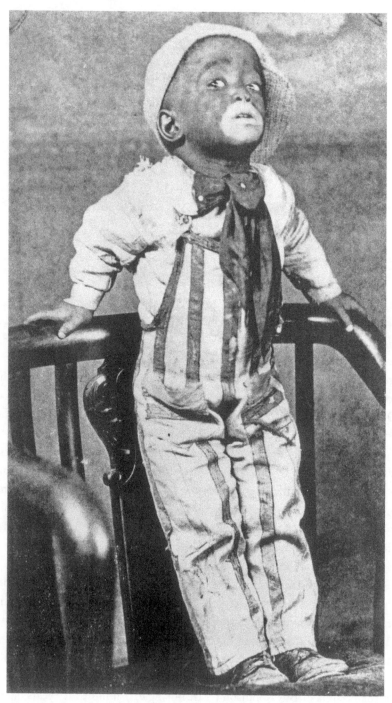

FIG. 2. Sammy Davis, Jr., c. 1929. Photo: Hulton Archive/Getty Images.

years older than Sammy Davis Sr. This is roughly the vintage that stamped Davis as a fully formed vaudeville performer with no childhood—the vintage of that "forty-four year-old midget." When Davis carried parts of his vaude-ville past into the second half of the twentieth century, including its social outlooks, its hoofing styles, its comedic routines, its variety and stage patter, he was embodying a style that even predated his own 1930s childhood and reached all the way back to the days of Bert Williams.

It is of great significance that it was the tap dance, of all possible forms, that carried Davis into the mid-twentieth century. Like many other African American dance forms, tap was an expression of freedom and self-possession in a setting where both were denied—a joyous use of the body itself as an instrument of liberation under circumstances of oppression, fugitivity, and Jim Crow humiliation. "The Negro, strictly speaking, never had a jazz age," wrote Alain Locke in *The Negro and His Music* (1936), "he was born that way. . . ."[2] The "Africa" in jazz-associated cultural forms of music and dance, according to an unnamed critic cited by Locke, was in the fusion of movement and sound, the musical practices that transformed the body itself into an instrument. It began "in the restless feet" and "rippled through his limbs and communicated itself to every instrument upon which he could lay his hands."[3] At the same time, tap was steeped in performance traditions that had emerged from the minstrel stage, making it as hated and suspect as the cakewalk among genera-tions of African Americans who came up too late for that moment when tap still defined the cutting edge of creative expression, of "the modern."

A number of forces account for the decline of tap in the middle decades of the twentieth century. The rise of cinema drastically cut the number of urban dance venues in the 1930s; changes in the tax code on entertainment establish-ments cut away at what was left in the 1940s. The rise of youth culture, rock and roll, and bebop—a jazz that was "insistent on being music for listening" rather than dancing—altered the nature of the dancing public, each in its own way, in the 1950s. Television was also a notoriously bad medium for the quick, flash styles that had developed, as neither its sound, its picture, nor the cumbersome wielding of its early studio cameras were well suited to capture the crispness and speed of tap. Whether tap died or, as Sandman Sims argued, "only went underground,"[4] it had traveled the entire arc from being the very epitome of "the modern" when *Shuffle Along* hit Broadway in 1921 to being the very epitome of "old timey" by the 1960s. And these temporal appellations carried powerful racialized meanings in the context of long-tailed minstrel traditions and emergent Civil Rights consciousness. Tap was becoming one of the markers of generational conflict in the African American community, just as Davis's career began its meteoric rise.

Even if the Negro "was born that way," Locke warned of "the ever-present danger of commercialization" to African American arts of music and dance. As a purely "Negro dialect of emotion, [jazz culture] could not have become the dominant recreational vogue of our time ... the most prolonged fad on record," if it had not also become "diluted and tinctured." Emerging from the "primitive rhythms of the Congo" and revolting "against the hardships and shackles" of an enslaved life in diaspora, jazz music and dance spoke forcefully to a more general (white) "revolt against Puritan restraint," becoming "the Western World's life-saving flight from boredom and over-sophistication."[5] As a young performer, then, Davis sat at the intersection of many different worlds. He was a child of the Great Migration, though he was schooled in a set of sensibilities and performance practices that we might more readily associate with the nineteenth century. He mastered forms of song and dance that were syncretic to begin with—products of the Atlantic slave trade, with its colliding and fusing cultural exchanges from Africa to the Caribbean to North America—but fraught, too, with histories of appropriation, mimicry, and parody, Cedric Robinson's "relentless juggernaut of Black inferiorization."[6] And his early years, from child performer in the 1920s to rising star in the 1950s, coincided precisely with the curve of tap dance in America from "modern" to "passé." "Show business teaches you," as Davis's mother, Elvera Sanchez, would put it; and the lessons Davis took "on the tag end of vaudeville" were at once his ticket and his burden through the middle decades of the twentieth century.[7]

RUFUS JONES FOR PRESIDENT

Born in Harlem in 1925, Davis was raised in lean economic conditions but also amid the protean cultural flowering of the Great Migration. His father, Sammy Davis Sr., was a song and dance man from Wilmington, North Carolina, a veteran of traveling shows like *Shake Your Feet* and *Struttin' Hannah from Savannah*. His mother was a Cuban chorus dancer from New York, though in his own account Davis later switched out Cuba for Puerto Rico, amid Cold War currents of anti-Castroism. The two first met while working a show called *Holiday in Dixieland;* Davis was "the group's fastest man on taps" and Sanchez, "the comeliest chorus girl." The troupe leader was

Will Mastin, a long-familiar vaudeville name from Huntsville, Alabama, who had "danc[ed] his way on soft shoes from country minstrel platforms to the big city stages," as the *New York Post* later put it.[8] Before *Holiday in Dixieland,* Mastin had worked with a "Texas Tommy" act called California Poppies ("Texas Tommy" was the name of a popular dance, taken from the slang for a prostitute).[9] Elvera Sanchez left the Mastin group to have her second child, Ramona. This was ultimately a break-up story, and bitterness emerged on both sides over the years. The Davises resented what they saw as Sanchez's Cuban-inflected colorism—a certain air of superiority based on her lighter complexion—and for her part, Sanchez later resented the exclusions she experienced as one of the "east coast people," when the geography of her son's life became bifurcated between east and west. In any event, Mastin and the Davises, Sr. and Jr., took to the road. Davis made his debut at the age of two at the Standard Theater in Philadelphia. "'Five girls and seven men were in the act then,' Sammy Sr. recalled. 'One was a comedian called Rastus Airship. Will was his straight man. Little Sammy would watch them every time they went on. One night he did Rastus' dance—right on the stage. He was a regular on the act from then on.'" A chorus girl named Salina (no one remembers her last name) was the person who first had success in teaching Sammy the time step.[10]

Davis's repertoire, his versatility, the scope of his talent, and his performance persona were all indelibly shaped by the long history of African and African American cultural forms, and the ways these had travelled and evolved across space and time in both unadulterated form and minstrelized parody. It has been said that Davis "sang 'white' and danced 'black.'"[11] We will return to the "singing white" later on; but this "dancing black" embodied certain Africanisms, self-emancipatory practices in diaspora, and negotiations with white power and white cultural institutions that amounted to a *politics,* whether or not one ever had a particular wish to be "political." It was in this sense that Bill "Bojangles" Robinson could consider himself a "race man"—"I do all in my power to aid my race. I strive upon every turn to tear down any barriers that have existed between our two races"—while to some his on-screen dancing alongside Shirley Temple was the epitome of racialized bowing and scraping.[12] Black audiences were already heckling Robinson in the 1940s with "We don't want to hear that old Uncle Tom stuff."[13] Davis would come under similar suspicions in the Civil Rights years.

Davis's little seven-year-old performing self has been preserved for posterity in *Rufus Jones for President* (1933), a two-reeler featuring Ethel Waters.[14]

Rufus Jones was one of a cycle of African American shorts produced by Vitaphone in the 1930s, uneven vehicles designed primarily to capture black sound in a visual medium: *The Symphony in Black* with Billie Holiday, *Black Network* with Nina Mae McKinney and the Nicholas Brothers, *Bubbling Over* with Ethel Waters, *Pie, Pie Blackbird* with Noble Sissle and Eubie Blake, *Syncopation Sermon* with Hall Johnson, *King for a Day* with Bill Robinson and Dusty Fletcher, *The All-Colored Vaudeville Show* with Adelaide Hall, *Hi De Ho* with Cab Calloway, and *Dixieland Jamboree* with Eunice Wilson.[15] Typical of the genre, *Rufus Jones* was dreamt up by a white creative and production team (written by Dorian Otvos and Cyrus Wood, directed by Roy Mack, and scored by Irving Berlin's right hand, Cliff Hess), but executed by an all-black cast that in addition to Waters included Hamtree Harrington, Dusty Fletcher, Edgar Connor, The Will Vodery Girls, and Russell Wooding's Jubilee Singers. *Rufus Jones* is a cringeworthy piece of racial libel from today's perspective, to be sure, but as in so much minstrelsy, it is also a contested terrain on which African American performers have left their own stamp of resistance.

The film begins on a porch, where Ethel Waters is hanging laundry. Little Sammy appears, having been hurt in a scuffle with his friend Sinbad. "That Sinbad Johnson sure is going to be sorry when he finds out what a great man you is," Waters soothes, as the boy sits in her lap. "Yous gwine to be president.... They has kings your age, I don't see why they can't have presidents.... The book says anyone born here can be president." She then sings him "All God's Children Got Wings." This loving scene gives way to Rufus's dream, as the child drifts off to sleep with the assurance *yous gwine to be president* evidently echoing in his mind. A jubilant crowd arrives at the porch in an Election Day parade, ready to draft Rufus for President. A brass band plays and numerous placards are bobbing aloft: "Vote first and last for Rufus Jones," "DOWN WITH THE REDS, PUT IN THE BLACKS." "We want Rufus for the president," announces the parade marshal. A member of the procession hoists Rufus onto his shoulders, and the parade continues to the strains of "Dixie," Daniel Emmett's 1860 ode to the plantation South. The procession arrives at a polling place, marked by a giant sign reading "Vote Here for Rufus Jones: Two Pork Chops Every Time You Vote."

When Rufus Jones's victory is announced, the scene shifts to an elaborate, and elaborately minstrelized, parody of black governance, a crazy quilt of cultural references that seems to combine the Reconstruction legislature scenes from *Birth of a Nation* with the pomp of African American election-

FIG. 3. Davis with Ethel Waters and Dusty Fletcher in *Rufus Jones for President,* 1933.

day celebrations in nineteenth-century New England. "I am happy to announce that Rufus Jones has been elected the pres-i-*dent*," intones the marshal. "Come here, Prez, you gotta say something to your constitu-*ahn*-say." At this point young Sammy Davis sings "I'll Be Glad When You're Dead, You Rascal You" (which had been a hit for Louis Armstrong in 1931 and for Betty Boop in 1932). The grown-ups surround the boy as he sings, patting juba, keeping time with their bodies; Hamtree Harrington bobs in a gentle, flat-footed Charleston in the background. Davis finishes with a nifty little high-kicking time step—a tap dance of enough dexterity and flash that we glimpse the plausibility of Will Mastin's "forty-four year old midget" ruse—before shouting "Yeah!" with an Armstrong-like flourish and biting with gusto into a piece of fried chicken.

Fade to the swearing-in. Devotees of the Broadway hit *Shuffle Along* might have recalled a similar scene involving the election of a police chief:

PECK [SHOUTING TO THE CROWD]: Is I fit?

CROWD: Yes you IS. You bet you're fit![16]

Now decked out in an academic cap and gown, Hamtree Harrington swears in the child President, who has donned a tuxedo and top hat.

HARRINGTON: Now first of all, swear to me / from now on pork chops will be free.

DAVIS: I do, I do!

. . .

HARRINGTON: Now make a law without no loops / there'll be no locks on the chicken coops. / And swear to me that you will choose / as the national anthem "The Memphis Blues." . . .

DAVIS: I do, I do!

Next we see the Senate chamber, a veritable gallery of stereotypes: a sign on the cloakroom reads, "Check Your Razors"; senators in top hats and tails are kneeling on the floor of the entryway shooting craps. Announced with pomp and circumstance, the child president enters, still in tuxedo and top hat, escorted by Waters and a young man in a ceremonial military uniform (epaulets, feather plume, sash, medals). The senators all sing "Hallelujah." Waters rises to make a speech:

Now, Senate, listen here. I don't want my child comin' home with no head-aches from runnin' this government, so I nominated myself to the office of the President-ESS. [Applause.] And I'm also rarin' to take up with y'all some matters of the most inconspicuous importance.

Such matters include establishing a Commissioner of Poultry "to see that all the padlocks is first removed from the coops," and a Watermelon Investigator "to plant the watermelon vines near the fence instead of in the middle of the patch." An objection from the floor ("Are we going to sit around here with all our *supremeority* and let her tell us what to do?") insults the President-ess, who then sings "Am I Blue?" followed by "Underneath the Harlem Moon," a vaude-ville minstrel number by Jewish immigrant lyricist Mack Gordon (b. Morris Gitler): "There's no fields of cotton, picking cotton is taboo/We don't live in cabins like our old folks used to do. . . ." The number's minstrel lineage becomes clear in the final verse, an ode to the happy-go-lucky (but no longer plantation) Negroes, who "just live for dancing" and are "never blue and forlorn"; it's no sin "to laugh and grin / That's why we *shvartzas* were born."[17]

Soon another objection is raised from the floor: "When we elects a President, we elects him to *do* something. This President just sits in the chair and don't do nothin.'" "I'll do something!" Davis replies, and flashes a quick minute-and-a-half dance number, moving from a flat-footed time step and "BS chorus"—standard steps from vernacular jazz dance—to more complex combinations and "up on the toes" moves that cite contemporaries like the Nicholas Brothers, a modified "falling off the log" move and a prideful, strutting little "walk around," all delivered in the "class act" style of a top hat and tails presentation. "There you is," Waters says with a mother's pride; *"You ain't never had a president what could do that."* It is worth mentioning here that the number is bound to be slightly misread from the twenty-first century perspective. While the seven-year-old Davis was a talented dancer who had fully mastered the mugging cuteness that had won him a spot with Will Mastin's troupe, it is also true that child performers of this genre and skill were fairly common on the black vaudeville circuit. There were performance conventions in place, that is, and there was also a kind of bouncy immaturity to Davis's performance that would have almost certainly led 1930s audiences to react more coolly than today's YouTube audiences do.

Harrington next announces a group of "ambassadors and diplomats and such like," and the Will Vodery Girls perform a lavish rendition of "Putting It On." The pop and smoke of a photographer's flash wakes the sleeping Waters, now once again on her porch with the young boy, and she realizes, "My pork chops is burning." She returns to "All God's Children Got Wings," and the film ends with the gentle ode to segregation, "Just you stay on your own side of the fence / and no harm will come to you."

Rufus Jones captures many important elements of the entertainment world in which Davis came up. His remark that he "was raised on the tag end of vaudeville" places him on a historical timeline, to be sure, but it places him in a very particular social setting as well. The "on" invokes the *how* of his rearing in addition to the *when* or *where,* as in "I was raised on cornbread and religion." As relayed in *Rufus Jones,* this was a segregated world where any production anticipating a white or a mixed audience was firmly under white control, and therefore where black talent often faced tough choices between embodying insufferable racial caricatures and unemployment. It was a world with a lot of watermelon and fried chicken, and a lot of jokes about chicken thievery and razor violence—much like the world of the "coon song," as described by Alain Locke, still rife with relics of "the worst minstrel days."[18]

But it was also a world in which black actors learned to play *through* the thick racial stereotypes, making the images their own by going over the top and thus subtly subverting the racialized commentary they had been enlisted to ventriloquize, as in minstrelsy, doing a parody of a parody. The last line of "Underneath the Harlem Moon" is typically rendered as "that's why darkies were born," for example, but Waters's use of the Yiddish *shvartsas* resolves the authorship more clearly, and so highlights the racial ventriloquism that was central to the white Vitaphone production. When she later says, "There you is, *you ain't never had a president what could do that*," the line comes across something like a hostage's compliance with explicit instruction. Riffing on precisely such moments, Phil Silvers would later do a scorching stand-up routine that depicted white lyricist Jerome Kern tutoring Paul Robeson in "proper" Negro dialect for his "Old Man River" performance in *Show Boat*.[19] In any case, *Rufus Jones* remains one of the most complete portraits extant both of the young Sammy Davis Jr. and of the entertainment world that reared him.

TAP

Black performance styles in blues, jazz, comedy, and tap were of necessity developed in conversation with such white-over-black imperatives, whether in accommodation or resistance. For comedians, this meant a minstrelized style of self-abnegating humor. For female dancers it meant oversexualization. For male dancers, it often meant an enforced clownishness that undercut the virtuosity and athleticism of the dance and of the dancers themselves. When not *over*-sexualized (Gus in *Birth of a Nation*), that is, the black male body in American entertainment tended to be *de*-sexualized (Hamtree Harrington in *Rufus Jones*). The Rufus Jones character himself emerged from among the legions of children known as "pickaninnies" or "picks" on the vaudeville circuits, though on the stage they typically accompanied a white star. Will Mastin himself had been a "pick," for example, and in film this tradition ran all the way back to one of Thomas Edison's first shorts, *The Pickaninny Dance* (1894).[20] In this regard a film like Vitaphone's *Rufus Jones* not only emerged from the minstrel stage, but shared a family tree with the acreage of racist advertising and postcard images and the "coon song" sheet music iconography that descended from Reconstruction-era slanders about Negro self-governance, which in turn descended from the caricatured "Bobalition of slavery" broadsides of the 1830s.[21]

There are four distinct contexts of differing historical scale—horizons of interpretation—in which to locate the performance styles that Davis was beginning to hone in *Rufus Jones* and the circumstances he inherited. The first is the deep historical past that stretches back centuries to Africa, cultural "retentions" transported through the Middle Passage. Tap dancing was among the styles that evolved from a long history of social dance in Africa, and from syncretic cultural exchanges in port cities throughout the Americas, where African jigs and European forms like the hornpipe and Irish step dancing converged in a "double helix" of traditions.[22] The repertoire of the enslaved included what later publics knew as the pigeon wing, buck dance, buzzard lope, ring dances, quadrilles, cotillions, reels, and water dances, among others. The African step dance called "Giouba" (typically rendered as "Juba," and later, "Pattin' Juba"), according to dance historian Marian Hannah Winter, "somewhat resembled a jig with elaborate variations, and occurs wherever the Negro settled, whether in the West Indies or South Carolina."[23] The Juba step has been described as a "sort of eccentric shuffle," fusing "steps and figures of the court of Versailles . . . with the hip movements of the Congo." Pattin' Juba consisted of "foot tapping, hand clapping, and thigh slapping, all in precise rhythm."[24] Early-twentieth-century anthropologists made all sorts of highly problematic pronouncements about African peoples, but in their zeal to create typologies and catalogues of African cultural "survivals," these scholars did render a wealth of observation on the continuities in dance elements across the diaspora. They saw "the Ibibio of Nigeria performing a shimmy to end all shimmies, the Sherbro of Sierra Leone executing an unreasonably fine facsimile of the Snake Hips, and a group of Hausa girls near Kano moving in a fashion closely resembling the Lindy, or Jitterbug." "Dahomean shoulder movements" were "antecedents of the Quiver, Shake, Shimmy, and similar dances." A Winti dance in Surinam featured "fingers tugging at the clothing, as though scratching to relieve an itching sensation," a gesture later known in North America as the Itch and made famous on the vaudeville stage by the popular duo Butterbeans and Susie, to the tune of "The Heebie Jeebies."[25]

The hallmarks of African dance wherever found included improvisation; call and response; the counter-clockwise circle dance; a taking of turns (soloist and ensemble—the "break"); the shuffle; a flexing or bending of the knees and waist that is quite distinct from anything in the European tradition; a centrifugal force, radiating outward from the hips ("Congo hip movements"); and a propulsive rhythm. It is typical in this tradition, wrote Alain Locke, "to embroider whatever basic rhythm is set—changing, doubling, skipping beats in a fashion bewildering to those less expert in rhythmic patterns and designs."[26] All of these elements tended to fuse movement with sound in such a way that the dancers themselves became musicians, and vice versa.[27] The polyrhythmic character of African musics also produced a common style of dance in which "the feet followed one drum, the hips another," in what one musicologist calls a "metronomic sense" of the regular pulse beneath highly complex and competing beats. In Africa and across the diaspora, it should be noted, all of this was to be accomplished by the dancer "with an air of ease and silent disdain," in Robert Ferris Thompson's words, that was to become in America the very hallmark of "cool."[28] The increasing commercialization of dance, beginning with the onset of Ragtime and Tin Pan Alley, enshrined these African "survivals," even while concealing them behind the modern American nomenclature of "Quivers," "Shakes," and "Shimmies."

The second horizon of interpretation concerns the evolution of African dance within the brutal context of Atlantic slavery. The percussive dancing that passed from plantation to stage—from Master Juba to Bert Williams and Bill Robinson to the Will Mastin Trio—not only retained the polyrhythms and adapted specific steps from earlier African social or religious dances like the Ring Shout, but were directly influenced by fugitive dance moves that had been developed within (and because of) the constraints and surveillance of slavery. When African drumming was outlawed, as Brenda Dixon Gottschild writes, for example, "The feet—as well as hands clapped together or patted on various body parts and 'found' instruments such as spoons, buckets, or brooms—had to carry out the function of drums."[29] Likewise, Protestant strictures against dance in parts of North America prompted slaves to improvise ingenious forms of their own religious dancing that avoided ever crossing the feet in a way that would *look* like dancing to the Euro-American eye. They would

> shift [their] weight from heels to toes, to insides and outer edges of the feet, moving the feet in various directions, turning toes and knees in and out, sliding, gliding, shuffling, stomping the feet—without ever crossing them or lifting them from the ground. On top of this they articulated the torso and limbs in counter rhythms and different directions, adding syncopations and improvised movements throughout the body. Thus they were not breaking white Protestant rules....

What this elaborate improvisation within the constraints of religious taboo would look like, writes Gottschild, is "an early form of pre-tap dance called buck dancing."[30]

The third horizon of interpretation has to do, not with specific gestures or moves, but with the *spirit* and the social relations of the dance. The Ring Shout or Juba crossed from the vernacular social world into the realm of commercialized entertainment already embedded in a set of friendly competitive practices—the hoofers' competition, the cutting or carving session—that mirrored other African-descended forms of competitive interaction such as the dozens, woofing, sounding, and signifying. Such forms richly combined individual expressive possibility with rituals of collectivity. One aspect of this inheritance was its masculinism. This is not "maleness," per se, as there were indeed brilliant women soloists like Katie Carter ("the Queen of the buck and wing dancers"), Alice Whitman, and Jeni LeGon, and also genius soubrettes among the chorines, like Florence Mills and Josephine Baker. *Masculinism,* rather, is a competitive bravado rooted in distinctly gendered sociality, privilege, and exclusivity, as in Harlem's famous "Hoofer's Club." "The older guys came with blood in their eyes," said Honi Coles, "always looking to cut you up. But that's how tap is."[31]

On the black side of the color line the masculinist aspect of this inheritance was imbricated with a broader, communal, race-based understanding of the dynamic relationship connecting the soloist to the ensemble—a cultural sense of individual expression amid mutual caretaking, a deep feeling of responsibility among members of the ensemble that critics have called *jazz ethics.*[32] Sammy Davis Jr. and his circle of old time hoofers paid homage to precisely this ethos in *Tap* (1989). The jam session (musicians) or the cutting session (dancers) is "the jazzman's true academy," as Ralph Ellison wrote. "It is here that he learns tradition, group techniques and style.... [He] must then 'find himself,' must be reborn, must find, as it were, his soul."[33] This is what Ellison had in mind when, in response to the proposition that African Americans "lacked cultural institutions to protect our cultural gains," he famously replied, "No. We *do* have institutions, we have the Constitution and the Bill of Rights, *and we have jazz.*"[34] At once metaphor and philosophy, Ellison's formulation posits a direct relationship between jazz and democracy in the dire dependence of both upon absolute freedom of self-expression and absolute commitment to the wellbeing of the ensemble. It was in this "jazzman's academy" sense that—in spite of the negative connotations bequeathed from minstrelsy—tap dancing could be a joyous expression of self-emancipation, "an act of black beauty and power," "a means of survival," as historians of dance have put it.[35] The improvisational interlude—the *break*—whether in dance or in sound, is the foundation of African American performance practices whose rhythm, angularity, asymmetry, and dynamism are deeply expressive of identity, both on individual terms and as a member of a collectivity and a link in the chain of tradition. Art itself, wrote Ellison, "the blues, the spirituals, the jazz, the dance—was what we had in place of freedom."[36] The dancing body became an instrument of liberation. "Setting a high value on the community-strengthening powers of rhythmic synchronization came with the slaves' African heritage," writes dance historian Brian Seibert, while "associating dance with freedom became part of their American one."[37] This principle of self-possession and self-emancipation has been on regular display in performance settings from the Time Step to the Shimmy to the Lindy Hop to the Moon Walk—to that monument to masculinism itself, the NFL end zone dance.

Ah, but those negative connotations. This brings us to the fourth horizon of interpretation, the evolution of tap dance forms in the North American entertainment context, and in particular the practices and the long shadow of the minstrel stage. Tap as "what we had in place of freedom" was immensely complicated and has been frequently misjudged because of its entanglement with minstrelsy, where, as Alain Locke put it, black performers had to make themselves over into "Pseudo-Negroes," producing "a decoction of their own slap-stick, caricature and asininity," "superficial types of uncles, aunties, and pickaninnies" echoing in the "minstrel and vaudeville stereotypes of Negro half-clowns. . . ."[38] As the jig became associated with Negro dancers, the very word "jig" became a racial epithet, as in "jigaboo," or "Jig Top," the segregated tent of the traveling circus. The percussive moves of the diaspora were first brought to the American stage by black entertainers like William Henry Lane (known as Master Juba), but from the mid-nineteenth century onward, many African-descended dance and music practices in North America became best known not under the proper authorship of African American performers, but only when circulated in ridicule by white performers in blackface.[39] Among white audiences, these burnt-cork forms often passed as originals rather than copies. The cakewalk—North America's first genuine "dance craze," around the turn of the twentieth century—nicely captured the racial house of mirrors that American entertainments had constructed. Here white dancers took to parodying their African American compatriots in an elaborate, ritualized quadrille that was in truth already a black parody of *them.*[40] "Us slaves watched white folks' parties," an elder remembered at the turn of the century, where guests "danced a minuet and then paraded in a grand march, with the ladies and gentlemen going different ways and then meeting again, arm in arm, and marching down the center together. Then we'd do it, too, *but we used to mock 'em,* every step. Sometimes the white folks noticed it, but they seemed to like it; I guess they thought we couldn't dance any better." Referring to herself as "an old strut gal," she also recalled that slaves could win special privileges if their dancing pleased the master.[41] The highly stylized cakewalk (or walk around)—including the contest and the prize—became a standard finale in the minstrel show from the Civil War until the early decades of the twentieth century. Bert Williams and George Walker brought the cakewalk to Broadway around 1900. It was "through minstrelsy that the dances called jigs, juba, shuffles, and breakdowns became theater," writes Seibert. "It was through minstrelsy that they became tap."[42]

The minstrel mask was worn to quite different effect by black and white entertainers. As Thomas Riis has observed, "Afro-American tricksters, used to wearing the mask for white slave owners, could show the white minstrel audiences what they wanted to see. . . ."[43] George Walker, for instance, would articulate his participation in minstrelsy in a fairly sharp language of proprietary right: "We thought that as there seemed to be a great demand for black faces on the stage, we would do all we could to get what we felt belonged to us by the law of nature."[44] Though white and black performers wore the mask quite differently and to disparate effect, the songs, dances, and comedic routines associated with minstrelsy circulated widely in American culture from the early nineteenth century onward, first in the minstrel show proper, but later in revues, operettas, burlesques, road shows, tent shows, medicine shows, circuses, small carnivals called "gillies," and vaudeville.

In such a context of mutual mimicry amid steep and dangerous power differentials, racial parody became written into the forms themselves in such a way that, even when performed by African Americans (often in blackface), they took on an aura of racial disparagement—the Jump Jim Crow and Zip Coon caricatures in early minstrelsy, the "happy darky" of the sentimental plantation formula or "plant show," the flash and grin of the Hollywood dance number. White entertainers in the minstrel era fought to preserve their place of privilege by excluding black performers through the mechanics of Jim Crow itself: "Blackfaced white comedians used to make themselves look as ridiculous as they could when portraying a 'darky' character," said George Walker.

The "fatal result" was that black performers "imitated the white performers in make-up as 'darkies.' Nothing seemed more absurd than to see a colored man making himself ridiculous in order to portray himself." Several generations of black performers had to contend with "the conflict between self and stereotype that existed in the minstrel dancing body."[45] Even Williams and Walker, who chafed and rebelled against the minstrel stereotypes, billed themselves as "The Two Real Coons." Alain Locke would observe of Bill

"Bojangles" Robinson's vaudeville dancing, "What the eye sees is the tawdry American convention," even if "what the ear hears is the priceless African heritage."[46] Some combination of "tawdry American convention" and "priceless African heritage" is precisely what is on display in the tap and juba scenes of *Rufus Jones*.

MINSTRELSY AND BLACK PERFORMANCE STYLES

The dances that had developed in this Atlantic World context were carried, copied, and modified by both black and white bodies across multiple performance venues and generated myriad styles and variations, as vernacular dance became professional entertainment between, say, Juba's 1830s and the Will Mastin Trio's 1930s. It was precisely on the layered terrain of these four historical fundamentals—the importation of African styles, their evolution within the harsh circumstances of slavery and tragically incomplete emancipation, the social relations among the dancing ensemble, and the residues of (and resistance to) the minstrel tradition—that "the jazzman's academy" was built. It was also here that the world of tap took shape in its American heyday, not only as a popular form, but as a singular element in the "grammar" of African American culture.[47] As historian Jacqui Malone writes,

> The dances that began on the farms, plantations, levees, and urban streets of colonial America, evolved through minstrelsy and moved onto the 'stages' of traveling shows, vaudeville, musical theater, cabarets, and night clubs. The development and growth of this country's preeminent vernacular dance paralleled the evolution of African American music and took a giant leap forward in the twenties, thirties, and forties, when the connections between black singers, dance acts, and jazz musicians revolutionized American culture.[48]

These forms encoded the tremendous optimism of the Great Migration and a rising ethos of the New Negro, even if minstrel conventions persisted. Like the Great Migration itself, the evolution of African American music and dance represented a stride toward the center of the republic and toward the "modern." African Americans were no longer the only enslaved people in a "free" republic, nor the most rural, agriculture-bound group in a rapidly industrializing one. This was of vast significance for a black public sphere in the urban north, where the optimism wrought by the Great Migration, the self-assertion of the "New Negro," and burgeoning post-Victorian institutions like the cabaret and the nightclub forged a different kind of black citizenship in close relation to a changing politics of representation.

Despite our association of the "New Negro" with Alain Locke's iconic 1925 volume of that name, this political and social figure properly began to coalesce closer to 1900. A cycle of black productions beginning around 1900 newly gave black popular culture a professional sheen and a critical—even political—edge. Black performers and critics alike sought to deploy artistry itself in the name of a politics of racial representation and respect; as critic Lester Walton wrote in the *New York Age* as early as 1903, "The stage will be one of the principle factors in ultimately placing the negro before the public in his true and proper light." Walton also saw that each black performance became either a gateway or an obstacle to the next. Such were the social stakes of black artistry on the long tail of minstrelsy. It was this generation of performers whom James Weldon Johnson credited with compelling "the public to recognize that they could do something more than grin and cut pigeon wings."[49]

The limitations on black freedom were stark, as Bert Williams, Bill Robinson, Josephine Baker, and (later) Sammy Davis Jr. could tell you. The North had a tremendous power to disappoint, and even to endanger. But a vibrant voice and a new critical edge emerged in African American performance in the closing years of the nineteenth century and the opening decades of the twentieth. Will Marion Cooke and Paul Laurence Dunbar's *Clorindy—The Origin of the Cakewalk* (1897) proved the viability of African American theater, not only as a commercial success, but as an expansive social space in a context where the color line continued to define the movements and opportunities of the city. Mounted amid the many minstrelized counterfeits of the cakewalk (a phenomenon partly of their own making), in *Clorindy* Cooke and Dunbar dispensed with the usual plantation romance and aimed to tell a more realistic story about post-emancipation life in 1880s Louisiana.[50] *Clorindy*, according to Alain Locke, was where "the American ear was just being broken in to the Negro tempo," though "its subtleties were missed in the consternation over the new fast pace of 'raggin' tunes."[51]

At the same time, Robert Cole and Billy Johnson's *A Trip to Coontown* (1898) cloaked racialized grievance in "ragtime insouciance," and even within the trappings of minstrelsy proved a vehicle for Cole and Johnson's "Colored Actors' Declaration of Independence," a claim on opportunity and dignity.[52] The "flurry of sound and movement" that was George Walker and Bert Williams's *In Dahomey* (1902), as Daphne Brooks writes, was a "sardonic subterfuge" that "set a precedent for yoking broad strokes of romantic whimsy with black political intent and activist vision. Indeed, the musical's 'incoherence' to some is in fact a cue for us to pay close attention to the ways this black theatrical production broke new ground and challenged the terms of representational coherency in relation to race." Critics at the time lauded the play's success in "lifting Negro music above the plane of the so-called 'Coon' song," and introducing the public to "another side of the varied, yet admirable character of the American Negro, who insists on entering every field of art, and becoming master of it."[53]

Darktown Follies (1911) "marked the turning point in the relations between the white stage and the colored stage," and in particular the era of frank white fascination with "authentic" black culture, absent its translations through the minstrel mask.[54] *Shuffle Along* (1921), created by lyricist Noble Sissle and composer Eubie Blake and starring the burnt-cork comedy duo of Flournoy Miller and Aubrey Lyles, as well as Florence Mills, offered "the most joyous singing and . . . the most exhilarating dancing to be found on any stage in the city," in James Weldon Johnson's estimation.[55] *Shuffle Along* augmented the fashion for black shows that *Darktown Follies* had inaugurated, and fueled a white "vogue" for all things Harlem that, despite its exoticism, still opened avenues of black opportunity and respect.[56] *Shuffle Along* was "the first outstanding Negro musical to play white theaters from coast to coast," propelled by the excitement of the dance itself—shuffles, slides, marches, struts, shimmies, strolls, slow drags, tangoes, one-steps, two-steps, and foxtrots.[57] And *Black Birds of 1928* delivered Bill "Bojangles" Robinson across the threshold to the notice of "serious" dance critics, who lauded the "true esthetic emotion" of his performance and who saw his steps as "extraordinarily beautiful." Indeed, Robinson was "the first Negro dancing star on Broadway," alone among black performers to break entertainment's "two colored" rule that promoted duos, trios, and foursomes over the prospect of true (singular) stardom. Putting an exclamation point on the politics of performance that ran across the three decades from *Clorindy* to *Blackbirds,* Robinson described the latter as "a safe and sane advertisement for a better understanding of my people."[58]

In this commercial context, particularly after the popularization of the polyrhythms of "ragged" music or ragtime, tap styles evolved in complexity, grace, and speed. They moved from the flat-footed hoofing of the buck dance, to the "up on the toes" style of Bill Robinson, to restless innovations like Robinson's stair dance ("the first tap masterwork of the twentieth century") to the "safety-be-damned acrobatics" of the Nicholas Brothers, to the boundless energy of flash acts like the Will Mastin Trio featuring Little Sammy.[59]

The tap dancer's credo, "Thou Shalt Not Copy Another's Steps—*Exactly*," conveys both the cross-fertilization and the long, unwavering memory that constituted the central tension of the dance tradition in tap across these years. Commenting on the Jazz Jasmines and Syncopating Sunflowers (the chorus in *Shuffle Along*), Eubie Blake said "it was like they learned from George Walker" himself. The tap world in the early part of the twentieth century was fast moving, to be sure, but it had a long and proprietary memory.[60] "Stealing steps" was strictly forbidden: a dancer's innovative moves amounted to livelihood itself, as everyone understood. But in the vernacular, "stealing steps" was also how the collective project of jazz dance proceeded and evolved. King Rastus Brown could copy a step, and then reproduce its entire genealogy. John Bubbles would study a step by asking a younger dancer to repeat it a few times ("That reminds me of a step I used to do"), and then top it by adding his own variation. The history of tap is "the history of stolen steps." This is part of what dancer Buster Brown meant when he said, "When you're dancing, I'm dancing with you."[61]

Around 1910 dancers fixed steel taps on their shoes for a sharper percussive effect, and the drumming that was tap, constantly subdividing, doubling, and tripling the beat, propelled the musicians and the music itself ever forward— speed, speed, speed. By the mid-1920s, according to critics, steps had become "more intricate, daring, perilous." Innovations on Broadway were braided with "stolen steps" from acrobats and circus acts and Russian dance troupes on the vaudeville circuit—kazotsky kicks, flips, somersaults, cartwheels.[62] The radical spirit among the chorines (Jayna Brown's "Babylon Girls," Saidiya Hartman's "beautiful experimentalists"), the human technology of the chorus as a whole, and the folding in of elements from classical dance and ballet now marked tap as the very apex of the modern.[63] "As the decade progressed," Seibert writes, "dance directors piled on references to modernity in crankshaft dances and skyscraper routines. They arranged people like pistons and made metal strike metal."[64] In his "Spirit of the Machine, and Negroes in the U.S.A.," architect and designer Le Corbusier (Charles-Édouard Jeanneret) noted both the iconic status of the jazz dancer as *the* American modern, and also a tantalizing relationship between the American present and the African past. "Tap dancers are very popular in the U.S.A.," he observed,

> silent Negroes, as mechanical as a sewing machine, inexhaustible, holding your interest by beating out a rhythm poem on the stage with the soles of their shoes.... The popularity of tap dancing shows that the old rhythmic instinct of the virgin African forest has learned the lesson of the machine and that in America the rigor of exactitude is a pleasure.[65]

Honky tonks, saloons, circuses, carnivals, burlesque houses and small vaudeville theaters, cabarets, and grand theater palaces. White spaces like Radio
City Music Hall, black spaces like the Apollo. Nightclubs like Small's
Paradise (Harlem), Club de Lisa (Chicago), Club Plantation (Detroit), and
Club Harlem (Atlantic City). Theaters where black talent could take the
stage but not sit in the audience; "integrated" theaters where black audience
members had to enter through the side or back door and sit in "black" seats
at the rear or up in the balcony. From the 1890s, when acts like Williams and
Walker or Cole and Johnson crossed over from minstrelsy onto the "legitimate" stage, black singers, dancers, and comedians found opportunities in a
wide range of performance venues and touring circuits. The borders between
the forms and venues that were minstrelsy's legacy had become quite porous,
and both the syncretism and the experimentation of styles accelerated as
performers moved from one show or genre or circuit to another.[66]

The variety that was these entertainments' stock in trade was conducive to
creative freedom and experimentation on the part of performers. It also put
a high premium on versatility. In addition to singers, dancers, and comedians, some of these traveling shows included jugglers, acrobats, ventriloquists,
magicians, animal trainers, impersonators, jubilee singers, yodelers, weight-
lifters, balancing acts, and lariat throwers. George Walker started out in
medicine shows, where his ability to "dance and sing, rattle bones, and beat
the tambourine drew large crowds"; Eubie Blake performed as a buck dancer,
singer and musician on the portable wagon stage of Dr. Frazier's Medicine
Show; and jazz drummer Jo Jones found that "when musicians were advertised for they had to do more than just play. You might have to be a dancer or
a straight man. . . ." Long before the Trio, Will Mastin's act had carried a
contortionist "who played clarinet lying on the floor with a flaming lamp on
his head."[67] These entertainment circuits were an extraordinary setting in
which to learn and hone one's craft, so rich and varied were the talents to be
found. Pigmeat Markham (the vaudeville comedian whose "Here Come de
Judge" routine became famous a full generation later, when recycled in the
1960s by Sammy Davis Jr. on *Rowan & Martin's Laugh-In*) observed:

> In the old days show business for a colored dancer was like going through
> school. You started in a medicine show—that was kindergarten—where they
> could use a few steps if you could cut them, but almost anything would do.

Then you went on up to the gilly show, which was like grade school. . . . If you had something on the ball, you graduated to a carnival—that was high school—and you sure had to be able to dance. College level was a colored minstrel show, and as they faded out, a vaudeville circuit or even a Broadway show.[68]

One sees in the structure of these forms and their relationship to one another the very things that Davis would eventually become famous for: his ability to combine performance styles and a versatile repertoire that included song, dance, comedy, impersonations, acting, musicianship in the form of drums, brass, and vibes, and a few oddball talents like gun-handling and juggling. If the standard vaudeville tour represented "a life of drudgery, with long railroad jumps, long hours, and small salaries," it was not necessarily a *lonely* life. A big-time vaudeville touring company usually consisted of eight acts: a "dumb" or non-verbal act involving acrobats or animals that allowed for the house to continue to fill after the curtain went up; a song-and-dance duo or trio; a sketch comedy act or one-act play; one or two headliners; a plush musical act with chorus girls; the top of the bill; and another "dumb" act as the show wound down and the theater emptied. The performer's goal was to develop eight to fourteen good minutes, and to be ready to repeat this act as many as eight to ten times daily.[69]

It was here, in the vaudeville setting of the 1930s, that Davis must have first thought of learning Markham's "Here Come de Judge" routine. When he was coming up, he explained in a later interview,

the kid that sang a song backstage or off-stage later came out and played the straight man or he was the juvenile in the scene. If you were a performer—and I put myself in the category happily, with the last three guys that came out of vaudeville in this way, and that was [Mickey] Rooney, [Jack] Carter, and myself, you sort of had to learn *everything*. You learned everything because it was definitely a prerequisite. . . .[70]

"He was like a sponge," dancer DeForest Covan said of this child hanging around in the wings. "Anything he could see, he could do." Davis later summed up his own cardinal rule this way: "stand in the wings and watch. If you ever have the privilege of performing with someone great, watch what they do and file it away. . . ."[71] Prince Spencer recalls crossing paths with the Will Mastin Trio (including the twelve-year-old Sammy) on the Keith circuit in Detroit. "I sang and told one-liners. Whoever told a joke in front of me in some other town, I told it in my act!"[72] It may have been Spencer's own "exit step," featuring

FIG. 4. and FIG. 5. Davis was reared in an entertainment tradition where versatility was at a premium. Opposite page: Don Smith/Radio Times via Getty Images. Above: REPORTERS ASSOCIES/Gamma-Rapho via Getty Images.

a Russian kick-out, that Davis in turn made famous in his own nightclub act and in his TV debut on *The Colgate Comedy Hour* years later.

By the time Davis was traveling the circuits with Will Mastin and his father, the United States boasted some 5000 vaudeville theaters, including 368 Negro theaters, according to *Billboard*.[73] These were organized by ownership and booking firms into multicity circuits; the best known included the Keith, Leows, Orpheum, Gus Sun Time, and Pantage circuits, but into the 1920s the most significant for black vaudevillians was the Theater Owners Booking Association (TOBA). TOBA controlled a majority of the theaters where black traveling companies and revues played, including jewels such as the Pekin in Chicago, the Howard in Washington, DC, the LaFayette and the Lincoln in New York, the New Standard and the Dunbar in Philadelphia, and the Booker T. Washington in St. Louis. According to the *Chicago Defender*, TOBA "reached from Galveston to Jacksonville and from Cleveland to Kansas City."[74] "[T]o many black entertainers," writes performance historian Mel Watkins, "the acronym TOBA became widely known as 'Tough on Black Asses.'" But TOBA proved "the principal transition from minstrelsy's rigidly maintained stereotypes to a performance style that more accurately reflected the majority tastes of the black community."[75]

There were many ways into the business—whether busking on street corners like Flash McDonald, passing the hat in clubs like Lavaughn Robinson, gaining local fame in an amateur contest like Jimmy Cross, or being raised in the wings, like Sammy Davis Jr. and any number of vaudeville "picks"—and there were many routes through the business once you were in. There was no such thing as a "usual" path along these routes, so precarious was the life and so capricious was success. Dancer Pegleg Bates's itinerary conveys something of the contours of this world and the way it might be traveled. "I was around fifteen," the one-legged dancer recalled,

> and people started complimenting my tap dancing. I went into amateur shows, and I won every first prize! It was definitely encouraging. I liked it, I liked to hear the applause. Then I went into minstrel shows. From minstrel shows I went to carnivals. And from carnivals to the T.O.B.A. I was with T.O.B.A. from 1922 until 1926.... And it was through them that brought me to the Lafayette Theatre in New York, one of the most important black theaters in Harlem. While there, I was seen by Lew Leslie, who at that particular time was the producer of *Blackbirds of 1928*, and that started me on my career as a professional tap dancer.

After a three-month stint with *Blackbirds* at the Moulin Rouge in Paris, Bates returned to vaudeville, traveling the Keith, the Leows, and the Fanchon and Marco circuits, eventually working his way up to fine theaters like the Paramount, the Roxy, and the Strand, as well as uptown nightclubs like the Cotton Club.[76] What is so evocative here is not only the map that Bates draws from one professional station stop to the next, nor the variety of performance spaces that he implies, but also the brushes of luck that forged his fate and that he was able to coax into a "career." An amateur buck dance prize was parlayed into a run in a minstrel show; a chance sighting by a producer on a TOBA tour landed him at the Moulin Rouge, alongside Bill Robinson in *Blackbirds*.

The heyday of black vaudeville was fairly short-lived. TOBA was established in 1920, and both the circuit and the genre were already in decline a decade later, assaulted by the talking picture show and the conversion of theaters for cinema on the one hand, and by the Great Depression on the other. Many of these newly converted movie theaters continued to book live talent, but the balance of power—the *draw*—was shifting as film itself went from the add-on novelty to the main event. Even major TOBA stars like the Whitman Sisters found themselves shortening their acts to fit "between the halves," the two films that were now the real headliners.[77] Adaptation to this new feature on the entertainment landscape prompted a transition from traditional vaudeville to "presentation" shows, which now showcased the music. The band moved from the orchestra pit onto the stage for the entire show (as in your standard nightclub act of the 1940s and after), and the presentation unit now consisted of a chorus line, a singer, a comic, and a tap dance act, most often traveling under the name of a leading musical act, like Tommy Dorsey, Duke Ellington, Cab Calloway, or Billy Eckstein (whom the Davises referred to simply as "B"). The best known presentation circuit, "Round the World," ran from the Lafayette Theatre in New York, to the Earl, Standard, Uptown, or Pearl in Philadelphia, to the Royal in Baltimore, finishing up at the Howard in Washington, DC. At the end of this four-week tour, the unit would retreat to the rehearsal hall back at the Lafayette for a week before embarking on the next tour with a new show.[78]

These, then, are the years of Davis's childhood. He "celebrated his first birthday in the dressing room of the old Hippodrome Theatre in New York," according to materials pushed out by a publicist in the 1950s.[79] When his mother Elvera went off "chorus girling somewhere," as Davis's grandmother would put it, a very young Davis took to the road with his father and "uncle" Will Mastin.[80]

His first amateur contest was at the Standard Theatre in Philadelphia in 1929, and he appeared with Mastin's group as a regular at the Gibson Theater in Los Angeles that same year. The trail goes cold after that for a while, until the Will Mastin Trio opens for Tommy Dorsey at the Michigan Theatre in Detroit in 1941. The first known reference to Sammy as a performer was a newspaper clipping from 1929 or 1930: "Sam Davis, Sr. is a remarkable dancer but his little four year old son, Sam Jr., puts the old man in the shade when it comes to catching the crowd."[81] Donald O'Connor, a child star traveling the white side of the circuits during the same years as Davis, once remarked that "I was never impressed with myself being different than any other kid. Although I never knew what other kids were like, because I was always with adults." The same must have been true for Davis. There was never any normal schooling for him; he spent his youth traveling from theater to theater, hiding from truant officers and learning to read and write from someone the elder Davis and Mastin had found to tutor him in the dressing room between shows.[82]

As cinema's "talkies" began to overtake vaudeville, Davis Sr. abandoned his show *Holiday in Dixieland,* which had traveled with a combined band and troupe of fifteen performers, now stripping down to a stage act eventually called the "Will Mastin Trio" in order to work the "vaudeville half" of picture shows. Vaudeville theaters everywhere were converting for film. But they still needed talent on the stage while projectionists set up the cumbersome equipment. It was here, at the dawn of the 1930s, that the Davis "family" first became "Will Mastin's Gang, Featuring Little Sammy," who had demonstrated his ability to absorb and master the entertainer's craft through observation.[83] He first attracted wide attention with his parroting of Louis Armstrong's "I'll Be Glad When You're Dead, You Rascal You" (repeated for *Rufus Jones*), but traveling the entertainment circuits gave him plenty of opportunity to learn more. "He had his own suitcase, his own shoe bag," writes biographer Wil Haygood. "His own set of little drums. He had numerous outfits—a white suit jacket, a white hat, plaid slacks, and white buck shoes made up one dandy sartorial number. Another was a little boy tuxedo, satin lapels and all."[84] As for his youth—and the fact that Sammy was not in school—Davis Sr. remarked, "Don't give no thought to that. . . . We been workin' Sammy under the cork. We blacks him up, he's got a Jolson suit and we bills him as 'Silent Sam the Dancing Midget' and the way he dances there's no chance of anyone catching wise."[85]

"It was those depression years that honed Sammy's already blade-sharp talents," ran Davis's publicity copy in the 1950s, and turned him into the incredibly versatile entertainer that he is today. The Trio played in vaudeville, in burlesque, in big cities and tank towns. Sometimes they were broke, sometimes stranded, sometimes stranded *and* broke, but they always managed somehow to get to the next date. And always Sammy was learning, learning. Once at a theater in Michigan, for instance, the late, great Bill Robinson caught the act, was vastly impressed with its youngest member, and asked Will Mastin to bring the boy to him for some extra tutelage. For countless hours Sammy absorbed the skill and wisdom and showmanship that flowed from every move that 'Bojangles' ever made, and the mark of those early, well-remembered lessons is still plain in his dance routines.[86]

For his own part, in *Yes I Can* Davis placed the tutorial with Robinson at the Plymouth Theater in Boston, not in Michigan, recalling the way Robinson "had his hands in his pockets and he was going up and down a flight of stairs and around the stage like he was taking a stroll set to music." When Robinson saw Sammy dance, he instructed the boy, "That's good. But make it so the people can understand it. Make it look easy."[87]

Despite the heavy accent of romance in these retrospective narratives, these were tough years for a vaudeville act like this. For one thing, the Trio was traveling—often sleeping, too—in their "ninety dollar LaSalle," across Jim Crow America. Finding accommodations was always tricky for black travelers. It was "hard" even in large cities, according to African American travel writer Alfred Smith in the 1930s, but "a gigantic task" in small towns and "sheer luck" anywhere else. "In spite of the unfounded belief to the contrary," Smith wrote, "conditions are racially identical in the Mid-West, the South, the so-called Northeast, and the South-southwest."[88] Though Davis Sr. and Mastin did their best to shield young Sammy from the harshest edges of the racism they encountered on the road, still he recalls the Michigan hotel where they were told, "We don't have rooms for you people." At a restaurant in Joplin, Missouri, "the countertop was painted white halfway around and brown on the other half." A counter man brusquely told the three black entertainers, "'You niggers'll have to sit on the other side.' He was pointing to the brown section." Their white friend's objection "'But we're all together'" fetched the blunt reply, "'Sorry, bub, you ain't together in here.'" The episode prompted the younger Davis to ask, "'What's a nigger?'... The way Will and my father were so angry and hurt I knew the word must have meant just us and it must have been terrible." Such moments, highlighting the omnipresent undercurrents of danger, were among the typical occupational hazards of black vaudeville in the 1930s and early 1940s.[89]

But beyond the racial indignities of the road experience, the pall of the Depression and the threatening rise of Hollywood as a chief competitor in the era of the "talkie" rendered this a period of particular desperation for vaudeville. Davis later asked Alex Haley,

> Listen, baby, have you ever had a *mustard* sandwich? Just mustard spread on bread—and then tried to dance on the nourishment from that? Will Mastin, my dad and me, we used to heat a can of pork and beans on the radiator, when they were nice enough to *have* heat in the radiator, and split it three ways, eating right from the can. There were times when for a meal we had a Mr. Goodbar apiece. Or a grape soda. I remember our filling our stomachs with nothing but water! I mean, I paid my *dues,* baby. . . . We starved. About literally starved. If we got two little one-nighters a week, we were lucky![90]

"Months passed and we went nowhere but to the pawnshop," Davis recalled. "With vaudeville dead and even the Palace running movies, variety acts like ours were moving into nightclubs."[91] The top tier on the nightclub route included truly elite venues like New York's Copacabana—a height the Will Mastin Trio eventually did attain. But the road to that triumphal moment meant years of struggle and uncertainty. "We moved from New England into the Midwest, working steady, covering most of Michigan in theaters, burlesque houses, and carnivals, changing the size of the act to as many as forty people depending on what the bookers needed."[92] At one stop,

> There was a silence in the room, the same sad and hopeless kind of quiet that I'd been hearing since we'd come to town. Vaudeville was dying. Wherever we went, for meals, or between shows in the Green Room, backstage, there was none of the usual atmosphere of clowning around that had always been so much fun. Everybody seemed afraid and they spoke of acts that had been forced to quit the business.

Once when young Sammy was practicing his drums, Davis, Sr. exploded, "Practice for *what?* To be in a show business there ain't gonna be?"[93] Wil Haygood's lyrical, smart biography, *In Black and White,* nicely parses the mixture of romance, excitement, and hardship in this vaudeville childhood: "Watching men slide nickels across countertops for the morning newspaper. Smiling at the pretty women who'd smile at him. Falling asleep as the covers were pulled up close to his shoulders in bed, all the while staring into the whites of the eyes of those who cared so much for him—his father, Will Mastin. The little boy was so free—and yet so caged in the world of show business." Davis, Sr. and Will Mastin, Haygood has to conclude, had "bartered away his childhood" one piece at a time.[94]

One sees encoded in the cultural forms themselves—dance, song, comedy, film—the racial currents and crosscurrents that complicated the era of the New Negro and the Popular Front. "Colored folks are mighty glad / 'Cause they've got rhythm for sale," sang John Bubbles in 1933, at once giving voice to the tremendous optimism of the Great Migration *and* the troubling commodification of blackness, often in the minstrel tradition, that continued to texture American entertainments well into the twentieth century. Think again of *Rufus Jones,* whose black political revelry drew subtly upon African American parodies of white comportment even as it trafficked in centuries-old comic stereotypes of misplaced black dignity. As cultural forms go, tap dance was perhaps uniquely vulnerable to the racial slanders that the white industry had in reserve for black talent. The impromptu spirit essential to tap made the dancing look effortless, natural, unstudied. Not only was the genius of the form often underappreciated as a result, but a conception of "natural" talent fed all too easily into a more general set of assumptions that assigned cerebral qualities to whiteness and bodily ones to blackness. Even when significant achievement was noted or credited among black dancers, it was often minstrelsy's old canard about mimicry and the gift for imitation—"a bad imitation of what was not a very good imitation in the first place," as the *New York Sun* put it in 1930. That same year, critic George Jean Nathan wrote in *Judge,* "These darkies, like most darkies, simply go on repeating the one or two little tricks that they have, and get pretty tiresome after you've been looking at them for a number of years." If belittlement was one version of the slander, total erasure was another, as when *Life* magazine actually credited Fred Astaire with the invention of "patting juba," calling him "the first American tap dancer consciously to employ the full resources of his arms, hands, and torso."[95]

Hollywood played an especially important role in disseminating minstrelsy's codes and ethos into the 1930s and beyond, doing a grave disservice to tap, and to black tap dancers in particular. For one thing, the technology of early sound pictures was ill suited to capture tap. Synchronization was always a problem for a form so forged in the aesthetic precision of sight and sound. Worse still, the moment of the sole's "strike" might fall entirely between exposures, and fully disappear amid the imperfect magic of moving frames. But beyond these technical difficulties, Hollywood had a racial dynamic of its own, rooted in the segregated white spaces of Los Angeles. It tended to fall back on convention—Southern convention—in its handling of race. The increasing centrality of film in the overall constellation of the culture industries meant the perpetual centrality of old plantation stereotypes that pleased white audiences below the Mason-Dixon line. In Hollywood the tap dancer's "Jim Crow persona was reinvented over and over," writes Jacqui Malone. "Black dancers were depicted as excelling in creative energy but mindless," and "tap dance sequences were usually staged in a way that made this difficult art form appear to be nothing more than spontaneous outbursts erupting from one's nature instead of one's culture"—or, we might add, from one's rigorous *work ethic*.[96] Hollywood might have made Bill Robinson's "stair dance" a cultural phenomenon on a mass scale in *Harlem Is Heaven* (1932), but more memorably it put Robinson side by side with Shirley Temple in "the humanized servant tradition," forever branding tap as servility itself and spreading its defanged images of the black male body far and wide.[97]

. . .

Between 1925 and 1949, as a popular form with a robust cultural infrastructure, tap was both flourishing and slowly dying at the same time. "Up until three or four years ago . . . it didn't seem as if I could get enough tap-dancing," wrote Robert Benchly in *The New Yorker* in 1931. "But I did. More than enough. With every revue and musical comedy offering a complicated routine every seven minutes throughout its program, and each dancer vying with the rest to upset the easy rhythm of the original dance form, tap-dancing lost its tang." Giving name to the deep contradiction that had been written into tap as a commercialized form, Benchly observed, "They are all good, and are getting better each year, so there is no excitement in seeing a good one any more."[98] This even though just a year before, sales of tap shoes had gone through the roof and Dancing Masters of America had announced, "America has gone tap-crazy." Davis was learning his first time step in the wings of the Plymouth Theatre while Bill Robinson was making his "stair dance" famous in *Black Birds of 1928*. And he would be achieving success as an opener for Sinatra just as Robinson died in 1949, and vaudeville along with him. Buster Brown dates the fall of tap quite precisely to the death of Bojangles: "After that, everything fell. Bang. No more jobs."[99]

These were Sammy Davis Jr.'s formative decades, from a childhood in vaudeville to a budding stardom touring nightclubs. Both his repertoire and his styles reflect the richness of the protean setting of his training. The hardship of the vaudeville circuit schooled Davis in a very particular vision of what "making it" in show business might or should look like; one cannot help but recognize in this early privation the thirst that would express itself in Davis's professional drive, but also in his attachment to all manner of hard-won and gaudy extravagance. The encrusted, fossilized, vintage 1930s show biz of his bartered youth, meanwhile, also outfitted him with tastes that the later twentieth century would not treat kindly. His vaudeville pedigree would pose many challenges, as the postwar public—and especially the black public—moved further and further away from the core performance elements and the core social assumptions that had been handed down from minstrelsy. Davis "was one of a fading breed," the *Christian Science Monitor* would later eulogize; Lerone Bennett called him "the last exponent of a dying art."[100]

But those who became acquainted with Davis only much later in his career—whether on the Vegas Strip, on Broadway, or on prime time TV—were still getting a good dose of the vaudeville that reared him. Davis's otherwise conventional Broadway musical *Mr. Wonderful* (1956), for instance, included a nightclub set piece in the middle, whose flurry of tap, singing, impersonations, and drumming replicated the act that had brought Davis to the top tier of the nightclub circuit in the preceding years. It was in this portion of the show that Davis "pays a glowing tribute to the late Al Jolson," as the Philadelphia *Evening Bulletin's* reviewer wrote. "And there are lots of things about Sammy that reminds one of the great black-face comedian. He even goes so far, reviving one of the Jolson songs, of going upstage, back to audience then, turning, hustling down to a Jolson runway out over the orchestra pit—and letting fire with the old Jolson verve."[101]

This act consisted of "a reprise of his 'Old Black Magic' recording hit; a show-stopping rendition of 'Birth of the Blues,' a nostalgic bit about Jolson and some stirring drum riffs," according to the *Philadelphia Inquirer*.[102] A few years had already passed since Langston Hughes very publicly derided Jolson for "only recently" discarding blackface.[103] But if Davis's Broadway act incorporated vaudeville-era material, so did it invite vaudeville-era critiques steeped in white racism. *Mr. Wonderful* is "a monumental hunk of showmanship [that] doesn't belong in a theater," sneered one New York critic. More pointedly, another added, "Big time show business, the Broadway kind, just ain't as easy as those Las Vegas dice parlors. . . . *Everything he does is reminiscent and imitative. Dancing, he uses Ray Bolger's trademark tricks. Singing, he's Johnny Ray.* . . ." This was precisely the white supremacist rap on black ability-as-mimicry that had greeted the first black minstrels a century before.[104]

Similarly, as late as 1968 Davis would still be bringing to network television some of the gags he had bitten from the vaudeville stage of his childhood. When Dan Rowan introduced "The Right Honorable Samuel Davis Jr.," those who were old enough (and, most likely, black enough) to remember were no doubt surprised to see a reprise of a decades-old Pigmeat Markham routine from the Chitlin' Circuit. In powdered wig and a judge's robe, Davis came on stage, half strutting and half dancing, swinging his arms from side to side wildly but rhythmically, chanting in minstrel fashion, "Here come de judge, here come de judge. . . ."

> If your lawyer's asleep, better give him a nudge,
> Everybody look alive, 'cause here come de judge.[105]

Or,

> You can testify but you just can't win
> 'Cause I'm here to tell you you're guilty as sin.
> Here come de judge. . . .[106]

The bit was so popular that it worked its way into American culture in a thousand ways. White children in schoolyards chanted the tag line each morning after it aired on *Rowan & Martin*. It generated three hit records—funk/soul tunes by both the Magistrates and the Majestics, and charting at #4 for Shorty Long. It provided the nickname for the 1968 Pontiac GTO ("The Judge"). And it gave Markham himself—a comedian who had started out in Bessie Smith's Traveling Revue in the 1920s—the miraculous opportunity for a 1960s comeback. His talking blues album later that year, *Here Comes the Judge,* has been credited as a precursor to rap, alongside *The Last Poets*.

Davis's signature number over the years, "Birth of the Blues," however, is his most significant sustenance of vaudeville sensibilities. By the time his nightclub act was taking off in the late 1940s and early 1950s, Davis had settled on "Birth" as his closer, though it never charted for him. The song had been written in 1926 by Tin Pan Alley composer Ray Henderson and lyricists Buddy DeSylva and Lew Brown for the Broadway revue *George White's Scandals,* a production more steeped in the appropriation and commodification of blackness (and in an exculpatory articulation of whiteness) than in "the blues" in any meaningful way. By the time the song resurfaced as a hit for Bing Crosby in 1941, it had transmogrified into a plush, up-tempo, swinging celebration of big-band-styled whiteness, still retaining its opening line from 1926: "Oh, they say some darkies long ago. . . ." Davis would change this (as Sinatra had) to "They say some people long ago," and then to "They say *my* people long ago" in later versions of the song. But in tone, Davis mostly retained Crosby's big-band sound, both in nightclubs (when he ended his set with "Birth of the Blues," the "applause was like a kiss on the lips," he wrote in *Yes I Can*) and on his debut album in 1955, *Starring Sammy Davis Jr.*[107] Davis did make the opening verse a quieter, more melancholy affair than the Crosby version, complete with some sustained "bent" or "blued" notes connecting the song to the African American blues tradition. But by the time Morty Stevens's orchestra rolls into the spirited second verse—"They heard the breeze in the trees / singing weird melodies"—Davis's version swings every bit as much as Crosby's and Sinatra's.

Most striking, though, in the song's journey across the decades from *George White's Scandals* in 1926 to Davis's Vegas act in the 1960s, is the extent to which the lyrics jar against the shifting cultural backdrop. Few other African American performers ever touched "Birth." Louis Armstrong once performed it in a duet with Frank Sinatra, singing through gritted teeth in an affective register that looks either like an effort to inject some honest, jagged-edged blues gravitas, or maybe just an imperfectly concealed resistance to the song.[108] The Oscar Peterson Trio recorded an instrumental version in 1959; that they chose to jettison the lyrics might be a statement in itself. The person who recognized that "darkies" had to be switched out for "my people" might have thought to ask some further questions about the song. What does it mean, for example, to say that "the blues" were inspired by "the breeze in the trees" or "a whippoorwill out on a hill" in "the Southland," and to sing this in the triumphal, uptempo spirit of an anthem as Emmitt Till was murdered or Bull Connor's dogs attacked black Civil Rights protesters in Birmingham? Lena Horne recalls being challenged by Café Society proprietor Barney Josephson on precisely this issue over her rendition of "Sleepy Time Down South," another "pretty" song based on false southern idylls. "Do you know what you're singing?" pressed Josephson.[109]

There is no evidence of Davis's ever grappling with this sort of challenge over "Birth." "The blues is an impulse to keep the painful details and episodes of a brutal experience alive in one's aching consciousness," wrote Ellison, "to finger its jagged grain, and to transcend it, not by the consolation of philosophy but by squeezing from it a near-tragic, near-comic lyricism. As a form, the blues is an autobiographical chronicle of personal catastrophe expressed lyrically."[110] It is "impossible to say exactly how old blues is," added LeRoi Jones

(Amiri Baraka) in *Blues People* (1963), "—certainly no older than the presence of Negroes in the United States. It is a native American music, the product of the black man in this country ... blues could not exist if the African captives had not become American captives."[111] It is one thing for a white, Tin Pan Alley team in the 1920s to pen a song about "darkies" taking inspiration from whippoorwills and calling it the blues—even long after W. E. B. Du Bois's writing on the "sorrow songs" in *The Souls of Black Folk*. But it is quite another for an African American singer to continue to peddle this line long after *Blues People;* after the Chaney, Goodwin, and Schwerner murders; after the Birmingham church bombing; after Selma. This is a song whose outlook and logic was wearing thin even when Bing Crosby picked it up in 1941. It could not help Sammy Davis Jr.'s cred as a "race man" that he dragged "Birth of the Blues" along with him all the way to 1990.

Summing up "the black culture industry"—by which he meant both the African American business of performance *and* the white trafficking in "black" culture—Ellis Cashmore wrote of the palette of the performance and representation bequeathed by minstrelsy:

> It is irony to some, theft to others, cultural syncretism to still others: the fact remains that African American culture fascinates whites and, without such a fascination, its destiny might have been to be overlooked. The minstrel took to whites an insight into black culture that was at once satiric and reverent. While it derided blacks, it also paid them an almost unwitting respect. It opened many eyes to the fact that blacks actually had a culture. It may have borne little resemblance to the one portrayed by the blacked-up minstrels; but it did recognize *something.*

Blues, Cashmore immediately adds, "for the most part resisted such parody. There was nothing to laugh at: its central narrative was misery and pain."[112] If "Birth of the Blues" is not *laughing* exactly, it is definitely swinging and it does seem to be smiling. Commentary like that of Ellison, Baraka, and Cashmore has to comprise the site within which we locate and make sense of Sammy Davis Jr.'s singing "Birth of the Blues" beyond the mid-twentieth century. This is not to censure Davis, but merely to underscore the historicity of his own, vaudeville-derived sensibilities and to note how important it was that at the outset of his entertainment career "I appeared in blackface."

TWO

———————

"A Concentrated Bunch of Haters"

WAR TIME IN WYOMING

> Here are all these 'niggers' ready and willing to go out and try to kill Hitler, and maybe get themselves killed, but they can't sleep in the same barracks with the white guys or go to the same movies or hardly get in officer's training. Made me start thinking.
>
> —JOE LOUIS

> On these USO tours I received a most unpleasant education in the niceties of segregation, Army style. The basic, terrible irony was plain to see. Here were Negro men drafted to fight for their country—for freedom, if you will—and forced to accept the discipline and customs of a Jim Crow army.
>
> —LENA HORNE

> I had been drafted into the army to fight, and I did.
>
> —SAMMY DAVIS JR.

BY HIS OWN ACCOUNT, Davis was first introduced to the full hostility and the violent undercurrents of American racism at the very moment he had been conscripted to defend American democracy. Traveling the vaudeville circuits, Davis Sr. and Will Mastin had been able to steward their young stage partner through the Jim Crow world, protecting him from danger and from racial insult at most turns. But he was all on his own when he reported for duty.

Davis had initially tried to enlist at the onset of the US entrance into the war after Pearl Harbor, imagining his soldiering as "a montage of movie scenes: I was marching with thousands of men singing 'You're a Grand Old Flag.' Pat O'Brien was my Captain and Spencer Tracy was the chaplain of our outfit.... I saw myself zooming off on dangerous missions, bombing enemy ships and dog-fighting with Zeros." Davis was rejected as too young on that first go-around, but at age eighteen in 1943 he received his draft notice, while playing the Fortune Club in Reno.[1] He passed the Air Corps cadet test—that dog-fighting dream of his—but was Jim Crowed into the infantry instead. Rejected for overseas duty because of a medical condition called "athletic heart" (an abnormally low heart rate), he served out his tour stateside, assigned to Fort Francis E. Warren in Cheyenne, Wyoming, a partially integrated base even before the military's official desegregation in 1947.[2] Here Davis quickly learned that he had enemies much closer to home than the Axis.

One should always be wary of assigning "watershed" moments. Major historical changes are usually a longer time coming than it seemed at a glance, continuities between the before and the after turn out to be robust, and on close inspection the old, dying ways can be discerned living on for generations. But World War II was an inflection point in the racial history of the United States, in that the world geopolitical situation, the rise and defeat of Nazism, and the emerging political requirements attending the United States' claims as "leader of the free world" all colluded to push democratic ideals with a new urgency and to put the federal government itself on the record as *anti-racist*. Racism was not defeated in these years, quite obviously, and in fact there is a strong case to be made that the Pacific theater represented a full-on race war against the hated "Japs" (including the 120,000 Japanese-Americans who were imprisoned in camps across Western states), even as the European theater was touted as a war against bigotry itself, embodied by Nazism and the Nuremberg Laws.

But Presidents Roosevelt, Truman, and Eisenhower did put the federal government on a different Civil Rights footing beginning in 1941, and it is no accident that—even despite the howling, hateful Dixiecrats and continuing racial violence from Birmingham to Detroit to Redwood City, California—for the first time ever *both* major political parties adopted at least mild Civil Rights platform planks in 1944, and Truman issued his Executive Order 9981, *To Secure These Rights,* on behalf of a desegregated military in 1947. The qualifier "modern" Civil Rights era distinguishes the 1940s from the long, continuous African American freedom struggle of earlier years precisely because this shifting context lent the struggle a new claim on federal conscience and a new fulcrum to leverage real gains through federal intervention. In 1941 A. Philip Randolph's threatened March on Washington over racist hiring practices in the war industries capitalized on FDR's public relations need of American democracy's highly buffed appearance. Though this particular victory was won without the march itself ever taking place, the tactic of street-level agitation aimed at a pro-Civil Rights *federal* response became the basic playbook up through the passage of the Civil Rights and Voting Rights Acts of the 1960s. The United States did not magically become anti-racist, but the geopolitical imperatives of World War II and the ensuing Cold War did give rise to "official" pronouncements that were not without their uses.

His time as a soldier from 1943 to 1945 gave Davis some close experience with all of these contending forces. The war years became a watershed in his own life in that Fort Warren was his introduction to the full-on cruelties of American racism, yet the Army also afforded him an opportunity to hone his skills as a performer independently of the Will Mastin Trio. Performing in the Special Services camp shows, Davis came of age both literally and figuratively as an entertainer, away from the surveilling eyes and judgments of his father and surrogate uncle. He emerged from the service with the experience, confidence, and performing chops that would quickly win him recognition as "the kid in the middle" when he rejoined the Trio after the war. Meanwhile, his Army experience outfitted him with the working philosophy that would characterize his cultural politics for decades to come, the certainty that *talent* would be the weapon in the war against racism. In this, Davis perhaps took a political turn in the opposite direction of many others who had watershed experiences with racism during the war. "The treatment accorded the Negro during the Second World War marks, for me, a turning point in the Negro's relation to America," wrote James Baldwin.

> A certain hope died, a certain respect for white Americans faded. One began to pity them. You must put yourself in the skin of a man who is wearing the uniform of his country, is a candidate for death in its defense, and who is called a 'nigger' by his comrades-in-arms and his officers; who is almost always given the hardest, ugliest, most menial work to do; who knows that the white G.I. has informed the Europeans that he is subhuman (so much for the American male's sexual security); who does not dance at the U.S.O. the night white soldiers dance there, and does not drink in the same bars white soldiers drink in; and who watches German prisoners of war being treated by Americans with more human dignity than he has ever received at their hands. And who, at the same time, as a human being, is far freer in a strange land than he has ever been at home. *Home!* The very word begins to have a despairing and diabolical ring.[3]

In this respect Davis is almost the anti-Baldwin. The two were reared by the conditions of the same time and place, Harlem in the mid-1920s (Baldwin was one year Davis's senior), and they would later become unlikely friends.

Baldwin once observed sympathetically that Davis had to choose between greatness and madness, and chose greatness.[4] In *No Name in the Street* (1972) Baldwin also recalled sitting in the pew right behind Marlon Brando, Eartha Kitt, and Davis at the Martin Luther King Jr. funeral, and it was Davis who caught him by the arm when Baldwin stumbled as they came out of the service.[5] But the two emerged from the life-bending crucible of the war oriented in different directions entirely. "If the war didn't happen to kill you," George Orwell once observed, "it was bound to start you thinking."[6] James Baldwin emerged from the war a lifelong dissident, and by his mid-twenties an expatriate, too. Davis emerged a can-do believer in the anti-racist power of his own abilities as a singer and dancer—"he felt the haters could not withstand his talent"—and therefore an odd believer in the American project, even if on occasion he did hear its "diabolical ring." In this Davis carried with him a good dose of the minstrel tradition that had nurtured him. It was the popular nineteenth-century minstrel performer, Billy Kersands, who once said "If they hate me, I'm still whipping them, because I'm making them laugh."[7]

PATRIOTISM, RACE, AND WAR

There are two distinct historical layers to African Americans' military participation and their fight for full citizenship in the 1940s. One is the general masculinist logic that had defined citizenship since the words "We the People" were first uttered in the eighteenth century. That the "voting public" ought to be the "fighting public" was a common conception. It was trotted out regularly in response to women's suffrage in the nineteenth century, for example. It pointed back to a time and a logic that rendered the "citizen-soldier" as a particular ideal for a settler democracy whose chief citizenly duties might well include arming for Indian Wars on the one hand and for slave revolts on the other. The same exclusions that rendered "We the People" as *white* in dominant ideology also rendered it *male* and *armed*.

It is therefore not coincidental that African American struggles for inclusion and equality have often imbibed masculinst assumptions regarding the citizen-soldier, since overcoming the exclusion by race would mean adopting the *inclusion* by soldiery. And thus it was that African American participation became a salient feature of every US military engagement beginning with Crispus Attucks in the Revolutionary War, which would establish the white republic. The Buffalo Soldiers fought on the plains and helped extend the domain of that white republic. In Cuba and the Philippines, black soldiers joined a war that solidified the white supremacist bargain that restitched the nation a generation after the Civil War. The 1898–99 wars in Cuba and the Philippines were ultimately imperial wars of subjugation (even if advertised on humanitarian grounds); but many African Americans nonetheless sought the civic payoffs of military participation and valor, while others may have dreamed of opportunities for themselves in tropical climes after the wars.[8]

The promise of the Great War was more explicit still: Woodrow Wilson had called it a "war for democracy" in his April, 1917 speech before Congress, prompting many African Americans to seek their "civil rights through carnage," as one historian put it.[9] But when black soldiers joined the Great War, they found leaflets distributed by the US government mentoring European allies in the Jim Crow treatment of black soldiers. In *The Crisis,* Du Bois famously announced after the war, "We return. We return from fighting. We return fighting," thereby announcing the arrival of the postwar period's "New Negro," a militant, rights-conscious figure who was on view in the pitched battles of the Red Summer in 1919, and celebrated in the Renaissance-era arts, like Claude MacKay's poem, "If We Must Die":

> Like men we'll face the murderous, cowardly pack,
> Pressed to the wall, dying, but fighting back.[10]

In a letter to his draft board, one returning soldier rather forcefully asked, "You low-down Mother Fuckers can put a gun in our hands, but who is able to take it out?" Others saw the matter as soldier Elisha Green did: "it would be better to die in France as a man than to die in America as a nigger at the hands of a despicable evil white man."[11] In all of this, there was an ineluctable nexus between the national imperatives of war and the race-based understanding of—and aspirations for—equality and citizenship.

The second historical layer of the military-Civil Rights nexus had specifically to do with World War II. The culture of the American left, beginning within the Communist Party but including the Popular Front more generally, had long equated fascism and racism. Flashpoints included the passage of the anti-Jewish Nuremberg Laws in Germany and Mussolini's invasion of Ethiopia, both in 1935, but the analysis was wider than this. The genesis of the Double Victory campaign—victory against fascism abroad and against racism at home—once the United States had entered the war resided in precisely this analysis of the echoes of American Jim Crow that reverberated throughout Europe as Nazism. Josh White's rendition of Langston Hughes's antifascist song "Freedom's Road" underscored this connection. In his triumphal promise of "marching down freedom's road," Hughes had written,

> Ought to be plain as the nose on your face,
> There's room in this plan for every race. . . .

White rendered the same line as, "there's room in the *land* for every race," thereby shifting the meaning of the following lines:

> Some folk think that freedom just ain't right
> Those are the very people I want to fight.

In performance White also subtly altered the line "Ain't no fascists gonna stop me, no Nazis gonna keep me / From marching down freedom's road." His version asserts, "no fascists gonna stop me, no *Natchez* gonna keep me," again heightening the connection between the epic battle against fascism abroad and the ongoing struggle for freedom at home.[12] American hypocrisy became a politically galvanizing force. African American pilots may have hoped that "Europe's skies would prove Jim Crow's graveyard," as historian Kimberly Philips writes. "At 27,000 feet, Nazi flak and fighter pilots are deadly accurate in knocking down Jim Crow," but back on the home front, according to the *Defender*, "Dixie prefers Nazis to Negroes."[13]

The geopolitics of World War II generated a contradictory amalgam of racial ideas that rendered struggles for justice on the home front at once dynamic, hopeful, desperate, and hazardous. This two-theater war represented contending propositions on the racial front. On the one hand, the fight in Europe was frankly billed as a "war against racism." Though never as keen on drawing a strict equation of Jim Crow and Hitlerism as activists of the left, nonetheless even for political centrists, and ultimately the apparatus of federal government, Nazi legal systems became an apt symbol of injustices that were "un-American." Blaring, front-page *New York Times* reporting on the passage of the Nuremberg Laws had defined this moment as Germany's "[flinging] down the gauntlet before the feet of Western liberal opinion."[14]

But meanwhile, in the Pacific war, race itself supplied the very language of enmity. In Europe the United States fought to remove hostile and dangerous regimes—to free Germany and Italy from the evil political parties who were advancing fascism. In Asia, the United States did not merely fight a regime or an emperor, but an entire *people*. In popular discussion and official oratory the Japanese were "vermin," "lice," "monkey-men," "cockroaches or mice," "vipers," a "yellow serpent," a "veritable human beehive or anthill," whose total "extermination" or "annihilation" was consistently favored by a significant percentage of the US population.[15]

The domestic project of Japanese-American internment depended on the Orientalist assumption that, while the ordinary German might be extracted from the project of Nazism, there was no such redemption for the Japanese nor even the Japanese-American. On the matter of US loyalty, according to California Attorney General Earl Warren, "when we deal with the Japanese we are in an entirely different field [in distinction to 'Caucasians'] and we cannot form any opinion that we believe to be sound." The Japanese in America, Warren implied, were in some sense *unknowable,* which is why, unlike German- or Italian-Americans, they had to be interned en masse. John L. DeWitt, head of the Western Defense Command that oversaw internment, flatly declared, "a Jap is a Jap."[16] The idea of the Pacific war as a race war found expression unabashedly, loosely, and broadly in every arena of American life and discourse in the war years. It turned up in political oratory and reportage, in pro-Ally print cartoons by Theodore Geisel (Dr. Seuss) or animations like *Bugs Bunny Nips the Nips* (1944); in US Army propaganda films like Frank Capra's *Know Your Enemy—Japan* (1943) or Chuck Jones's *Spies* (1943); and in popular songs pressed on shellac and beamed over the airwaves, including "Let's Take a Rap at the Japs," "We've Got a Job to Do on the Japs, Baby," "You're a Sap, Mr. Jap," "We're Going to Have to Slap that Dirty Little Jap," "We're Going to Find a Fellow Who Is Yellow and Beat Him Red, White, and Blue," and—in an ode to the multiethnic US platoon—"When Those Little Yellow Bellies Meet the Cohens and the Kellys."[17]

And then of course there was the fact of a segregated military. "The efforts of African Americans to withstand the violence *within* the military were as significant as their efforts to endure the horrors of combat," writes Kimberly Philips.[18] Though the services had initially been slow to recruit across the color line, by 1944 there were nearly a million African Americans serving in uniform, including 702,000 in the Army and 165,000 in the Navy. Most either served in all-black units under white officers, or served in "white" units as cooks, porters, laborers, or servants.[19] While the administration argued that "Negroes might be inspired to take pride in the efficiency of Negro units in the Army, as representing their contribution to the armed forces," the point of segregation was never merely *separation,* but degradation and the production of racial hierarchy in a thousand ways, great and small.[20]

The segregated military not only enforced the degraded status of black soldiers as second-class citizens, but as a pamphlet on *The Negro March on Washington* pointed out, "Negroes in separate regiments can more easily be assigned to dirty work or extremely dangerous work than they could if they were with white soldiers in mixed regiments. It is [also] much easier to pick out a Negro regiment as a 'suicide squad'. . . ." In "Four Freedoms at Home," Albert Parker noted that "Hitler is retreating on the eastern front and Mussolini is an ex-dictator. But Jim Crow is as brazen and aggressive and powerful as he has ever been during the twentieth century."[21] The late historian David Brion Davis once recounted that, as a private in the Army during the war, one day on the troop ship to France he had been ordered to "go down and make sure the niggers aren't gambling." The young white soldier registered shock on two counts: the nature and vulgarity of the order, but also the fact that they had been at sea for several days and he had never seen any African Americans aboard ship. Venturing down to the bowels of the mechanical rooms, as he was instructed to do, he discovered several African American sailors, naked and shoveling coal in what seemed like hundred and twenty degree heat in the boiler room. "That scene could not been more than a whisper away from slavery," he told me.[22] This was the first reckoning of the man who went on to write *The Problem of Slavery in Western Culture,* among others.

Such inequities within the military—and the struggle against them— were everywhere discussed among African Americans, in the black press, and occasionally in the white press as well. A letter writer to *Yank, The Army Weekly* described how German prisoners of war at Fort Huachuca (Cochise County, Arizona) were treated with more dignity and accorded more rights than African American soldiers. "Are these men sworn enemies of this country? Are they not taught to hate and destroy . . . all democratic governments? Are we not American soldiers, sworn to fight for and die if need be for this our country? Then why are they treated better than we are? Why are we pushed around like cattle?"[23] A black soldier wrote in to the *Cleveland Call & Post* to protest conditions at Camp Claiborne (Louisiana): "Now right at this moment the woods are swarming with Louisiana hoogies armed with rifles and shot guns even the little kids have 22 cal. rifles and BB guns filled with anxiety to shoot a Negro soldier." The place is "a living hell," he wrote; "I am a Northern boy and we feel that we can't tolerate these conditions any longer. I hope there's some way the Negro people of Cleveland Detroit Chicago & New York the individuals who understand a better Way of life would instigate an investigation of this place. . . ."[24] Though far too old for service himself, Bill "Bojangles" Robinson intervened directly with Mayor Fiorello LaGuardia to protest the Army's quartering white soldiers in Atlantic City and segregating black soldiers at the Hotel Theresa in Harlem. "America had become a stranger to my earliest dreams," wrote John A. Williams of his own wartime experience, which included coming under armed threat from a white fellow-soldier in the New Hebrides. As the writer at Camp Claiborne concluded, "they say fight for democracy in foreign lands and islands we have never heard of before when it doesn't exist here."[25]

These ripsaw crosswinds—war against racism, war for white supremacy—buffeted the politics of the home front, ultimately birthing what we know as the modern Civil Rights movement, especially its claims against—and its purchase on—the federal government. Some of the most radical formulations concerning race, democracy, and anti-fascism emerged even before US entrance into the war, calling into question the world-saving claims advanced by the Roosevelt Administration. "I am not afraid to fight," C. L. R. James wrote. "Negroes have been some of the greatest fighters in history. But the democracy that I want to fight for, Hitler is not depriving me of."[26] Under the pen name J. R. Johnson, James published a ten-installment brief against the war in the *Socialist Appeal* in the fall of 1939, "Why Negroes Should Oppose the War." Elaborating an analysis of race, rights, and political economy that ranged from the Jim Crow South to colonized Africa to the black experience as pawns in that first "war for democracy" in 1917, James laid out a radical critique that increasingly found voice in more mainstream black discourse.

The hypocrisy of it all, for James and others, resided at the center of the question.

> When Roosevelt and other so-called lovers of 'democracy' protested to Hitler against his treatment of the Jews, Hitler laughed scornfully and replied, 'look at how you treat the Negroes. I learned how to persecute Jews by studying the manner in which you Americans persecute Negroes.' Roosevelt has no answer to that. Yet he will call upon Negroes to go to war against Hitler.[27]

Similarly the *Pittsburgh Courier* cautioned, "Before any of our people get unduly excited about SAVING DEMOCRACY in Europe, it should be called to their attention that we have NOT YET ACHIEVED DEMOCRACY

HERE. We cannot save what DOES NOT EXIST."[28] A. Philip Randolph's first March on Washington Movement, also before the US entrance into the war, sought to at least partially right these wrongs by challenging discriminatory practices in the federally-backed and already burgeoning defense industries. The mere threat to Roosevelt—alter the racist hiring practices in factories that thrive on federal dollars, or we will embarrass you before the world with a monster black rally on the National Mall—resulted in Executive Order 8802, prohibiting discrimination in the defense industries. The order was often defied, but it represented a victory for grassroots struggle that would set the pattern for a generation.[29]

The March on Washington had originated in a mass meeting in Chicago, where a member of the Women's Auxiliary of the Brotherhood of Sleeping Car Porters had argued, "We ought to throw 50,000 Negroes around the White House, bring them from all over the country, in jalopies, in trains and in any way they can get there. . . ."[30] This spirit persisted throughout the war years, and outlasted them as the anti-racist critique that underpinned black discourse on the war carried over and intensified. The *Pittsburgh Courier* launched the famous Double Victory campaign in January of 1942, only weeks after the attack on Pearl Harbor. That campaign began with a letter to the editor by one James G. Thompson. Among the questions he posed were:

> Should I sacrifice my life to live half American? Will things be better for the next generation in the peace to follow? Would it be demanding too much to demand full citizenship rights in exchange for the sacrificing of my life? Is the kind of America I know worth defending? Will America be a true and pure democracy after this war? Will Colored Americans suffer still the indignities that have been heaped upon them in the past?

Referencing the common "V for victory" sign displayed in public places, Thompson suggested adopting "a double VV for a double victory. The first for victory over our enemies from without, the second V for victory over our enemies from within."[31] Black newspapers like the *Pittsburgh Courier,* the *Amsterdam News,* the *Baltimore Afro-American,* the *Richmond Afro-American,* and the *Chicago Defender* were laced with stories about the inequities of military life, from separate and unequal facilities on base; to rules and regulations unequally applied; to exclusions from the PX or the base church; to servile work assignments with no chance of advancement.[32] They were laced, too, with reports of violence against black soldiers—a shooting in Beaumont or a stabbing in Corpus Christi; murder at the hands of a bus driver in Alexandria, Louisiana, or even at the hands of the Military Police. In a "Statement to the Nation" in 1943, the NAACP decried "the continued ill treatment of Negroes in uniform, both on military reservations and in many civilian communities.... Negroes in the uniform of the nation have been beaten, mobbed, killed and lynched."[33]

Reflecting on the travails of African Americans in *An American Dilemma* (1944), Swedish sociologist Gunnar Myrdal predicted, "The present War will, in all probability, increase their discontent with their status in America."[34] Indeed, the rhetoric of the war and the national mobilization on behalf of "democracy" convinced many African Americans that Roosevelt's vaunted "Four Freedoms" might be made to have something to do with *them*. Freedom from want, for example. Struggles for equitable treatment in the military and the defense industries, skills picked up in the context of war, black women's escape from domestic work into skilled positions in the shipyards and aircraft and munitions factories: all of this suggested that horizons were widening.

Freedom from fear was tougher; as American history has shown again and again, conditions are never quite as dangerous for African Americans as they are in those moments when the promise of change is in the wind. White supremacist backlash almost always turns out upon closer inspection to be *frontlash* as white insistence on racial primacy rears its head *in advance* of significant gains or of promises fulfilled. Take the imposition of Jim Crow in the decades after Emancipation; the anti-black violence during both World Wars; and later on the "segregation now, segregation forever" politics of the Civil Rights-era South or the escalating pace of hate crimes in the Obama years. In 1943 the Social Science Institute at Fisk University monitored racial violence in forty-seven US cities, many involving "hate strikes" of white workers to keep African Americans out of defense plants or violent eruptions around the integration of worker housing, as when the Sojourner Truth Housing Project for black workers was constructed in a white neighborhood in Detroit. At first driven away by white throngs wielding clubs, knives, and guns, the black workers were able to assume occupancy at Sojourner Truth only with the protection of 1,750 state and local police.[35]

The worst of the wartime racial violence occurred in Detroit and Harlem. The Detroit riot in June of 1943 began with a skirmish at Cadillac Park, where tens of thousands of black and white residents had gathered in close proximity. As in Chicago in 1919, the violence escalated and spread quickly, from the original antagonists to large numbers of combatants on both sides whose fury derived from longstanding frictions and grievances but was now unleashed amid rapidly advancing libels and rumors. Eventually there was full-on urban warfare. Between Sunday and Tuesday (June 20–22), hundreds of people were injured, thirty-four were killed, and scores of fires, overturned cars, and looted businesses added up to over two million dollars in damage (equivalent to $29.5M today). In a postmortem that will haunt today's reader, the *Crisis* reported on the complicity or even full participation of Detroit police in anti-black violence:

> Three quarters of the Negroes killed were shot by police. Not a single white person was shot by police. More than 90 percent of those arrested for rioting were Negroes. Yet all the pictures showed white people chasing, kicking, and beating colored people. There were many graphic and horrible pictures of the riot, but the most meaningful to the theme of this piece was the one showing a Negro being struck in the face by a white rioter as he was being escorted by *two* policemen![36]

A writer in the *Christian Century* was quick to contrast the violence in Detroit and the lofty claims attached to the war effort: "The nation is at war, according to the President, in order to make possible a world in which there shall be, for all people, freedom from fear." *Freedom from fear,* he scoffed, "with mobs sweeping up and down the streets of cities, shouting 'Kill the d—n niggers!' 'Kill the d—n greasers!' 'Kill the d—n Japs!' Freedom from fear! Will not the words stick in our throats?"[37]

Several weeks later, on August 1, the tinderbox that was Harlem erupted as well. "What happened in defense plants and Army camps had repercussions, naturally, in every Negro ghetto," wrote James Baldwin.[38] When a soldier on leave from a nearby base in New Jersey, Robert Bandy, intervened in a scuffle between a white police officer and a black couple in the lobby of the Braddock Hotel on West 126th Street, the officer shot him in the shoulder. Rumors quickly spread through the neighborhood that Bandy had been killed and huge crowds gathered, both at the hotel and at the Sydenham Hospital two blocks away, where Bandy was being treated. Rage overflowed, and the multitude began smashing store windows along 125th Street. "It would have been better to have left the plate glass as it had been and the goods lying in the stores," Baldwin wrote. "It would have been better, but it would have been intolerable, for Harlem needed something to smash. To smash something is the ghetto's chronic need."[39] Mayor Fiorello LaGuardia hurried to Harlem to plead in person for calm on both sides of the blue line, and to combat the rampant rumors of Bandy's death. The Mayor continued his pleas over the radio as well, but by the time calm prevailed a day later some 500 people had been injured and six killed; 550 had been arrested; and 1,450 stores had sustained damages totaling $5 million ($74 million today). It took over 7,000 police and nearly as many from the National Guard to subdue the rebellion.

In *Marching Blacks* (1945), Adam Clayton Powell Jr. referred to the Harlem uprising as "the last open revolt against a bastard democracy [and] the whole sorrowful, disgraceful bloody record of America's treatment of one million blacks in uniform."[40] But if Powell and others were inclined to emphasize the "blind, smoldering and unorganized resentment against Jim Crow treatment of Negro men in the armed forces" alongside resentments of "the unusual high rents and cost of living forced upon Negroes in Harlem," what made the uprising in Harlem a *political* event was the breadth of consensus and even participation across Harlem society.[41] This was not just a masculinist uprising against the injuries of the Jim Crow military, it was a *community* outpouring. Martin Luther King Jr. would later define rioting itself as "the language of the unheard." Ann Petry's short story "In Darkness and Confusion," written soon after the violence but published only after the war, portrays this vividly.[42] The buttoned-up protagonist William Jones initially takes a dim view of his niece Annie May and her friends—"Too much lipstick. Their dresses were too short and too tight. . . . They were all chewing gum and they nudged each other and talked too loud and laughed too loud. They stared hard at every man who went past them."[43] By the end, Annie May has won his understanding and even grudging respect, as the entire community is united in the rage of the riot. One wonders, with Farah Jasmine Griffin, whether these "too-too girls" might have been the female analogue to the zoot suiters, a disaffected subgroup whose hip style, in Ralph Ellison's words, "conceals profound political meaning." Did forms like bebop, the Lindy Hop, or "too short and too tight" dresses embody energies and frustrations of the sort that were unleashed in the chaos of the wartime riots? This seems to have been Petry's view, and the moral of her story. After Jones witnesses the hotel-lobby confrontation that would spark the day of violence in Harlem, the work becomes, in Griffin's words "the story of the crowd."[44]

Petry renders the dynamics of the riot with awesome power and economy. Much of this work is accomplished by a tight constellation of characters, whose relationships stand in for the entire wartime black community. These are Jones, a straightlaced middle-aged man who works at the corner drugstore; his church-going wife, Pink; Annie May, who has been living with them in Harlem since her mother (Pink's sister) passed away; and their son Sam, a soldier now stationed down in Georgia. A certain foreboding surrounds the latter, who has fallen out of communication with the family entirely. "Sam's being in the army wasn't so bad," Jones thought. "It was his being in Georgia that was bad." A child of the Great Migration, Jones could not help but dwell on his mother's long-ago warnings. "The very sound of the word Georgia did something to him inside. His mother had been born there. . . . 'They hate niggers down there. Don't you never let none of you children go down there.'"[45] Sure enough. At the barbershop, amid congenial talk of how the "only thing to do, if you ask me, is shoot all them crackers and start out new . . .," Jones learns that Sam himself has been shot by a white MP because "he wouldn't go to the nigger end of a bus." He was then court-martialed for wrenching the gun away and shooting the MP in the shoulder.[46]

Later, in a hotel that stands in for the Braddock of the actual Harlem riot, Jones witnesses a scuffle between a white cop and a "frowzy-looking girl." The cop pushes her roughly; she calls him a "white son of a bitch." When a black soldier comes to her aid—the Robert Bandy of this equation—the cop shoots him. A "tall thin black man" standing next to Jones comments, "That ties it. It ain't even safe here where we live. Not no more. I'm goin' to get me a white bastard of a cop and nail his hide to a street sign."[47] The action from there follows the general geography of the August riot, around 125th and 126th streets.

> Now there were so many people in back of [Jones] and in front of him that when they started toward the hospital, he moved along with them. He hadn't decided to go—the forward movement picked him up and moved him along without any intention on his part. He got the idea that he had lost his identity as a person with a free will of his own. It frightened him at first. Then he began to feel powerful. He was surrounded by hundreds of people like himself. They could do anything.[48]

Petry's sociology of the black community in action is carried in Jones's rapid education among the throngs—not only his shifting sense of identity as it melds with a community whose members he had judged quite harshly, but in his observation and new understanding of black unity, as he witnesses Pink throwing a bottle through a storefront and Annie May pulling a mannequin out of a display window as another store stands gaping and looted.[49] Jones had earlier judged Annie May something of a "Jezebel," and for her part every time the girl looked at him "there was open, jeering laughter in her eyes."[50] But Jones looks at her differently amid the unfolding scene of the riot. "She had never had anything but badly paying jobs working for young white women who probably despised her," he reflects. "She was like Sam on that bus in Georgia. She didn't want just the nigger end of things." Finally, observing bitterly that "White folks got us comin' and goin,'" even Jones himself participates in the looting.[51]

All the elements of the modern Civil Rights era were apparent during the war. There was the political strategy, as enacted in the threatened March on Washington to force FDR's hand. There was also the dissonant promise and dashed hopes embodied in the "war for democracy" as conducted by a Jim Crow Army and the Northern disaffection on display in Detroit and Harlem, an arsenal of outrage on behalf of a struggle that white Americans would like to think of as distinctly Southern. But also, as in Petry's rendering of those who took to the streets of Harlem, there was an entire community galvanized and in motion. A headline in the *New York Times* on August 3, 1943 blared, "500 Are Arraigned in Harlem Looting: 100 Women Among Prisoners Crowding Courts After Night Disorders."[52] It was an apt window onto the era of mass mobilization that was just taking form.

DAVIS'S WARTIME FIGHT

Davis's description of his own experience during the war is pivotal to his personal narrative. His travails in the service became a centerpiece in his retelling. This was not only because his service experience broke the protective shell that Davis Sr. and Mastin had established for him personally. It is also because it invoked the continuing power of that emblematic contradiction in postwar culture, the black soldier toiling amid the humiliations and dangers of a race-stratified military on behalf of a country that knew neither racial justice nor true democracy. Davis's Fort Warren experience featured prominently wherever his story was told as his star rose in the 1950s, whether in *Life, Ebony, The Saturday Evening Post,* or the *New York Post,* and it provides a foundational moment in his first autobiography, *Yes I Can.*[53] When he went into the Army, he told Tony Brown on PBS's *Black Journal* (1971),

that was my first taste, really, of racism, ever, because I had never been exposed to it, being in show business.... As a kid being in show business, I didn't learn until later why we had to sleep in bus stations, or why we had to go to the police and say, where is there a colored family that you could stay with, because you couldn't get into hotels, things like that, and you couldn't eat in this restaurant. But there was a very close fraternity between most of the black and white performers at that time.[54]

But his protective wall crumbled as he was mustering into the service in California, before even arriving at his assigned base. Davis was standing in a line among new recruits in Monterey when a white soldier challenged him: "where I come from niggers stand in the back of the line." Davis swung his duffle, knocking the man down, to which the reply was, "OK you knocked me down, but you're still a nigger." "That laid with me, you know, because that's so venomous," Davis recalled, "that's the kind of cat that you ain't never going to reach." In other recollections Davis transposed this episode to the base in Wyoming, but it remains plausible either way. As biographer Gary Fishgall notes, it is difficult to square some details with what is known of the military sites Davis is describing. But overall Fishgall endorses the temper of the Davis Army narrative, accepting that "Davis's military service provided the crucible for the extreme consciousness-raising he described. . . ."[55]

Fort Francis E. Warren (now a US Air Force base), was a complex of low, wooden buildings a few miles outside Cheyenne, built in the 1860s to provide military protection for the project of laying transcontinental railroad tracks through Indian lands. Warren had started out as a small western outpost, but by World War II had grown to over two hundred hastily constructed barracks and housed tens of thousands of soldiers. Although in the nineteenth century the fort had been home to three of the Army's four African American regiments (the so-called Buffalo Soldiers), racialized relations were never easy on the base. The commanding officer at the post, Brigadier General John A. Warden, was notorious for creating an inhospitable climate for black soldiers. An aide to the Secretary of War reported in 1942, "I found the Negro soldiers very bitter with reference to alleged manifestations of racial prejudice" on the part of the General, including his unwillingness to promote black soldiers into the ranks of noncommissioned officers and his loose deployment of the n-word. The first group of black trainees during the civilian call-up in 1941 was transferred out due to racial tensions locally.[56]

The wide-open Wyoming landscape might have been familiar to Davis, who had already spent some time in Vegas, but the tight, tense quarters were not. "When I walked in the barracks," he recalled, "the cats were all sleeping. I finally went up to one guy, woke him, and asked which was my bunk. This guy just looked up at me and said, 'Why you asking me, you—?' That did it. This was the first time I'd ever in my life been away from Dad and Will, and I just started to cry."[57] But over time, the real problem for Davis was the close contact at Fort Warren between black and white troops, and in particular the unrelenting cruelties of a certain contingent of white Southerners—like the offending soldier in Monterey—who seemingly could not get enough of tormenting their black comrades-in-arms.

> I met some prejudiced cats—all right? I got pushed and banged around some, got my nose broken twice—all right? But the roughest part wasn't that: the *roughest* was psychological.... Until the Army, nobody white had ever just looked at me and *hated* me—and didn't even *know* me. From the time I got into the basic training center ... from the first *ten minutes,* I started hearing more "nigger" and seeing more sneers and hate looks than I'd ever known all my life. Walked inside the *gate,* asked a cat sitting on some barracks steps to show me how to get to where I had to go: "Excuse me, buddy, I'm a little lost—" Cat told me, "I'm not your buddy, you black bastard!"[58]

"I had been drafted into the Army to fight, and I did," he wrote in *Yes I Can.*[59] Until his own talents as a performer rescued him and he was reassigned to a Special Service unit devoted to "entertaining the troops" (a forerunner of the USO), Davis's Fort Warren experience involved plenty of fisticuffs and some truly harrowing encounters with white soldiers. "Look, we got a problem," he heard one white soldier complain upon his arrival. "These niggers out there are assigned to this company."[60] If the war against Nazism was a war against racism, many in the US Army had not received that memo. White soldiers complained of having to sleep in proximity to black soldiers; they balked at using the same latrines; they hurled epithets—"I didn't join no nigger army"—and they picked fights at every opportunity. The worst of them bullied the best of them into submitting to a racist regime within barracks; potential white allies were effectively silenced.[61]

Fistfights and brawls in the barracks or the club typically began and ended as good, old-fashioned white-on-black mob actions. The most vicious of the assaults on Davis usually involved a white Texan ringleader named Jennings. They included white soldiers serving up a beer bottle full of urine, and then pouring it over Davis. Another gang assault, as recounted in the preface, ended with the words "I'm a nigger" and "Coon" in white paint across Davis's chest and forehead. "Dance, Sambo," came the order under armed threat. "I started moving my feet and tapping...."[62] As Davis was always outnumbered, the results of these clashes were predictable, though a sympathetic commanding officer did bust Jennings to KP duty on occasion. But Davis sometimes gave as good as he got, actually knocking out his assailant at one point. ("I had sent Jennings to the infirmary. What beautiful news.")[63] Although he was slight of build, Davis did possess the athleticism of a dancer, and he had seen enough "cutting sessions" in his day to fully understand the codes and the violence of masculinist bravado. And besides, he added in a 1978 interview, "I knew how to fight. My dad and my friend Sugar Ray Robinson taught me."[64]

Significantly, on this question of vulnerability Davis did once intimate that he might have been raped at Fort Warren, though his account was ambiguous. Davis's fluid sexuality was a topic of open discussion in Hollywood circles later on, though Davis himself never exactly came out. A current website devoted to "out and proud bisexual celebrities" includes Davis, along with the note that he had once told Paul Anka, "Hell, man, I'm living my life the way I want to. No restraints, no hang-ups. It's my time and I'm gonna do it the way I want to."[65] One of Davis's few public comments on the subject was in a 1978 interview in which it is difficult to say whether he is attesting to sexual experimentation or reporting a sexual assault: "You make a choice. I was in the Army. I was 17, and I was little. A friend once warned me, 'Hey, Sammy, don't ever do anything that'd get you busted. Little cats don't make it past the front door in prison.' I didn't know what he meant. I learned in the Army." Although he had edged into this discussion as a story of "a homosexual experience" that he was "not ashamed" of, *I learned in the Army* carries an implication of coercion that matches much of his service experience, minus the explicit racial component.[66]

Suggesting the always potentially violent confluence of sexuality and race on base, the vicious attack that ended with racial epithets painted across Davis's body was the consequence of Jennings and his gang misinterpreting Davis's attentions toward a white Women's Army Corps officer as *romantic*. The truth was, Davis was trying to pitch an act for a stage show that the WAC captain oversaw. Engagement in such base entertainments, it turned out, was Davis's ticket into relative safety. His performances on the base also poured the foundation of his philosophy that talent could overcome racism, that his brief hour on stage could undo the hatred that ran through the ranks. "I lived twenty-four hours a day for that hour or two at night when I could stand on that stage, facing the audience, knowing that I was dancing down the barriers between us."[67]

A corporal named George M. Cohan Jr., known for his postwar work on *Robert Q's Matinee* and *The Ed Sullivan Show,* approached Davis about a collaboration. Though ten years his senior, Cohan, like Davis, had grown up in and around show business. He was the son of a vaudeville actor who by this time had become famous as the composer of "Yankee Doodle's Come to Town," "Over There," "Give My Regards to Broadway," "Stars and Stripes Forever," and "You're a Grand Old Flag." (Davis would later stoke his own fame with an imitation of James Cagney, whose 1942 *Yankee Doodle Dandy* brought the Cohan biography to screen. Small world.) Cohan Jr., perhaps as a result of his pedigree, had developed some pull in the world of US service entertainments. Spotting Davis's talent, he introduced the idea of co-writing some material for an inter-camp entertainment competition. The other acts would be using canned material "out of the Special Services books," he said, and perhaps Cohan and Davis could make a splash with original material. Davis's audition for this competition represented his first attempt at a Sinatra impression.[68]

His collaboration with Cohan was a success, and Davis was classified as an "entertainment specialist," spending the remainder of his time in the army with a group devoted to entertainment and morale. "For eight months I did shows in camps across the country, gorging myself on the joys of being liked," he wrote. The "camps across the country" piece is an unsquareable detail: his personnel record locates him at Fort Warren throughout.[69] But the entertainment piece, and the significance of *being liked,* seems accurate. The theme of overcoming humiliation through the force of his talent had surfaced before in Davis's narrative, when he was slighted on a date in Harlem by a woman who ditched him in a movie theater. It was not just racial injury, then, but gender or sexual injury, too, whose salve was to be found in success on the stage. "Nothing could change the fact that I had been so unimportant to her that she couldn't even remember I was waiting for her. . . ." But a little daydreaming showed the way forward. "I closed my eyes . . . I was headlining the Paramount. She was sitting up front waving at me, hoping I'd notice her."[70] This twinning of race and sex is important to Davis's conception of categories like "dignity" and "indignity," and so whenever Davis faced racial affronts, concerns about masculinity were never very far behind.

A second point about Davis's formulation "gorging myself on the joys of being liked" is that it underscores an emerging personal philosophy of anti-bigotry, self-possession, and manhood that would characterize his life at the intersection of culture and politics for many decades to come. In the Army, he later told Alex Haley in his famous *Playboy* interview,

I met the most concentrated bunch of haters I ever experienced: On that stage, for the eight months I was in Special Services, that spotlight erased my color. It made the hate leave their faces temporarily. It was as if my talent gave me a pass from their prejudice, if only temporarily. And when I spotted haters in the audiences, I tried to give extra good performances. I had to *get* to them, to neutralize them, to make them recognize me. It was in the Army that I got the conviction that I had to become a great enough entertainer that the hatred of prejudiced people couldn't touch me anymore. See?[71]

ENTERTAINING THE TROOPS

To say that Davis escaped into the entertainment detail is not to say that he fully escaped the racism of the US Army. Throughout the war, the project of "entertaining the troops," by both tradition and by GI regulation, was rooted in the project of the minstrel show. Although the whole point of Cohan's tapping Davis at Fort Warren was to get away from the "stuff out of the Special Services books," and although we cannot know exactly what Cohan and Davis came up with and what Davis was actually doing on stage, we do know that in taking the stage on base he was entering a world very much defined by the conventions of blackface minstrelsy. One government-issue guidebook for such on-base entertainments produced by the USO, unabashedly titled *Minstrel Shows* (1942), begins with quite meticulous instructions regarding the fabrication and application of burnt cork:

> We recommend . . . that 'burnt cork' be used because it is easy to apply, does not damage clothing and is easy to remove. Several handfuls of corks should be placed in an old, tin pail which can serve as a furnace. . . . After the corks have been thoroughly burned, they should be crushed and reduced to a powder by hand. This powder is then moistened with water and ground fine; the resultant paste can be . . . smeared over the features of the face, as if applying cold cream. Carefully apply it around the eyes and outline the lips. Comedians leave a wider white margin around the lips.[72]

Nor is this instruction incidental. *Minstrel Shows* in its entirety is devoted to the requisites of wartime minstrel shows as the US Armed Services saw them. Though Special Services devoted some time and energy to the question of "how soldiers see the Negro," here the instructions for mounting military entertainments proceed quite comfortably upon the assumption that it is white soldiers who are being addressed, and the perspective of black soldiers is of no account. Indeed, the syntax distinguishing "soldiers" and "the Negro" is all you need to know.[73] The scripted introduction welcomes the troops to "the magic realm of minstrelsy," noting that, "Our fathers and grandfathers found enjoyment in this native American type of entertainment. . . ." In addition to the handbook's elaborate instructions on preparing burnt cork and blacking up, scripts for two different shows are presented with precise instruction on the character of the four "end men" or comedians.

> END MAN #1, whom we have called 'Ephus,' is the small, meek, nervous type. . . . END MAN #2, who answers to the name of 'Asbestos,' is the 'Brother Crawford' type in the 'Amos and Andy' radio program. . . . END MAN #3, whose name is 'Chinchilla,' is the typical 'Andy' of 'Amos and Andy'. . . . END MAN #4, called 'Macbeth,' is the overbearing, domineering type. He should be, if possible, tremendous in size.[74]

A typical routine includes a monologue by one of the end men, a phone conversation with his "Uncle Tom" up in heaven: "How's the new cabin coming along?"

> . . . Well, it must be awful nice up there, just sitting around all day, listening to those comics like me and eating fried poultry.—(*Listens*) Huh? (*Registers surprise*) You don't eat poultry?? (*He is horrified*) You're not allowed to eat chicken up there? (*Almost pleading*) Not even one little innocent drumstick? (*A look of bewilderment covers his face for an instant*) Uncle Tom, are you *sure* you're in Heaven???[75]

Here and elsewhere, the unselfconscious and exclusive *whiteness* of the text bespeaks a thick attachment to prewar assumptions, even as the United States embarked on its "war against racism" in Germany.

The fullest surviving record of this genre of the Special Services' work is the African American set piece in *This Is the Army,* a Warner Bros. musical from 1943 featuring Ronald Reagan and George Murphy as the interlocutors or emcees.[76] Based loosely on a similar patriotic venture during the Great War in 1918, Irving Berlin had originally pitched the idea to General George C. Marshall of organizing a Broadway show whose proceeds would go to the Army Emergency Relief Fund.[77] The film version has a thin plotline but is mostly vaudeville variety, complete with elaborate plantation scenes of white actors in blackface. Sammy Davis Jr. does not appear in this film; the breakout black dance number is led by another of the Special Services recruits from the black vaudeville circuit, Jimmy "Stump" Cross.[78] Five years Davis's elder,

Cross had first made his name with a Louis Armstrong impression at a talent contest at the Lincoln Theater in Philadelphia.

Cross was known among his vaudeville peers as the most brilliant comedian and best dancer of his generation. In fact, Davis himself felt that it should not have been he, but Cross who "made it" out of black vaudeville and into the wider entertainment world. But alas, Cross's Hollywood work was mostly uncredited—as it was in *This Is the Army*—and his vaudeville act was among the casualties of early television. Cross's work in *This Is the Army* conveys the racial ambivalences and ambiguities embedded in the Special Services' wartime efforts. Staged as though the company had been unwillingly conscripted into making a statement on African Americans' wartime patriotism, the "black" section of this otherwise all-white film reads like a begrudging acknowledgment of black citizenship, whose main purpose is to put whites at ease over the prospect of arming their black compatriots. "What the Well Dressed Man in Harlem Will Wear," Irving Berlin's exuberant song and dance ode to Harlem's soldiers, is also a stand-alone, Jim Crow set piece, easily excised for the film's distribution in the South.

In both its heavily syncopated beat and the substance of its central motif—how certain people dress—"What the Well Dressed Man in Harlem Will Wear" represents Berlin's return to his 1929 hit "Puttin' on the Ritz." A medley or mash-up would be simple to arrange, so close are the two songs in style and tone. This is significant because the 1929 version of "Puttin' on the Ritz," sung by Fred Astaire, is decidedly *not* the version that would become famous after the war in *Blue Skies* (1946, also by Astaire), but is a frankly racist ditty about going up to Harlem and mocking black people. The sanitized and now best-known version talks about the "well to do" up on "Park Avenue / where fashion sits."

> High hats and narrow collars,
> White spats and lots of dollars

The now forgotten (and closely guarded) 1929 rendition was set "Up on Lenox Avenue / where Harlem flits." These are not fleeting or insignificant local references but are central to the meaning of this Harlem Renaissance-era denigration of African Americans and their culture, including a minstrelized break with tap dancing and black dialect patter between two "end men" types from the minstrel tradition. This earlier version skewers the "spangled gowns" on the crowd of "high browns"—"all misfits / Puttin' on

FIG. 6. Harlem setpiece in *This Is the Army,* 1943.

the ritz."[79] And tasked with writing a song about black patriotism during World War II, Berlin created yet another song about what "the men of Harlem" wear, revisiting his frankly racist hit from fourteen years earlier, about "LuLu-Belles" "swell beaus," and their ludicrous black "Jubilee."

Racial "ambivalence" may be too mild a term here. Implicit disparagement of African American citizenship is carried in the production aesthetics of *This Is the Army's* setpiece as well. The design is dominated by several giant, twenty-five-foot, colorfully zoot-suited and thoroughly minstrelized cut-out figures who tower over Joe Louis, Jimmy Cross, and a battalion of servicemen/dancers throughout the number. Though the purpose of these coon-like monstrosities may be to depict the disaffected zoot that the "well-dressed" man has now turned in for his GI khakis, these figures haunt the scene, as if to say that the men of Harlem can wear whatever they wish—*we* know who they are (and who they must always be). Before this set, Cross executes his comic dance routine, a virtuosic but also grinning and eye-rolling tap epic that is punctuated midway through by "Brown Bomber" Joe Louis rhythmically pounding away at a punching bag on stage.

The modern eye might scout Cross's clowning as a product of the number's white authorship and direction, but it speaks as well to complicated African

American entertainment traditions bequeathed from the minstrel stage and vaudeville, in which comedy often blunted the dangerous edges of black masculinity for the benefit of a white audience. Extant clips of Cross's earlier comic dancing with the duo "Stump and Stumpy" suggest that the number in *This Is the Army* is as much Jimmy Cross as it is Irving Berlin. What is concealed in either case is African American *seriousness,* evidently a commodity that white Americans were not ready to contemplate in 1943. As Danielle Fuentes Morgan writes, "Minstrelsy undertaken by African American performers had a subversive element and was often structured as Black comedy for Black audiences even in the presence of white viewers. . . . Black performers and audiences laughed at the foolishness of white audiences for believing in the myth of docile Blackness."[80] At least one film critic read this set piece not only within the Jim Crow presentation of the film, but within a Jim Crow *logic* of talent. "Negro cast members make it unmistakably clear that Negro rhythm is an inborn gift and that white men might as well give up trying to acquire it," opined the *New York Times,* in what someone probably thought a piece of racial liberalism or magnanimity.[81]

For the scores of black entertainers traveling the Special Services and USO circuits during the war, if the minstrelized material did not get them, then some version of Jim Crow probably would. All-black camp show units toured across the country, performing shows under titles like *Swing Is the Thing, Harlem on Parade, Swingin' on Down, Sepia Swing Revue, Keep Shufflin',* and *Rhythm and the Blues.*[82] These performers were effectively Jim Crowed out of overseas entertainments. There were no black entertainers among the 266 performers in forty-five units traveling overseas for the USO in 1943, according to the *Afro-American;* five had joined the show in Italy by 1944. "Separate but equal" was the more common paradigm. A segregated overseas "Foxhole Circuit" was established, and the US Office of War Information's Radio Section ran a program for black soldiers called *Jubilee* beginning in 1943. Over the years this featured headline entertainers like Hattie McDaniel, Billie Holiday, Ethel Waters, Lena Horne, Butterfly McQueen, and the International Sweethearts of Rhythm.[83]

But the USO's show personnel were subject to all the strictures and humiliations of Jim Crow as they traveled under the auspices of the Army, as when Hazel Scott was refused service at a stop in St. Louis. Asked why she did not identify herself to staff as the Government Issued celebrity she was, she replied, "I don't want any special privileges. There are 13 million Hazel Scotts in America. They just don't play the piano."[84] Worse, Lena Horne found herself entertaining a group of soldiers—whites in front, African

Americans in the back rows—only to discover that the white soldiers in premium seats were *German prisoners of war.* (She cannily moved to the center of the seating area, performing to the black soldiers with her back to the Germans.)[85] And in a restaging of Marian Anderson's famous 1939 dust-up with the Daughters of the American Revolution, Hazel Scott was refused the venue of Constitution Hall on racial grounds in 1945. Asked to intercede, President Truman said forcefully, "We have just brought to a successful conclusion a war against totalitarian countries which made racial discrimination their state policy. One of the first steps taken by the Nazis when they came to power was to forbid the public appearance of artists and musicians whose religion or origin was unsatisfactory to the 'master race.'" Finally, though, Truman bowed to "the impossibility of any interference by me in the management or policy of a private enterprise" such as the DAR. Like Anderson before her, Scott was barred from Constitution Hall.[86]

Jim Crow practices, however, were decidedly not the salient piece for Sammy Davis Jr. when he contemplated his experience in US Army entertainments. Along with some important mentoring by a white sergeant named Williams, taking to the stage had been Davis's escape from the worst of his torments in barracks life, and he talked about it this way. We know little about the kinds of sketches and routines that he and Cohan were dreaming up, and this brief chapter in the Davis canon has left but a light trace on the historical record. But to whatever extent he encountered the Army's stubborn adherence to minstrel traditions—burnt cork included—and to the "separate but equal" staging of events and seating in clubs and theaters, putting on shows became his version of "dog-fighting with Zeros." From this point on, talent would be his arsenal.

. . .

Though Davis had little to say about the Army beyond its having taught him the bitter realities of American racism, he did revisit the military a few times over the decades. He twice played soldiers on screen, as an ex-soldier and the unlikely army buddy to the otherwise white Rat Pack in *Ocean's Eleven,* and as an ex-slave aspiring to ride with the cavalry in *Sergeants 3.* He also toured Vietnam with the USO in 1970, playing before as many as fifteen thousand troops at Long Binh. As a member of Richard Nixon's Committee on Drug Abuse, Davis visited Vietnam specifically to observe the military's drug rehab program and to "report on race relations."

Traveling with his band and a group of dancers that included his then-wife Altovise Davis (whom he had married in 1970 in a ceremony officiated by Jesse Jackson), Davis played sets that gestured toward the rock and roll sensibilities of the Vietnam soldier in numbers like "Spinning Wheel" and "Lucretia MacEvil" by Blood, Sweat & Tears alongside his standards like "Impossible Dream." A documentary film crew captured him reflecting on the social distance traveled between his own military service and the Vietnam generation. "The army, being an 'establishment' of its own, it is very hard to make a step forward, to change things—because it is a system," he said.

> But when I see the changes in the army and in the military between 1943 and 1970, I am amazed because I thought we had made *half* that kind of a step—if that much. But it is just so much better than I ever expected.... If you're going to ask me, is the Army a country club—hell no. Is it going to be a drag on the average cat who's on the street whether he be black or white to get into the military, I say *yes it is,* because we live in a society that promotes total freedom. But everybody better thank God that the military has its head where it is and is trying to improve itself, as opposed to where it was before. This is all I'm saying.

Finding race relations in the military "maybe forty percent better than in the civilian life" in 1970, Davis was impressed by the "recourse" the Vietnam-era soldier enjoyed. "He has more avenues to make vocal the complaints, because somebody's listening," as compared with his own World War II experience.[87]

The change Davis was noting here, whether or not he realized it, had begun in the World War II years that had been his own personal torment. The very hallmark of the racial liberalism that emerged from the war was Truman's desegregation of the military in 1947. Among its chief icons in the postwar years were the sacrificing black member of the (ahistorical) multiracial platoon and the wronged African American soldier, returned to injustices on the home front that he had fought to defeat in Germany and Italy. Even within a national context of bitter and stubborn hatreds—Jim Crow, white citizens councils, anti-black violence both North and South—in liberal discourse after the war, nothing captured the country's failures more powerfully than the image of the Negro servicemen and women wronged by the country they had fought for. Writing of "the boy whom the Japs had failed to kill," the white writer Ray Sprigle (whose *In the Land of Jim Crow* was a forerunner to the more famous racial imposter project *Black Like Me*) reflected,

On Resurrection morning when they call the roll of Americans who died to make men free, add to that heroic roster the name of Private First Class Maceo Yost Snipes, honorably discharged soldier of the armies of the Republic—black—citizen of Georgia, USA. Death missed him again and again in the rotting jungles of New Guinea, where he served his country well. He came back home to be shot down in the littered dooryard of his boyhood home because he believed that freedom was for all men, black Americans too, and he tried to prove it. . . . The ballot cost him his life. That's why the white folks murdered him.[88]

After the spectacular violence of the Monroe Massacre—the murder of four African Americans, including US Army veteran Roger Malcolm, on a back road in Georgia—the *Defender* cited a black observer: "They're exterminating us. They're killing Negro veterans and we don't have nothing to fight back with except our bare hands."[89]

The institutional history of "official" anti-racism in postwar America comprised a web of relationships that had been forged during the war among the NAACP, the Associated Negro Press, the Office of War Information (OWI) and its Committee for Mass Education in Race Relations, and progressive groups like the American Film Center Incorporated. In his executive order *To Secure These Rights* (1947), President Truman added the anti-discrimination machinery of the federal government. "The Axis has utilized Race as a cardinal principle in its arsenal of propaganda," Walter White had written during the war. Hollywood must repudiate "the Negro as a barbaric dolt, a superstition-ridden ninny . . . a race of intellectual inferiors, cowardly, benighted, different from the superior group." This move was not only "to identify the mood and temper of the American people today." Rather, "in the name of those ideas for which all of us are now fighting, we ask that the Negro be given full citizenship in the world of the movie."[90] Black filmmaker Carlton Moss likewise wrote to the Office of Facts and Figures (later the OWI), "Unless we answer the just grievances of the Negro people [the Axis] will use them to sow disunity and confusion." Moss's own film *The Negro Soldier* (1944) was a signal production in this effort. Moss plays a preacher, offering up a scorching sermon that rehearses the long history of African American military valor, from Crispus Attucks on down, before reading chapter and verse from the hateful pages of *Mein Kampf* as a way of excoriating Nazism and rousing his audience to something like the American Creed.[91] Though shot at a time when American forces were still segregated (and still putting on blackface minstrel shows), *The Negro Soldier*

FIG. 7. The Kid in the Middle, c. 1946. Photo: American Stock/Getty Images

is largely credited with winning America's hearts and minds—or at least Hollywood's—for the idea of an expanding national role for African Americans. It was this wartime *rhetoric* of anti-Nazism, a visual vocabulary of multiracial democracy more than the realities on the ground, that presaged the postwar Hollywood liberalism whose mixed-platoon heroics, enacted in picture palaces across the country, established the racial field of "cultural events that *mattered*."[92]

In a sense, the camp entertainments made the Sammy Davis Jr. we now know. He emerged from the war a grown man; when the Will Mastin Trio re-formed after the war, "the kid in the middle" had come of age as an entertainer in his own right. He had found his own voice (even if that voice was Sinatra's). He quickly became the star of the Trio. But more importantly, World War II created a cultural surround in which someone like Davis could thrive—a social context, indeed, in which someone like Davis was *required*. Virulent racism would persist. But the "official anti-racism" first occasioned by the nation's fight against Nazism and now urged by Cold War imperatives and the geopolitics of decolonization meant that white America was newly in need of some black people to ostentatiously "tolerate," even to adore. Jesse Owens, Joe Louis, and Jackie Robinson would be the first; entertainers like Davis, Harry Belafonte, Sidney Poitier, Pearl Bailey, and Diahann Carroll would follow. Straight-up blackface minstrelsy would largely be discredited in mainstream American culture by the late 1940s, even if blackface would keep surfacing like a bad drug habit into the twenty-first century. The most defamatory depictions from the minstrel era would be tempered in postwar representations, even if Poitier, Belafonte, and Bailey had to take some demeaning roles and walk some difficult tightropes.

But what America did *not* seem to need in these years were entertainers who were outspoken and strident in their social justice concerns, like Paul Robeson, Hazel Scott, Josh White, and Canada Lee, all of whom were blacklisted. Enter Sammy Davis Jr. *Metronome* magazine named him the "Most Outstanding New Personality of 1946," and he was perhaps a figure ready-to-order for this moment: black, multitalented, and yet non-threatening in his manner and politics, seemingly deferential in his assimilationism.[93] "Sammy Davis Jr. is a young Negro entertainer of inexhaustible energy who has had an amazing success in recent years," wrote one critic as *Mr. Wonderful* opened. "He has built the most fanatic following of any star. To his own people he is more than just a star; he seems to be a symbol, a representative who has proved something that everybody, of any race or color, wants to prove."[94] In some very important ways, this is the racial cosmos that World War II had delivered. It was a world where America might perform its own democratic *bona fides,* even while not fully enacting them.

THREE

The All-Negro Cast, and Other Black Spaces

> We still live, alas, in a society mainly divided into black and white. Black people still do not, by and large, tell white people the truth and white people still do not want to hear it. By the time the cameras start rolling or rehearsals begin [for *Porgy and Bess*], the director is entirely at the mercy of his ignorance and of whatever system of theories or evasions he has evolved to cover his ignorance.
>
> —JAMES BALDWIN

FROM THE MOMENT HE LEFT THE ARMY, Davis pursued a version of success in the entertainment industry that was dependent upon breaching the Jim Crowed spaces of the nightclub and casino, network television, and Broadway. But he also passed through a postwar Hollywood whose own experiments in desegregation were halting, uneven, contradictory. American cinema was confused enough that its epic monuments to racial egalitarianism included several "all-Negro" pictures whose notable lack of integration might be pleasing enough for Southern distributors and viewers. "Hollywood will be glad to give good Negro actors good roles as decent human beings," wrote Langston Hughes during the war, "in the new pictures Hollywood will make when Hollywood really understands what democracy is all about—as, of course, Hollywood will when we all get through fighting for democracy." His judgment changed several years later: "Uncle Tom did not really die. He simply went to Hollywood."[1]

"Good roles as decent human beings" on anything like a consistent basis would be a long time coming, but American cinema's shifting understanding of "what democracy is all about" did generate some interesting experiments. Amid the postwar crosswinds of a changing racial politics, one such experiment was a brand of all-black production, updating the "folk" or homiletic elements of earlier black films like *Green Pastures* (1936) and *Cabin in the Sky*

(1943). These were not the prewar era's "race movies," but films intended for a mixed-race national audience and that, perhaps above all, were meant to engage good liberal intentions. Chief exemplars include *Carmen Jones* (1954), *Anna Lucasta* (1958), *Porgy and Bess* (1959), and *A Raisin in the Sun* (1961), two of which featured Sammy Davis Jr. I would also add here *A Man Called Adam* (1966), which was a departure from the genre in also featuring white headliners like Frank Sinatra Jr., Mel Tormé, and Peter Lawford alongside Davis and a mostly black cast. It did, however, focus on "black" life and had a seriousness of purpose in parting ways with the industry's standard white-over-black priorities. This is not a monolithic genre, certainly, consisting as it does of big- and small-budget entries, studio and independent. It was also cobbled from properties that had been successful in pre-cinema forms—two as operas, two as stage plays. But these were films that, good or bad, were ostentatiously black in a cinematic cosmos whose operational rules in every register were white. Such productions did not often live up to the collective vision, the politics, or the social aspirations of their black cast members. This was in no small part because despite their black casts almost all of these films were "white" productions, under white direction and attuned to the white gaze, in any meaningful measure of that phrase. *A Raisin in the Sun* stands out as an exception in its artistic and political vision.

The "black spaces" of *Anna Lucasta* and *Porgy and Bess* may have come chronologically later than the "white spaces" described in the next chapter—Davis's *Colgate Comedy Hour* appearance was in 1954, while *Lucasta* and *Porgy* came at the end of that decade. But nonetheless these later texts are in some sense logical antecedents, in that the black spaces of all-Negro films, like the black spaces that Jim Crow enforced and policed, were expressive of an earlier era's social codes. They took shape as much in deference to a worldview that was on its way out as the one that was on its way in. The black space of *Anna Lucasta* precedes the white space of Ciro's or *The Colgate Comedy Hour,* that is, precisely as segregation precedes desegregation in US political culture.

RACIAL LIBERALISM IN POSTWAR FILM

In his *New York Times* review of *Anna Lucasta* in 1959, the acerbic critic Bosley Crowther broached the broad subject of race and Hollywood norms, starting with the oft-expressed concern—misplaced, as he saw it—that "a virtual curtain of neglect and indifference is drawn against the Negro" in

Hollywood's casting and subject matter. Though knocking this down as a "large exaggeration," Crowther did begrudgingly concede that "for every 'Jackie Robinson Story'. . . there have been fifty white society dramas, family comedies, Walt Disney animal pictures, Westerns and monster films." But he went on rather too comfortably to resolve the question in Hollywood's favor by appealing to the logic of the market: "If experience had shown that pictures about Negroes were generally popular—and there have been enough good ones to go by—they'd be making more of them right now." In the view of this longtime critic in the nation's leading metropolitan newspaper, no great opprobrium was due the moguls, producers, or casting directors of the industry for neglecting black life.[2]

A few days later a *Times* reader dissented in a letter to the editor: "As a Negro, I enjoyed 'Anna Lucasta.'" The film "brought to the screen a new concept, taking the Negro out of the stereotype of eye-rolling, arm-waving musicals and depositing him in a dramatic world of his own." This was a modest "step in the direction that screen democracy should have taken ages ago. It would seem to me that the seed has been planted, and if allowed to grow, then the Negro will come of age in the cinematic world and enjoy his full birthright in this medium." For this viewer, the film represented nothing less than "an oasis in the desert of bias that the Eartha Kitts, the Sammy Davis Jrs. and the rest of their clan have been trying to cross these many generations."[3]

Setting aside the merits of *Anna Lucasta* itself, the exchange was important for the heavy lifting it identified for the 1950s "Negro picture," and for the relationship it identified between "screen democracy" and democracy pure and simple. The give-and-take identifies two distinct strands in cultural politics, as the film industry adapted to emergent codes of public anti-racism—or at least plausibly deniable racism—in the wake of World War II. One was the racialized politics of hiring in American film, Crowther's question regarding whether or not "a virtual curtain of neglect and indifference is drawn against the Negro." A second, distinct strand had to do, not with the *shall* of representation, but the *how*: not to what extent will African Americans be depicted, but will African American representations be dignified and egalitarian, or not? Will American film shed the conventions and tropes that have made it a "desert of bias"? African Americans' "full birthright in this medium," in the letter writer's formulation, had to do with *both* a black screen presence *and* a screen egalitarianism in the depiction of blackness itself. But these were separate battles.

One can identify African American activity—indeed, activ*ism*—along both of these axes through the middle decades of the twentieth century. Figures like Paul Robeson, Harry Belafonte, Ossie Davis, and Ruby Dee fought the industry along the "inclusion" axis. On the "representation" axis we might find NAACP's protests of *Birth of a Nation,* the Associated Negro Press and the Screen Actors' Guild's (SAG) committee work against Hollywood's durable and demeaning "servants-and-savages" black casting, or a postwar generation's squeamishness with the stage and screen personas of older figures like Step'n Fetchit, Butterfly McQueen, Louis Armstrong and—later—Sammy Davis Jr. But the fights for inclusion and for dignified representation were distinct, and the relationship between them could be vexing. In the post-war years, SAG discovered that their insistence upon dignified roles amounted to a *threat* to black employment. Clarence Muse, a well-known actor in the Step'n Fetchit mold, condemned Walter White and the NAACP for disrupting the potential to "build ourselves into" the movie industry through their efforts to expel racist depictions, since for many studios to jettison demeaning representations would mean dropping black actors altogether.[4]

As already noted, the war and the early Cold War years represented a period of intense racial crosswinds in the United States, and—for the culture industries—a period of significant contest and readjustment. In 1942 the NAACP struck a deal with several Hollywood studios, codifying changes in representation and production staffing that were meant to alter the approach to blackness that had to that time mollified white audiences in the Jim Crow South. "BETTER BREAKS FOR NEGROES IN H'WOOD," screamed *Variety.*[5] Wartime newsreels and documentaries (often in collaboration with the Office of War Information) led the way toward a cinematic vision of a desegregated America. Amid the urgent anti-Nazi imperatives, depictions such as Carlton Moss's *The Negro Soldier* had dared to imagine black dignity, if not equality. "We must emphasize that this country is a melting pot," directed the OWI in a sponsored column in *Variety.* The United States was "a nation of many races and creeds, who have demonstrated that they can live together and progress. We must establish a genuine understanding of alien and minority groups and recognize their great contribution to the building of our nation." Wartime narrative films that echoed *The Negro Soldier*'s sense of duty to this melting-pot pluralism included *Crash Dive, Sahara,* and *Bataan* (all 1943).[6]

After the war, emergent ideas about what material should be produced and what it should look like were reflected in a notably "liberal" cycle of race-themed films, including *Home of the Brave, Pinky, Intruder in the Dust, Lost Boundaries,* and *No Way Out,* in addition to treatments of anti-Semitism in *Crossfire* and *Gentleman's Agreement.* Race now made its way into serious films with a "classical Hollywood pedigree," bearing "from script to screen . . . the marks of institutional life," as film historian Thomas Cripps writes. "In effect, the entire infrastructure of the industry signaled its readiness to resume the retailing of race-angled material the war had once made necessary." By the end of the 1940s, *Ebony* could assert that postwar film had broken out of "the prewar rut of Dixie-minded presentation," and was now traveling a postwar cultural path where "racism was made unpopular by Hitler."[7] The NAACP cast its lot with Hollywood majors to produce a new kind of narrative film, while the "race movie" producers fell from favor by the quality of their films and the unchanging social vision of their segregated theater spaces and racial imagery.[8] Among progressives in the industry and their allies in Civil Rights groups or the USIA, debates persisted about whether black characters should be rooted in black communities, black culture, and realistic situations—the kind of treatment that would make *Raisin* such a progressive statement—or whether they should follow Kenneth Stampp's opposite, universalist formula: "Negroes *are,* after all, only white men with black skins."[9]

But the sharper conflict during these years did not reside in philosophical disputes over representation, but at the level of politics and institutions, where the NAACP and progressive filmmakers of many stripes came under new scrutiny and were subject to the rising power of anti-communism and the House Un-American Activities Committee. These were, after all, the years when Popular Front activities of the 1930s—anti-racism included— were being redefined in retrospect as *"premature anti-fascism."* Racial liberalism may have been patriotic, but so was it dangerous. As Walter White put it to Countee Cullen and Arna Bontemps, "we have a racial stake . . . which can be lost or tragically damaged if we make the wrong movies."[10] And despite the pressures to advance the vision of America's true democratic egalitarianism in a global context of Cold War hostilities and decolonization, on the domestic front Southern censors still challenged liberal hegemony by cutting certain black figures from otherwise "white" popular films. Eddie Anderson was excised from *Brewster's Millions* for his "familiar way"; Lena Horne from *Words and Music* out of personal animus; and Cab Calloway from *Sensations of 1945* as "inimical to public welfare."[11] In this inconsistent climate, Disney could still produce a travesty such as *Song of the South* (1946), built upon minstrelized tropes of the "happy darky" and Confederate anguish over the

Lost Cause. But Bosley Crowther could also accuse the studio in the columns of the *Times,* for all to view: "You've committed a particularly gauche offence in putting out such a story in this troubled day and age. One might almost imagine that you figure Abe Lincoln made a mistake. Put down that mint julep, Mr. Disney!"[12]

It was amid this postwar climate of contradiction that the cycle of all-Negro films appeared, beginning with *Carmen Jones* in 1954. The results were mixed for an actor like Davis, who was just getting a shot. As Ronald Jackson II writes, public discourse had long scripted the black masculine body as "(1) exotic and strange, (2) violent, (3) incompetent and uneducated, (4) sexual, (5) exploitable, and (6) innately incapacitated."[13] This postwar cycle can hardly be said to have cracked these libels. One can map the male characters of *Porgy* onto Jackson's six categories quite literally, for instance. But these films did represent a singular liberal project within the industry and an exceptionally hard-working genre in the wider cosmos of postwar racial discourse. Political expectations around these films were high; they pulled a very particular kind of attention and sparked a genre of social criticism as much as they represented a genre of cinematic storytelling.

ANNA LUCASTA

To say that *Carmen Jones* and *Anna Lucasta* were culturally significant in their Civil Rights moment is not exactly to say that they were *good*. In his brilliant, wry review of *Carmen Jones,* James Baldwin wound through the mazes of problematic racial logic at work in that production, "the first and most explicit—and far and away the most self-conscious—weddings of sex and color which Hollywood has yet turned out." In this "Negro" remaking of Bizet's *Carmen,* he writes,

> the implicit parallel between an amoral Gypsy and an amoral Negro woman is the entire root idea of the show; but at the same time, bearing in mind the distances covered since *Birth of a Nation,* it is important that the movie always be able to repudiate any suggestion that Negroes are amoral—which it can only do, considering the role of the Negro in the national psyche, by repudiating any suggestion that Negroes are not white.[14]

For Baldwin, an all-black production like *Carmen Jones* was bound to end up impossibly boxed in, if not by the implicit racial logics of the script and score themselves, then by the attitudes of the director, the baggage dragged into the theater by white audiences, or the daily-ness of the headlines bearing contextual news of segregation, desegregation, racialized violence, and the nascent movement for Civil Rights.

In Baldwin's reading, *Carmen Jones* preserves its claim to racial liberalism *only* by the effect of its all-black cast. The absence of white folks here "seals the action off . . . in a vacuum in which the spectacle of color is divested of its danger. The color itself then becomes a kind of vacuum. . . ." The absence of any white figures, that is, allows for an unruffled and decidedly ahistorical understanding of blackness itself—a blackness decoupled from its US context and from both a present and a deep past characterized by violence, pain, inequality, and struggle. But this soothing pseudo-universalism has its costs, in the ledgers of pure democratic thought. The result of *Carmen Jones'* strange de-blacking of its black cast through the removal of all white referents is "not that the characters sound like everybody else, which would be bad enough; the result is that they sound ludicrously false and affected, like ante-bellum Negroes imitating their masters." The sets, too, "could easily have been dreamed up by someone determined to prove that Negroes are as 'clean' and as 'modern' as white people and, I suppose . . . that is exactly how they *were* dreamed up."[15] Though *Carmen Jones* is "one of the most important all-Negro movies Hollywood has yet produced," it is finally a spectacle of erasure in which genuine, living blackness is the thing that is actually erased. The film stages a falsified image that one can only hope *against* ("since they have until now survived public images even more appalling"); and it implies a broader American outlook that is "very deeply disturbed."[16] The *Carmen Jones* project carried a palpable social energy on the part of black cast members, reaching back to the American Negro Theater and figures like Canada Lee and Paul Robeson. But screened at the time of the *Brown* decision, it also represented a collective reverie on the part of white producers and white audiences about a blackness that was *not* in dissent or rebellion, and that had no cause to be.

Both the tenor of *Carmen Jones* and the hazards it fell into provide a key to later "all-Negro" efforts like Sammy Davis Jr.'s first films, whether the modest production of *Anna Lucasta* or the studio behemoth *Porgy and Bess*. Like *Carmen Jones, Anna Lucasta* was an all-black rethinking of an earlier property that had nothing to do with African Americans, in this instance a 1944 Philip Yordan play about a Polish-American family in Chicago. In its serpentine production history, *Lucasta* had undergone "more color changes than a traffic light," as *Time Magazine* put it.[17] Following its initial incarnation as a stage play based loosely on Eugene O'Neill's *Anna Christie, Lucasta* enjoyed varied rebirths. It had a production in Harlem, in which "the white trash became black trash, and caught fire," one critic wrote. It reappeared as a pulp novel (1945) and an Arthur Laurents vehicle for Paulette Goddard (1949), both about Polish immigrants again. And finally it had an African American redux in the 1958 film, as Yordan "tried the old black magic once more," according to *Time*.[18] Interestingly, it was not the original but the Harlem stage version whose success perhaps paved the way for those that followed, though none ever quite rose to that level again. Ruby Dee, then a young actress with American Negro Theater, recalled the feverish improvisation and rewriting as the black cast retooled Yordan's Polish family drama. Ossie Davis was among the ANT actors who took *Lucasta* out on the road, where "the black community ... pounced on *Anna* like a leopard from ambush.... Actors were treated like demi-gods, we could do no wrong."[19]

Anna Lucasta was a peculiar candidate for this treatment. On the one hand, there was almost no ethno-racial specificity or grain to the family drama, even when cast as a "Polish-American" story, and so the requirements for translation from an immigrant to an African American story were minimal. But on the other hand, its blank-slate, generic character—absent the layers of improvisation and rewriting added in the American Negro Theater production—was bound to make it a superficial rendering of African American life, lacking any reference to a wider community or to an encompassing history. The cast of the film generated plenty of excitement in the black community, but there is no sociological thrust to *Anna Lucasta*. In Yordan's novelization of the first (white) film version, for instance, there is but one line that even marks the Lucastas as an immigrant family.[20]

For the rest, *Lucasta* as written tells a story bleached of ethnic culture, history, and context—it is instead a tightly psychological family drama centering on a possessive, vicious drunk of a father, Joe Lucasta, and his wronged and now wayward daughter Anna. The full ensemble includes Anna's would-be boyfriend, a footloose sailor named Danny Jackson; a second suitor, Rudolf Strobel, son of an old Lucasta family friend who is said to possess a small fortune; and the crass, conniving members of Anna's family, who willingly play Anna as a pawn in their game to get ahold of Rudolf's wallet. But the core of the story is Anna's fall (when we first meet her, her lips are "painted" and she is leaning against a lamp post) and her hope of redemption, a trajectory that begins with Joe Lucasta's aberrant possessiveness and desire. Anna had been harshly turned out of the Lucasta home (hence the painted lips, the lamp post) when her father found her in a sexual embrace with a boy in the woodshed. Joe's violent rejection of her is laced as much with incestuous jealousy as it is with religious prudery.

> She hadn't been thinking about him in that woodshed, the night he'd caught her there with that boy pawing her and kissing her! Her red mouth had been ripe for those bawdy kisses, all right. The way her body had been arched against his, young and strong and yielding and glad—

Anna later reflects that her father tended to look at her "with red-rimmed eyes that seemed like they were stripping every shred of clothes off her back and loathing the nakedness that was left."[21]

The 1958 film, with Eartha Kitt as Anna and Sammy Davis Jr. as Danny Jackson, hewed closely to the 1949 script.[22] There are a few throwaway references to the Great Migration ("Where would we be if we'd stayed down in Alabama?"), but there is little that is specifically African American in the text of this highly touted "Negro drama." As with *Carmen Jones,* the absence of white characters and of any wider social frame strips out whatever contextualization there might be for the Lucastas' post-Migration struggles. The ensemble arranges itself around the central father-daughter conflict in precisely the way it had when the family was Polish. Anna's mother is a loving Pollyanna, always hopeful that Joe will find forgiveness in his heart and Anna will find happiness. Anna's brother-in-law Frank is grasping and craven, and powerful enough to orchestrate the rest of the family's movements. Rudolf is good-hearted and pure, if something of a rube. Danny Jackson is as hard-boiled as Anna herself, but, like her, shows occasional tenderness underneath. In the role of this "jazzed up, high-flying, free-spending ex-sailor," Davis's on-screen energy won plaudits in some quarters, denunciations in others. Crowther complained that Davis's Danny Jackson came across as "jive talking, snapping his fingers, jump-walking and rarin' to go . . . so completely overacted that it is grotesque and ludicrous. Mr. Davis does sixteen wiggles for every one that the role requires." Davis may have been over-compensating. He was commuting between the *Lucasta* set in Los Angeles and his nightly stage act at the Moulin Rouge in Las Vegas, and at one point he actually collapsed from exhaustion on set.[23]

This rendition of *Anna Lucasta* does make two very modest and perhaps ambivalent nods to its specifically black retelling. One is when Danny returns from his military tour at sea and finds Anna at her favorite haunt, a dive bar called Noah's Ark. He introduces her to a small idol of the Haitian god of the sea, Agwe, whom he calls "Papa." It is not readily apparent why this textual detail has been added. It may be a token of "blackness" straight from Hollywood's limited repertoire, perhaps suggesting Danny's paganism, perhaps a symbol of Danny's constancy and his genuine intention to trade in the sailor's life for a landlocked future with Anna. He does say that "Papa" will now "ride the radiator cap" of the taxi Danny plans to buy. But Agwe—who is neither present in earlier versions nor, obviously, Polish—seems one tiny sign of Danny Jackson's Afro-descended sensibility, and not necessarily a positive one, given the place of Vodou in Hollywood symbology.

The other addition comes later, during an alcohol-soaked and jazz-infused delirium montage meant to chronicle a wild stretch of debauchery. Anna has temporarily cast aside her plans with Rudolf and run back to her "fallen" life with Danny. Here the musical score—heavy on the drums, with a hot and frenetic horn section—sets a tone of "urban" wildness. "You'd go crazy in a week without the lights and the swing and a guy who gets you in the groove," Danny has told Anna, precisely previewing this later sequence. The jive-talk and jump-walking musical score, the lights and the swing, is accompanied by fast-paced, jagged, disorienting cuts of Anna drinking booze, Danny dancing in a frenzy, Anna drinking more and more, Danny furrowing his brow over her sodden excesses, Anna laughing sloppily, Danny playing drums as if in a fevered vision, Danny playing the trumpet, Danny dancing virtuosically, wildly, his wardrobe changing from sailor uniform to street clothes and back again, as the pace and the jump-cutting illogic of the sequence becomes more and more hallucinatory and mad. This bender comes to an end only when the two have run through all of Danny's cash—presumably in a week's time or so—and retreat to Noah's. "What are you using for money?" the bartender asks. "If I had money, I wouldn't be here," is Danny's exhausted, tart reply.

Anna's delirium sequence may propel the plot along the familiar lines of every other version of *Anna Lucasta,* but it draws upon a distinctly "black" aesthetic. It is also the one place where Sammy Davis Jr.'s stage talents are on full display, as even Eartha Kitt's never are in this film. In this respect it is Davis, above everyone else in the cast, who is made to carry the cultural codes of "blackness" in this all-black production, a circumstance at once acknowledged and misconstrued in the conspicuous critical attention paid him as "jazzed up" and "jive talking." *Time Magazine* remarkably commented that there are several scenes where "Sammy, with superhuman energy, takes over the screen like a blackface Bugs Bunny"—oblivious to the fact that Bugs Bunny himself was basically a sort of blackface Bugs Bunny.[24]

FIG. 8. Davis in the delirium scene, *Anna Lucasta*, 1958.

So, what of the serious "racial statement" in a work like *Anna Lucasta*? What of "screen democracy," in this instance? One historian describes the film as suspended between its aspirations toward an emerging, racially liberal market and its own outmoded racial ideas, between "reaching for values that television could not handle and adapting ... to TV's bland tastes." "Perversely," according to a contemporary critic, films like *Lucasta* had "chewed on more than they had bitten off."[25] But like *Carmen Jones* before it and *Porgy and Bess* after, *Lucasta* garnered much serious commentary as an important racial *event* in a nation where federal troops had recently been called to desegregate southern schools. "There is no particular feeling that this is a 'Negro' film," doted *Daily Variety*, in firm approval of precisely the generic ethno-racial qualities of *Lucasta*. "The racial character dwindles as the human characters come through. The people are not humorously Negro or pitifully Negro, but people, funny and sad."[26] *The Catholic World* similarly lauded the film's "vivid and altogether credible sense of human reality that transcends considerations of race and nationality," even if the tale's "sordidness tends to overbalance good intentions."[27] Score one, then, for the "anti-defamation" work that the film was said to accomplish, even if it set out—just as Baldwin feared—to do that work by erasing, and so conflating, and so radically misunderstanding both whiteness and blackness. Score one also for the film's accomplishments along the hiring axis of anti-racist agitation in Hollywood. As *Newsweek* swooned, *Lucasta* "has tendered more employ-ment to Negro actors than any ten other plays calling for such racial casts."[28] These were all credible liberal *bona fides,* and *Lucasta* therefore held a place in African American culture that perhaps outstripped the merit of the work itself. "Thirty yards away," wrote Toni Morrison in *Love,* faithfully recalling its status in the community, "a group of women lolled in the shade of the porch drinking rum punch. Two were actresses, one of whom had auditioned for *Anna Lucasta.* . . ."[29]

But *Lucasta* did run up against the limits of its historical moment, and also the limits of its execution as a work of serious cinema. Under the banner "Negro Cast Scores in 'Anna Lucasta' Film Drama," the *Los Angeles Times* applauded the film, first of all, as a "rarity" in that "it is cast entirely with members of the Negro race, [yet] it is not a musical." The review went on to predict that, since *Lucasta* "contains no racial problem or conflict—the white folks are nonexistent in this movie—it should be popular even in the South."[30] But as Eartha Kitt would later note, "two thousand five hundred cinemas across America would not accept the film. I was told that the South—which was responsible for fourteen per cent of a film's revenue—was confused because I looked too white on the screen. This was not the right time for an integrated exercise, apparently."[31] Setting aside the irony of Southern whites' objections to integration in this all-black production, there was certainly enough free-floating racial animus at large in the culture to hinder the success of a project like *Lucasta.*

This is just to say, even if critics and well-intentioned audiences wanted to hail the film as a major social event on behalf of a rising racial liberalism, it was going to have to be *good*—much better than the "mediocre movie" that so many critics found. "*Anna Lucasta* provides dignified professional employ-ment for a distinguished cast of Negro performers whose opportunities in films are all too frequently limited to stereotyped minor roles," wrote one. "Since the picture has this laudable feature to its credit, I wish there were more about it to recommend than there is."[32] Crowther tried to parse the issue more finely, noting the impossible terrain of American taste and opin-ion on the matter of race. A film could well elicit the "resentments and irrita-tion" of the Jim Crow South *at the same time* as it disappointed or offended "the extremely sensitive predilections of the militant race-advancement groups." He held up *The Defiant Ones,* starring Tony Curtis and Sidney Poitier, as an example, denounced for its "chain-gang stereotype" in some quarters and for its theme of "brotherhood" in others. But *The Defiant Ones* was *an excellent film.* "Unhappily, 'Anna Lucasta' . . . is one of those films about Negroes that will do no one good."[33]

PORGY AND BESS

Before work on *Anna Lucasta* had even wrapped, Davis signed up to play the dope peddler Sportin' Life in Samuel Goldwyn's next epic, big-deal, all-black production, *Porgy and Bess.*[34] By Davis's own account, he "pulled out every stop to land the part." "Mr. Davis went after the role with all the vigor of a politician seeking election," reported the *New York Times;* Goldwyn said that "he was flooded with letters urging that Mr. Davis get the role."[35] Davis's campaign included personal lobbying with Goldwyn on the part of mutual friends Frank Sinatra, Jack Benny, and George Burns. A possibly apocryphal story has it that Davis even bought Goldwyn a watch. "I'm touched. What's this for?" the mogul asked. The chance to do a "wonderful dance number," Davis replied. After knocking himself out with an extravagant hoofing routine, Davis asked, "How do you like it?" Goldwyn snapped the watch shut and said, "It's too long." On another occasion Davis stopped his show at the Moulin Rouge to announce, "Ladies and gentlemen . . . Samuel Goldwyn and his wife are up there. Mr. Goldwyn, I'll do the role of Sportin' Life for free."[36] Ira Gershwin's wife Lee reportedly found Davis "repulsive," and Goldwyn himself favored Cab Calloway for the role. But when Calloway was unavailable, Goldwyn went ahead and signed "that monkey" Sammy Davis Jr.[37]

Davis's enthusiasm for *Porgy and Bess* set him at odds with many in the black artistic community. As the *New York Mirror* reported, "for a quarter century [*Porgy*] has been offered as Americana (and also has been condemned in some quarters as a mockery of the Southern Negro)."[38] Harry Belafonte turned down the part of the disabled beggar, Porgy, as the *Pittsburgh Courier* reported, because "he'll never play any role which demands that he spend all his time on his knees."[39] Sidney Poitier, who finally took the role, tried assiduously to avoid it, but was outfoxed by an enterprising agent and by Goldwyn himself. The latter boxed the actor in by threatening to withhold his muchdesired role in *The Defiant Ones,* and making a splashy public announcement that Poitier would indeed be the next Porgy. Goldwyn called *Porgy* "one of the greatest things that has ever happened to the black race," but even after signing on, Poitier thought that judgment "outrageous bullshit."[40] If

Goldwyn's pronouncement says something about the enduring status of the production as a social and political *event,* at least in white eyes, Poitier's speaks to a common African American outlook, especially in the post-*Brown,* post-Montgomery, post-Little Rock world of 1959.

The first iteration of *Porgy and Bess* was the 1925 DuBose Heyward novel *Porgy.* Like Davis himself, born in the same year, *Porgy* was a product of the Great Migration, though from the sending region, not the receiving. Also like Davis, its sequential iterations bridged the blackface and Civil Rights eras, played across the color line in complicated ways, and generated adoration among white audiences even while being reviled among many African Americans. In addition to the spectacle it presents of squalor, gambling, drug use, prostitution, adultery, violence, and murder in a Carolina neighborhood called Catfish Row, *Porgy* thrives on the kind of racial essentialisms that had propped up the solid South since Reconstruction. Porgy himself was "black with almost the purple blackness of unadulterated Congo blood," and his outward appearance was a direct reflection of timeless inner qualities. In the semi-tropical midday sun, "he would experience a pleasant atavistic calm, and would doze lightly under the terrific heat, as only a full-blooded negro can."[41] Like myriad minstrel performers and coon shouters before him, Heyward laid claim to sociological authenticity through a heavy-handed deployment of supposedly genuine Negro or Gullah dialect.

—Dat all right, Auntie. Le's you an'me be frien'.

—Frien' wid yuh? . . . One ob dese days I might lie down wid er rattlesnake, and when dat time come, yuh kin come right up along an' get intuh de bed. But till den, keep yuh shiny carcase in Noo Yo'k till de debbil ready tuh take chaage ob um.[42]

Heyward came by his views honestly: his mother, Janie DuBose Heyward, had made herself locally famous in Charleston as a "darky recitalist" and author of popular blackface song and sketch books in the 1910s on into the 1920s. Heyward inherited a nostalgia for the old South and the old Negro *and* a cultural repertoire for rendering that South as both portraiture and argumentation. In his case, the argumentation was *against* the Great Migration from places like Catfish Row to the predations of the far-away city. His was a "poetic anti-modernism" that had much to suggest about the social order and about the Negro staying in "place." White critics loved the paternalism of Heyward's vision, and in particular the Job-like stoicism of Porgy himself, who, as the *Columbia State* had it, "reconciles himself to his lot with the patient endurance typical of his race, but in his face there is a look of eternal waiting."[43]

Porgy was not necessarily a more serious or artful property than *Anna Lucasta,* then, but *Lucasta* never did find its George Gershwin. The composer had long shown an interest in—rather, he claimed an *affinity for*—African American culture. Among other instances he had written *Blue Monday,* a "blues opera" that Gershwin referred to as his "nigger opera," for *George White's Scandals of* 1922. (Incidentally, here Gershwin collaborated with lyricist Buddy DeSylva of Davis's signature "Birth of the Blues").[44] Gershwin was drawn immediately to Heyward's novel as rich source material, and the discussions leading up to his own, operatic rendering would last many years. But first Heyward and his wife Dorothy would adapt the novel for the theater in 1927. The Heywards' play was very close in tone to the novel, merely streamlining the action to take place on Catfish Row rather than across various sites in Charleston. The play also augmented the character of Sportin' Life—the dandified, Zip Coon, cocaine-pushing figure who is Bess's ruination—and the anti-Migration themes he represented. As a basically faithful rendering of the 1925 novel, the 1927 play landed pretty much as expected. White audiences continued to love the "authenticity" of the portrayal of black life; "I spend much of my time living down the rumor that I am a Negro," said Heyward. African American audiences remained split between resentment toward the stereotypical themes and images on the one hand, and excitement over the all-black casting and the opportunity for black talent on the other.[45]

These color-line reactions extended to critics. White critics appreciated the play's "clear impression of African Negro life lived as a totally separate, untouched thing within our civilization . . . real darky life, of the most primitive sort." They also applauded the authenticity of the black cast, often going so far as to assert that "there is no acting," "the Negroes who form the cast of 'Porgy' . . . do not act—they just seem to live their parts as if their places of residence were Catfish Row."[46] African American critics, once again, saw the play as a mixed blessing at best, voicing great excitement over the professionalism of the cast and the power of the acting, even as they quibbled over everything from the colorism of the casting, to the burlesque notes of the staging and plot, to the indignities and "cyclonic buffoonery" of the characterizations, to the frequent and easy use of the n-word, to the likely misunderstanding of white audiences. Ironically, all-black extravaganzas like Eubie Blake and Noble Sissle's *Shuffle Along* had paved the way for *Porgy* by demonstrating the market viability of such a production for white audiences. But the particularities of the Heyward property raised the perceived stakes for black actors, critics, and audiences alike.[47]

Part of what was at stake for the black image in *Porgy* would be revealed in 1932, when Al Jolson made a failed bid to produce a blackface version of the play for the Theater Guild.[48] And part, too, would be revealed with the appearance of George and Ira Gershwin's own opera in 1935, perhaps in better taste than the proposed Jolson project, but no less problematic. It could not have been a foregone conclusion that the Jewish composer (born Jacob Bruskin Gershowitz) would cotton to a novel like *Porgy*, whose Anglo-Saxon racial essentialisms extended beyond the black denizens of Catfish Row, to "the little, dark Russian Jew in the next shop, who dealt in abominably smelling clothing."[49] But in this period racialist understandings of Jewishness could carry romantic, positive valences, too, and there was a robust popular discourse available to locate Gershwin's "natural" feel for African expression in the "common Oriental ancestry in both Negro and Jew." Duke Ellington might lament the "lampblack Negroisms" of Gershwin's *Porgy and Bess,* and choral director Hall Johnson caution of the "short and sickly life" that awaited the hybrid product of such cultural appropriation, now "transplanted into strange soil." But others (typically white and Jewish) thought it the very "Jew in Gershwin" that made him "our foremost writer of American-Negroid music."[50]

Gershwin himself embraced his role as a uniquely placed expert in Negro expression, and set out in his opera to develop a method of pastiche through which "to utilize the drama, the humor, the superstition, the religious fervor, the dancing and the irrepressible high spirits of the race."[51] It was Gershwin's racial ventriloquism which—even if an improvement on blackface—caused jazz critic Rudi Blesh to remark that *Porgy was* "not Negro opera" but merely "*Negroesque,*" despite its cast, its "artificial coloration," and its deployment of some "street cries." *Porgy* carried all the "earlier travesty of minstrelsy," but in a form even more insidious. "By enlisting actual Negroes for the public performance of the Tin Pan Alley potpourri, a new stereotype . . . is being fitted to the Negro in which he is set forth as an able entertainer singing a music that the white public finds to be just like *its own.*"[52]

Still, Gershwin's work carried a great deal of authority in certain circles. Gershwin and folklorist Henry Botkin had gone down to South Carolina to visit Heyward and to carry out several weeks of "fieldwork" in Folly Beach in 1934. The stories of this visit—pumped pretty hard in publicity materials for *Stage* magazine by Heyward himself—lent a cast of authority and "authenticity" to the resulting work. By 1934 this kind of fieldwork was understood less in the context of minstrelsy's longstanding practices of "study" among "genuine" American Negroes, and more within the Depression era's documentary impulse to gather up and represent "the folk." Heyward's promotional materials situated Gershwin and himself as true folklorists in the mold of Zora Neale Hurston or Alan Lomax, setting up camp off the Charleston coast, where "its large population of primitive Gullah Negroes . . . furnished us with a laboratory in which to test our theories, as well as an inexhaustible source of folk materials." Indeed, such an authority did Gershwin become that upon his return to mount the show in New York, it fell to him to teach Negro dialect to black actors "born and educated in the North, [who] hadn't the slightest trace of the essential Negro lingo, and were obliged to learn the dialect of the South."[53]

The 1935 opera left a major mark on American culture, including accolades for an extremely gifted cast led by baritone Todd Duncan (fresh off of a production of Pietro Mascagni's *Cavalleria Rusticana)* and Julliard-trained Anne Brown in the title roles. Vaudeville veteran John Bubbles was Sportin' Life. None, however, won more praise than Gershwin himself, "the Abraham Lincoln of Negro music."[54] As had been the case in two iterations over the previous decade, white audiences responded with enthusiasm and predictable condescension to the "racy and congenial" depiction of Negro life, its "primitive emotions" and gallery of long-familiar types—"the languid and lazy roustabouts; the tongue-lashing women folk; the dope-selling smart guy; the longword-slinging lawyer; the song-singing mammy; the sing-song crab-seller; the strawberry lady; the police-fearing inhabitants . . . [and] terror-stricken savages." "'Porgy and Bess,' it seems, was concocted for white folks," wrote white critic Robert Garland. "Old Massa Garland adores it!"[55]

Porgy was imported—largely unwanted—into the modern Civil Rights era via United States Information Agency tours of Europe beginning in the 1950s, but it was Samuel Goldwyn's Hollywood production in 1959 that reintroduced *Porgy*—or tried to—as a viable tale for the heightened Civil Rights sensibilities of American audiences in the post-*Brown,* post-Emmett Till period. White people in the industry still tended to look very kindly upon the property (the film's producers "have better than a portfolio; they have 'Porgy and Bess,'" gushed *Variety*).[56] Goldwyn lavished an enormous production budget on *Porgy,* estimated at $7 million, or $62M in today's dollars. He also unleashed a perpetual publicity machine that hyped the epic proportions of the endeavor, "this historic movie," including its production "in Todd-AO, Technicolor, and six-track stereophonic sound." Todd-AO was a 70 mm widescreen process and format that had only recently been developed, but whose expense and presumed technical wonder became a standard feature of pre-release publicity for the film, calculated to impress before the fact.[57] Goldwyn gathered a stellar cast that included Pearl Bailey, Brock Peters, and Diahann Carroll in addition to Poitier, Dandridge, and Davis. Lesser roles were filled by soon to be famous figures like Scatman Crothers, Maya Angelou, dancer Geoffrey Holder, and Nichelle Nichols, *Star Trek's* future Lieutenant Uhura. The *Porgy* project became such an industry-wide spectacle and attracted so much attention that it generated an entire cottage industry of *Porgy and Bess* recordings in 1959. This "rash of LPs," as the *Los Angeles Times* called it, included records from Louis Armstrong and Ella Fitzgerald, Pearl Bailey, Diahann Carroll, Harry Belafonte and Lena Horne, and Miles Davis and Gil Evans, in addition to the movie cast's album. A separate Sammy Davis Jr. album with Carmen McRae also appeared that year. It was widely panned, but Davis had been forced to skip singing on the film's soundtrack album for contractual reasons.[58]

There was considerably more disquiet among black onlookers than white as Goldwyn's *Porgy* came over the horizon. "Do movie stories like 'Porgy and Bess' reflect unfavorably on the Negro?" one black journal polled its readers in 1958. The question was not at all a new one, but it did have a different ring now than it had two decades earlier. The NAACP elected to stay out of this particular fray: "The Association has taken no official stand on the proposed 'Porgy and Bess' film," they announced while the film was still in production. The organization did promise to continue exposing any film or play that was "demonstrably malicious or harmful," but would only "exercise this kind of judgment in narrow rather than broad limits.... We have no wish to set ourselves as censors."[59] The stance communicated the NAACP's general disengagement from cultural politics, in contrast to its 1940s struggles with Hollywood. It may have also been a well-considered nod to the older problem of a politics of casting and hiring that ran directly against the progressive politics of narrative dignity and representation. In either case, it was left to others to make the stronger case. Harry Belafonte, for one, was not about to betray the Civil Rights struggle for the sake of the "crap shooting and razors and lusts and cocaine" that constituted *Porgy's* "old conception of the Negro." "DuBose Heyward wrote a very racist story," he said. "The leading man was on his knees. The second leading man was a cocaine pusher. The third man was a hustler. The leading lady was a prostitute."[60] If *Lucasta* was problematic in being not at all black, *Porgy* was problematic in consisting of a blackness

FIG. 9. Davis as Sportin' Life in *Porgy and Bess,* 1959. Photo: ullstein bild/ullstein bild via Getty Images.

routed through the white, minstrelized imaginations of the Heywards and the Gershwins.

The set of *Porgy and Bess* was "a cauldron of conflicts and accusations" from the start, according to Poitier biographer Aram Goudsouzian, in no small part because of the off-camera, Civil Rights challenges of such a production. These included both the racial dynamics on set, and a heightened sensitivity and sophistication about the potentially degrading aspects of the opera itself and the politics of how Hollywood got its work done.[61] A fire destroyed the soundstage before filming even began, and at least one LA paper suspected an arson that may have been the handiwork of "minority groups [who] had been bitter over the studio's plans to produce the Gershwin musical."[62] Soon after, Goldwyn fired the film's original director, Rouben Mamoulian (who had also directed both the 1927 Broadway play and the 1935 opera) because of pre-production problems and delays. The real trouble began when Otto Preminger was named to take Mamoulian's place. Cast member Leigh Whipper, president of the Negro Actors Guild, quit the project, saying, "I believe that the proposed *Porgy and Bess* is now in hands unsympathetic to my people." Preminger, he said, was "a man who has no respect for my people."[63] Other cast members—comically—said that Preminger was not a racist, but merely a tyrant. Conflicts on set between cast members and the new director began with fights over the use of Negro dialect. When Poitier challenged Preminger on the interpretation of a particular line, Preminger, for his part, demanded, "What am I dealing with here—children?" Pearl Bailey angrily refused to play any female character who wore a bandana; Dorothy Dandridge threatened to walk off the set over a fight with photographer Leon Shamroy. "It wasn't like a soundstage. It was like a guerrilla war," said one observer. Almena Lomax, of the Council for the Improvement of the Negro Arts, took out a two-page ad criticizing Goldwyn's paternalism.[64]

Sammy Davis Jr. was the outlier throughout all of this. He was "happy as a lark" on the *Porgy* set, as jazz singer Keely Smith recalled.[65] Not only did he campaign to work on a production that others refused (Belafonte) or tried their best to escape (Poitier), but with the exception of one, mostly comical flap over whether or not Davis would work on Yom Kippur ("A black Jew. This I can't fight," said Goldwyn), he remained unbothered by the on-set and on-screen controversies of the project.[66] He and Preminger got along famously where many others chafed at the director's leadership and social style. "You made lampshades out of my people," Davis joked with the Austrian director, during one light exchange.[67] But beyond his ease on the set, Davis had a respect for *Porgy* as a work—and for Sportin' Life as a role—that was not widely shared among the other black cast members. As the first to assume the role in 1935, dancer John "Bubbles" Sublett had transformed Sportin' Life "from a sinister dope peddler into a humorous dancing-villain."[68] Davis set out to reverse this way of inhabiting the role, recouping the ominous element and portraying Sportin' Life as "the epitome of evil," even though he confessed that at the time he was unaware that "happy dust" was cocaine. Davis loved the challenge that the part presented, initially seeing Sportin' Life as "the rogue; the man you booed in burlesque," but later coming to a deeper understanding of how he wanted to portray his villainy. "I worked it so that I never simply walked on or off the set. I would leap on, or suddenly appear from nowhere, giving that Shazzam quality of the appearance of sudden evil. And I got off the set like a whiff of smoke."[69]

The real spine of the role, and of Davis's performance, consisted of Sportin' Life's two songs, "It Ain't Necessarily So" and "There's a Boat That's Leavin' Soon for New York." In and among many American standards by Rodgers and Hart, Cole Porter, Irving Berlin, Sammy Cahn, and Frank Loesser, Davis had already recorded several Gershwin numbers for Decca Records, including "A Foggy Day" (on *Here's Lookin' at You,* 1956), "Fascinating Rhythm" (*Forget-Me-Nots for First Nighters,* 1957), "But Not for Me" and "Someone to Watch Over Me" (*It's All Over but the Swingin',* 1957), and "I've Got a Crush on You" (*Mood to Be Wooed,* 1958). In *Porgy and Bess* he rendered "It Ain't Necessarily So" in a sly and knowing tone, punctuated with soft, sardonic laughter, an anthem to irreligion.

> The things that you're liable to read in the Bible
> It ain't necessarily so.

This is the number that is best remembered in Davis's *Porgy* repertoire, notwithstanding the full LP of ten songs he released later in the year with Carmen McRae. But in the context of the film, the more interesting performance is "There's a Boat That's Leavin' Soon for New York." This is Sportin' Life's drug- and vice-laden seduction of Bess, all lies and insinuation about a better life in the big city: "Come with me, there you can't go wrong, sister." Davis renders this in a voice that is not typically his own—rasping, slightly lisping, urbane, a syrupy overpromising sweetness only imperfectly covering the harshness of an underlying betrayal-in-waiting. He sings in character, that is; this was the "serpentine" of one critic's estimation of Davis's performance of Sportin' Life.

> And through Harlem we'll go struttin'
> We'll go a struttin',
> And there'll be nuttin' too good for you . . .
> There's a boat that's leavin' soon for New York,
> Come with me, that's where we belong,
> Sister, that's where we belong!

The song is fascinating in its multilayered meaning, all the more in the way Davis renders it. This urban/urbane seduction is at the heart of the "old Negro" nostalgia of DuBose Heyward's vision, though in *Porgy* the novel, modernity and its evils reside in Savannah. It was Gershwin who added distant New York City later, for the Broadway musical. But if this snakish urban seduction is a warning against modern evils within the philosophical economy of *Porgy*, it is still carrying the water for Heyward's "old South" nostalgia. "The Negro" had best stay in place, Heyward felt. But on the other hand, this Catfish Row articulation of the promised life over the horizon in the far away city also embodies the very real contours of the Great Migration—Heyward's anti-urban cautions disregarded *en masse*. "Come with me, that's where we belong" is not just a false promise to be resisted, but a generational truism to be registered. It is in the context of these contending meanings that a certain codeswitching Davis performs over the course of the song is most significant. He departs from his rasping, serpentine articulation of Sportin' Life's seduction at two junctures in the final verse, the phrases "come along" and "that's where we belong." For these two fleeting moments he sounds like Sammy Davis Jr., in what we might read as a breaking-the-fourth wall commentary—performed as disruptive sincerity—upon the place of New York in African American history. "That's where we belong" may be Sportin' Life's seductive Catfish Row lie to Bess; but it is also Davis's own post-Migration truth.

In general Bess has generated more artistic ingenuity than any of the male parts in *Porgy,* as Daphne Brooks has argued. The role has attracted a cavalcade of actresses, from Anne Brown to Leontyne Price to Dorothy Dandridge, who devised ways of playing *through* or *against* or *beyond* the limiting, even demeaning role in order to portray something complex, suggestive of interiority, and solemn in a manner that neither Gershwin nor Heyward themselves ever dreamed. Brooks is interested in the "undertheorized genealogy of black women musical geniuses who . . . confronted and covered, immersed themselves in, but also resisted, re-wrote, and re-inhabited the behemoth albatross that is *Porgy and Bess.*"[70] The male roles were perhaps less open to such counter-interpretation, or at least there is less of a tradition of the male leads capturing and rearticulating the roles in this particular way—Sportin' Life perhaps least of all. Though it is hard to discern Davis's precise intentions in the codeswitching verse of "Boat" (his ingenuity did not necessarily run in the same direction as that of Anne Brown or Nina Simone) still the disruption in the song creates a little ripple that might have broken the spell of Gershwinian "blackness" for some 1959 viewers.

The accolades for Davis's performance began to accrue early on. Musical director Andre Previn told Davis after seeing some of the rushes, "You're going to steal this picture." And long before the film had opened, Preminger could be overheard raving about Davis all over town.[71] The critics' response bore Previn and Preminger out, even amid an otherwise lukewarm reception for the film. "Sportin' Life makes the screen jump for joy" (*McCalls*); "Sammy Davis Jr. is a sensation" (*Chicago Daily News*); "serpentine, acrobatic, evil incarnate—is the finest Sportin' Life yet" (*Cue*); "he exhales sulpher and brimstone as the devilish dope peddler. In two words HE'S GREAT" (*New York Mirror*); "a source of great fascination as he twirls and springs and minces through the role of Sportin' Life, lively as a rubber ball, evil as the 'happy dust' he leaves in his wake" (*Saturday Review*); "a new movie star is on the rise ... [Davis] packs a potent sex appeal"(*Chicago Daily Tribune*).[72] Bosley Crowther was no less effusive in the *Times*: Davis "is the sharpest and most insinuating figure in the show," he wrote. In previous productions "Sportin' Life has come through as a sort of droll and impious rascal with the bright, lively quality of a minstrel man. . . . But there's nothing charming or sympathetic about the fellow Mr. Davis plays. He's a comprehension of evil on an almost repulsive scale." Even the *Pittsburgh Courier* noted, "There are quite a few folks out in Hollywood pushing [Davis] for an Academy nomination. . . . I'm with them."[73]

Davis hit his mark among critics, proving his chops as a screen actor, and his own judgment of his performance held over time. "I think it is ultra important for any all-round entertainer to have one really good classic film part behind him," he later reflected in *Hollywood in a Suitcase*. "My definitive piece of movie acting was Sporting Life, and if I make nothing else I'll let that stand on my record without a shadow of regret." Elsewhere he was more economical: "the part was the gasser of my life."[74] But Davis's performance aside, there is the broader question of what it meant to put *Porgy* on the screen amid the Civil Rights struggle. Critic Wil Haygood, like many others, remembers *Porgy* as "the last of the old mammy musicals produced by the Hollywood studios."[75] Poitier numbered *Porgy* among only two regrets in his career (the other was *Long Ships,* a disastrous Viking picture that became infamous for being shot in Tito's Yugoslavia), and he was long criticized for taking on such an Uncle Tom role. As Baldwin put it, "African Americans relied on public expressions of racial dignity, and their most prominent leading man was on his knees singing, 'I got plenty o' nuttin', and nuttin's plenty fo' me.'"[76]

Lorraine Hansberry made quick work of the film, too, famously calling it "bad art" in her debate with Preminger on Irv Kupcinet's Chicago TV show, *At Random*. "The artist hasn't tried hard enough to understand his characters," she argued. But far beyond an objection to mere stereotypes, Hansberry, like Baldwin, saw *Porgy* accomplishing more pernicious ideological work on behalf of American racism. We had apparently decided that within American life we have "one great repository where we're going to focus and imagine . . . exaggerated sensuality," she said, "—and this great image is the American

Negro."[77] Texts like *Porgy* executed a kind of iconographic and racialized division of labor by which definitions of "blackness" not only signified "inferiority," but mapped more complicated notions of character and "nature" that underwrote, justified, and so stabilized a socially stratified status quo. Baldwin elaborated the argument: "at the time I was watching Bess refuse Sporting Life's offer of 'happy dust,' Billie [Holiday] was in the hospital. A day or so later, I learned that she was under arrest for possession of heroin and that the police were at her bedside." In linking the cinematic spectacle of Bess and Sportin' Life's "happy dust" in *Porgy* with Billie Holiday's real-life addiction, arrest, and death, Baldwin was laying out a significant principle in the racial politics of art and also of life.

> Though we disclaim all responsibility for the failure of an artist, we are happy to take his success or survival as a flattering comment on ourselves. In fact, Billie was produced and destroyed by the same society. It had not the faintest intention of producing her and it did not intend to destroy her; but it has managed to do both with the same bland lack of concern.[78]

Here precisely was the "the saddest and most infuriating thing about the Hollywood production of *Porgy and Bess*," Baldwin summarized. Preminger "has a great many gifted people in front of his camera and not the remotest notion of what to do with any of them. The film cost upwards of six, or sixty, millions, or billions, of dollars but all that was needed for the present result was a little cardboard and a little condescension." It is not just that Porgy is on his knees, Bess is a prostitute, Crown is a killer, and Sportin' Life is a pusher. Nor is it enough that Catfish Row has been all scrubbed up to be put on Hollywood display. Rather, these images and narrative elements exert their force in the real world offscreen. "What has always been missing from George Gershwin's opera is what the situation of Porgy and Bess says about the white world," Baldwin wrote. "It is because of this omission that Americans are so proud of the opera. *It assuages their guilt about Negroes and it attacks none of their fantasies. Since Catfish Row is clearly such a charming place to live, there is no need for them to trouble their consciences about the fact that the people who live there are still not allowed to move anywhere else.*" White producers defend their production, as Preminger said, "as taking place in 'a world which does not really exist.' This is an entirely illegitimate defense, and, in any case, the people in front of the camera keep reminding one, most forcefully, of a *real* Catfish Row, real agony, real despair, and real love." This is what art does—even "bad art."[79]

Whatever sentimentalized depictions of Heyward's "old South" and "old Negro" *Porgy and Bess* was still peddling twenty-five years after Gershwin's composition, the world Goldwyn's *Porgy* met was itself in the midst of epic change. When the *Pittsburgh Courier* ran its year-end round-up for 1959, it set "'Porgy and Bess,' in its $8 million MGM motion picture version" on a timeline alongside the year's heroic Civil Rights accomplishments and its harrowing instances of racialized violence and danger across the United States. A "stone and bottle throwing" white mob had attacked a black family in Collins Park, Delaware, for the crime of moving into their neighborhood. Meanwhile, a twenty-three-year-old was "snatched from Poplarville, Miss. Jail . . . and lynched." A group of "white Chicago young 'toughs' brutally beat a Negro amputee." The NAACP leader Samuel Quinn was "killed at his farm by a mysterious shot-gun blast," also in Mississippi. "White mothers in Queens High School district in New York City" protested a "newly integrated school." And "Rev. Martin Luther King Jr. says Negroes must be willing to go to jail in quest for complete integration."[80] *Porgy* itself was swept up into this historical maelstrom: in early 1960, members of a black youth group were turned away from a screening of *Porgy and Bess* at the Brown Theater in Louisville, Kentucky; the NAACP picketed, and a Unitarian Church organized a bus trip to Indianapolis for the group to see the film. Chapel Hill, North Carolina, likewise saw pickets. Goldwyn eventually pulled the film from theaters throughout the South, remarking, "I just don't want to be responsible for any race riots."[81] The white South may still have been ripe for presentations of DuBose Heyward's minstrelized Catfish Row—just not in desegregated theaters.

A MAN CALLED ADAM

Davis's 1966 jazz-themed film, *A Man Called Adam,* is a very different sort of project from either *Anna Lucasta* or *Porgy and Bess*. It was not translated from whiteness—neither Philip Yordan's Polish ghetto nor DuBose Heyward's minstrel South—but written fairly self-consciously as a Civil Rights meditation by Lester Pine.[82] Davis later told Alex Haley, "I think we said some things never said before in a picture."[83] Pine is best known for his later *Claudine* (1974), a sophisticated, socially conscious work of Great Society art about a single mother living in poverty. *Adam,* too, depicts a politicized black world that has very much been shaped and perhaps disfigured by the white supremacy and the white violence that envelops it. Nonetheless, *Adam* was "the first major film in years with predominantly Negro talent," as the *New York Times* positioned it. From the start critics framed its reception within postwar industry traditions that ran from *Carmen Jones* to *Anna Lucasta* to *Porgy and Bess* to *A Raisin in the Sun*.[84] Once it became clear that the film was going to be greeted with less than enthusiasm, its failures, too, were assessed within this context of the "Negro film." "One of the terrible inequities of life in these United States is that the Negro artist cannot enjoy the luxury of a casual, quiet flop," wrote a reviewer in *Newsweek*. Had *A Man Called Adam* been run-of-the-mill Hollywood drivel about white jazz musicians, "it would have come and gone almost unnoticed." A black production, though, "takes on, willy-nilly, the proportions of an important failure." No social harm is done if white actors have shoddy material and poor direction. But when "Negro actors do the same, their unconvincing make-believe serves to confirm the contemptible condescension of whites who have been so amused that their Negro maids and clerks pretend to have real private lives of their own. . . ."[85]

The politics of *A Man Called Adam* perhaps invited this kind of serious critical consideration in the shadow of the Civil Rights Act and the Watts Rebellion. But they also represent an odd mash-up of the varied political stances of the ensemble. Davis himself remarked that his character "only happens to be a Negro"—a classic Davis line. "In a way, there's a lot of me in him. I insisted on that. . . ."[86] This outlook on race is best conveyed in a scene between the established jazz phenom and a struggling white horn player played by Frank Sinatra Jr. "You know all that jazz about how colored cats play so much better jazz than ofay cats?" Adam asks the kid.

> I got a theory about it. I say the reason why colored cats got more soul is that they never took time out, see, to take lessons. They either stole a horn, found a horn, or someone gave them a horn and they had to start from scratch. So they had no other story to tell but what was inside of them, which was their soul. Now whether you're white or black, everybody's got a soul. So [gesturing to the horn], blow your soul.

After the white kid plays a bluesy bridge that is obviously meant to be understood by the audience as "soulful," Adam asks, "You sure you ain't colored?" "Maybe a little." Classic Davis here, too.

Cast members Ossie Davis and Cicely Tyson were already well known for their Civil Rights politics. Ossie Davis had been among the organizers of the

March on Washington for Jobs and Freedom in 1963, and had served as that event's emcee. More recently he had offered the eulogy at Malcolm X's funeral. Though her greatest fame was yet to come, Tyson had nonetheless become associated with a forward-looking racial politics for her role in Jean Genet's edgy exploration of race, identity, and justice, *The Blacks: A Clown Show*. Their Civil Rights concerns were not only layered into *Adam* via their off-camera activism and personas, but written into the roles of Claudia Ferguson, a young Civil Rights worker, and Nelson Davis, a family friend and caretaker for Claudia's grandfather, an aging, old school jazz great played by Louis Armstrong. Lester Pine's script laid out a range of positions far beyond Sammy Davis's own brand of integrationism and "happens to be a Negro" racial interchangeability. *Adam* boasted "a CORE sampling of injustices that supposedly explain the color-conscious hero's heavy drinking and bad temper," as *Time Magazine* had it. Each of the film's primary figures— Adam, Claudia, Nelson, and the Armstrong character, Sweet Daddy Ferguson—presents a particular social type or political mood within the wider question of how to navigate the politics of race. The film's message, according to *Time,* was "the distressing thought that non-violence, man, will get you nowhere." This is not necessarily an insightful or accurate summation, but is an arresting emblem of how race was being read in 1966.[87]

At the center of the drama is Adam Johnson, a brilliant jazz trumpeter in the Miles Davis mold. We see immediately upon being introduced to him that he is a brooding genius, temperamental and quick to anger. We will know soon enough just how vicious and destructive this streak is. The film opens with a violent eruption in the middle of a gig, when a drunk white audience member disrupts the set with a request for "some happy sounds" instead of the dark and cerebral style Adam has on offer. Adam throws a wad of cash at him in a fit—"go find your happy sounds in a jukebox"—and storms off stage. Backstage his agent and the other band members take him to task for his lack of professionalism, fetching yet another violent outburst, including a punch to the jaw of the band's blind pianist. "You're scary, man," warns the drummer before Adam exits. The next scene endorses this conclusion, as Adam finds that the Louis Armstrong character has been put up in Adam's apartment on the mistaken information that Adam would be out of town that night. In anger Adam roughly ejects the old jazz legend, Sweet Daddy Ferguson, as an unwelcome squatter, not even allowing him the chance to change out of his pajamas. "That man is crazy," Sweet Daddy says to his granddaughter and agent (Tyson and Ossie Davis) when they turn up to sort things out. Although there is enough evidence scattered throughout the narrative of Adam Johnson's complexity and inner contradiction, and even of an underlying gentleness and generosity—as when he mentors the kid trumpet player—much of the film is simply an explication of his particular versions of "scary" and "crazy."

The first layer of excavated meaning around his unruly temper has to do with a deep background of personal tragedy and of mistreatment at the hands of white society. This is where Adam has much more in common with Lorraine Hansberry's Walter Lee Younger than with any of the characters in *Lucasta* or *Porgy*. The first glimpse comes during a set at the club, when Nelson and Claudia sit at a back table talking about Adam. Adam's wife and child had been killed in a car accident ten years ago, Nelson explains. "That's when he really flipped." Adam himself fills out this story later on. The accident, he relates, took place in a southern town after a concert. A stage door crowd of admirers had gathered—"white kids, colored kids, just jazz fans"— and a "big ofay cop" took offense at the intermingling, and especially the white women's adoration of the black musician. When one of them approached Adam with a giftwrapped bottle of champagne, the cop demanded to know who it was for. "Mr. Johnson," she replied. The cop smacked the bottle out of her hands with his billy club and growled, "I don't see no Mr. Johnson, all I see is a bunch of niggers." It was *then* that Adam got stone cold drunk—self-medication after a racist affront—and got behind the wheel in the ill-fated drive that would end up killing his family and blinding his piano player.

Adam's confrontation with the white world is thus the framing backstory to all that follows. It is also dramatized in two on-camera scenes of tremendous tension and potential violence. In the first, Adam, Claudia, and the kid trumpeter are staying out at a country house owned by Adam's white manager. Their suspicions clearly aroused by the visitors' blackness, local police show up at the door to check them out, implying that they would need some confirmation that these "guests" indeed belonged in this tony retreat. Adam identifies himself as a musician, a client of the homeowner, which the cop greets first with an insult ("You don't impress me being a musician. We put more of you people in jail than anyone else") and next with a demand that Adam roll up his sleeves in a spot-check for heroin use. Adam predictably explodes; a scuffle ensues; and Adam is arrested. At the Justice of the Peace in the next scene, Adam pays his $50 fine by ostentatiously plucking a fifty from an enormous wad of bills, a dig at the white authorities. Afterwards, outside the station, Claudia scolds Adam for his hotheadedness. "Save your heroism for something important," she says. Here is precisely where the personal becomes political, and where the distinct layers of Adam's politicized backstory and his idiosyncratic character come together. "It *is* important," he insists, "don't you know that, Claudia? They take a piece of you here, a piece of you there, someday there ain't nothing left, except 'Yassir, boss.'"

The second explicit racial confrontation follows hard after, in a contract negotiation between Adam and a powerful talent agent played by Peter Lawford. The agent is going to send Adam down south to play a tour, as implicit punishment for the musician's bad behavior of late. "You said I need discipline," Adam objects, "why do I have to have it in the South?" Manny's response is steeped in the luxury of white ignorance as to what this might mean for the black performer. "Look, you're a musician," he says flatly. "You go down there and you blow, and then you get on the bus—in the back if necessary. Now, sign these contracts or get out of my life." At which point Adam, taking a liquor bottle from the bar in Manny's upscale office, breaks it to a jagged, threatening edge. He menaces the agent with it until upon command Manny is crawling and groveling on his hands and knees. "*There's your discipline,*" Adam hisses, turning on his heel.

These conjoined themes of the *psychological* or individual temperament, as inflected by the injuries and affronts of the *social,* are further encased in Pine's screenplay within the realm of the *political,* represented by a varied gallery of characters who have each made their own kind of political sense of the injustices they witness and endure. Nelson speaks the language of respectability politics, insisting on dignity as a principle but smoothing over tough situations with a pragmatic concern for keeping up appearances. The band members represent a kind of retreat into the sociality of their jazz artistry. Both the music they produce and the nightclub spaces they inhabit are cordoned off from the "real world" of racial injustice and rage in some way, which is one reason they resent the particular disruptions of Adam Johnson's smoldering resentments. Their bands and their clubs are integrated in ways that the rest of the society seemingly is not; and they have no use for the racial trouble that Adam's rage introduces into these safe spaces.

The Louis Armstrong character represents both a musical style and a politics whose day has passed. Adam chides Nelson that the "comeback" he has planned for Sweet Daddy is unfair to the old man: after the novelty of his old-school Dixieland wears off among the younger audience, Ferguson will not only be unable to play clubs anymore, but unable "to go back home to his rice fields" too. He will end up begging drinks (in a predicted scenario that actually anticipates the "Mr. Bojangles" narrative that Sammy Davis Jr. would popularize in Jerry Jeff Walker's song years later). Adam's beef here is actually with Nelson and his do-gooder instincts rather than with Sweet Daddy himself. But as a sociological observation, his warning does mark the old man as a kind of hapless victim of history whose out-of-date view of the scene outfits him for neither hipness, political activism, nor Adam's own brand of vintage-1966 nihilism and rage. By the time blaxploitation had emerged as a genre just a few years after *A Man Called Adam*, Sammy Davis Jr. himself would read to many as being much closer in type to Louis Armstrong than to the Miles Davis of *Adam's* inspiration. But in 1966 Adam's comments on Sweet Daddy Ferguson voiced an important acknowledgment of social change and generational difference, and the *back* of "back home to his rice fields" is loaded with meaning about pre-Civil Rights era realities and accommodations. Armstrong's appearance is all the more interesting in that years earlier Sammy Davis Jr. had criticized the real-life Armstrong for his willingness to continue appearing before segregated audiences even while presenting himself as a "Negro spokesman" on the issue of integration in Little Rock. Davis also criticized Armstrong for retaining the word "Darkies" in a *1957* recording of the 1927 hit "Mississippi Mud." When Satchmo presents himself as "a champion of his people," said Davis at the time, "I must in all honesty read the statement and smile and chuckle to myself."[88]

At the center of this muted political debate in *A Man Called Adam* is the Adam-Claudia relationship. Their conflicts, their sexual interest in each other, and their uneven courtship all unfold within a philosophical contest between the musician's nihilism and the activist's idealism. On the evening when they first meet (after Adam has so rudely kicked her grandfather out of his apartment), he speaks in belittling tones of Claudia's accomplishments and aspirations as a Civil Rights worker. "Nelson makes a big deal out of you being in jail. Says Martin Luther won't make a move without you," he says in disparagement. In another of his anti-social or even misanthropic moves, he forces himself on her and kisses her roughly and then demands that she slap his face, a demand she will not gratify. "Passive resistance, huh? The new Negro. Love your enemy. Thanks to you I can buy a hotdog at any dime store in the country." This last line is enunciated with plain contempt for her and for the entire SNCC project that she represents. Claudia's initial reaction oozes contempt right back: "You're acting just like they say we act," she spits.

"And you don't want to act that way because that's what they say, huh?" he returns, as if to say, *you're still dancing to the tune of the master, whatever it is you think you're doing.*

But behind the anger a certain fascination lurks—a fascination with Adam Johnson and his charisma and his tortured genius. "Did he ever marry again?" Claudia asks Nelson after first hearing the car accident story.

"No, lots of women though."

"*I bet.*"

The more we learn about Claudia Ferguson, the more we see that she also has a certain fascination with the spiritual reclamation project that Adam presents the social worker in her:

> I know what I am. I know what I've got to give. You don't. I'm not interested in kissing your tears away; I don't want a seat at your funeral; and I won't let you be any less than what you are. Ever.

Nelson later warns her that Adam "just wants to rack you up like a pool ball." He is incapable of real love. "But there's something in that man—something in his soul that's screaming to me," says Claudia. "'Help me, help me, I don't want to die.'" Even Adam himself has to doubt her ability to rescue him from himself and from the social conditions that have created and then wrecked him. "Come on, Claudia, let's face it. It won't work, baby. Why don't you go back to school and write your plays, and write about the dignity of man and save humanity. I just drag you down, baby."

The lifting up and the dragging down—the philosophical and psychosocial tug of war between Claudia and Adam, between idealism and nihilism, between optimism and despair—frame the latter half of the film. After one of his trips to rock bottom, Adam goes to find Manny in an upscale Manhattan restaurant. He grovels, offers to shine his shoes, and pleads, "Anything you want me to do, Manny, I'll do." Manny relents, and Adam's ensuing upswing and successful tour are conveyed in the familiar form of biopic montage: shots of spinning tour bus wheels, stage door crowds, club and concert snippets, highway lines streaming by, all laid under a hot jazz soundtrack. The triumphal vibe of the tour is disrupted on the last stop, when a couple of white toughs in the audience jeer and throw things at Adam and the white kid trumpeter, hurling the presumably homophobic cry, "Hey, lovers!" In sharp contrast to the combustible figure we have come to know, Adam keeps his cool, later telling the stage manager, "You tell Manny I'm disciplined—I did my job, the audience didn't."

In the dressing room after the last show, he credits Claudia with his success on the tour and proposes marriage in what turns out to be his final hopeful moment in the light of her idealism. But as they leave the venue, the toughs from the audience return to assault the white kid trumpeter in an alley by the stage door. Adam freezes, doing nothing to help. Claudia will later confess to Nelson that she blames herself for Adam's paralysis, for taking the fight out of him. "I would rather he had fought on that street corner and died. . . . He loved me, and he gave up his manhood for me." (This is undoubtedly the plot point that caused the *Time Magazine* reviewer to cull the moral of the story as "non-violence, man, will get you nowhere.") Adam's final demise comes, some unspecified time later, when he turns up at the club where his old band is playing. They have taken his horn out of hock for him, and they invite him to join them on stage. But Adam is defeated in his solo by some impossibly high, unreached notes, and his violent break and collapse on stage. He has perhaps "blown his soul," as he had put it earlier, in all the potential meanings of that phrase. The final, terse eulogy offered in his honor: ". . . peace to his soul, and all that jazz."

Reviews were mixed. The *Los Angeles Times* wrote that "the screen all but bursts with [Davis's] intense talent," but archly concluded that, at the end of the day, *Adam* is "one of those instances of the parts being greater than the whole." The leading African American paper, the *Chicago Daily Defender,* on the other hand, saw *Adam* as nothing less than "a suitable landmark in the Negro's bid for social expansion." Even the *New York Times* opined that "this little picture dares—that is the only word—to unfold a simple, tender love story between two Negroes . . . as though it were the most natural everyday thing in the world."[89] What had "always been missing from George Gershwin's opera," as James Baldwin wrote, "is what the situation of *Porgy and Bess* says about the white world." *A Man Called Adam* at once carried forward the Hollywood tradition of the "Negro film" as a singular cultural event that fixed the society's gaze on questions of race, but in a way that *did* address what the central figure's situation "says about the white world." Actors in a production like *Porgy* had to play *through* their roles in order to convey a racial reality that was unavailable to the white imagination of the libretto. *A Man Called Adam* was Lester Pines's and Sammy Davis Jr.'s attempt to bend the conventions of the "black" film toward precisely the "real agony, real despair, and real love" that Baldwin said was missing from *Porgy.* "For the Negro is not a statistic or a problem or a fantasy," wrote Baldwin; "he is a person and it is simply not possible for one person to define another. Those who try soon find themselves trapped in their own definitions."[90]

Aside from his work on *Lucasta, Porgy,* and *Adam,* Davis's postwar career was not much characterized by work in "black" spaces. But it is worth pausing for just a moment to consider the black space of the "alternate public sphere" created by Jim Crow, as historian Adriane Lentz-Smith puts it.[91] "Some colored people claimed that they welcomed the change," wrote Henry Louis Gates Jr., recalling the waning sociality of Jim Crow's black spaces in his West Virginia town as integration dawned. "It was progress . . . it was what we had been working for so very long, our own version of the civil rights movement and Dr. King. But nobody really believed that, I don't think. For who in their right mind wanted to attend the mill picnic with the white people, when it meant shutting the colored one down?" "I sat at a lunch counter for nine months," joked Dick Gregory. "They finally integrated and didn't have what I wanted."[92] The black public sphere that Jim Crow created is something that is lost in much post-Civil Rights discussion, just like the significance and majesty of Negro League Baseball as a black institution. "The soul of that world was colored," recalls Gates.

> Its inhabitants went to colored schools, they went to colored churches, they lived in colored neighborhoods, they ate colored food, they listened to colored music, and when all that fat and grease finally closed down their arteries or made their hearts explode, they slept in colored cemeteries, escorted there by colored preachers. . . . They dated colored, married colored, divorced and cheated colored. And when they could, they taught at colored colleges, preached to colored congregations, trimmed colored hair on nappy heads, and, after the fifties, even fought to keep alive the tradition of the segregated all-colored schools.[93]

Ballplayer Ferguson Jenkins similarly recalls with some nostalgia the nightlife on the black side of the tracks as he traveled the minor league circuits of the pre-Civil Rights Act South with the Miami Marlins, the Arkansas Travelers, and the Chattanooga Lookouts. While it was true that black players had to stay in shabby rooming houses (or even in African American funeral homes, in some towns) while their white teammates stayed in nicer, all-white hotels, he also recalls hanging out poolside in the Overtown section of Miami with James Brown, Etta James, and other African American celebrities who were likewise barred from the white hotels. It was here that a young Jenkins would see "a blonde haired black woman, or a shark skin suit" for the first time, he recalls with a certain fondness.[94]

For Davis, "the black section" meant mostly Harlem, a site he identified with a harsh past that one could only hope to escape, as he later immortalized in "Don't Forget 127th Street." But it also came to mean the Westside area of Las Vegas, for which he felt the same kind of warmth that Jenkins felt for Overtown. West Las Vegas was created by Jim Crow housing and social practices as oppressive as any in the country, but what the African American community made of it was something else again. "We had Jackson St. which was lit up and was just jumping every which way," recalled Ruby Duncan in an oral history of this thriving area. Joe Louis's Cove Hotel, in which Davis held stock, was "a flourishing nightspot" where Davis, Nat King Cole, Pearl Bailey, and other billboard black performers would stay while playing the white spaces of the Strip. Other Westside clubs included the El Morocco, the Town Tavern, and Club Alabam.[95] The Moulin Rouge, on Bonanza Road at the edge of West Las Vegas, became an icon of integrated casino and nightclub culture in Las Vegas, but it was integration of a slightly different sort. It was not a "white" club whose barriers fell to allow black entertainers and guests, but rather, as a Westside establishment opened on the black side of town in 1955, it was by local geographic custom a "black" club frequented by the cool white crowd—Frank Sinatra and Dean Martin among them. Its white investors capitalized on the "thrill" of interracial mixing. But the Moulin Rouge was in important ways a fixture of Las Vegas's black culture. Part owner Joe Louis greeted guests at the door. All employees were black, including managers and security guards; the single exception, at the outset, was card dealers, who had had no opportunities in this town to get experience in that trade. A late night show called the Tropi Can featured the only all-black chorus line in Vegas. Headline acts included Lionel Hampton, Gregory and Maurice Hines, Dinah Washington, the Mills Brothers, the Platters, and a range of black entertainers who came over from the Strip to perform after hours, including Harry Belafonte and Sammy Davis Jr.[96]

All of this vibrant Westside nightlife was a casualty of desegregation— like Negro League Baseball, a heartfelt loss to the community amid the political triumph over Jim Crow. After *de jure* segregation fell, the formerly humming Cove Hotel eventually sat "closed and empty, a hulking building with a swimming pool full of trash and five stories of cracking windows." Like Henry Louis Gates Jr., Ruby Duncan felt a certain sadness at the black world that was lost to integration, even though that had been the dream.

"There was action and fun in West Las Vegas. And people was more happy and more sound-minded I think at that time," she told historian Annelise Orleck. "When integration came through, we all lost that closeness. We all just started going someplace else to spend our money. And when that happened everything dried right up."[97] For Davis's part, he had done his best to dance down those barricades, and when they finally fell, he tried his best to never look back. But the "all-Negro" productions he participated in between 1958 and 1966 document something terribly important about what it took to crack the color line in American film. The distance in political temperament between *Lucasta* and *Porgy* on the one hand and *A Man Called Adam* on the other gauges both the pace and the nature of cultural adjustment atop the seismic social changes of the Civil Rights years.

FOUR

The Vegas Strip, Network TV, and Other White Spaces

I wish I worked places you could go. I'd take you with us.

—LOUIS PRIMA TO SAMMY DAVIS JR.

If Donald O'Connor can do it, man, I'm gonna do it.

—SAMMY DAVIS JR.

THE LONG AND CONTINUING HISTORY of de facto segregation in American neighborhoods, schools, state assemblies, commercial districts, and corporate boardrooms is such that, not only are most social spaces in this country *raced* in one way or another, but a color line is at work in the very way that we are likely to perceive and experience a given space. The presence of one person of color in a classroom or restaurant, for example, will lead white parties uniformly to judge that the space is "integrated." Meanwhile that lone person of color is apt to experience this as the "whitest" of spaces. In this respect it is significant that from the early 1950s, when he first began to headline on the Vegas Strip, to his Rat Pack residency at the Sands, to later 1960s appearances on *Batman, I Dream of Jeannie,* and *The Beverly Hillbillies,* Sammy Davis Jr. himself alone represented "integration" almost everywhere he performed. This had the peculiar double effect of rendering Davis among the most important barrier-breakers and racial pioneers of his generation while at the same time associating him in the public mind with white spaces and with whiteness itself. As activist George Jackson observed, "If we are not enough like [the white man] to suit his tastes, it's because he planned it that way. We were never intended to be part of his world."[1]

Davis very much *did* intend to be "part of his world." In addition to garnering death threats from Nazis, his penchant for the industry's white spaces generated no end of sharp critiques from many African Americans, too. They called out his comportment, his "assimilationism," his accommodation to various forms of disrespect or second-class treatment, including by Frank

Sinatra and his other so-called friends in the Rat Pack. "I think what he is really trying to do is get away from being a Negro," opined a 1960 letter to the editor of *Ebony*. "When the whites are through with Sammy Davis Jr.," said singer Sam Cooke, "he won't have anywhere to play."[2]

Whatever his relationship to the broader African American community, Davis experienced his own trajectory as a series of incursions into the kind of forbidden white spaces whose heavily defended boundaries were of a piece with Jim Crow racial exclusion. These were the spaces of Miami Beach or Las Vegas clubs, of Beverly Hills neighborhoods, of the Broadway stage, of the Hollywood western or the television sitcom. "We must wait, we are told, until the hearts of those who persecute us have softened—until Jim Crow dies of old age," Paul Robeson wrote of the enforced gradualism of the post-*Brown* years. "But the idea itself is but another form of race discrimination: in no other area of our society are lawbreakers granted an indefinite time to comply with the provisions of law."[3] The nation was moving with "all deliberate speed" in mandated desegregation, which signified decidedly more "deliberation" than "speed," as the Civil Rights community was finding. But Davis himself was hurtling forward through gate after gate. His crashing of Ciro's, the Sands, *The Colgate Comedy Hour,* or the sound stage of *The Rifleman* may have offered some a glimpse of a desegregated future, but so might it grant the kind of alibi that postwar liberalism so sorely needed, providing a fundamentally racist culture the grist for plausible deniability. "When confronted with egalitarian and democratic social movements," George Lipsitz writes, "people in power always hold out the lure of individual escape for selected individuals."[4] Davis represented precisely this sort of "escapee," a metaphor he used himself: "somewhere along the way, without my being aware of it or knowing when, I had escaped," he wrote in *Why Me?*, after a catalogue of prior insults and slights.[5] And so he might be seen as doing some heavy lifting on behalf of both desegregation *and* persistent whites-only privilege. To many, his successes did not seem to translate to the black community at large. His exceptionalism was, well, exceptional.

While the tendency has been to write about Davis in the either/or terms of accommodationism versus Civil Rights heroics, it is the *both/and* that is the more important historical feature. Davis's Broadway show *Mr. Wonderful* (1956), for instance, was an intentional, thoughtful attempt to meaningfully desegregate Broadway *and yet* it staged a set piece honoring Al Jolson. Davis's aspiration had been "to say something racially . . . we should do a 'modern' musical. That means an integrated show with a mixed chorus." Not eight dancers with a single African American, Davis insisted, but more like half and half. "Nobody's ever done it right and we of all people can and should be the first ones."[6] The show was about the nightclub rise of a character named Charley Welch, loosely based on Davis's own story. Writers and producers had struggled with the show's treatment of race. The producers were aiming for a show that was not "too racial." At one point Davis objected that, "Instead of a story about a sophisticated, sensitive guy who doesn't want to live with prejudice, Charley Welch has become a schnook who doesn't have the guts to try for success. Why spend $300,000 to do a show about *that*?" We've "got lots of entertainment, lots of flash, some good songs, dances, jokes," he noted bitterly. "Yeah ... everything but integrity."[7] In retrospect, the most striking thing about *Mr. Wonderful* is its resurrection of Jolson, despite the fact that he had long been disparaged among black audiences for his blackface fame in *The Jazz Singer* (1927), and later minstrelized performances in *The Singing Fool* (1928), *Mammy* (1930), and *Big Boy* (1930, which not only put Jolson in blackface as a minstrel, but as a genuine "Negro" character). Ironically, though, when *Mr. Wonderful* opened, some critics from the right "slaughtered us on the racial thing" saying, "let Western Union deliver the messages."[8]

Here as elsewhere, Davis's incursion into white spaces does not suggest some kind of Manichaean melodrama pitting a clear right-mindedness against a countervailing wrongheadedness. Rather it points out the complex and contradictory texture of social change, as Jim Crow began to collapse. It casts into relief the institutional structures, generational dynamics, and cultural logics that gave form to both liberalism's gradual gains and racism's stubborn resistance. Which is just to say, integration alone was never enough to make "white spaces" anything other than "white."

WHITE SPACES AND THE KID IN THE MIDDLE

Black vaudeville was dead by the time Davis got out of the Army, and so when the Will Mastin Trio picked up after the war, their aspirations were hitched to a version of success that meant opening for white headliners in white clubs like Slapsy Maxie's, Ciro's, and—God willing—the Copacabana. This was the beginning of the "kid in the middle" stage of Davis's career. The young, flashy, fast, extraordinarily energetic Sammy was flanked by the now-aging Sam Sr. and Will Mastin, who dance at a fraction of his speed, as in the

FIG. 10. Ciro's nightclub, late 1940s. Photo: Michael Ochs Archives/Getty Images.

Paramount short *Sweet and Low* (1947).[9] Having outgrown his *Rufus Jones* child stardom, the twentysomething Davis had lost some (but not all) of his mugging cuteness. His act was now a solid flash routine built on conventional moves (boogie back, boogie forward, shorty George, roll, flash step, trenches), an unoriginal but *fast* dance vocabulary that greatly excited audiences on the white side of the tracks. The Trio had opened for Tommy Dorsey before the war, and had briefly met Frank Sinatra and Mickey Rooney, both of whom had been impressed enough by Davis to become important allies and mentors after the war. The Will Mastin Trio opened for both stars in 1946. Davis was also adding more and more arrows to his quiver in addition to the singing and dancing—drums, vibes, trumpet, comedy, and impressions.

This latter skill became a sensitive issue, and Davis's aspirations as an impressionist spoke to the layers of meaning and danger laced into Jim Crow's social codes. This was not just a matter of white *space,* in other words, but of codes of propriety and conduct at every level. Davis started out doing impressions of black stars like Louis Armstrong and Step'n Fetchit, but soon branched out to try bits on white figures like Humphrey Bogart, James Cagney, and Jimmy Stewart. Mastin and Davis Sr. were the first to react; their caution on this question bespoke the growing generational differences that were widening within the Trio. "You want to do impressions of *white* people?" Mastin stormed. "You just can't. . . . They'll think you're making fun of them. No colored performer ever did white people in front of white people. . . . You just stick with Satchmo and B [Billy Eckstein] and Step'n Fetchit." Davis Sr. was blunter still: "If you ever do that again I'm gonna kill you. . . . Don't you know there ain't no colored person got no business imitating white people?"[10] It was one thing for a black performer to don the burnt cork in order to imitate white people imitating black people; but this was different. Even white performer Larry Storch—"the best ear in the business"—warned Davis away from doing white impressions, as he coached Davis on the art of impersonation when the two crossed paths at the Last Frontier in Las Vegas. "I told him, 'Sammy, those voices will never work coming out of a black face.' This was in the days when blacks weren't allowed in the casinos. They could entertain there, but they couldn't enter them. But he insisted, and I showed him what I knew. And of course he was a tremendous hit.'"[11]

The Trio's old dance act plus Sammy's comic routines, musical numbers, and impressions: this was the seventy-five minute set that killed at Ciro's on the Sunset Strip when the Trio opened for Janis Paige in 1951. Paige was three years Davis's senior, a rising white star who was best known for musical films like *The Time, the Place and the Girl* (1946), *Romance on the High Seas* (1948), and *One Sunday Afternoon* (1948), and who had recently appeared in the Broadway hit *Remains to Be Seen* (1951). The Will Mastin Trio, by virtually all accounts—including Paige's—stole the show. Entertainment royalty like Dean Martin, Jerry Lewis, and Danny Kaye turned up backstage to congratulate them. "We didn't even have a dressing room," Davis Sr. recalled. "We were . . . up some spiral stairs, where they stored stuff."[12] Herman Hover, the manager of Ciro's, made his way up the spiral stairs, too, to tell the Trio that he was switching the billing—they would be the headliners going forward.

It is not always possible to point to one particular performance as a turning point in a career, but the Ciro's performance with Janis Paige was exactly that. "Once in a long time," wrote *The Hollywood Reporter,* "an artist hits town and sends the place on its ear." *Daily Variety* hailed the performance as a "walloping success." The *Los Angeles Times* breathlessly announced that "The Will Mastin Trio, featuring dynamic Sammy Davis, Jr., are such show-stoppers that star Janis Paige has relinquished the closing spot to them."[13] The splash at Ciro's translated immediately into appearances in a range of other venues on the white side of town: Chez Paree, the Riviera, the Beach Comber, the Copacabana. Jack Benny invited the Trio on tour. One of the most important doors to open was a rare opportunity on Eddie Cantor's NBC variety program *The Colgate Comedy Hour*. Cantor briefly remarked on his own recent visit to Ciro's, before introducing Davis as "one of the greatest hunks of talent I've ever seen in my life." "In my twenty years of going around these cafes," he gushed, "this is the greatest act I've ever seen."[14]

Much early television programming sounded like radio and looked like vaudeville. The omnipresent television variety show was basically a vaudeville revue well into the 1960s. Pegleg Bates tap-danced on the same *Ed Sullivan Show* that featured the Rolling Stones invasion in 1964. In the early years of *The Colgate Comedy Hour* or Milton Berle's *Texico Star Theater,* television was pumping life into the styles and performance standards of vaudeville, even as it closed down vaudeville theaters.[15] The Will Mastin Trio opened their *Colgate* act by trading moves on the dance floor. Mastin, then Sr., danced for about the first two minutes before giving way to an outsized and energetic performance by the younger Davis—again, *fast,* with some legomania and acrobatics thrown in for good measure. Davis danced for about a minute and a half, flanked by his elders, before adding a five-minute comedy routine, "Ira Grizzle, Private Eye." He featured impressions of James Cagney, Jimmy Stewart, and Billy Eckstein, both speaking and singing. He also sent up Edward G. Robinson, with Robinson's signature fedora pulled down almost over his eyes, and wagging a comically large cigar. Cantor came on stage briefly to wipe Davis's brow, before the young performer wound up with an impression of tenor Mario Lanza, and a Jerry Lewis bit that included the comic's exaggerated facial mugging and physical humor. When Cantor rejoined Davis on stage, arm affectionately draped around the younger man, he prodded the audience with a mixture of enthusiasm and pride. "Am I right? Is this the greatest hunk of talent you've seen in years?" On the spot (and on-camera, evidently without warning either the network or his sponsor), Cantor invited Davis back for his next show four weeks hence. Finally, he reintroduced Sr. and Mastin, who took quick turns tapping. Then Davis finished the act with the kind of crazy Russian leg kicks that would have been long familiar on the vaudeville stage.

FIG. 11. The Will Mastin Trio with Eddie Cantor on *The Colgate Comedy Hour,* 1954.

In all this, the moment that really landed and made its mark in the American psyche was the fleeting shot of Cantor mopping the young Negro's brow. A flood of hate mail came in. "Dear lousy nigger, keep your filthy paws off Eddie Cantor he may be a jew but at least he's white and dont come from Africa where you should go back to I hope I hope. I wont use that dirty stinking toothpaste no more for fear maybe the like of you has touched it. What is dirt like you doing on our good American earth anyway?" NBC, Colgate-Palmolive, and Eddie Cantor himself all received such letters. "Where do you get off wiping that little coon's face with the same handkerchief you'd put on a good, clean, white, American face?"[16] Cantor refused to be intimidated, however, and took a strong stand before the seriously cowed network executives and sponsors. "No one is taking my show away from me," he told Davis. "I told Colgate-Palmolive to either take me, my show and the guest stars I choose or I'm gone. I also told them that only some people from the South were offended by what I did; and if they didn't like it, they could go and buy another brand of toothpaste."[17]

The exchange is a fascinating little piece of social history. Cantor explicitly cited his own Jewishness as the template for his understanding and approach to the bigotry Davis was facing: "as a Jew, I know the feelings you have." Cantor also gave Davis his mezuzah (a decorative case—in this instance a locket—containing a piece of parchment with a line from the Torah). According to Davis this gesture, and the object itself, were critical to his later conversion to Judaism. But as important was Cantor's connection to Davis as a vaudevillian. "Let me tell you a story," he said to Davis in the wake of the *Colgate* controversy,

> something that happened to me back in my vaudeville days, when I was just one of the opening acts in the Ziegfield Follies. You probably know there was a great Black singer, comedian and dancer named Bert Williams who was the first Black person to star in the Follies. One night between shows, we went up the street from the theater to a little bar. We were the only customers in the place and sat at the bar. Bert and I both ordered a whiskey. As the bartender set my drink down in front of me, he said, 'That will be fifty cents.' As he set Bert's drink down he said, 'That'll be a hundred dollars.' Without batting an eye, Bert pulled out his wallet, laid down four one hundred dollar bills and said, 'I'll take three more.'

Cantor told the bartender who Williams was, and the bartender apologized profusely. "Always remember the cheers and the applause," Cantor told Davis. "As long as there is prejudice, you will just have to keep knocking the doors down or blowing on the houses until they cave in, which someday, God willing, they will."[18]

Unlike the TOBA tours of earlier years, the postwar nightclub circuit brought the Will Mastin Trio to all-white clubs and resort towns where African Americans' movements were under stricter surveillance and constraint, or to "sundown towns" where their presence after dark was forbidden altogether, literally illegal. Davis's first booking south of the Mason-Dixon line was at the Beach Comber in Miami Beach. "Sammy was scared to death to go down there," recalls Arthur Silber, "and Will didn't want to go at all. . . ." The Trio stayed at the Lord Calvert Hotel, one of those other-side-of-the-tracks Meccas that Ferguson Jenkins described, where black musicians and comedians on the entertainment circuit mingled with traveling sports figures like Sugar Ray Robinson and Roy Campanella. On the white side of the tracks, meanwhile—from the train station to the white resorts—black sociality was policed and affronted at every turn. At the train station they were met with "WELCOME TO MIAMI . . . BLACKS TO THE LEFT AND WHITES TO THE RIGHT"; at the hotel, "No Niggers—No Dogs"; in a store window, "Everybody welcome but the Nigger and the Jew."[19]

The Trio and their entourage discovered that African Americans were subject to a special curfew in Miami Beach, and that taxis were not allowed to bring them across the water to the strip from downtown Miami, but had to drop them at the causeway, unless they secured a special performers' pass. While they were there, a newspaper circulated with the headline, "NIGGER ON THE BEACH." One busker, who was shouting out the headline as he hawked the paper, was promptly punched out by Milton Berle. The ironies of this Jim Crow arrangement were captured most starkly in a confrontation with two white cops as Davis traversed the territory from Miami Beach back to the Lord Calvert late one night. "What're you up to? You know you've got no right to be here?" But one of the cops recognized Davis as the figure whom his kids had admired on TV. "What's he do?" "I guess he tap dances." The tense confrontation ended this way:

'Hey, c'mere a minute, boy.'

I walked to the car. He handed me a slip of paper and a pencil.

'Put your autograph on here for my kid.'[20]

Davis's experience in the rising resort town of Las Vegas was no less fraught, but was even more important to his profile, his reputation, and his stage repertoire. Vegas had sprouted like a neon mushroom in the desert in the years after the war—or like a mushroom cloud, is more like it, given the significance of defense contracting around atomic testing in the region. The population had been just over five thousand in the early 1930s, when work began on the nearby Boulder Dam and gambling first became legal. By 1960 the city had grown to over sixty-four thousand, and its gambling establishments were hosting upwards of eight million tourists each year. Dancer Flash McDonald remembered the early days performing in Vegas, when it was a little dirt-road town with a couple of casinos. After Meyer Lansky's proxy Benjamin "Bugsy" Siegel added the upscale Flamingo to Route 91's western-themed El Rancho and Last Frontier in 1947, gambling investment (and organized crime) from the east flooded into the town. Soon it had established what we know as The Strip, with the additions of the Desert Inn, Sahara, Sands, Royal Nevada, Riviera, Dunes, Hacienda, Tropicana, and Stardust casinos and resorts. Old Route 91 went from "wild west" to "sunbelt modern" in a little over a decade.[21]

By the 1950s some were calling Las Vegas the "Mississippi of the West," less for the significant number of migrants from the Delta than for the city's strict segregation and its unremitting hostility to black residents. Black workers from Mississippi, Arkansas, and Oklahoma had been brought in for work on the Boulder Dam and were recruited in even greater numbers in the 1940s for work at a new defense plant, Basic Magnesium Incorporated. Service jobs exploded with the growth of the casino and tourist industry, providing thousands of kitchen, housekeeping, and custodial jobs for the former agricultural workers of the cotton South. By 1960 the black population stood at about eleven thousand. But Las Vegas was a solidly Jim Crow town, both within the ecology of the casino industry, which catered to and was eager to please a largely white, Southern clientele, and in systemic citywide segregation in schools, housing, and public facilities. African Americans did the invisible work of Las Vegas tourism, washing dishes and cleaning rooms, but never the better paying and more public work of waiting tables or dealing cards. Then they went home to the all-black Westside, whose premodern squalor matched the poorest regions of the South or Appalachia. The city failed to provide even the basics of running water and electricity. "No Niggers, no Chinese, and no goats," specified one typical deed on the white side of town. Mary Wesley, a chambermaid at the Sands, told oral historian Annelise Orleck, "When I got to the Westside, I saw all these little shacks made of cardboard and metal, in rows as far as you could see. I thought they were chicken coops. That's how people was living." City officials not only enforced a brutal, second-class citizenship, but seemed to believe—and hope—that the black population was not in Las Vegas to stay. A survey in 1949 assessed that 80 percent of Westside homes failed to meet minimum federal standards. A "Concrete Curtain" had descended between the black and white sections of town.[22]

This was the Vegas that Sammy Davis Jr. first experienced, even as his star was rising—"I was a Negro in a Jim Crow town." "We can't let you have rooms here," he was told, the first time the Will Mastin Trio was booked as an opening act at the El Rancho. "House rules. You'll have to find a place in the—uh, on the other side of town." On the Westside the Trio were fleeced by a black boardinghouse keeper, who charged them twice the rent of the El Rancho for a "Tobacco Road shack."[23] This was a town where a performer like Davis could take the stage, could even have his name up in lights and be adored, could rake in a fortune for the house, but then be quickly and decisively banished from the kingdom, made to exit through the back door and to retreat across town for his own food and lodging. "In Vegas, for twenty minutes, twice a night, our skin had no color," Davis wrote. "Then, the second we stepped off the stage, we were colored again. . . . We had to leave through the kitchen, with the garbage, like thieves in the night." Davis and other black entertainers "couldn't even eat in the kitchen," recalls Morton

Saiger, an employee at the Last Frontier in those days. "There was a picnic table outside the kitchen. I had to bring out sandwiches for them to eat there."[24] According to Geraldine Branton, when the Nicholas Brothers opened for Sinatra at the Sands, Fayard Nicholas was instructed that he had to withdraw to the dressing room, out of patrons' sight, whenever he was not on stage. White performers took to rubbing his head for good luck. "You're white, but I'm talented," he finally exploded. "Don't ever dare treat me as less than a man." The response this provoked from the casino brass: "We're going to make Sammy Davis the star, and you'll never work again." "I don't care if he's Jesus," the manager of the Tropicana once said, when told that the man he had just ejected from his dining room was Nat King Cole. "He's black and he has to get out of here." Turned down himself for a dinner reservation at the Desert Inn, Davis concluded, as he always did, "I had to get bigger, that's all. I just had to get bigger."[25]

The story is too often told that Davis singlehandedly desegregated Las Vegas, perhaps behind the important influence (and mob ties) of Frank Sinatra. It is true that Sinatra had long aligned himself with progressive causes. These included his short film *The House I Live In* (1945), for which director Albert Maltz was later blacklisted, based on the anthem by Abel Meeropol, the lyricist who also produced "Strange Fruit." Sinatra had a long record of traveling with black acts like the Trio and fighting for integration in travel, dining, and accommodations arrangements.[26] It is also true that Davis was among the first black entertainers to insist upon the principle that he should be able to stay at any establishment that booked him on stage, winning that argument at the Old Frontier in 1955. "If Vegas could open up to us like that then it was just a matter of time until the whole country would open up," he wrote, articulating the close connection he always saw between performing in white spaces and knocking down all of Jim Crow's barriers.[27] He tells a Civil Rights victory story about being warned away from the Old Frontier pool by a manager who Davis assumed—hackles up—to be policing the hotel's color line. As it turned out, the manager's concern, rather, was that having such a big star lounging at the pool might draw hotel guests away from the gaming tables. "I've already got my tan," Davis joked, consenting to leave the poolside. It is worth noting, though, that in Las Vegas to this day another, very different story is told, about how the Sands Hotel drained its pool after Davis became the first African American swimmer to enjoy a dip there.[28]

Change was very slow to come to Las Vegas, even long after the *Brown* decision and Little Rock, and long after Davis himself had won the right to book a suite in the hotels where he performed. "We were still impotent," he reflected, when his friend Finis Henderson declined an invitation to join him ringside for his show, well into the 1960s.

> Black people did not come to see me in Las Vegas because if black people didn't arrive at the hotel with the special safe-conduct of 'Sammy's guest,' they didn't get in. And who wanted *that?* Who wanted to be 'allowed in' and then sit there . . . feeling the stares against the back of your neck? . . . All of the dealers had white hands. I saw cocktail waitresses, change makers, maintenance people. All white. At the front desk of the hotel, nobody, nobody was black.

"Sammy," explained Jack Entratter, the manager of the Sands, "antagonizing our high-rolling Southern clientele is not smart business."[29]

Davis did indeed accomplish important political work in Las Vegas, and he remained committed to it to the extent that years later a Welfare Rights organization there continued to cherish a life-sized cardboard standup of Davis in their entryway.[30] But importantly, too, Davis and Sinatra were *not* alone in desegregating the Strip. They were building on the important and tireless work of local activists, and they were joined in their efforts by a number of other outspoken entertainers, from Lena Horne to Harry Belafonte to Josephine Baker. Prior to Davis's victory at the Old Frontier, Bugsy Siegel had allowed Lena Horne to stay at the Flamingo as early as 1947 (though reportedly he treated her as being under house arrest). Siegel allegedly also deferred to Hazel Scott, when his effort to eject her from his lounge fetched the angry challenge, "What are you going to do, kill me?" Harry Belafonte broke the color barrier at the gaming tables at the Sands, and Josephine Baker threatened to cancel a second show at the El Rancho unless black patrons were allowed to see it. "I'm not going to entertain. I'm going to sit right here until you make up your minds."[31]

But more significantly still, in the months and years after the Montgomery bus boycott the NAACP and other local activists challenged Jim Crow practices in Las Vegas entertainment, both the older western-themed "sawdust" parlors like the Last Frontier and the rising "red carpet" establishments like the Sands. Mary Wesley recalls daily acts of resistance by black maids, porters, and kitchen staff in this period: "You mean I can make your beds, I can touch up your pillow but I can't walk through the front door?"[32] It is critical to understand both the grassroots agitation and the commitment of fellow celebrities as the infrastructure of Davis's fight against Jim Crow in Las

Vegas. A key juncture in the fight came in the spring of 1960, when *Las Vegas Sun* publisher Hank Greenspun brokered a deal between the NAACP, the resorts on the Strip, Governor Grant Sawyer, and Las Vegas mayor Oran Gragson. The resorts would accept African Americans as guests, city and state government would form a race relations committee, and the NAACP would call off their planned marches and conspicuous public agitation.[33] In this respect the grassroots push for desegregation in Las Vegas continued the long tradition of political work that had begun in A. Philip Randolph's March on Washington movement and the Double V campaign, and that had made headlines just a month before in the sit-in movement in Greensboro, North Carolina.

THE RAT PACK'S RACIAL LIBERALISM

Davis's name in lights as a headliner on the Strip was a highly significant marker of racial progress, as was his conspicuous presence in the otherwise all-white Rat Pack, alongside Frank Sinatra, Dean Martin, Peter Lawford, and Joey Bishop. Their fame and their frequent appearances at the Copa room at the Sands cemented and codified the 1950s gains when it came to Jim Crow in Las Vegas. Their act also became the most complete text extant of Davis's complicated navigation of "performing while black" in stubbornly white spaces. Comedian Billy Crystal has remarked, "Hanging out with Sinatra and those guys increased his 'cool factor.'" But Ruta Lee, who worked with the group in the film *Sergeants 3*, seemed closer to the mark when she observed that Davis had allowed himself to be the Rat Pack's "wind-up toy. He was the pet."[34] In fact the stage show that the Rat Pack developed in their famous "Summit" at the Sands—a hard-drinking circus of ad-libbing and carousing and boys-will-be-boys "antics" peppered in between the headliners' lavish musical numbers—created an illusion of integration while demonstrating just how *uncool* mid-century liberalism could be. Even in its multi-ethnic inclusion (Italian, Jewish, English, African American) the Rat Pack maintained a white-over-black dynamic at every moment. They broke silence on race, but fell back on stereotypes and crass humor as their default. As one analysis has it, "There wasn't a cushier, crazier gig on earth and coon-calling was just part of the schtick."[35] Jokes about the KKK might communicate a heady sense of triumphal liberalism, but so did they carry a quiet violence.

FIG. 12. The Rat Pack at the Sands, 1960. Photo: Michael Ochs Archives/Getty Images.

Crystal's characterization of the Rat Pack as "cool" is instructive, but complicated. "Cool" held a very particular place in postwar American culture. It was a brand of rebelliousness or non-conformity, "grace under pressure," "a public mode of covert resistance." It had roots in Depression-era and postwar masculinism and film noir aesthetics on the white side of town (Humphrey Bogart, Marlon Brando), but an even more precise derivation and set of connotations in African American jazz culture. "I play it cool / and dig all jive," wrote Langston Hughes, "That's the reason / I stay alive." Cool was a "survival technology," according to critic Albert Murray; it was an "ideal emotional mode of balance—a calm, cerebral space of relaxation." For Ralph Ellison, too, "resistance to provocation" and "coolness under pressure" were "indispensable values in the struggle [for freedom]."[36] (Think bebop, but also think Billie Holiday.) The "aestheticization of detachment" that was the "cool mask," according to historian Joel Dinerstein, was adopted by jazz artists like Lester Young, Miles Davis, and John Coltrane as a political improvement on the Step'n Fetchit smile. "African American cool was a psychological and stylistic repudiation of the racial performance of Uncle Tomming. . . ."[37]

However "cool" Sinatra and his buddies were in the white register, in the Sands Summit performances Davis himself rather pointedly refused "the cool mask" in the *black* register. As a result he was forced back to something akin to the minstrel mask and to a problematic role as the butt of all jokes. If cool was "defined by individual black males daring to self-define rather than be defined by others," in bell hooks's memorable formulation, then the Rat Pack's stage act was all but founded upon the white performers' ability to do all the defining.[38] Davis may have "kept his cool," but the survival technology he adopted was *not cool,* in that it embodied neither resistance nor defiance nor critique nor self-definition.

The ethnic patter of the Rat Pack on stage was constant, to explosive white laughter, and often to Davis's own exaggerated laughter.

BISHOP: This is Sammy's night. Let's bring him back out, and we'll stay in the background.

SINATRA: No, there will be no segregation.

MARTIN [CARRYING DAVIS IN HIS ARMS LIKE A CHILD]: I'd like to thank the NAACP for this wonderful trophy.

SINATRA TO DAVIS: Keep smiling, Smoky, so everybody knows where you are.

Sinatra and Martin throw a tablecloth over Davis as they unveil an on-stage bar. With Davis covered in a white sheet,

SINATRA: Alright folks, put on your sheets and we'll start the meeting.

DAVIS [REMOVING THE SHEET]: Oh, come on!

MARTIN: Go bore a few holes in that and be somebody.

DAVIS: I'm one of the great Jewish Mau dancers.

LAWFORD: Sure Sam, I'm not prejudiced. I'll dance with you.

DAVIS [LAUGHING]: I know your kind. You'll dance with me, but you won't go to school with me.

DAVIS: Nat King Cole was a merry old soul . . . a merry old *colored* soul. . . .

SINATRA: Hurry up, Sam, the watermelon's getting warm.

SINATRA: Why don't you be yourself and get some ribs?

DAVIS: How come I ain't never seen no colored people on *The Millionaire?* I've been watching that program for five years, it's ridiculous.

SINATRA: I saw one once, but they wouldn't cash his check.

Davis tap dances.

BISHOP [FROM OFFSTAGE]: Look at this, Frank, a Jewish woodpecker.

SINATRA: I'd like to see them try this in Little Rock.

Davis and Lawford trade barbs, Davis in a British accent, Lawford in a thick minstrelized black caricature.

They would often close the show with Davis's signature, "Birth of the Blues," an unsettling landing for this particular quintet amid the racial banter, given the song's white, appropriative, and politically sanitized rendition of the blues' origin story.[39]

It is easy enough in hindsight to see the racism—however "friendly"— running through these performances, and one might cringe, along with Ruta Lee, that Davis had been made his white colleague's "wind-up toy." The more challenging point is twofold. First, the Rat Pack's racism itself was meant to perform a kind of *liberalism* that was a fairly new thing in the post-*Brown* moment.[40] There was not necessarily a vision here, or much thought at all, even though Sinatra and Lawford were close to the John F. Kennedy campaign, which was then in the process of rolling out a Cold War-inflected argument about the "stain" that discrimination represented for the nation's reputation globally. The Sands performances were not "produced" in any meaningful way, and the rudderless, writerless, hard-drinking chaos on stage was in fact part of the appeal. Each night the (white) audience was invited to carouse with the boys for a time. The act developed organically, as a product of the kaleidoscopic relationships among the five men, and in their boys-will-be-boys drive to top one another in good-natured hijinks. What was on display was indeed a brand of integration that was novel for its time, complete with equal billing for Davis and with genuine friendship across the color line. But in expressing their ease with Davis's black presence in this white space, white members of the Rat Pack often crossed a line, drawing upon racism itself as the very idiom of "ease." A later generation might have called these attempts at humor "edgy." On stage at the Sands in 1960, there was no need felt to justify this kind of language, and so no such explicit disclaimer. Everyone was meant to feel good that Davis was there, and to feel good that his blackness was the stuff of comfortable laughter. And to feel good that he appeared to feel good, too.

Secondly, therefore, the stakes for Sinatra, Martin, Bishop, and Lawford were quite different than they were for Davis when it came to the politics of the Sands performances. This would go for the Rat Pack's films, too, like *Ocean's Eleven,* whose heist plot cast Davis as a garbage truck driver while coolly offering jokes about blacking up. If Sinatra and Martin's role was to stage a jocular (white) open-mindedness that was still a rarity in this place and time, Davis's burden was to make everything—*everything*—okay. He saw himself as still very much in the business of breaking down barriers, so he had to be more conscious of the racial project that was afoot than his white colleagues, wrapped as they were in the invisible cloak of their privilege. The first half of the burden for Davis, then, was to accept whatever came down the pike during a show and to make sure that it worked as good-natured ribbing and as comedy.

Davis would try to draw an explicit link between his theory of racial humor on the one hand and the racial *schtick* of the Rat Pack on the other. The Rat Pack had at one time been known as "the clan," for instance, a subject that Davis brought up on stage:

> DAVIS: Hold it, . . . I want to go on record that I ain't belongin' to nothing that's called a *clan.*
>
> MARTIN [NODDING TOWARD SINATRA]: You'd better discuss it with the leader.
>
> DAVIS: Maybe he's *your* leader but *my* leader is Martin Luther King![41]

The second half of Davis's burden was to make the white audience feel at home with an integrated act and a free-flowing racial discourse that was new to many of them. It was often he who broke the racial ice, for instance.

> Let me say what an honor it is to represent the ethnic groups. I'm colored, Jewish, and Puerto Rican. When I move into a neighborhood, *I wipe it out.*

He would say to pianist George Rhodes, "I know how sensitive you are, but would you mind playing on some of the *white* keys?" Or, "George, there are too many white guys in the band."[42] Or, as Michael Silva began to pound a beat on the kettle drum, "Play steady—and no messages." Such jokes were self-consciously meant as a kind of racial caretaking, to make white audiences comfortable not only with his blackness but with their own thoughts about his blackness. This move could sometimes be quite elaborate. He would launch into a lengthy monologue about how "hatred won't die of old age ... it can't stand light, it has to breed in secret, like cancer." It was important to discuss race and racism openly, no matter how hard. Then he would add, at last, "*However*, needless to say, I ain't goin' to Mississippi to do this."[43] Cue laughter.

Davis's acceptance of the Rat Pack's rank racial humor became a calling card, as was his willingness to be the butt of jokes, including his own. This is neither to castigate nor to redeem Davis, but rather to render the grain and historicity of the choices he made in Rat Pack settings. Some friends were upset by the Rat Pack dynamic, but Davis saw it as part of the political chimera of "getting bigger" in the business—ironically, his indemnification against racism. "Many hurtful things happened with the Rat Pack," wrote longtime friend and publicist Arthur Silber Jr.,

> and I am sure the public didn't even realize what was happening. . . . But the things Frank and Dean said and did to Sammy under the guise of humor were painful, mean and infuriating. Not being Black, and not being Sammy, Frank and Dean might not have even realized just how hurtful they were to Sammy. The members of the Rat Pack were friends, and that made what they did hurt Sammy even more, right down to his very gut.[44]

An emerging Davis signature in these years was the exaggerated, silent laugh—an over-the-top, thigh slapping kind of laugh that looked like a mask and that could almost become a grimace. Black laughter has lost "the threatening overtones it once had," wrote critic Mel Watkins. "In fact, when employed by professional entertainers it may even become a comic signature, a source of comfort and instant recognition for the [white] audience, and a critical part of the entertainer's comic arsenal. . . . Sammy Davis Jr.'s thigh-slapping, foot-stomping laughter was, of course, as broad and expansive as his legendary talents and almost as extravagant as his jewelry."[45] Columnist Donna Britt likewise recalled that, when Davis appeared on the talk show circuit, "Nobody else on the show would be more convulsed by the host's feeblest jokes."[46] One observer described him as "a courtier to Ivan the Terrible, [he] would bend over laughing and make sure his liege saw it: his

FIG. 13. Davis with Dean Martin and Frank Sinatra. The over-the-top laugh. Photo: Bettmann via Getty Images.

face stretched in desperate mirth, literally slapping his knees, yet not a sound coming out of his mouth."[47]

The caretaking labor performed here was important to Davis's act, and never more so than when he took the stage with Sinatra and Martin in Las Vegas. But there could also be a rage to it that is terribly important. "Sammy just kept slapping his knees," wrote Silber, "making believe he was laughing—but no sound came from his mouth. It was easy to tell what was going on."[48] Significantly, Davis himself describes that very laugh in *Yes I Can,* at the juncture of a series of racial slights at the Copacabana. Sinatra had set him up as a special guest at a ringside table. The first night, Davis heard a man say to another guest at Davis's table, "I saw you sitting down there—in Africa." The next night, another referred to the "little nigger in front of me"—"you can understand my surprise when I find my wife and I seated behind the little jigaboo." "Baby," Davis said to Jules Podell, the manager of the Copa, "if you'll excuse a little well-earned bitterness: colored people don't really have big lips, we just look that way from *keeping* them stiff for so long." Soon Joey Bishop took the stage to start his set, "and I played the scene of enjoying myself, laughing, stamping my feet hilariously."[49]

The arc of Davis's career between 1946 and 1960—from the Trio's opening for Sinatra at the Capitol Theater, to Davis's hamming it up with the Rat Pack in Las Vegas a decade and a half later—is the story of a meteoric rise, to be sure. *Time* magazine wrote him up in 1955 as the next big "socko" thing, and he was.[50] His climb encompassed broken racial barriers at white night-clubs like the Copacabana, triumphal breakthroughs at Ciro's or on network TV (*Ed Sullivan, Milton Berle,* and *Steve Allen* in addition to *The Colgate Comedy Hour*), rising Las Vegas notoriety, overcoming a serious car accident and staging a dramatic comeback (also at Ciro's), and finally seeing his name in lights on the Vegas strip alongside Frank Sinatra, one of the brightest stars in the firmament. The path says a great deal about Davis's idiosyncratic drive and desire, about his "I must get bigger" approach to Jim Crow. But it also illuminates quite a lot about the *textures* of Jim Crow and about the grada-tions of accommodation and resistance in the postwar years. His climb from the Capitol Theater to the Sands also represents the period from the Double Victory campaign to the Greensboro sit-ins.

Strikingly, even amid Davis's undeniable professional successes and his Jim Crow victories, his fight against the cultural undertow of racism was limited by contrast. Watching another black act from the wings at the Strand Theater in the 1940s, where the Trio was opening for Count Basie and Billie Holiday, Davis critiqued their deference and their minstrelized patter: "I listened to them saying, 'Ladies and Gen'men, we's gwine git our laigs movin', heah.' Must we be caricatures of cotton field slaves? We don't all pull barges up the Mississippi. Can't we entertain and still keep our dignity?" In the moment, Davis realized that the Trio, too, tended to perform in this genre, deferring to the color line, cutting off a kind of straight, look-in-the-eye con-nection with white audiences. "The jokes weren't done like Milton Berle was doing them, to the audience, they were done between the men on-stage, as if they didn't have the right to communicate with the people out front. . . ." By habit and tradition, Davis recognized, "we were still doing *Holiday in Dixieland.*" Around that time Davis shed his zoot suit for the same reason. "I was saying, 'Gen'men' with those clothes just as loud and clear as if I'd come shuffling on singing 'Old Black Joe.'"[51]

What to make, then, even many years later, of "Hurry up, Sam, the water-melon's getting warm"? Patterns of white hostility (even if disguised as presumption) and black strategy (whether resistance, accommodation, or full-on deference) persisted, both in the industry and in the street. Indeed, as historian Jonathan Holloway notes, the situation for African Americans was often more dangerous after barriers *did* begin to fall.[52] One dimension of this was certainly the white-over-black structures of the industry. Even post-*Brown*, spaces like the Sands or Broadway's Majestic Theater were built to coddle and kid-glove the sensibilities of white people, and white Southerners in particular. There was also continuing white control of the entertainment product. As soon as "one of the Negro artists reaches the top rung of the ladder," Memphis's *Tri-State Defender* commented, "he must have a white manager, a white press agent, a white secretary, a white booking office and a long list of white phonies to follow him around." Lena Horne points out, "at that time a Negro manager could not get jobs for his clients, because the agencies that had Negro talent under contract were not about to let a Negro personal manager in."[53] Another dimension of this, as the Rat Pack's good-natured hijinks suggested, was the extent to which racism was so deeply rooted as to inflect the very *logic* of American culture, including—and perhaps especially—American liberalism.

DESEGREGATING THE WESTERN

Hollywood and network television were among the white spaces—and increasingly important ones, nationally—whose gates Davis was intent on crashing. In Hollywood, even the fantastical all-black space of *Porgy and Bess,* as we saw, was the disguised white space of DuBose Heyward and George Gershwin's imagination and of Otto Preminger's direction. Davis's own experience with the Eddie Cantor handkerchief incident was enough to underscore the whiteness of television, but the principle was conspicuously at work everywhere one tuned in. "Anyone ever think of giving [Davis] a Como-type quarter hour to sing a lot, and dance a little?" asked *Post* critic Barry Gray, shortly after Davis's *Colgate* appearances. "Hardly seems necessary to point out that with all the great Negro talent around, not one is seen on TV in a regularly scheduled spot." Gray, a longtime (white) critic of American racism, was taken by Davis's Copacabana performances, he said, but also by the rumor that ABC had recently failed to follow through on a TV contract with Davis.[54] Later, when Davis filmed a successful appearance on *General Electric Theater,* CBS delayed airing the episode, ultimately holding it for release opposite *The Dinah Shore Show,* which was the network's way of killing it in (and for) the South. After months of frustrating dealings with the network, Davis bitterly concluded, "my dreams of glory of being a trailblazer for my people were hanging in shreds on the fucking Mason-Dixon line."[55]

This became common knowledge and a more common sentiment when Nat King Cole was forced to pull the plug on his own show in 1957. The *Nat King Cole Show* had originally aired without commercial sponsorship, because companies were afraid of upsetting white Southern sensibilities. NBC paid for the show, confident that its success would eventually bring sponsors around. It did not. "The collapse of the *Nat King Cole Show* served only to reaffirm what many felt to be true," writes one historian. "Television was no place for Afro-American talents to seek success." For his own part, Cole merely quipped, "Madison Avenue is afraid of the dark."[56] Television had actually become *whiter* since 1952, when changes to FCC licensing practices expanded the footprint of Southern stations and affiliates. Jan Willis recalls huddling around the TV with her family in Docena, Alabama, to watch Sammy Davis Jr. on *The Ed Sullivan Show.*

> We leaned in close as stiff-necked Ed began his introduction. But just as Sullivan threw wide his arms to greet Davis—like so many times before—the card came on with its message of denial . . . 'Trouble along the cable.' Every time a black person appeared on television, we saw only this card.[57]

Television "did not invent the 'whiteness' of America," writes Alan Nadel, but it did "impressively help codify and deploy whiteness as the norm for the United States in the nuclear age."[58]

The cinematic and television *texts* Davis helped to create as he fought these battles may have been problematic, from a Civil Rights standpoint ("Yeah, everything but integrity"), and this is indeed how he is often remembered. We will return to this. But his thinking about racial equity and the airwaves was in some ways ahead of the curve. As he demanded of his agent, Sy Marsh, "why do I have to play the part of a Negro?" The question itself implied a radical proposition.

> Why do I have to play a part that depends on color? Why can't I play something where the fact that I'm a Negro has no bearing on the script in any way? Why must a special part be written for a Negro? Or else, an entire script switched so they do *Abie's Irish Rose* with an all-Negro cast? Y'know something? I *die* every time I hear some cat on Broadway who says, 'What we need is integrated theater. Authors should write in more parts for Negroes.' That's

not integrated theater. *Really* integrated theater will be when an actor—colored or white—is hired to play a part. Period. Not when a Negro is hired to play the part of a Negro who's in the story strictly *as* a Negro, like when they're doing a scene in a Harlem bar and the producer tells Casting, 'Send up one Negro bartender, one Negro bar owner, and some Negro extras for customers.'[59]

He went on to launch a critique that would become far more common much later on, during the culture wars of the post-Civil Rights era. "According to dramatic television there are almost no colored people in America," he observed, charging that sponsors were too timid to do anything that would risk "jarring customers in Southern markets." "Baby," he challenged Marsh, "have you any idea how jarring it must be for about five million colored kids who sit in front of a television set hour after hour and they almost never see anybody who looks like them? It's like they and their families and their friends just plain don't exist."[60]

The politics of representation—"images"—is no doubt crucial, as we have seen from the battles over everything from minstrelsy's images to *Porgy*. "Any black is every black," writes critic Ann duCille, when it comes to the power of mass-mediated representations of blackness to frame real-world understandings. "Stigmatic blackness," in her formulation, constitutes African Americans as at once "socially peripheral" and "symbolically central"—disposable to society and yet a critical "repository of salacious fantasies and dark desires."[61] But *total erasure* is another thing altogether. Wryly noting the "clear and present absence" of African Americans on a show like *Perry Mason*, a girlhood favorite, duCille describes another of those family moments huddled around the console, when "we keenly felt the presence of our own absence as human beings worthy of a Perry Mason defense."[62] Television and film not only mediate dominant images of groups for both main- and small-stream audiences, that is, but create a portraiture of the nation at large, upon which hinges our understandings and expectations of citizenship. The cosmos projected in American television and film has the power to create and police a normative whiteness, not just reflect it.[63]

Davis was bent not only on desegregating institutions (network and Hollywood studios), but on desegregating storytelling *genres* as well. One of the genres that interested him most was the Western. The Hollywood Western was still a popular draw, having been adapted as Cold War allegory after a generations-long run from the silent era's *Train Robbery,* to the prewar years' *Big Trail* (John Wayne), *Dodge City* (Errol Flynn), *Destry Rides Again* (James

Stewart), or *Union Pacific* (Joel McRae and Barbara Stanwyck). On television, Westerns made up fully 80 percent of the top ten shows and 50 percent of the top twenty throughout the 1950s, including *The Lone Ranger* (1949–1957), *Hopalong Cassidy* (1949–1954), *The Cisco Kid* (1950–1956), *The Roy Rogers Show* (1951–1957), *Death Valley Days* (1952–1970), *The Adventures of Kit Carson* (1951–1955), *The Adventures of Wild Bill Hickock* (1951–1958), *Annie Oakley* (1954–1957), and *Gunsmoke* (1955–1975).[64] If a black actor were looking to break out of the traditional song-and-dance ghetto or the occasional all-black extravaganza, serious acting on a Western might be the place to do it.

Davis did pitch a race-themed plot idea for Rod Serling's *Twilight Zone,* where a garden variety white bigot awakes to find himself transformed into a black man. But much of his agitation was aimed at the popular "horse opera," as it was called. "I'll play anything except an Uncle Tom," he told Sy Marsh, "but don't brush off the western thing so fast. . . ."

> It happens there were a lot of colored cowboys. . . . The guys who wrote the history books happened to be white, and by a strange coincidence they man-aged to overlook just about everything any Negro did in and for America except pull barges up the goddamned Mississippi. But I've got books on the early west. . . .[65]

He was right. Not only were there black cowboys in the nineteenth century (as many as one out of four), but there were regions where the term "cowboy" was widely understood at the time to name someone who likely *was* black.[66] We now have a more multi-vocal and sophisticated understanding of the American west than the one that was mythologized and handed down from Buffalo Bill's traveling Wild West shows (1880s), to Hollywood spectacles like *Stagecoach* (1939), to 1950s television westerns like *Gunsmoke.* These renditions were heavily racialized melodramas about the advance of white, masculinist "civilization" on the way toward national greatness (whether cast as gun-slinging or as cavalry heroics), and the Hollywood and broadcast-era depictions of cowboys and Indians were often thinly veiled allegories of the titanic Cold War struggle against those other "reds," the Soviets. This genre in its starkest white supremacist codes would begin to unravel precisely as the Civil Rights movement crested and the Cold War consensus became frayed. Consider the motley, inclusive gang of *Cat Ballou* (1965), for instance, as narrated by black troubadour Nat King Cole, or the demise of *Butch Cassidy and the Sundance Kid* (1969) before an army—conspicuously—of soldiers of color in Bolivia.

Davis was not the first actor to undertake this project of getting African Americans the hell into Dodge. Jazz musician Herb Jeffries had starred in a number of black-cast westerns in the 1930s: *Harlem on the Prairie* (1937), *Two Gun Men from Harlem* (1938), *The Bronze Buckeroo* (1939). Jeffries was drawn to the genre for much the same reason as Davis after him. He once saw a black child in Cincinnati crying because his white friends would not let him be Tom Mix in their cowboy game, "because Tom Mix ain't black." Jeffries determined to go to Hollywood and "somehow instigate a black cowboy picture that could play in thousands and thousands of segregated black theaters throughout the south. I said, 'I gotta make that cowboy picture somehow.'"[67] Interestingly, Jeffries's own racial identity was a matter of some question. Raised by his single Irish mother, he claimed an African American father early in life, revising that to "three eights Negro," "Moorish," "Ethiopian," or "Sicilian" later on. The US census had him down as "mulatto."[68] But in any case, like Davis after him, Jeffries saw challenging the casting norms of the Western as an important racial project.

The culture industries' whitewashing rendered this an exercise that had to be repeated with each generation, and it was Sammy Davis Jr. who led the charge into the industry's "west" in the 1950s and 1960s. He had assembled an impressive personal gun collection and studied to become a master at gun handling. He added a quick-draw and gun-spinning exhibition to his stage act when he was still with the Will Mastin Trio. He showed off his gun-handling skills in some of his earliest television appearances, including on *The Colgate Comedy Hour* and during a 1955 interview on Edward R. Murrow's *Person to Person*. In 1957 he and Arthur Silber Jr. shot an amateurish short western film called *Captured,* featuring two bandits and their prey fighting to the death on some barren western range over a satchel of gold that looked suspiciously like a leather, mid-twentieth-century women's handbag. Perhaps it was Davis's fascination with gun-handling that drew him to the western genre, or perhaps it was his well-known expertise in this field that caused producers to look to him to desegregate the all-white "west" of both the big and small screen. Regardless, Davis worked on his first western project for *Zane Grey Theater* in 1958. Perhaps predictably, production hit a snag when sponsors balked at the idea of a black deputy shooting white people. Script doctors rewrote the episode to include a separate "black" plotline involving a unit of "Buffalo Soldiers" at war with the Comanche nation (and casting Davis as a bigot, to boot).[69]

Episodes of *The Rifleman* followed in 1962 (twice) and *The Wild, Wild West* in 1965.[70] Each time Davis was the lone black figure in a white west. The

Rifleman episodes are notable as artifacts of the early Civil Rights years in American television. As the first African American gunslinger on network TV, Davis merited a mention from George Lincoln Rockwell, head of the American Nazi Party, as a symbol of "the degeneration of American culture."[71] In "The Most Amazing Man," Davis plays a big-talking spinner of yarns named Wade Randall, whose tall tales take in the rifleman's teenaged son, Mark, to the extent that the boy writes a school composition on Randall. After talking himself into a spot of real danger (challenged to a gun fight over a real-life betrayal implied in one of his tall tales), Randall is exposed as a fraud. In truth he is a railroad cook known as Cookie, who will surely perish in this gunfight unless somehow rescued by the rifleman, which he is. The notable thing in the context of 1962, and the "liberalism" of the liberal project here, is that Cookie's blackness is never a salient piece of this story of his humanity. Rather it speaks, and is meant to speak, volumes that he is drawn in a sympathetic light, for all his imperfections, and that a white boy in this town would see him as "The Most Amazing Man." The role is not written as "black," in other words, which was its power for Davis and his collaborators. While playwright August Wilson might later propose that to cast black actors in white plays was "to cast us as mimics," Davis's *Rifleman* appearance here, like Diahann Carroll's appearance that same year in Broadway's *No Strings,* advanced racial *interchangeability* itself as a progressive proposition.[72]

Davis's other *Rifleman* episode is more striking still, operating from the opposite principle of embedding the lone black character in a broader African American world, at least by implication. In "Two Ounces of Tin" Davis plays Tip Corey, a drifter who shows up in the rifleman's New Mexico Territory town to avenge the "law" that had failed him. Here again Davis's blackness goes unmentioned, but this time his character's backstory does suggest the relevance of race through its implicit, racialized patterns of violence. When Corey was a young boy, his father had been killed by a bunch of drunken ranch hands while trying to protect a young Indian woman they were harassing. The father sent Tip to fetch the marshal for help, but this marshal turned his back on the endangered Indian woman, on the elder Corey, and on the law. The ranch hands—unmistakably coded as "white" in this backstory—then killed Tip Corey's Pa, knowing there would be no recrimination. "My Pa believed in the law," Tip asserts, having now returned to the town years later to take on the marshal and symbolically to hold "the law" accountable.

Like "The Most Amazing Man," this episode is chiefly about empathy, though here the cross-racial aspects are drawn in bolder lines. Tip Corey finally fails in his quest for justice, and the episode ends with rifleman Lucas McCain and his boy Mark laying flowers at the graves of both Corey and his father, as Lucas somberly intones the closing line, "There but for the grace of God go I." This particular disruption of the television western's whiteness was effectively censored by ABC, which pulled "Two Ounces of Tin" at the last minute in favor of a rerun of *The Loretta Young Show*. This incident demonstrates how live the battle was in 1962 not only to create dignified roles, but to simply get black faces onto the screen. As one Freedom Ride activist noted of the Sammy-for-Loretta switchout at the time, "This is typical of what seems to be a general policy of keeping out appearances of Negroes when possible."[73]

Davis's work on *Sergeants 3* (1962), another reprise of the Rat Pack's Sands Hotel antics, represents a more elaborate foray in the western vein.[74] The film is an Americanized update of the Gunga Din tale, a Rudyard Kipling poem (1890) about three British soldiers and a native water-bearer in India, who protect the empire from a murderous Indian cult called the Thuggees. In this revision Davis's character, an ex-slave named Jonah, figures as the water-bearing Gunga Din, making him a central pillar in this saga of white imperial righteousness, as black critics like Matthew Stelly were quick to point out. Stelly later wrote of Davis as a "Gungamima," a gender-neutral epithet combining the native betrayal of Gunga Din with the minstrelized stereotype of Aunt Jemima.[75] There is a dose of familiar Rat Pack antics here, mostly consisting of heavy drinking among the three sergeants (Sinatra, Martin, and Lawford), and their standard martini-soaked jokes about the playboy bachelor life in a subplot about Lawford's impending marriage. But anyone expecting broad comedy is apt to be taken aback by the sober brutality of *Sergeants 3*, and by the film's "straightness," its fidelity to the western genre.

The film opens with a ruthless attack on a small white settlement in the 1870s. Kipling's Thuggees are translated here into Northern Paiute or Lakota—never named, but implied through a plotline centering on the dangerous spread of the purportedly anti-white Ghost Dance. The opening violence against so many white "innocents," which the viewer is meant to understand as unprovoked, is not unprovoked at all, then. The white settlers and their cavalry are the invading force here. But the tacit logic that immediately establishes the melodramatic line between whites and Indians as the line between good and evil holds in the film from beginning to end. In this respect, *Sergeants 3* never strays from the fundamental conventions of the mid-century Hollywood western, regardless of whatever schtick the Rat Pack heaped into the mix. It is worth noting that these stories of colonial and anti-colonial violence on the plains were (and are) not simply fossilized and "past," as Native scholar Nick Estes argues. Indigenous resistance has never come to an end, and neither have the colonial practices by which the United States continues to occupy North America with a regime of normalization. Indian relocation was unfolding in real time even while the Rat Pack played cowboys and Indians for *Sergeants 3*, as the Army Corps of Engineers oversaw the many "necessary" dislocations of a sprawling river and dam project across Lakota territories in the 1950s and 1960s. Yet another generation further along, Wasté Win Young would announce at Standing Rock, "We are the protectors of our nation, of Oceti Sacowin, the Seven Council Fires. *Know who we are.*"[76]

"Invasion is not an event, but a structure," writes Patrick Wolfe—an ongoing structure of military power and administrative management, a juridical structure of imposed rules and police powers, a structure of logic and understanding by which some claims have standing and others do not, a structure of historical understanding itself, ever partisan in its parsing of "honor," "glory," and "righteousness," and of the "natural" order of things.[77] The "innocence" of this continuous occupation in North America is something that has to be reproduced and reestablished over and over again, as the intervening scholarship on settler-colonialism has shown. Popular narratives like *Sergeants 3* are among the very things that have performed this ideological work. The audience's facile assumptions about Indian "treachery" and the superiority of white "civilization" are not only reinforced and rewarded in a film like *Sergeants 3*, but are crucial to its very coherence. The redemption and recognition of the Sammy Davis Jr. character in the eyes of the white officers *only* makes sense and works as "entertainment" if we are able to regard the project of white settlement, Indian-hating, and violence as a just one.

It is into this racialized melodrama that Davis's Gunga Din figure wanders. He is an ex-slave who wants nothing more than to enlist in the US cavalry and take his place as a soldier alongside those in the three sergeants' command. Jonah is introduced in the film's third scene, that disturbing bit of racialized barroom bullying—played partly for laughs—in which the ex-slave is made to tap-dance at gunpoint on a bartop while playing the bugle, amid the jeers and hoots of a crowd of rowdy white patrons who loudly express their mixed enjoyment and derision. Later we learn that Jonah's master had given him this bugle and a mule when he freed him at the Civil War's end: "I'm ruined, so you git. You're a free man." Jonah tells Sergeant Mike

Merry (Sinatra) in humble tones, "I'm looking for a home," to which the sergeant replies flatly, "There ain't no home for you where we're going." In response to Jonah's plea to be allowed to join the US Army and ride with them, Merry says simply that, "it can't be done . . . regulations." But Jonah turns up at the fort as an uninvited guest anyway, and Merry finally agrees to turn a blind eye, reminding him nevertheless, "you're a civilian, you're not part of the military." Jonah later steals along with the military detail out on patrol, and when discovered he pleads, "There are so many horses to take care of. And I can carry water, too." All of this establishes the logic and the narrative line of the Kipling saga. The two stories share a colonial project, complete with its unforgiving boundary between the included and the excluded, the rulers and the ruled, and a water-carrying subaltern who is determined to serve the empire and thus make a separate peace with colonial power and win his own humanity through its recognition of his loyalty.

Jonah finds something of an ally in the Dean Martin character (named, with a wink at the Sands, Chip Deal), who advises him to stay out of sight but makes clear that he will help the ex-slave in his quest. "That's pretty good," he says with kindly paternalism, as he watches Jonah practice his military drills. This alliance between ex-slave and cavalryman becomes critical to the unfolding Indian war. On a patrol to the sacked white settlement, they have their first violent encounter with the Indians, a stock action-genre Hollywood firefight complete with the requisite hand-to-hand combat aboard a speeding buckboard wagon. This is mixed in with some comic touches involving a cache of fireworks and—significantly—a series of achievements in battle on Jonah's part, missed or misrecognized by Sergeant Merry. But the narrative background on the regional violence begins here. A lone Indian named Mountain Hawk is able to call forth legions of attacking Indians by enunciating the single mysterious word, *Watanka!* The actor cast as Mountain Hawk, Henry Silva, is himself an interesting symbol of Hollywood's racial dealings in an era of unabashed redface, brownface, and yellowface, even as blackface had passed from fashion. He was of Sicilian and Portuguese parentage, but his racial indeterminacy had long been pressed into the service of dark "exoticism" by various Hollywood casting directors. By this time Silva had played a Mexican peon in *Viva Zapata!* (1952), "Chink" in *The Tall T* (1957), an indigenous Venezuelan named Kua-Ko in *Green Mansions* (1959), and the Korean houseboy Chinjun in *The Manchurian Candidate* (1962). He would go on to play an array of characters with evocative names like Salavtore Giordano (*Johnny Cool*, 1963), Mr. Moto (*Mr.*

Moto, 1965), Garcia Mendez (*The Hills Run Red,* 1966), and Crazy Knife (*The Plainsman* 1966).[78]

It turns out that Mountain Hawk's dramatic clarion call offers the key to the recent Indian raids. The attackers are followers of a Medicine Man named Watanka, a Ghost Dance prophet preaching "the dance of death." After a few convoluted twists of plot and subplot, Jonah and an Indian scout named Caleb bring in important intelligence on the Ghost Dancers. Chip Deal urges Sergeant Merry that patriotic duty dictates that their unit must take on "the biggest danger this country is in right now." Merry himself dismisses any intelligence furnished by Caleb and Jonah as "a stupid idiotic rumor." But Sergeant Deal is all in, and Jonah, Caleb, and Deal ultimately set out to discover the murderous Ghost Dancers, despite Merry's orders to stand down. The Indian scout Caleb turns back at the border of his people's territory. But the soldier and the ex-slave press onward, the one out of duty and the other out of an earnest hope of being accepted as an enlisted man in the all-white army. The two find a cave corresponding to the "golden temple" in *Gunga Din,* then get trapped when the Indians return, ominously speaking about killing off the whites and bringing back the days of old when the buffalo were plentiful. Sergeant Deal creates a diversion—grandly stepping forward to put the Indians under arrest "in the name of the President of the United States, Ulysses S. Grant"—so that Jonah can escape to fetch Sergeant Merry.

From this point on, we are back to the Gunga Din tale with some fidelity. Jonah serves as loyal scout to Mike Merry, showing him the way back to the cave and to captive Sergeant Deal. Along with the mightily outnumbered soldiers, he enters the battle against the Indians ("I'm a soldier now, ain't I?"). Having been shot through with an arrow and taken away from the action, at a moment of supreme desperation for the soldiers Jonah creeps up through a chimney at the top of the cave and blows his bugle as a call to the distant cavalry, saving the day. The film's closing scene depicts a commendation ceremony, conferring the Secretary of War's personal "certificate of merit" upon the three sergeants and "a civilian named Jonah Williams, now Private." In this version, unlike the original *Gunga Din,* the water-carrier lives to enjoy his own recognition by the colonial administration.

Sergeants 3 is indicative of the complexities and the deeply layered history inhering in a disarming term like "the white space of the Hollywood western." On the one hand, the film would seem immediately but *merely* to denote the jagged edges of a vintage 1960s racial liberalism. This might applaud "inclusion" of the sort that Sammy Davis Jr. represented in this context, while still insisting on both a servility in the Jonah Williams role as written *and* on the continuing second-class status of Davis himself vis-à-vis the rest of the Rat Pack. Though the racial politics of *Sergeants 3* are apt to make the twenty-first-century viewer squirm, it is true that black actors in American westerns were few in these years, as were representations of enslaved or recently freed people in American popular narratives of any sort. Disrupting this norm was the cultural politics of race that Davis himself was attuned to and that Frank Sinatra would take some pride in during the Kennedy years. In response to criticisms of the Step'n Fetchit mode of some of the Jonah role, Davis replied, "*Sergeants* wasn't to be taken seriously. It was a fun-type show that people could enjoy without getting all wrapped up in morals and points. That was one of the biggest reasons I took the part. . . . I have never done or said anything in my professional life that I thought was a hindrance to my race."[79]

Davis's defensiveness suggests that he was perhaps not as sanguine as he claimed to be about this "fun-type show." And in fact the film thoroughly naturalizes a brand of white supremacism and violence in its narrative framing, more Hollywood mythologizing at a moment when a generation of US soldiers was soon to be referring to free-fire zones in Vietnam as "Indian country." As Jonah Davis not only reprises a familiar role as the never-quite-emancipated slave, an enforced servility that had haunted black-white relations on the screen from the silent era on down, but he also quite literally carries water on behalf of a colonial project that had haunted white-*red* relations since 1492. These social and political relations, embedded in the sovereignty and counter-sovereignty of the settler-colonial situation, had been rendered nearly invisible in the conventions of Hollywood mythologizing, just as surely as living, breathing indigenous peoples had been effaced by the casting of Sicilian Henry Silva in the lead indigenous role. Quite aside from the potential slights of the Jonah role, in other words, it is the genre's colonial buy-in—and all that it renders invisible—that is more deeply at issue. Assimilation into *what?*, is the question properly asked of Jonah. There was a reason that, as comedian Dick Gregory recalled, "We [African Americans] used to root for the Indians against the cavalry," in other words. "When the cavalry won it was a great victory, but when the Indians won it was a massacre."[80] Hollywood's mythic west was a metaphysical project in its power to render such moral inconsistencies invisible to a white audience. Perhaps *Sergeants 3* further upped the ante on this, in the plotline that brought an ex-slave neatly into the cavalry fold.

Davis would try his hand at the genre again in the 1970s, in *The Trackers* (1971) and *Little Moon and Jud* (1975). By this time, while the American western was still a decidedly all-white enterprise (with the occasional white actor in redface), the racial discourse had shifted significantly in both US politics and popular culture. *The Trackers*, a TV pilot co-produced by Davis and Aaron Spelling, was particularly self-conscious in its racial justice themes, drawing conspicuously upon gestures and motifs from the 1967 Sidney Poitier/Rod Steiger film *In the Heat of the Night*.[81] With *The Trackers* Davis became the first-ever black producer of a network TV movie. He also garnered top billing above co-star Ernest Borgnine, an obvious departure from his days as the Rat Pack's "wind-up toy." The plot commences when a Texas rancher's son is murdered and his daughter kidnapped, apparently by Apaches, and their father sends for a US Marshal he knew in his old "ridin' days" (in the Confederate Army, it turns out). The "tracker" who answers the call is not the Borgnine character Sam Paxton's old friend Charlie Gordon, but instead the African American Ezekiel Smith, a Deputy US Marshal from Abilene. "That ain't no Charlie Gordon," Paxton grumbles, squinting into the distance, as Davis approaches the ranch. Another white man in Paxton's posse will observe, "Sure ain't nobody like that around these parts."

Race remains central to the plotlines of *The Trackers* in ways both tacit and explicit. Davis's project here is not only to *desegregate* the screen's mythic west as a lone black figure (as in *Sergeants 3*), but fully to comment on questions of race and equality. This commentary is immediately set in motion by the Charlie Gordon backstory: "One of the best officers in the Confederate army, sending me a—," Paxton exclaims, breaking off an implied epithet in racist incredulity. "I sure thought better of him." Gordon's note of introduction for Ezekiel Smith anticipates as much, lauding Smith as "the best damn tracker and lawman I ever met, excepting me." But it adds, "Pay no mind to his manner," by which Gordon means Smith's *uppity* manner, noting "I could never whip it out of him." Paxton at first rejects the black man's expertise and his aid, until his own wife intervenes on Ezekiel's behalf: "I don't care what this man is . . . I want my baby back." From this point on, the impetus of the narrative is twofold: the rescue story, in which a mystery must be unraveled and a young woman rescued; and the racial story, in which the black man will gradually prove himself and the white man will grudgingly be won over. It is in this second narrative line that the debt to *In the Heat of the Night* is most evident. The plot device of Ezekiel's status as a racial and regional outsider mimics Poitier's Virgil Tibbs, a Philadelphia detective enlisted to solve a murder in a small Mississippi town as he is passing through. The dynamic between Ezekiel and Paxton also replicates quite precisely—if in somewhat tepid form—the quiet friendship and admiration that grows between Tibbs and the icon of a snarling, tobacco-chomping southern sheriff played by Rod Steiger.

Just as in Virgil Tibbs's sojourn in Mississippi, the black marshal's ride from Texas to Mexico with Paxton's posse is marked at nearly every turn by the region's overt racism. At a dangerous juncture along the trail, a white member of the group suggests that they should let "the black" ride point, because it "wouldn't be a loss if he caught [an arrow]." When Paxton and Ezekiel go into a saloon on their way toward the Mexican border, their order for a whiskey is met with the bartender's refusal. Gesturing to Ezekiel, he says gruffly, "We don't serve them in here." Paxton takes the drink that is offered him, shrugging apologetically to his black riding mate, "I'm too old to change." A furious Ezekiel Smith storms out. Having it out over this incident later on, Ezekiel challenges the white man: "I reckon I'm about all you got, Mr. Paxton . . . but I ain't your slave, and I sure ain't your friend. Now why don't you just tell me, what am I, huh?" Paxton responds, "Nothin' like I ever saw before."

Here he acknowledges both the "uppity" of Gordon's introductory letter for the black marshal, and the off-camera, post-Black Power cultural politics that conjoins *The Trackers* with a film like *In the Heat of the Night* and separates it from Davis's earlier forays in *The Rifleman* and *Sergeants 3*. The corresponding scene in the Poitier/Steiger film is when a local white patrician, finding himself accused by Virgil Tibbs, slaps the black detective across the face *and is immediately slapped back*. This piece of theatricality announced a major change in the world. The accused man then turns to Sheriff Gillespie and challenges him: "you saw that, what are you going to do about it?" Gillespie, between clenched teeth but in evident astonishment, says, "I don't know." This seems precisely the affective scale that Davis and Spelling were reaching for in Paxton's assessment that Ezekiel is "nothin' like I ever saw before." Neither slave nor friend, Ezekiel now insists that Paxton come right out and ask for his help, and Paxton does finally break down. "I'm askin'. Do you hear me, you black little Indian? I'm askin'."

Paxton is now officially on the path toward a hesitant admiration, but the racial tensions between the two persist. After they kill off a small encampment of Apaches, Ezekiel wonders at Paxton's stone coldheartedness, calling him a "pale-faced goblin" for his ability to calmly eat amid the dead bodies. Paxton counters with the charge that Ezekiel knows nothing about violence and the kind of pain that "savages" have caused, having never lost a son or daughter. "What do you know about it all?" he urges. This finally fetches Ezekiel Smith's full backstory: "I'll tell you what I know, Mr. Paxton. White men raped and killed my mother, burned down our house, shot my father—that was cowboys just *funnin'*. I know all about murder and killin'." Ezekiel is helping Paxton "because I owe a white man—your friend, Charlie Gordon. He took me in, he raised me," he explains. Gordon had also saved Ezekiel's life. Advance the peg another notch in the scale of Paxton's racial reeducation.

In the final slope of the narrative arc, the two cross the Rio Grande into Mexico, and they do in fact locate and rescue the kidnapped daughter, along with a few other white women who are imprisoned in some kind of trafficking operation. Perhaps another nod to a Civil Rights sensibility, the villains are *not* the presumed Apaches, but a gang of white Americans behind an urbane fellow named Barnes, who calls himself *El Grande.* The resolving of the mystery and the rescue of the prisoners requires a series of challenges that create an increasing racial understanding between Ezekiel and Paxton, and something like a dawning friendship. When they are deciding how to steward the newly freed prisoners to safety, for example, Ezekiel asks flatly, "How much chance do you think I got with a group of white women going through Texas? Now will you get going, please?" And when his daughter asks about Ezekiel, Paxton identifies the black marshal as "a friend." At the film's end, upon their safe arrival back at Paxton's ranch, Ezekiel tells Paxton that it is time he be heading back to Abilene.

"I wanna thank you," says Paxton.

"There's no need," returns the marshal.

"When you get back, say hey to Charlie Gordon, *Zeke.*"

"I'll do that, *Sam.*"

They then part ways, each taking a furtive moment to glance back, Paxton with a smile, Ezekiel with a tip of his hat. Their use of first names in the closing lines—a first in the film—again replicates the Tibbs/Gillespie parting in *Heat of the Night,* though absent the poignancy mustered by Poitier and Steiger. There, as Tibbs boards a train back to Philadelphia, Gillespie says with the full richness of a white Mississippian's glimmer of warmth and still reluctant respect, "You take care, hear?"

James Baldwin expressed considerable cynicism about this formula, noting that it required perhaps too much suspension of disbelief for any self-aware African American to engage in. It is "a species of cowardice, grave indeed," he wrote, for Hollywood "to pretend that black men do not know [certain] things." The "brotherhood" between Tibbs and Gillespie—"the achievement of which state of grace is exactly what [the film] imagines itself to be about"—requires the characters to behave in ways that history itself suggests they never have and never would. There is not only decency and egalitarianism on the white side, but also credulousness and inexperience on the black. "The history which produces such a film," Baldwin writes,

> cannot, after all, be swiftly understood, nor can the effects of this history be easily resolved. Nor can this history be blamed on any single individual; but, at the same time, no one can be let off the hook. It is a terrible thing, simply, to be trapped in one's history, and attempt, in the same motion . . . to accept, deny, reject, and redeem it—and, also, on whatever level, to profit from it.[82]

The same might be said of *In the Heat of the Night's* direct and self-conscious descendants. Ezekiel Smith would not have survived Paxton and his Texas posse for a single day, and it is, at best, a disingenuous brand of obfuscation to suppose that he would have, knowing what we do of our own history. It is, at worst, yet another piece of whitewashing propaganda meant to sell a vision of American egalitarianism that is not only historically false, but had plainly been *shown* to be a lie in the contemporary post-Civil rights moment of COINTELPRO and Nixon's "law and order."

The Trackers might therefore not represent cinematic excellence, nor ethical clarity of the sort that Baldwin would wish for. It does show Davis—as actor, and importantly here, also as producer—trying to accomplish something in the all-white space of television in general, and of the western in particular, that is quite different in both tenor and intent from his original forays into the white spaces of *The Colgate Comedy Hour*, the Sands Hotel, or *Rifleman*. Ezekiel Smith embodies none of the problematic shuffle of the Jonah character in *Sergeants 3*. Even his backstory—not a slave, but a talented tracker—conveys command. But what Baldwin is onto here is that the earlier tensions of the anti-defamation project in the culture industries had persisted, though now in slightly different form. Whereas originally the struggle had been between the politics of casting (getting into pictures at all) and the politics of representation (embodying on-screen dignity), the Civil Rights era and its aftermath saw an added layer of tension, asking whether it was sufficient to have acceptable characters embedded in problematic (hi)stories. Narratives embody a *logic*, Baldwin reminds us. Thus even an upright, realistic, admirable, and decently-drawn character like Ezekiel Smith might share far more than one suspects at first glance with the "renegade Negroes" of

Birth of a Nation. He does so much heavy lifting in support of the project of getting white people "off the hook," as Baldwin put it—a white supremacist rendering of American history just as surely as the KKK's ride to the rescue as written "with lightning" by D. W. Griffith a half-century earlier.[83]

INTEGRATION AND ITS DISCONTENTS

"I could never satisfy the people I was trying to appease," Davis wrote of one of his many low points in the battle against racism. "Appease" is an interesting choice of words here, and an important one, given Davis's social location in a generation for which "appeasement" could only conjure images of Neville Chamberlain lying prostrate before Hitler. "How could I not offend them by what I do when my very existence was offensive to them? There could be no end to it. Don't be seen at the same tables with white people. Stay away from white women. Don't touch Eddie Cantor. What next? I wanted to make it, but if that was the price, it was too high."[84] The price could be high indeed, as Davis continued to catch hell from critics on both sides of town—the whites he could "never satisfy" as well as the African Americans who were offended by his "appeasement" itself.

But *too* high? Davis never did stop crashing the ongoing white parties in American popular culture. On the heels of his Rat Pack films and *Rifleman* episodes, he became one of the most ubiquitous and familiar figures on primetime television, often cast not as a fictional character, but as none other than "Sammy Davis Jr., as himself." This had been a common formula in Hollywood going back to the 1930s and 1940s—"Ethel Waters, as herself," "Lena Horne, as herself," "Cab Calloway, as himself"—and had been denounced by black critics and actors alike as an unacceptably lazy approach to black hiring: it required nothing in the way of rethinking white-centered plotlines and creating an American cinema that reflected America itself, nor did it require a white production team to actually learn something about African American life. As exceptional figures, "stars," actors in "as herself" roles could (technically) desegregate the screen while (actually) doing nothing for "the race." A generation later, television was making the same move. Sammy Davis Jr. "as himself" was called upon to almost singlehandedly desegregate primetime television, appearing on *Ben Casey, The Patty Duke Show, I Dream of Jeannie, Batman, The Courtship of Eddie's Father*, and *Here's Lucy.*[85]

But another strand in this dual storyline of racial pioneering and racial appeasement was the persistence of the performance styles that Davis developed in the Rat Pack's Vegas shows. Davis "sang 'white' and danced 'black,'" as mentioned earlier, modes that were longstanding aspects of his style.[86] "Singing white" was in part a matter of genre, hitching his star to the American songbook and showtunes rather than rhythm and blues. "If a cat's grooving to Wilson Pickett, and Otis Redding, and Ray Charles, and James Brown," even Davis had to admit, "then Sammy Davis Jr. is not his cup of tea...."[87] In part it was a matter of technique: in timbre, register, phrasing, diction, he sang a lot like Sinatra. In part it was a matter of repertoire. He chose songs like "The Lady Is a Tramp" (a 1937 Rogers and Hart tune from *Babes in Arms,* later made famous by Sinatra); "Hey There," (a 1954 Adler and Ross song that charted for Rosemary Clooney at #1 at the same time it hit #16 for Davis); Anthony Newley's "What Kind of Fool Am I?" from the 1962 show, *Stop the World—I Want to Get Off,* which Davis also revived in the 1970s; or Sinatra's hit, "My Way"(1969). All of these songs owed a debt to African American musical traditions, as almost all American popular music does, but they were self-consciously "white-styled" in that the aesthetics of their orchestration, arrangement, and performance was calculated to occlude or deny that debt. The Davis repertoire also included old-fashioned "black" numbers like Jerome Kern's "Ol' Man River"; Al Jolson's "Rock-A-Bye Your Baby with a Dixie Melody" (1932, re-popularized in later iterations by Dean Martin, Judy Garland, and Jerry Lewis); and, as we have seen, "Birth of the Blues," from *George White's Scandals of 1926.*

Even when he was solo, Davis's live performances through the 1960s routinely featured the kind of jocular racial patter that first emerged in Rat Pack settings, lines like, "When I move into a neighborhood I wipe it out," or "Could you play on the white keys?" He was still caretaking his white audience. More interesting than the tendency toward racially themed humor in these performances were some of Davis's aesthetic choices, even while generally "singing white." His 1960s renditions of "I've Got You under My Skin," for instance, featured a near *a capella* arrangement of voice and drums that read artistically as *black*—all the more in an all-white space like the Cocoanut Grove or St. Louis's Kiel Theater. "*Ow-di-DONG-ging-GI-gong-TI-gong-TI-gong,*" Davis began, setting the beat before Michael Silva's drumming rolled in. This is where the Africa joke was always inserted, and always to white laughter: "Play regular, and no messages"; or, "If you get an answer...." Then, over the top of the drumming, Davis gave a brief vocal intro that was half jazz scat, half soulful wail, which fell somewhere between Harry Belafonte's Caribbean "Day-O" shout and a Native American chant. This chant became more and more "Native" over the years—in a 1967 performance he threw in the comic line, "Gonna keep singin' this 'til it rains."[88] Once the verse began, Davis was back in his Sinatra-styled phrasing and timbre, a very conventional vocal rendering of "Under My Skin," even while the African drumming rolled on underneath. *Don't sleep on my blackness,* this arrangement seemed to say to the all-white audience. Davis's endless ethnic/ racial jokes included those tucked *into* the song: "Don't you know, little *Schmuel,*" Davis sang, substituting the Yiddish for Sam for the original "little fool." Alongside the patter, the aesthetics of the song's "ethnic" arrangement serves to remind the audience at each turn that—despite the general assimilationism of Davis's presentation— this is still an *integration* project. As he joked in every show from the Rat Pack performances onward, "I am thrilled to represent the ethnic groups."

When it comes to the longevity of the Rat Pack's racial bearing, perhaps most surprising in retrospect is the *Dean Martin Celebrity Roast* of Davis in 1975. This is a date far enough out from the height of the Civil Rights movement to be safely considered *post,* and yet it was a show no more sophisticated or enlightened in racial terms than the Rat Pack Summit fifteen years earlier. It was a special night, host Dean Martin told his Friars Club audience in his opening comment: "even the NBC peacock is wearing an Afro." Davis's blackness was at the very center of the festivities from that moment forward, from Milton Berle's calling him the "original model for the Oreo cookie," to Frank Gorshin's calling him "the world's only dancing fudgsicle" and a "Brillo pad with legs."

> DEAN MARTIN: His family was so poor, until the age of three he slept in a hollowed out watermelon.
>
> MARTIN: Sammy's first booking was in Atlanta. As he stepped off the plane, he was met by the Governor—and a rope. Even the Ku Klux Klan took note of Sammy. They voted him most likely to be—next.
>
> MILTON BERLE: In honor of all the blacks on the dais tonight, the hotel didn't put any silverware on the table. . . . Getting tired, Sammy? Want to take a watermelon break?
>
> MARTIN [READING A TELEGRAM]: Dear Sammy, we'd like you to come pose nude for our magazine. Signed, *The National Geographic.*
>
> PHYLLIS DILLER: One time in Mississippi Sammy told the bus driver he wanted to ride in the front of the bus. So the driver tied him to the bumper.

JAN MURRAY: [If you anger Sinatra by singing his song, 'My Way'], you'll wake up with the head of a watermelon in your bed.

MURRAY: Sammy did travel life's highways [as the lyric of "My Way" says], but he was on the back of the bus.

DON RICKLES: I laugh at the blacks, the whites, the purples. Mostly the blacks.

RICKLES: All peoples are alike. You live in my neighborhood and I'll live in yours, right, Sam? [pause] *Are you crazy?*

RICKLES [KISSES DAVIS]: Any black on my lips?

When Davis finally took the podium himself, there were no jokes at all. Rather, in fairly solemn tones he explained away and excused the preceding spectacle. "The day they don't make fun of you," he said, "it means they don't love you."

There are several dimensions to this. One is generational, certainly. Most of this crew was born between 1908 and 1918. Davis and Rickles were the among the youngest, born in the mid-1920s, and Freddy Prinze, born in 1954, was the outlier. Much of the roast represented a vintage 1930s and 1940s racial sensibility, then, expressed with a vintage 1960s openness. Like the Rat Pack itself, it was "cool." There is also a second dimension of pure, unadulterated, and unflappable *whiteness*. The Friars Club was historically a very white space. Bert Williams had been the club's first black member, and Davis was only its second. Even with Dionne Warwick, Freddy Prinze, Nipsey Russell, and Wilt Chamberlain on the dais, it was *still* a white space. By this I mean here that the space was characterized by a white obtuseness regarding how a certain joke might land—and more, an obtuseness that itself rests on privilege, the *luxury* of obtuseness. Further, it demonstrates a white incapacity to locate humor as anti-racist critique. The joke never takes down the Klan, for instance. It only makes light of the fact that there *is* a Klan.

But most significant of all is the third dimension, a cultural confusion that the roast's white participants express again and again over what racial egalitarianism should (or would) actually look like. This roast took place just up the road from the Sands at the MGM Grand. No less than the Rat Pack's act, the racial banter—the steady stream of all-in-good-fun insults, the retreaded stereotypes, the casual jokes about watermelon, segregation, the Ku Klux Klan, and even about *lynching*—all of this good-natured "humor" sought wishfully to bury the racial past beneath the sheen of a new era. But more, the style of performativity and sociality on display here represents a blind groping toward *egalitarianism* in a setting where, over the span of centuries, there had been precious few authentic models for this. Milton Berle had been an important mentor to Davis, and had once decked a Miami Beach segregationist on Davis's behalf. When he asks, "Want to take a watermelon break?" he is saying in a single breath:

1) We live in an enlightened age when I can speak "race" out loud, even with Sammy sitting right here;
2) I always thought that watermelon jokes were funny; and
3) I got nothin' else.

It would take comics of color like Dick Gregory, Richard Pryor, and later Chris Rock or Margaret Cho to forge a comedy around race that could be funny to diverse audiences *and* anti-racist in its political spirit of critique. Like so much of post-Civil Rights US culture, the Friars Club in 1975 was rich in white institutional power but impoverished in its sociological insight.

. . .

"I and I alone am responsible for Sammy's conversion to Judaism," said Joey Bishop on this occasion. "He wanted me to turn colored, and I said 'Go to hell. I got a bad back—I can't march.'" Another "colored" joke, sure, but here Bishop also indicates what was among the most famous and talked about of Davis's incursions into "white" space, his conversion to Judaism shortly after his 1954 car accident. Not only were American Jews overwhelmingly white-identified in these years, but in this immediate post-Holocaust moment they were almost obsessed with the stability of their own whiteness. Davis's conversion was the subject of much skepticism and speculation on both sides of the color line. Whites thought that he was not "really" Jewish, that perhaps this was just some sort of publicity stunt; more was demanded of Davis in this regard than perhaps any convert in the history of the faith. African Americans, on the other hand, suspected that his conversion was just another way of ditching his blackness and his people. "He must realize that he is a Negro," one *Ebony* reader opined.[89]

For his own part, Davis described his conversion as being overdetermined. It was part spiritual awakening at a moment of searching after his near fatal accident, when the teachings of Judaism happened to be nearer at hand than other religious traditions. It was partly due to his warmth and respect for the many Jews who had mentored him over the years, including Eddie Cantor, Milton Berle, and Jerry Lewis. Then there was his admiration for the openness and inclusivity of the Jewish tradition as he understood it, leaning heavily upon Isaiah's dictum that "My house shall be a house for all people." Most significantly in this regard, it was partly his interpretation of "the affinity between the Jew and the Negro."[90] Davis was subjected to many racist slights in Los Angeles; on one occasion someone painted *"Merry Christmas Nigger"* across the garage door of the Beverly Hills home he had purchased for his grandmother. He reported that after this incident "more than ever" he saw the affinities between his people and the Jews. "The Jews had been oppressed for three thousand years instead of three hundred like us," he wrote, "but the rest was very much the same."[91] More importantly, describing his attachment in terms that were as much historical as theological, he saw in Jewish tradition precisely the defiance that his own life of Jim Crow limit-busting aspired to. "The whole world kept saying, 'You can't do this' and You can't do that' but they didn't listen. It's beautiful. They just plain didn't listen. They'd get kicked out of one place, so they'd just go on to the next one and keep swinging like they wanted to."[92] Jews' refusal to listen to the world when told *You can't do this* was familiar to Davis, and indeed mirrored his own refusals.

Typical of the paradoxes attending his politics, in other words, while everyone else suspected that Davis had chosen Judaism for its whiteness, Davis himself was drawn to it as a model for *blackness*. In the pluralist culture of the Civil Rights years and after—our national life "beyond the melting pot"—we are fairly quick to ascribe some sort of self-loathing to identity expressions like Davis's, as Lenny Bruce did in a scathing early-sixties routine on Davis:

JUDGE: What do you do, Mr. Junior, to deserve forty thousand a week?
DEFENDANT [SINGS]: Racing with the moon . . . That old black magic . . . Hey, Dean, I gotta boo-boo!
JUDGE: Strip him of his Jewish star, his stocking cap, his religious statue of Elizabeth Taylor. Thirty years in Biloxi![93]

But there is an insistent philosophical premise at assimilationism's core that should not be lost. In a social context where "difference" is perceived to run so deep and where hierarchies are so firmly entrenched that it is unthinkable for people to transcend their own social categories, the assimilationist proposes to do precisely this—and in doing so to call the entire logic of categories themselves into question. This was the radicalism of Davis's desegregation project, such as it was. But he found again and again that hierarchy was policed, as was "difference" itself, by both the power of institutions and by the subtler workings of cultural logic and normativity. It takes more than mere inclusion to create a truly desegregated space.

FIVE

"Division Is Not Our Destiny"

INTERRACIAL ROMANCE AND *GOLDEN BOY*

The ban on intermarriage has the highest place in the white man's rank order of social segregation and discrimination. Sexual segregation is the most pervasive form of segregation, and the concern about 'race purity' is, in a sense, basic. No other way of crossing the color line is so attended by the emotion commonly associated with violating a social taboo as intermarriage and extra-marital relations between a Negro man and a white woman. No excuse for other forms of social segregation and discrimination is so potent as the one that sociable relations on an equal basis between members of the two races *may possibly* lead to intermarriage.

—GUNNAR MYRDAL

The atmosphere of fear and caution and compromise, of walking on eggs, was surrounding [May Britt], slowly dragging her into the web, stifling all love for life—forcing it into the prison of my skin.

—SAMMY DAVIS JR.

AT A CIVIL RIGHTS CONVENTION in Birmingham in September, 1962, Martin Luther King Jr. was just announcing an upcoming benefit featuring Sammy Davis Jr., when a "200 pound white youth" rose from his seat, strode to the front of the hall, and, as businessman A. G. Gaston and others would later report, "began punching King in the mouth." An extraordinary scene followed. A crowd of attendees led by ministers Joseph Lowery and Ralph Abernathy rushed to King's defense. King embraced and in fact protected his attacker from the advancing throng. And then the attacker himself, twenty-four-year-old Roy James, broke down in tears—still in King's embrace—while onlookers began singing Movement songs. When hauled away to city recorder's court by the police, James admitted to being involved with the

American Nazi Party, and explained that "he had been driven to his deed by the mention of Sammy Davis—a black man converted to Judaism who was married to a white woman."[1]

Stay away from white women. By the time King took this punch to the jaw on Davis's behalf, the star's interracial romances had been a matter of popular obsession for several years. But the general matter of interracial romance, sexuality, and marriage had been a foundational, explosive obsession of US political culture for a few centuries. It is not just that *Loving v. Virginia* had another few years to wait. In a setting where race-as-standing determined patterns of power and appropriation, whether settler-colonialism's appropriation of land, or Atlantic slavery's appropriation of labor, race-as-*lineage* became a crucial organizer of who was eligible for various goods and who was subject to various dangers and privations. If who could own property and who might *be* property were keyed to race, then the regulation of sexuality and reproduction was critical to the political economy.[2] These strong established logics of race and intermixture did not always have identical effects. For indigenous peoples, intermixing *diluted* racial identity and so loosened the grip on tribal land holdings. But intermixing cut in precisely the opposite direction for African-descended slaves. For them, intermixture could *never* dilute racial identity, perpetuating bondage from one generation to the next no matter how much "white" heritage a person had, all the way to its logical conclusion, the "one drop" rule of black racial identity encoded in law.

In the case of the enslaved in North America, the political economy of race, slavery, and reproduction produced truly diabolical practices in the colonial and antebellum periods. These included the practice of rape as a means of coerced reproduction by which slavers might extend their holdings in chattel. But they also included practices of erasure, non-recognition, and denial, by which children born of such rape were *dis*owned as "kin" and therefore literally *owned* as "property." Pondering the meaning of a phrase like "kinship system" in the context of Atlantic slavery, Hortense Spillers famously reflected,

> the idea becomes useful as a point of contemplation when we try to sharpen our own sense of the African female's reproductive uses within the diasporic enterprise of enslavement and the genetic reproduction of the enslaved. In effect, under conditions of captivity, the offspring of the female does not 'belong' to the Mother, nor is s/he 'related' to the 'owner,' though the latter 'possesses' it, and in the African-American instance, often fathered it, *and,* as often, without whatever benefit of patrimony.

"Kinship" here loses all meaning, Spillers concludes, "since it can be invaded at any given and arbitrary moment by property relations."[3]

The knot of race and sex resides at the very heart of this monstrosity. As a result, both during slavery and after emancipation this regime of property relations established myriad projections, displacements, erasures, distortions, icons, and popular narratives designed to defend white power and to protect the white psyche. Narratives of black sexual excess and immorality were contrasted with myths of white innocence, racial purity, and virtue as against black predation, the most common being the imperative of defending white womanhood from the marauding black rapist. Once slavery had been swept away, the Jim Crow system of racialized segregation and hierarchy that grew in its place insisted even more fiercely on these projections, displacements, erasures, distortions, icons, and popular narratives. Here one might cast a quick glance backward to the longstanding comedic conventions of minstrelsy that did double duty in disparaging the prospect of black citizenship while also defanging the potent iconic figure of black masculinity that slavery's own depredations had conjured. It was the myth of the black rapist that underwrote the terrorism of lynching, which in turn policed white supremacy at every turn. But it was also the myth of racial purity that upheld the notion that Jim Crow segregation actually had a reified, scientifically proven and sustainable line to defend in the first place. As historian of marriage law Peggy Pascoe wrote of the "animating fictions" of white supremacy, "one constitutional, one scientific, and one popular," while the regime of slavery was still in place

> laws against interracial marriage didn't prevent masters from having sex with slave women or having mixed-race children, both of which were common occurrences. Rather, they prevented masters from turning slaves they slept with into respectable wives who might claim freedom, demand citizenship rights, or inherit family property, and so undermine the foundations of racial slavery.[4]

After slavery had been abolished, she continues, "the term 'miscegenation' helped transform the prewar skeleton of laws against interracial marriage into a postwar body of miscegenation law that emerged from the shadow of slavery to stand on its own." The post-bellum era of emancipation became even more feverish about love and sex across the color line, as "miscegenation law depended on judges drawing lines between legitimate marriage and illicit sex, then branding interracial relationships of all kinds *as* illicit sex."[5] The white Southern progressive writer Lillian Smith called this "the race-sex-sin spiral": "The more trails the white man made to back-yard cabins, the higher he raised his white wife on her pedestal when he returned to the big house." Then the white man "in a jealous panic began to project his own sins on to the Negro male. And when he did that, a madness seized our people."[6]

The notion of racial "purity" was enshrined in laws against interracial sex. But it also coursed through American scientific thought, from the arguments of the polygenists in the 1830s, who posited separate biological origins of the races, to the frank discourse of "mongrelization" in twentieth-century works like Madison Grant's *Passing of the Great Race* (1916) and Lothrop Stoddard's *Rising Tide of Color against White World-Supremacy* (1920). Before Nazi Germany gave eugenics a bad name, it was thinkers like Grant and Stoddard who framed the immigration debate in the early twentieth century, and who supplied the language and logic of "Nordic" superiority that underwrote the 1924 Immigration Act. But nowhere were such racial distinctions as sharply drawn and as politically powerful as in the creation and defense of the white/black binary during what Crystal Feimster has termed "the violent transition from freedom to segregation."[7] The very term *miscegenation* was coined on the cusp of Emancipation, in an 1863 pamphlet anonymously penned by *New York Daily Graphic* editor David Croley, a "hash of quarter-truths and pseudo-learned oddities" whose pro-amalgamation formula for freedom parodied racial egalitarianism in a fashion that was meant to scare white people away from abolition and emancipation.[8] During the Draft Riots in New York that same year, the *Herald* reported that a white mob had descended on "a house ... where negroes visited white women," "ambitious to regulate the races and to prevent amalgamation." As Feimster writes, Americans "understood citizenship in terms of manhood and patriarchal rights and prerogatives. ... [R]esistance to black citizenship, with its implied rights of political, economic, and social equality, took on a sexual connotation because of the association of equality with sexual license."[9]

Emancipation and the political convulsions of Reconstruction may have unleashed the late-nineteenth-century "madness" that Lillian Smith described—violent terror groups like the Ku Klux Klan and the White League, organs like the *Weekly Caucasian,* rumors of black-on-white rape, and two generations of rampant white-on-black lynch law. But the core logic of racial purity and its imperatives only increased in urgency over time, as theories of black citizenship threatened to become realities, and as the white power that had been slaveholding gave way to the white power that was Jim

Crow. As Ida B. Wells observed in *The Red Record* (1893), white men may have initially excused their own racial violence by arguing the emancipated slaves' propensity for "insurrection" or "riot." To this they later added the political argument—under cover of Supreme Court decisions like *Dred Scott*—that this was "a white man's government" and freedmen "had no rights that the white man was bound to respect." But more recently, Wells observed, once true citizenship had been stripped away in the counter-revolution that crushed Reconstruction, and once "Negro domination" was no longer a threat,

> Brutality still continued; Negroes were whipped, scourged, exiled, shot and hung whenever and wherever it pleased the white man so to treat them, and as the civilized world with increasing persistency held the white people of the South to account for its outlawry, the murderers invented the third excuse— that Negroes had to be killed to avenge their assaults upon women.[10]

The myth of the black rapist and the foundational linkage between white supremacy and the regulation of sex persisted well into the twentieth century. "Political equality means social equality, and social equality means intermarriage, and the mongrelizing of the American race," said Congressman Ellison "Cotton Ed" Smith of South Carolina in 1932. "We will resist to the bitter end, whatever the consequences, any measure or any movement which would have a tendency to bring about social equality and intermingling and amalgamation of the races in our states," said Senator Richard Russell of Georgia in 1946.[11]

This is the mythic narrative that gave us the "renegade Negro" Gus in *Birth of a Nation*. It is the miscegenated nightmare that was early rock and roll in the white southern imagination. "Rock 'n' roll is part of a test to undermine the morals of the youth of our nation," argued the North Alabama White Citizens Council. Specifically, "It is sexualistic ... and ... brings people of both races together."[12] This was also the sexual threat on the horizon in 1950s debates over school desegregation, part of what George Wallace was defending against when he shouted from the portico of the Alabama State Capitol in 1963, "In the name of the greatest people that have ever trod this earth, I draw the line in the dust and toss the gauntlet before the feet of tyranny, and I say segregation now, segregation tomorrow, segregation forever."[13] "Almighty God created the races white, black, yellow, malay, and red," opined the trial judge in the lower court that first heard the *Loving* case, "and he placed them on separate continents. And but for the interference with his arrangement there would be no cause for such marriages. The fact that he separated the races shows that he did not intend for the races to mix." The Virginia Supreme Court later added that the state's miscegenation statutes were valid because they "preserve the racial integrity of its citizens . . . regulate the marriage relation so that it shall not have mongrel citizens . . . [and] prevent the obliteration of racial pride, [that would] permit the corruption of blood [and] weaken or destroy the quality of its citizenship."[14]

Civil Rights groups had recognized in the postwar period that an inflammatory rhetoric of racial mixing was being deployed to defend segregation in general and school segregation in particular. The NAACP mounted a brave, sustained campaign against the laws that regulated interracial sex and marriage. Between 1951 and 1965, in the run-up to *Loving's* hearing in the Supreme Court, thirteen states repealed their miscegenation laws. All were west of the Mississippi, with the exception of Indiana. This left such laws on the books and fully in force in sixteen states.[15] When the high court did strike down Virginia's marriage law, it did so in the starkest possible terms: "There is patently no legitimate overriding purpose independent of invidious racial discrimination which justifies this [racial] classification. The fact that Virginia prohibits only interracial marriages involving white persons demonstrates that the racial classifications must stand on their own justification, as measures designed to maintain White Supremacy."[16] The Nazi Roy James— so enraged by Sammy Davis Jr. the race-mixer that he was compelled to assault King at the very mention of Davis's name—might not have been in "good" company in 1962, but he was certainly in a lot of it.

"THE 'WHITE GIRL' BIT"

The postwar culture industries were at once puritanical and cautious but also salacious and prurient when it came to questions of sexuality and race. Earlier on, even the pairing of eight-year-old Shirley Temple and fifty-eight-year old Bill Robinson bristled with sexual suggestion in a film like *The Little Colonel* (1935), such that their on-screen movements and especially any touching between them had to be carefully policed.[17] Now, more was possible. Darryl Zanuck's *Pinky* (1949) featured Jeanne Crain as Patricia "Pinky" Johnson, a light-skinned black woman who passes for white and takes up with a white doctor without his knowing her "true" racial identity. *Island in the Sun* (1957) was a Harry Belafonte/Joan Fontaine vehicle that explicitly examined the relationships among white, black, and mixed-race characters on the fictional island of Santa Marta. *South Pacific* (1958) was based on the Rodgers and Hammerstein musical whose subplots included both an interracial romance and mixed-race children. At once betraying conventional notions of racial "difference" even while preaching and popularizing a liberal view of racial "tolerance," the score argues that prejudice is not natural. One has to be "carefully taught" to hate "people whose eyes are oddly made / or people whose skin is a different shade."[18]

Both *Island in the Sun* and *South Pacific* revived an older Hollywood convention of blunting potential controversy by displacing racial titillation into overseas settings. "White man ... brown girl," shouted the press copy for King Vidor's *Bird of Paradise* (1932), starring Dolores Del Rio, a miscegenated story of the tropics where "blood runs hot and the heart is free." Black zombies were also popular, as Thomas Cripps wryly comments, because "they can carry off blonds without getting ideas in their heads."[19] But tropical or not, *Island in the Sun* was "enough to offend the South and disappoint ... the North," and stirred significant protest. Segregationists attempted to stop its release completely and lobbied the Defense Department to refuse to show the film on US military bases. In South Carolina a bill was proposed that would have fined theaters $5000 for screening the film, although it never passed. Joan Fontaine recalled reams of hate mail in her autobiography, *No Bed of Roses,* and *Look Magazine* reported on the letters at the time, quoting one: "How far into the slime will the race mixers sink?"[20]

Later entries in this genre would include Broadway's *No Strings* (1962), which centered on an interracial romance while—quite radically—never mentioning race or making race a plot point. *Guess Who's Coming to Dinner* (1967) smoothed the jagged edges of the intermarriage plotline through a reassuring liberal mix. The respectability politics represented by Sidney Poitier as the black suitor, a highly accomplished and world-famous doctor, joined white patriarchy, with Spencer Tracy as the white prospective father-in-law whose blessing cedes the point on intermarriage but gives not an inch on the question of white authority or control. But perhaps one of the most ingenious and subversive texts of this kind was an oblique sequence in *The Girl Can't Help It* (1956), featuring Little Richard performing "She's Got It" over the top of a visual sequence of Jayne Mansfield as she slays one (white) man after another with her raw sexuality, sashaying about the nightclub in a provocative bid for attention at the direction of her agent.[21]

> There's a sweet little girl that lives down the street
> Some people think she's square but I think she's sweet
> You can see her every day, strolling up and down the way
> Looking so pretty and this is what I say
> She's got it
> Ooh baby, she's got it.

The visuals never stray from the era's convention of racially segregated framing; unlike in *Island,* Jayne Mansfield never crosses into the same shot as the black performer. But Little Richard's lyrics—lustily delivered against the sexual energy of the strutting, runway-walking Mansfield—imply with a thick dose of risqué humor an interracial involvement that never actually materializes. Although the two never share the same frame, Richard's style, voice, and emotive power convey that the "I" of the lyrics is clearly the black singer rather than any of the white admirers in the visual montage.

> Ruby lips, shapely hips
> When she walks down the street all the cats flip
> She's got it
> Ooh baby, she's got it
> Ooh baby, she's got it
> I can't do without her

In a generative little riff on *Cowboy Canteen* (1945), film historian Thomas Cripps has commented on the miscegenated postwar culture that was created when black acts like the Mills Brothers provided the backbeat to white romance and desire with a hit song like "Paper Doll," a lyric "brimming with adolescent yearning." "Unwittingly," Cripps writes, "and without forethought . . . the war had cast black singers in the role of actors in the romance of white people."[22] The Little Richard/Jayne Mansfield sequence in *The Girl Can't Help It* is fully knowing rather than unintentional, and it toys boldly with the interracial line that Hollywood had just begun to test.[23]

It was in this gradually shifting but still fraught and dangerous social context that Sammy Davis Jr. would become notorious for his predilection for dating white women. When Davis Sr. told her that their son had fallen in love with a white woman, Sammy's mother Elvera Sanchez reportedly replied, "Why of course. What else does he know?"[24] She thus casually articulated the dirty secret that Jim Crow segregation was meant to at once conceal and deny: not that interracial sex was *unnatural,* but on the contrary, that the races had to be kept apart—schools had to be segregated, for example—

precisely *because* "of course" white and black youth would naturally find one another.

The press was not nearly so blase. "In the garden of love, Sammy Davis Jr. goes like a hummingbird," wrote Jim Cook in a lavish, multipart series on Davis for the *New York Post* in 1956. "In the last year, scandal magazines thrice have spattered him with stories about his friendships with comely Caucasians."[25] The "comely Caucasians" of rumor and innuendo in 1956 included Ava Gardner, Lee Sharon, and Meg Myles. Gardner was the most controversial because in addition to being white, she was very famous in her own right *and* she was Frank Sinatra's ex-wife. After a visit to the Apollo, Gardner posed for a publicity shot with Davis to go along with a by-line story, "Why I Dig Sammy Davis Jr.," as part of her attempt to connect with a black audience. Davis consented to the project, though he worried at the time that it could "cause trouble for her" if it were misinterpreted. Which it was. "WHAT MAKES AVA GARDNER RUN FOR SAMMY DAVIS JR.?" tabloid headlines screamed. "If they hated it when Eddie Cantor just put his arm around me," Davis worried, "they'll throw rocks at me for this." As early as 1955, a white supremacist city council candidate in North Carolina circulated the Davis-Gardner photograph in an effort to defeat a black candidate by roiling racial fears.[26]

A string of rumors and reports on Davis's interracial affairs followed in tabloids and gossip columns throughout the late 1950s, and in the black press, too, some fabricated (Marilyn Monroe and June Allyson), some real (Kim Novak and Joan Stuart), but typically with salacious, barely coded references to the "Honey-Blonde" or "the ash blond dancer-actress [who] has really made off with 'Mr. Wonderful's heart."[27] Davis chafed at "the scandals, the constant 'white girl' bit" in the press. He complained that some gossip rags hinted at racial transgression even in cases where Davis was with a black woman, like *Ebony* model Harlean Harris, or wrote up "the Negro girls at Sammy Davis Jr.'s dinner party at Danny's Hideaway" as if they were merely "cover-ups" for Davis's presumed white date. The black press, too, "started riding me harder than ever," as he recalled to Alex Haley. "Stuff like, 'Sammy Davis Jr., once a pride to all Negroes, has become a never-ending source of embarrassment.'"[28]

But amid the constant churn of lascivious stories, a few of these interracial relationships were very real, and they generated very real political fallout. The first was a brief relationship with actress Kim Novak, with whom Davis really did seem to be in love. "He was so enamored of her," recalls Jerry Lewis. "I said, 'They'll cut your knees off and you'll never dance again. Do you understand what you're doing?' He said, 'Yes, she's the best thing in my life.'" Agent Steve Blauner, too, warned Davis, "How long do you think it'll be secret? They'll kill you."[29] Though the two entered this relationship with the secretiveness and caution of a pair of co-conspirators ("I pulled up my collar, slipped out of the car and ran the last half block, ducking behind trees and slinking across her lawn"), the story broke in the *Chicago Sun-Times* on the first day of 1958. "Kim Novak's new interest will make her studio bosses turn lavender," one scandal sheet warned.[30]

Davis later minimized the trouble, even implying that he never heeded the industry warnings that this romance might damage Novak's career. "If I'd listened to what the whole world says I'd be in Harlem shining shoes," he said. But the truth is much harsher, and Jerry Lewis seems to have been right. Novak's studio did worry over what the interracial romance might do to her reputation and hence to her value. "Miscegenation jurisprudence was instrumental in stabilizing white property," historian Eva Saks reminds us, and Novak's whiteness itself was very much property, whether it belonged to her or to Columbia Pictures.[31] The dictatorial Columbia executive Harry Cohn had mobsters threaten Davis with physical harm if he did not break off with Novak *and marry a black woman* within forty-eight hours. In *Yes I Can* Davis downplayed the coercive aspect of this episode, but the fact is, in a whiplash overnight turnabout and seemingly out of nowhere, he really did marry African American dancer Loray White—a tragic charade of a marriage that lasted something short of two years.[32] His relationship soon after with "honey-blonde" Canadian dancer Joan Stuart avoided the drama and the danger of the Novak affair. Nonetheless it ended amicably but unhappily in a cancelled wedding when Stuart's parents objected to the marriage "because of racial and religious differences." "Naturally, we don't approve," Stuart's mother told the Associated Press, bluntly. "It's ridiculous."[33]

It was Davis's marriage in late 1960 to May Britt ("the blondest white woman alive," one journalist later wrote) that generated the most attention.[34] It was a union publicly marked in nearly every utterance for its interracial character, whether the couple was conspicuously but indirectly labeled as a "Negro entertainer" and a "Swedish actress" (*Life Magazine*), or the color line was explicitly named, as in "Mr. and Mrs. Sammy Davis Jr.: Self-Portrait of a Mixed Marriage" (Mike Wallace for the *New York Post Daily Magazine*). "Isn't this the first marriage between a Negro man and a blonde, white movie star?" asked an aggressive London reporter when the two announced their

FIG. 14. Davis with May Britt, 1960. Photo: Bettmann via Getty Images.

engagement. "Are you announcing it [in the UK] because you're afraid to do it at home?" Davis objected to the obligatory racial modifiers in describing the marriage, pointing out, "I had not said, 'Will you inter-marry me?'" Still, over time he had to acknowledge that "the atmosphere of fear and caution and compromise, of walking on eggs, was surrounding [May], slowly dragging her into the web, stifling all love for life—forcing it into the prison of my skin."[35]

That "prison" was founded both on the political fringe and in the political mainstream. At the fringe, their marriage brought the Davises into several close brushes with the Nazi Party, first in Europe (where they decided to make their wedding announcement as a way of putting a stop to the constant speculation in the press) and then back in the US upon Davis's return from his tour abroad. Before a performance at London's Pigalle Club, "pickets wearing swastika armbands were carrying signs: 'GO HOME, NIGGER.'

... 'SAMMY, BACK TO THE TREES.'" Back in the United States shortly after, American Nazi protesters likewise turned up at the Lotus Club in Washington, DC. "They were wearing khaki shirts with swastika armbands and carrying signs: 'WHAT'S THE MATTER, SAMMY? CAN'T YOU FIND A COLORED GIRL?' ... 'GO BACK TO THE CONGO, YOU KOSHER COON.'"[36] Soon the bomb threats and other threats of violence commenced. The Beverly Hilton began receiving phone calls: "We've got guns and hand grenades and we're coming to blow up the place." "There's a bomb in the theater right now." A drawing of a bullet was slipped under Davis's dressing room door. Davis added an extra security detail to his entourage and began carrying a gun himself. Nazi pickets showed up in other cities, too; a rash of bomb threats hit the Geary Theater in San Francisco; stacks of hate mail piled up, warning, "God will strike you down for what you are doing. You have sinned against God's will." Britt later recalled instances when she and Davis changed their plans at the last minute to avoid going out in public. His team started double-booking rooms for security's sake—a vacant decoy room to hold in Davis's name, and a second to safely occupy under an assumed name.[37]

But this was 1960, and where the fringe left off and the Democratic Party of Alabama, Mississippi, or Georgia picked up was never so easy to demarcate. Dick Gregory later quipped, "A Southerner is a person who thinks the Sammy Davis, Jrs. are just about the nicest couple ever—if it wasn't for him."[38] This made Davis's marriage to Britt a sensitive issue for the John F. Kennedy campaign, as one Rat Pack member (Peter Lawford) was JFK's brother in-law, and another (Frank Sinatra) was his most famous supporter. Davis was already present by implication in this Rat Pack-Kennedy alliance, and in fact he was an enthusiastic supporter in his own right, too, but how close would Kennedy's people dare let him get to the campaign? "Dear Nigger Bastard," one hate letter read, "I see Frank Sinatra is going to be best man at your abortion. Well, it's good to know the kind of people supporting Kennedy before it's too late. (signed) An ex-Kennedy vote." Another included a two-panel cartoon, the first depicting Davis as JFK's butler, serving a platter of fried chicken and watermelon; the second, Davis and Kennedy eating together. The caption read, "Will It Still Be the *White* House?"[39] The Davis-Britt marriage, it turned out, was precisely where the good old fashioned white supremacy of anti-miscegenation sentiment and the states' rights wing of the Democratic Party were conjoined. A Northern liberal like Kennedy had to be alert to the fact that a strong challenge to Southern tradition on race would lose the white south for a generation, in Lyndon B. Johnson's gross underestimation.[40]

When Davis was booed at the Democratic convention in Los Angeles, even he began to worry that he was going to cost Kennedy precious votes. Right or wrong, he assessed with grim realism, "my wedding was giving the Nixon people the opportunity to ridicule Kennedy and possibly hurt him at the polls." The press exacerbated things by their penchant for always reporting on Davis and Britt in close proximity to the Kennedy campaign story.[41] The first piece of fallout from this for the Rat Pack-JFK alliance was that Davis and Britt decided to postpone their wedding until after the election, so that everyone—especially best man Sinatra—would be spared the anxiety over what the optics might mean for the campaign. Having arrived at this decision on his own, Davis rehearsed how he would break the news to his bride-to-be: "We're postponing our marriage because it's so repulsive to some people that they won't want to vote for Kennedy. You understand, don't you darling?"[42] The second, far more hurtful development was that Davis and Britt wound up being disinvited from the Kennedy inauguration in January. Over the objections of Lawford and Robert Kennedy, the Kennedy team decided that the couple's attendance at the inaugural would set JFK off "on the wrong foot" with Southern Democrats. Kennedy's secretary Evelyn Lincoln called Davis to rescind the invitation.[43] "No, don't ask me to understand," Davis thought. "Don't do this. Don't humiliate me. Don't cut me in half. . . ." But he said nothing, only that he understood.

> And I did understand, that hatred got noticed and had to be neutralized, whereas love could be put on hold. I understood that in politics a thousand votes were exactly one thousand times more valuable than one friend. . . . I could handle it from the idiot in the street who pickets or calls me a name or writes a letter. But when the President of the United States does it? To someone he knows. Someone he shook hands with and told, "I won't forget your help. . . ." My God, if he'll do this to me, then what hope have the millions of invisible people got?

"It hurt like a motherfucker," he wrote in *Why Me?* For her part, May Britt tried to adopt a foreigner's detachment toward Jim Crow's codes and meted-out punishments, even suggesting that perhaps Davis could go to the inaugural alone. At the end of the day, she, too, was punished for this racial transgression, when—taking the opposite route of Harry Cohn at Columbia—the lawyers at Twentieth Century Fox let her contract expire shortly after the wedding.[44]

Amid Davis's explosive personal history with interracial romance, an opportunity emerged—amazingly—to mount a Broadway play centering on the explosive issue of interracial romance. As early as the spring of 1956 (around the time of the Ava Gardner rumors), the *New York Post* was reporting that Clifford Odets wanted to revive *Golden Boy* with Sammy Davis Jr. in the starring role.[45] In 1961, producer Hillard Elkins picked up the idea with the added wrinkle of remounting the property as a musical. So it was that Odets, a leftist playwright best known for Popular Front plays like *Waiting for Lefty* and *Awake and Sing!*, found himself revisiting this 1937 production about an Italian-American boxer as possible grist for an African American update and revival. Odets's theme "had always been the liberation of the soul from its social shackles," wrote William Gibson, who took part in executing the rewrite after Odets died in 1963, "and the Negro now was the equivalent of his cab-driver of the thirties."[46]

Davis signed onto the project early on, and both his enthusiasm for the work and his stage persona and repertoire became important to the rewrite as it took shape. As Elkins had pitched the idea to both Davis and Odets, "when translated in terms of an American Negro of today, it would have the same kind of statement and point as the original play. I feel that musicalization is the one way of making this point palatable." A "palatable" story about "the Negro of today," including an interracial romance, *on Broadway?* Davis was in—not least, because he saw it as a "chance to make up for *Mr. Wonderful*, artistically and racially."[47] The compatibility of Davis's view with Odets's on the matter is striking, considering how far to his left Odets actually was. But as Gibson later put it,

> Clifford rather identified with the Negro movement today as he did with the proletarian movement in the '30s. *The essence of it was that every individual who is oppressed has the right to grow, to flower, to become himself.* This was Clifford's theme all his life. He was very receptive to the idea of a Negro playing Joe Bonaparte. It would have pertinence today comparable to what it had in the '30's only in different terms.[48]

That *every individual who is oppressed has the right to grow, to flower, to become himself* was the very essence of Davis's own philosophy, even if he rarely used formulations like "oppressed."

Unlike the ethnically generic or bleached-out *Anna Lucasta*, in its initial incarnation in 1937 *Golden Boy* was quite specifically a "ghetto" narrative about an Italian-American boxer and his immigrant father. The Old World sensibility of the father, a modest fruit vendor, is conveyed in his heavily accented immigrant English and his hopes for his American son. One can almost hear his scratchy, 78-rpm Victrola record of Enrico Caruso in the background as he speaks of his own boy's musical gifts and hopes: "My boy'sa besta violin' in New York!"[49] The young boxer, in this iteration, is Joe Bonaparte, a promising fighter whose only liability is a tendency to hold back in order to protect his chief asset, the gifted hands of a violinist. As this was a Depression-era play written by a former Communist Party member, there is plenty here about capitalism, too. Against the simple decency of Bonaparte's immigrant father and the purer world of his musical aspirations, the grasping, brutal world of the boxing arena and the crude characters who people it offer a cautionary tale about all that this materialist, modern America has become. "We'll find some city where poverty's no shame," Lorna tells Joe in a fleeting moment of hope; "—where music is no crime!—where there's no war in the streets—where a man is glad to be himself, to live and to make his woman herself!"[50] In this sense Joe's Duesenberg coupe, whose combined lures of material magnificence and speed finally kill Joe and Lorna, embodies the rising, dangerous America. "Those cars are poison in my blood," he says earlier in the play. "When you sit in a car and speed you're looking down at the world."[51]

But the most striking thing about the original *Golden Boy*, when considered in the context of a 1960s revival featuring Sammy Davis Jr., is that the plot takes its tragic turn when Bonaparte accidentally kills another boxer in the ring—and his victim is an unnamed "colored" boxer referred to only as "the Chocolate Drop." In casting Davis as the Bonaparte character, Odets, Elkins, and Gibson made over the Italian ghetto into black Harlem and turned the Joe-Lorna romance into an interracial one, which became the most notable aspect of the 1964 production, fully what it was understood to be *about*. In doing so, they turned the script inside out, as it were, figuratively transforming an off-stage and unnamed "Chocolate Drop" into the play's central figure. This alternate-universe aspect of the revival, which asked what would happen if black stories commanded center stage, is undoubtedly what attracted Davis to the project, and perhaps Odets himself, too. "I'd give my right eye for a good black boy," manager Tom Moody muses in the original, as he ponders a suitable foil for the talents of his rising Italian star.[52] In the rewrite, his rising star *is* that "good black boy." The move might have been on Odets's mind for some time. The 1939 film version retains the Italian Bonaparte as its central figure, but emphasizes the racial injustice aspect of the story by bringing "Chocolate Drop" on stage. This version not only puts the black boxer on camera, but shots of the "colored section of the gallery" during the fight, and a powerful scene with his family and corner men after his death, fully humanize the black boxer's tragedy in a way that the stage version did not.[53]

The racial rewrite of *Golden Boy* was an immense challenge on several levels. First was the purely cosmetic issue, as Gibson noted, that "dialogue written for a white couple in 1937 was unbelievable in the mouths of a Negro youth and a white girl in 1964."[54] Much of what became the final script for the revived version started out as ad-libs by Davis, who according to Gibson "also suggested the content of many crucial moments, and hauled me out of more than one pitfall; he said to me one night, 'I leave you with two words,' and paused for me to guess what they were.... 'Write colored.'"[55] What Davis meant by this exactly we can only guess, but the layers are suggestive. In Davis's particular brand of integrationism, as expressed throughout his career and perhaps codified the following year in *Yes I Can,* the epistemological status of "colored" was always in question. (There is the white horn player "blowing his soul" in *A Man Called* Adam, too.) If there was in fact such a thing as "writing colored" for Davis, it was also true that a white writer like William Gibson could do it. *Golden Boy* thus resided squarely upon the *is* and the *ain't* of racial difference, even as the nation was becoming so thoroughly fixed upon race that it would soon burn itself down. The musical "invokes the question of in what measure will the white world accept the Negro," wrote the *New York Times.*[56] If acceptance is forthcoming, then what does race even mean? And if not, then *why not?* Race is meaningless, and yet race is destiny. In this respect, it is as generative to read *Golden Boy* against the contemporaneous Civil Rights Act of 1964 as it is to set it against the backdrop of miscegenation law in the run-up to *Loving v. Virginia.*

The unavoidable issue, as the team rewrote the Odets play, was that a central plot point in the original was a budding romance between Joe Bonaparte and his manager's girlfriend, Lorna Moon. If the leading role is now the black boxer Joe Wellington, then this romance has to be an interracial one—unless of course Lorna is also black, in which case her relationship with Wellington's manager Tom Moody becomes interracial. Or Moody is black, too, in which case you have a nearly all-black cast, something that financial backers on Broadway probably relished even less than the inflammatory plot point of an interracial affair. The learning curve for Gibson was incredibly steep, as the racial dimension of the Joe-Lorna romance became central. "For a Negro to make good in the world implied the *white* world," Gibson recognized, "and if the betrayal was of love, the allegory had willy-nilly changed into one of interpenetration of the races." As he noted, "Southerners saw the issue with clarity as a sexual matter," accurately setting miscegenation at the very center of the desegregation battles that were then raging around the Civil Rights bill. He added, in a remarkable piece of philosophizing for a white American in 1964, "and my own view was that with the act of love acceptable the racial problem qua racial problem would vanish; if sex was taboo, so was sitting together at a lunch counter."[57]

The contours of the revamped plotline are easily recounted. Joe Wellington, a talented up-and-coming boxer, is hungry for his shot at the title. He chafes at his treatment by both a white management team ("If ole black Joe beats Grant next week...."), and an overly protective father who wants more for his son and whose accommodationist streak really bothers the younger man.

> JOE: When I fight nobody spits on me, in that ring I'm as good as I am, no previous condition of servitude—
>
> MR. WELLINGTON: You know, your Ma wanted you to amount to somethin', not be just another colored fighter.

Or again, "What do he want, be a big shot with white folks where he don't belong?"[58] Against the backdrop of Joe's boxing ambitions and the racial realities that frame his quest, Act I establishes two plotlines through a triangulation of characters: a frayed relationship between manager Tom Moody and his mistress Lorna Moon, and a delicate, emergent romance between Joe and Lorna. Their feelings are coaxed to the surface when, as they chat on a city playground, they are set upon by a gang of white toughs. "Whatta, y'like coons, lady?" "Hands off the lady, nigger." After Joe and a late-arriving group of black teens dispatch the toughs in a brief skirmish, Lorna comments on Joe's seeming skittishness toward her.

> LORNA: Three at one blow, and girls scare you?
>
> JOE: White girls.[59]

It is here that Lorna gently begins to care for Joe—maybe something like love. She later defends Joe against the insults of her racist boyfriend. "Joe's a very nice-looking boy," she says. "You never looked." Tom replies gruffly, "What, that jig? We get off this tour I'm gonna have your eyes examined."[60]

The exchange significantly sets race at the center of the Tom-Lorna plot in addition to the Joe-Lorna story, in the form of the question as to how these two will each wear their whiteness. The first act crescendos with Joe's confidence that he can overcome the obstacles in his path—"Can I be what I want to be? / Yes, you can!"—and with his declaration of love: "You think I fight just for money and that mob of hyenas? I also fight for you, Miss Lorna Moon! . . . I'm offering *me!*"[61]

Act II picks up Joe's story after an unspecified time of continuing success, and amid a lot of racially-tinged jostling among the ring's management types to take control of the promising boxer's career. Joe was named "Fighter of the month," announces African American ring-man Eddie Satin. "I gave him a new Ferrari."[62] While Joe's career-making moment is still on the horizon, the arc of Act II focuses primarily upon the frank declarations between Joe and Lorna, Lorna's promise to break off with Tom, and then her cold-feet betrayal of Joe at the decisive juncture. The most dramatic moment here, given the history that envelopes it, is Broadway's first interracial kiss:

> Joe comes to take her face in his hands, and kisses her on the mouth, gently; the warmth of mouth to mouth steals over their bodies, their arms slowly enveloping each other's, until they are one figure, totally joined. The lights dim out on them.

Soon after, Joe confronts Tom and Lorna, momentarily confused that Tom does not seem to know about Lorna's love for Joe.

JOE: Tell him, Lorna.

LORNA: I love Tom. Tell him what?[63]

In a halting, emotional confession, Lorna later explains herself to Joe: "I haven't—the guts to—make a life—with you." After the big fight, Joe flees in that fancy Ferrari: "I gotta—get out, I gotta—run, move—. . . get in my car, speed—I gotta get out of my—skin." His last plea is, "Oh Lorna, why couldn't you love me right?" The play ends when Lorna, Frank, and the elder Wellington receive the news that Joe has been killed in a crash.[64] Not only has the Duesenberg been switched out for a Ferrari in the update, but in the Odets original Lorna and Joe Bonaparte perished together. Here the jilted fighter dies alone, in what might be read as the writers' faintness of heart, a refusal of the most radical possibilities inhering in the relationship.

The ascending significance of race and sex as Gibson and Elkins struggled to refashion *Golden Boy* wound up front and center in the show's branding.

Perhaps bravely so, for its historical moment, but problematically so, too. The album cover and posters for the soundtrack featured a stylized black, gold, and white block print of a couple in embrace. Neither face is visible. The man's enormous black hands wrap around the shoulders and cradle the long tresses of a woman whose whiteness is conveyed by the stark, blank-page absence of any features save her golden hair. The embrace is a loving one, upon closer inspection, but the momentum of the culture supplied enough prejudicial cues to suggest some kind of menace on first glance. This suggests the extent to which, as it developed, the *Golden Boy* project was haunted not only by Davis's very public relations—both real and imagined—with various white women, but by looming historical figures like Jack Johnson, the black boxing champion who was known for his "dandyish" taste in fine clothes and fast cars, and for his refusal of Jim Crow's laws when it came to sex and romance. Johnson had been arrested in 1912 for allegedly violating the White Slave Traffic Act (the Mann Act), which barred interstate and international transport of women "for immoral purposes." The allegation here, to be clear, involved a consensual relationship between Johnson and his then-lover Belle Schreiber. The charge was clearly trumped up to punish the famed boxer for violating "public sentiment" and "as a lesson to the black folk, the world around," as the *Indianapolis Freeman* noted in the wake of Johnson's conviction. "The pugilist as a citizen has not been given a square deal," ran one *Freeman* editorial. "As a Negro, a member of a despised race, he has been meted out a terrible punishment for daring to exceed what is considered a Negro's circle of activities."[65]

The point is not merely that the stylized poster for *Golden Boy* evokes Jack Johnson's physique more faithfully than it does the diminutive frame of Sammy Davis Jr. It is instead that the very image, like an effigy, carries the full burden of Johnson's history, along with *Birth of a Nation,* the post-Reconstruction rape libel, the displacement onto blackness of sexual impropriety, the bestial tropes and Mann Act mythologies. All of these things echo out alongside the tender Joe-Lorna plotline of this "liberal" project. And this is the baggage that many in the audience brought into the theater with them, critics included. The show toured in previews for fourteen weeks through the summer of 1964—Philadelphia, Boston, Detroit—as Elkins and director Arthur Penn continually reworked, revised, and adjusted the book. The cast, meanwhile, was bracing against the strong visceral reaction of audiences who were not fully ready for the storyline on offer.[66] "On the first day of rehearsal in Detroit," Davis recalled,

Arthur Penn watched the second act scene in which Paula Wayne [Lorna] and I discover we're in love and we're supposed to kiss. A white woman and a black man. But with race riots going on all over the city we were afraid to. He said, 'I've never seen a love scene in my life in which people don't kiss. Hold hands. Something. There's no declaration of love. . . .' He was completely right, of course. If we were a play with a message we'd better deliver it. That evening Paula and I grabbed each other and kissed. Full on the mouth. Embrace. Kiss. In Detroit, Michigan. All of us scared shit.[67]

The onstage kiss stirred the predictable outrage, "and Hilly [Elkins] got threats. 'We're gonna cut off that whore's tits. And the nigger's balls.' Paula had to be given a bodyguard. I already had one." In some performances, Davis remembered, "I got booed from the audience and in the scene when the white girl refused me people would applaud."[68]

Both during the previews and after the show had opened in New York, critics, too, tended to read *Golden Boy* against the Civil Rights moment without leaving their reflexive racial politics at the door. The *New York Times* rather applauded the show for taking up the challenge of the love story "of a white man for a white girl," now modifying it "to accommodate a Negro boy and a white girl."[69] It was undoubtedly liberal opinion, not just aesthetic judgment, in other words, that made the show a hit. By summer 1965 the *Los Angeles Times* could cite sales figures that put *Golden Boy* in a "charmed circle" of Broadway hits. Others were less sure, however. The *Wall Street Journal* saw a hint of sensationalism and opportunism in the venture, complaining that "The note of social protest at times seems to have been stuck in like the proverbial plum." The *New York World-Telegram and Sun* disparaged the work as "the short, shrill life of a Negro boxer," the word *shrill* here saturated in racial judgment.[70]

The *Washington Post, Times Herald* offered a different kind of dissenting note on the plotting of *Golden Boy*, but echoed the seeming distaste for the over-politicization of this art: "when the girl finally sends Davis away, we are moved directly into the stomping, injured Harlem chant of 'I ain't gonna bow down no more!'" The implication is that Davis has been rebuffed because of his race; the beat, the very presence, of the musical number depends upon it. But *"that isn't the way we saw it happen,"* this critic objects. Lorna was torn between two lovers, he explains, two life circumstances—one white and one black—and chose the one over the other not for racial reasons at all. "The old play and the new environment haven't quite joined hands."[71]

This is a remarkable reading, given that the lead actors of *Golden Boy* were under threat and had been forced to hire their own security details for the sake of an on-stage kiss. There is nothing neutral about the choice between the "two life circumstances" Lorna is contemplating here, that is, and that she did not have "the guts" to choose Joe even though we have seen the shabby treatment she is made to endure from Tom, including the broken promise that he will leave his wife for her, has *everything* to do with race. The danger that the black "life circumstance" would represent for Lorna begins with the white toughs at the park—"Whatta, y'like coons, lady?"—and their assault on Joe. But it spills beyond the fourth wall to the hate mail piling up in the dressing rooms and the bomb threats received at the cast's hotel, even to the opprobrium enacted by audience members themselves, whenever they booed Joe or applauded Lorna's refusal of him. Lorna's decision *is* made under the duress of racial threat. That is "the way we saw it happen."

The politics of *Golden Boy* are neither straightforward nor simple, however, and the *Washington Post* critic is onto something when he directs us to the score, in this instance the anthem-like quality of "No More." This is indeed the show's standout moment, musically. It is Joe Wellington's solemn and powerful statement of protest: "I ain't your slave / No more." This is the song that audiences most associated with the Civil Rights-themed material of the show. The *New York Times* hailed it as "an irresistible chorale of defiance."[72]

> Well, you had your way—no more.
> Well, it ain't your day—no more.
> Yes, I'm standin' up, I ain't on the floor,
> I ain't bowin' down—no more.

A similar register is achieved in "Night Song," another number whose Civil Rights themes are unmistakable.

> Where do you turn
> When you burn with this feeling of rage?
> Who do you fight
> When you want to break out
> But your skin is your cage?

For the most part, however, the score of *Golden Boy* is highly conventional and rather unremarkable Broadway. This might at first glance seem surprising, given the political charge of the show and the care with which Gibson and Elkins reworked the radical Odets material to make a statement for the 1960s. But recall that, for Elkins, the real work of "musicalization" was to make an explosive point more "palatable" for Broadway audiences. Despite the very significant appointment of an African American woman, Joyce Brown, to conduct the twenty-six piece orchestra, with the exception of a couple of very high profile moments like "No More" and "Night Song," the music is not the thing that is likely to strike with the most force about either the politics or the aesthetics of *Golden Boy*.[73] More characteristic than either of the score's anthems is a song like "Colorful," a playful little romp that fetishizes race as "chic" in a way that was becoming increasingly common in "liberal" America in the 1960s. One thinks of the Rat Pack's ease with racial humor at the beginning of the decade, for example, or Dr. Chegley's line in *Julia* at the decade's end: "Have you always been a Negro, or are you just trying to be fashionable?"[74] "Son, you make for colorful copy," a reporter says to Joe. "Colorful copy? Why, sir, you don't know how colorful I done been." Joe then launches into a veritable color wheel of metaphorical references (I had no experience, I was green; I'd get unhappy, I was blue; politically, I never turned red. . . .) before coming to rest on blackness: "I look at myself and black / suits me best."

> Black is chic
> Always correct for the house or yard
> Black is neat
> It goes with everything and doesn't try too hard
> Black is basic, you'll agree. . . .
> Black is me!

"Daddy, I ain't never turned white," Davis sings, in a line of such powerful self-allusion that it comes off as another breaking of the fourth wall.

> But black
> That's B-L-A-C-K, dig?
> Black suits me best
> And that's it!

The *Times* also singled out "Don't Forget 127th Street," a song that has not quite weathered the post-Civil Rights years. "It has been said that revolution could be buried in a song with no one the wiser," the *Times* reviewer wrote. But "the coming change chants its urgency from every beat of this number, and it's not meant to be a secret. . . . The swift, keen-edged lines about the Negro condition have bite and integrity." The number "describes with more burning zeal all the things that are wrong in Harlem" than has yet been achieved in our "grim sociological tracts."[75] An ensemble number devoted to upward mobility and African Americans' complicated relationship to Harlem ("H is for the heroin they sell here"), the "change" that is so urgently chanted in this song is decidedly *not* the one from Sam Cooke's contemporaneous hit "A Change Is Gonna Come." The problems with "Don't Forget 127th Street" are many, including some baffling little throwaway lines that disparage significant Harlem figures:

> Don't forget the cultural life on this here street,
> Richer than the outside world suspects.
> Hark! The cheerful patter of all the junkies' feet
> And the soothing tones of Malcolm X.

Or again,

> We got a right to howl
> We got Adam Clayton Powell.

At the center of the song is a highly problematic overlapping of the ethnoracial category "ghetto" with the economic category "slum." That is to say, the song conflates the optimism and excitement of the "Negro Metropolis" and the renaissance taking shape around the time that Davis was born with the "blight" that had turned out to be the Great Migration's betrayal. Ethel Waters's earlier ode to urbanization in "Underneath the Harlem Moon" had proclaimed, "There's no fields of cotton, picking cotton is taboo; / We don't live in cabins like our old folks used to do." "127th Street" symbolically reversed this, lamenting the life in "our dandy little ghetto." The song did not protest *conditions*—and certainly not urban *policy*—so much as graft conditions onto place such that it disparaged Harlem life in general. One verse of complaints spelled out "Harlem"—*H*eroin, *A*lleys where kids play, *R*ats, absentee *L*andlords, *E*ndless clean-up projects, and *M*oldy rooms. To some, including the *Times* reviewer, the song appeared to voice the kind of urban protest that would soon become nationally famous as Black Power, even though Civil Rights groups had been protesting *de facto* conditions in the North throughout the years that the SCLC was waging its assault on *de jure* conditions in the South. But the song's undergirding philosophy follows immediately in a highly significant tell:

> Put them all together, they spell 'Harlem,'
> The place that white folks think we love.

In collapsing unacceptable conditions into an unlovable *place,* "127th Street" refuses the political critique of what white America had allowed the "Negro Metropolis" to become, through white flight, tax policy, housing discrimination, and the *de facto* segregation of suburbanization. Instead it aligns itself with Davis's (and Joe Wellington's) quest to gain entrance into the "white" world. The urban social geography and the hope of escape spelled out here are of a piece with the kind of "freedom" that interracial romance stands in for in *Golden Boy,* as it often does in the Davis biography. As Joe sings:

> Sure, when I'm driving in my big Ferrari
> With some luscious rich chick as my pet,
> Believe me,
> How I'll miss this beautiful '27th Street,
> (Ladies and gentlemen, I assure you!)
> I'll miss it every chance I get.

The parenthetical "Ladies and gentlemen, I assure you!" breaks the fourth wall for a moment, fusing Davis's public persona and very public struggles with the sense of the song, and in so doing it fuses the issue of urban geography with the question of love across the color line. "They've got me down as Charley White Chicks Chaser," Davis would lament the following year in *Yes I Can.* The issues of Davis's dating choices and his restaurant, nightclub, and neighborhood choices were always closely aligned in the public mind, as he regularly got taken down by the *Amsterdam News* or the *Pittsburgh Courier* for choosing white neighborhoods instead of black, or eating downtown instead of in Harlem.[76] Just as these critics suspected of the Davis biography itself, "Don't Forget 127th Street" dreams not of freedom *for* a flourishing Harlem, but of freedom *from* Harlem. The twinned issues of crosstown urban geography and crosstown sexual license were an important indicator of Davis's own outlook on what freedom might mean, but also of the liberal symbology in which *Golden Boy* trafficked.

Davis was never at his most elegant on this subject, it is true. "I was dating anyone I wanted to," he wrote in *Yes I Can,* looking back on the period of early success around the time of his first *Colgate Comedy Hour* appearance in the mid-1950s.

> Not 'white girls' or 'colored girls'—girls! If I saw one I liked and got the nod and she happened to be white there'd be a voice saying, 'Hold it. She's trouble.' Then there was another voice that answered. He was the swinger. 'Go, baby. If she wants you and you want her then damn the torpedoes and full

speed ahead. *Go.*' And I went, playing both sides of town, each with its little extra kick: on one side, the satisfaction of knowing that nobody was telling me how to live, on the other, peace of mind and the joy I got out of the fantastic attention my own people were giving me. I hit those hot downtown bars empty handed, but when I left I was the Pied Piper of the Sunset Colonial, heading home with the freshest, best-looking, tomatoes in the whole grocery store skipping along behind me.[77]

Davis was very nearly the literal embodiment of the bell hooks axiom, "No matter the daily assaults on their manhood that wound and cripple, the black male is encouraged to believe that sex and sexual healing will assuage his pain." hooks noted that sex is "where the quest for freedom can be pursued" in a world that bars other forms of liberation.[78] The braiding and mutually constitutive nature of race, sex, and social geography in his own thinking—as in "Don't Forget 127th Street"—illuminate what lies at the core of *Golden Boy's* articulations of "freedom" and "transgression," including the show's Broadway transgressions themselves.

. . .

Richard Watts Jr., the well-known drama critic of the *New York Herald-Tribune,* was somewhat impatient with the racial politics of the show and with the perceived chip on Joe Wellington's shoulder. No longer a violinist, as in the original Odets play, Watts complained, the protagonist here "is driven into becoming a prizefighter . . . because he is determined to make up for the insults he has received due to his race by rising to fame and fortune in the brutal world of the white man."[79] But ultimately it was not the 1930s politics behind the original play, Odets's "shackles" of social categories, that marked *Golden Boy* as a political or politi*cized* production. Nor was it the 1960s Civil Rights sensibility embodied in Joe Wellington's rise and voiced in an anthem like "No More." Rather, the show became all about the interracial romance. It was *Golden Boy's* peculiar fate to come under the attack of Nazi groups and the KKK when in rehearsal in 1964, and of Black Power groups while on tour just a few years later. The one objection hearkened to a deep past in which the color line and the policing of sex propped up regimes of slavery and later Jim Crow. The other identified interracial romantic choices as signifying a brand of assimilationism, self-abnegation, or cultural betrayal that were coming in for bitter critique amid rising frank assertions of Black Pride.

Despite its 1930s Popular Front pedigree, it is impossible in retrospect to see Davis, Gibson, and Elkins's revival of *Golden Boy* outside of the immediate context of its Civil Rights moment. The play was in rehearsal as the 1964 Civil Rights Act was being debated in Congress; its run was interrupted in 1965, when Davis went to the Voting Rights march in Selma, Alabama, and again in 1968, when its Chicago rehearsals were suspended for several days for the King funeral.[80] All of this was in the run-up to and the aftermath of the *Loving v. Virginia* decision in June of 1967, which enshrined interracial marriage, under the Equal Protection clause, as a personal *right* "essential to the orderly pursuit of happiness by free men." As in so many other Civil Rights-themed enterprises in this era, the writers and crew of *Golden Boy* were on the right side of history, perhaps, but they were on the wrong side of the law until *Loving* and on the wrong side of common sentiment well after that. Dancer Lola Falana, among the original cast of *Golden Boy*, reflected on the significant political and physical courage that the show represented in its mid-1960s moment. No less a figure than Martin Luther King Jr., she said, "knew the battle was color. He knew Sammy was in the throes of that because of the show." King no doubt also recalled in vivid clarity the pop to the jaw he had once taken, in the name of "interracial sex," at the very mention of Davis's name at that 1962 Birmingham convention. King "saw Sammy as a brave warrior," Folana recalled. "They threatened to shoot Sammy down. While we were onstage, we would always be ready, listening for gunshots. Sammy had guts, that's the basic word."[81]

SIX

Writing Wrongs in Yes I Can

HALEY: Your night-club and theater audiences are predominantly white. Do you think there may be some element of
race consciousness in your compulsion to win their approval?

DAVIS: No question about it. I always go on stage anticipating
what people out there may be feeling against me emotionally.
I want to rob them of what they're sitting there thinking:
Negro. With all the accompanying clichés.

—ALEX HALEY
Interview of Sammy Davis jr., Playboy

Despite all my years of living with prejudice, so help me God, I'm
incredulous every time it hits me in the face. I never one day of
my life woke up thinking I'm colored, or I'm anything other than
just a guy. And then every day somebody reminds me.

—SAMMY DAVIS JR.,
Yes I Can

DAVIS'S 1965 AUTOBIOGRAPHY (with Jane and Burt Boyar) took its can-
do title from one of the songs on his then-current hit album, *If I Ruled the
World:*

> Got the feeling
> I can do anything
> Yes I can
> Something that sings in my blood is telling me
> Yes I can.

The book is suffused with this sort of brave optimism from beginning to end.
It is the story of how, by sheer will, Davis uses his extraordinary stage talents
to break down the racial obstacles and barriers arrayed in his path. It is
the same optimism that one glimpses in Joe Wellington's rendition of
"No More" in *Golden Boy,* but here we would do well to remember
that *Golden Boy* ends in tragedy. Despite Davis's repeated insistence that

black talent holds the power to break down segregation's walls, a recurring motif of *Yes I Can* is that the robust, stubborn, limiting forces of racism will endure.

Yes I Can is among the period's best-selling treatments of race and racism in America. In this respect, it is perhaps most revealingly read not in the context of the celebrity autobiography such as Lena Horne's *Lena,* published the same year, but alongside the other best-selling tracts on race in America in this period. These include John Howard Griffin's *Black Like Me* (1961), James Baldwin's *The Fire Next Time* (1963), *The Autobiography of Malcolm X* and Claude Brown's *Manchild in the Promised Land* (both 1965), and Stokely Carmichael and Charles V. Hamilton's *Black Power* (1966). Davis brought down barrier after barrier—in Las Vegas, in Miami Beach, in TV variety shows and sitcoms and westerns. But the autobiography is tragic in its constant thematic undercurrent that these successes never did secure the things he wanted most: true equality, whether in the industry or as a patron at the Copa, and a level of respect that was fully colorblind. *Yes I Can* ever turns in upon itself in a painful, unintended refrain of *No You Can't.*

The sprawling, six-hundred-page autobiography consists of a brief prologue and four parts, thirty-six chapters in all, covering the years from Davis's early memories of Harlem and the vaudeville circuit in the 1930s up to his marriage to May Britt in the early 1960s. Work developing the basic outline for the manuscript was actually completed in 1962; revisions and contractual difficulties postponed publication until 1965. My interest here is not especially in *Yes I Can*'s fidelity (or not) to factual events. Instead, it is revealing as a widely circulated text whose narrative logic and voice contributed to public discourses of race in the mid-1960s. The prologue is crucial in this respect. It would seem to indicate the biographical arc of a life bending from humble origins toward immense celebrity and fame. It also teases Davis's most challenging moment along the way—his career-threatening accident in 1954. But the prologue might better be read as setting the structure of an *argument* that the rest of the book will elaborate and advance. It opens on a scene of celebrity, the big finish to a 1954 performance at the New Frontier in Las Vegas. Davis ends his set with "Birth of the Blues," and the adoring audience's "applause was like a kiss on the lips."[1] He thanks them, not for the applause, he explains, but for "making it possible for me to walk through the world through the front door" (4). Moving nimbly off stage, Davis stewards us not only through the spaces of the casino, but across historical time:

I loved the way the crowds opened up for me and I circled the room twice, getting loaded on the atmosphere they'd kept us away from the other times we'd played Vegas, when there'd been a law against me, when it had been 'Sorry, but you're not allowed in the casino—you understand.' While the other acts had laughs and gambled, we went back to the colored side of town and we 'understood.' But now we didn't have to understand, and the joy of it swept through me every time I walked through that door . . . Now they wanted us enough so they were breaking their rules, *we were bigger than Jim Crow* (4–5, emphasis added).

There was a "big neon sign flashing my name across the desert," and its glow illuminated the chief lesson that Davis's life story served up: talent is a weapon, talent breaks down barriers, talent will overcome racism (5). Glad-handing as he moves through the casino, Davis casually plunks a roulette wager on red, evoking laughter with the line, "If you yell 'black' at me there's going to be a race riot." It was his way of enunciating race amid a sea of white faces, like the jokes that were later a staple of his routine, at once edgily marking the space as *raced* while also putting whites at a weird kind of liberal ease. This, incidentally, is almost certainly an embellishment from the post-Rat Pack moment of the book's creation rather than an accurate rendering of the New Frontier in 1954—one of the many clues that *Yes I Can* is more impressionistic composite than straight reportage.

Davis and his driver Charley light out across the desert in Davis's Cadillac, on their way to Los Angeles in order for him to record a song for the soundtrack of *Six Bridges to Cross*. A nice touch: he turns on the radio just as his own hit song, "Hey There," is playing. The references are just enough to tip off anyone in the know that this must be the night of Davis's near-fatal accident. Which it is. With "the grinding, steel-twisting, glass-shattering noise" of the collision still echoing in the reader's mind, as he lies in the wreckage Davis comes to the realization that will frame this life and this book: "I'm never going to be a star? They're going to hate me again" (8). The presumed but stunning linkage of stardom and hatred—a stardom predicated as racial hatred's one and only antidote—articulates the central thesis of *Yes I Can,* its liberal architecture.

Despite the manuscript's rough ride to publication, once it was out *Yes I Can* was something of a literary event. The book was excerpted in *Harper's Magazine* and *Ebony* in late 1965 and serialized in its entirety in the *New York Post* in the spring of 1966. The hardback sold a quick 100,000 copies at $6.95 a pop before the $.95 paperback appeared.[2] But the book landed strangely, precisely because of its odd mixture of anti-racist protest and hyper-individualized self-absorption. "Mr. Davis can recreate the 24-hour experience of what it is like to be black more vividly than most Negro literary types," wrote Eleanor Perry in the *New York Herald Tribune*. The *New York Post* similarly lauded the book for "walloping us with the pain that attends a Negro who faces discrimination head on."[3] Hazel Garland, the revered magazine editor of the *Pittsburgh Courier,* wrote that Davis "became a controversial figure because he dared to live his life not as a Negro but as a man." *Yes I Can* was about "more than Sammy's triumphs," it was "about a man who had the strength to live by his own rules." In some ways Davis's was a story ready-made for Garland's style of journalism: "I covered good news for years," she later reflected.

> But it was news none the less. It was what Black people felt was important to them. These are successful people who had the same obstacles placed in their way as others, but instead of complaining, or finding excuses they went out and did something about it. They didn't allow racism and prejudice to hold them back; they fought the odds and won.[4]

Among the immediate plaudits, the *Christian Science Monitor,* too, noted that Davis's "emphasis is less on life than on meaning. . . . I have the impression that the fact that this is his life means less to him than the fact that it is a life that demonstrates certain things." These included "color, prejudice, and human life inside a dark and famous skin." Even the *Chicago Daily Defender,* the colossus of the African American press, went so far as to say that this "could be the best book of its kind ever written," a book that "every American should read."[5]

Others were less certain. The book begins with an epigraph from Martin Luther King Jr.: "We ain't what we oughta be, / We ain't what we wanta be, / We ain't what we gonna be, / But thank God we ain't what we was." But there were those who questioned *Yes I Can* as a viable Civil Rights project. In a twisting, searching, unsettled piece for the *New York Times,* Martin Duberman set the book squarely within the political context of its moment. "We have recently heard much of the Negro's mistreatment, but the trials of a single man, when recounted as vividly as Sammy Davis Jr.'s are in his lengthy autobiography, renew and redouble the shock." But at the end of the day, for Duberman, Davis "has been unwilling or unable to make his story a depth analysis of self, and his history has been too special to serve as a prototypic tale of the Negro in America. And so we have a presentation that fluctuates between personal narrative and sociological suggestion, a fluctuation often absorbing, often unsatisfying."[6] Acerbic (black) writer George Schuyler, fresh off of his opposition to the Civil Rights Act, tipped his hat to Davis ("He had every handicap except mediocrity") before skewering the book as a piece of self-indulgence. Davis "overestimated the importance of such things as whether he would be welcomed at El Morocco or other smart supper clubs. He wasted a lot of time and energy and tears on trivialities," as far as the one-time author of *Black No More* was concerned.[7]

Any treatment of *Yes I Can* must begin by reckoning with the question of authorship, as the involvement of white journalists Burt and Jane Boyar in the project went somewhere beyond the typical "as told to" formula, fell somewhere short of ghostwriting, and landed closer to full co-authorship. The politics of the book have much to do with the nature of the collaboration among the three, as do the politics of its reception. Burt Boyar, a sometime actor, became a culture columnist and critic for the *Philadelphia Inquirer* and the *Morning Telegraph.* He was later known for his syndicated column *Beau Broadway,* featuring interviews and critical commentary on New York theater. Jane Feinstein had been a drama student in Manhattan when she met Boyar. She was a silent partner in his various critical pursuits long before being fully credited as a co-author for *Yes I Can.* Her annotations on the extant manuscripts attest to her status as a full partner in the project. She also earned significant deference from Davis, who once told Burt Boyar, "When I want your opinion on something I'll ask Jane," even if the gendered conventions of the industry pushed her from the limelight. Boyar had reached out to Davis for an interview soon after *Mr. Wonderful* hit Broadway in 1956. Over the ensuing years that interview grew into a major collaboration across hundreds of hours between Davis and the Boyars. So while Davis is the primary storyteller here—and it is his story to tell, after all—the collaboration, especially as it was across the color line, is critical to the final form that the book assumed.

Draft manuscripts of *Yes I Can* at the Library of Congress include one iteration that is subtitled *The Story of a Negro in a White World.*[8] This is a work of cultural ambassadorship, at its core. It is not just the rags-to-riches story of a black entertainer, but an exposé meant to pull back the curtain on American racism for the edification of a largely white readership. "He was very despondent," said Boyar of Davis. "Racism was absolutely deflating, so totally unkind, unnecessary."[9] The Boyars took it on themselves not only to get Davis's story out there, but themselves to learn about injustices they had

had the luxury of overlooking. When Davis exclaimed to the Boyars, "If people could just know what it's like!," writes biographer Wil Haygood,

> He meant the indignity, how you could be made to feel low and hurt even if you had crisp one-hundred dollar bills in your pocket. And suddenly, drawing in all of Sammy's pent-up pain in that comment—it was as if Boyar's mind had taken on a new engine—Burt Boyar realized that Sammy was talking not about joy, but about the slights and the pain, the sometimes awfulness of a life lived high one moment, then dragged to the depths of despair the next by doormen who were making a tenth of your salary. Who knew, out there in the hinterland, that beyond the opening nights, the champaign, the Vegas lights, the beautiful small-waisted blondes, the raw sweet sexual escapades, that he, Sammy Davis Jr., cried? That he hurt?[10]

The injustices described in *Yes I Can* of course represented no revelation at all to a black readership, and were clearly aimed at white readers safely ensconced in the privilege of their own unknowing. The Boyars' work as white translators can be read between the lines in addition to the narrative framing that their interviews provided. If *Yes I Can* embodies Davis's ambition to relay "what it's like," the Boyars' white shock at what lies behind the racial curtain proves an equal part of this narrative. Strangely, though, Burt Boyar reflected that, "We didn't write it as a racial book."[11] Here is precisely where Davis's own version of assimilationism intersected with the cross-racial narrative project that involved not only Davis telling his story, but the Boyars *hearing* it. In Davis's aspirationally race-free worldview the heart of the narrative is a series of *human* indignities, not specifically "Negro" ones. The Boyars, for their part, were especially drawn to colorblind humanism as a device for winning the empathy of the white reader. For Davis, that is, the point was to live a life beyond race: "How could the color of skin matter so much? It was just skin. What *is* skin?" For Burt and Jane Boyar, the point was to *narrate* a story beyond race—to evoke the empathy of a white readership by blunting any and all "difference" that might render Davis less relatable (70). This is what Boyar meant when he said *Yes I Can* was not a "racial book." It is probably also what Haygood meant when he said it was "an apolitical book."[12]

Of course the authors' choices and the nature of the narrative do not make this an *a*political book so much as they mark it for a particular brand of politics. "Make no bones about it," black radical critic Matthew Stelly caustically writes, "this book appeared in 1965; black people were waking up and becoming conscious. Most of the sales of this book went to white folks who felt that studying Sammy was a lot safer than turning on the TV and seeing their cities burning down, one by one."[13] Indeed, one white publisher even passed because "Davis had been far too quiet in the book about civil rights. He wanted anger, heat on the page."[14] But regardless of either its "heat" level or its authors' expressed views on the matter, it was its potential as a "racial book" that caused *Yes I Can* to be both celebrated and disparaged. To take a case, Beth Hillel in Los Angeles held a book event that paired *Yes I Can* with Claude Brown's *Manchild in the Promised Land*.[15]

In this convergence of Davis's brand of assimilationism on the one hand and the Boyars' notion of narrating "indignity" in human rather than racial terms on the other, one thinks of Saidiya Hartman's meditations on "the difficulty and slipperiness of empathy." Thinking through John Rankin's nineteenth-century writing against slavery, Hartman finds that empathy "confounds Rankin's efforts, because in making the slave's suffering his own, Rankin *begins to feel for himself rather than for those whom this exercise in imagination presumably is designed to reach*." Though *Yes I Can* is not about "shocking accounts of whipping, rape, [and] mutilation" under slavery, but about the racist slights and Jim Crow humiliations dished out long after emancipation, Hartman's provocative question holds. "Can the white witness of the spectacle of suffering affirm the materiality of black sentience only by feeling for himself?"

Empathy is "precarious" for Hartman, and the line between "witness and spectator" is a thin one, because in the mental exercise of would-be alliance the empathetic (white) self "becomes a proxy and the other's pain is acknowledged to the degree that it can be imagined, yet by virtue of this substitution the object of identification threatens to disappear.... Empathy is double-edged, for in making the other's suffering one's own, this suffering is occluded by the other's obliteration."[16] Whether enslaved or Jim Crowed, the African American is an apt object for white empathy *only* inasmuch as he is replaced by the white reader himself in the imaginative exercise—to the extent that he is conjured as not exactly being African American at all. Stepping into the other's shoes in order to walk a mile, in other words, makes the walk all about the (white) self and not about the racialized Other whose cause is being heralded. This dynamic is subtle but powerful in the assimilationist narrative that Davis and the Boyars crafted. Oddly aligned in its rhetorical strategy with *Black Like Me* (1961), *Yes I Can* tracks the affective prices to be paid and the damages that "occur to the heart and body and intelligence when a so-called first-class citizen is cast on the junkheap of second-class citizenship."[17]

It is probably this tortured bid for an empathy that trades blackness for racial *interchangeability* that deepened so many black readers' suspicions that Davis simply wanted to *be* white.

AUTOBIOGRAPHY AS ARGUMENT

Following its prologue, *Yes I Can* unfolds in four parts. Part I runs from Davis's early days in vaudeville to his discharge from the army in 1945. The second charts the Will Mastin Trio's rise from second-tier venues like the Cricket Club in the latter 1940s to Davis's celebrated stint at Ciro's after the car accident in 1954. Part III takes the reader from his post-accident comeback to a dark moment of near suicide in 1958, and the final part runs from *Porgy* to the birth of Davis's daughter Tracey in 1961, an optimistic note of accomplishment, contentment, and futurity. Though simple chronology would seem to govern the storytelling here, this is actually a book with a thesis, and each of the four parts has its thematic sub-argument to advance. The first part considers Davis's dawning awareness of racism and his discovery of raw talent as a weapon. The second turns to his fight against Jim Crow, and the allies and enemies he found on the white side of the color line. The third engages his attempts to find his own Civil Rights voice, and his tribulations with a black public that misunderstood him. And finally, the fourth reflects on finding a modicum of happiness straddling the color line—even if that color line continues to hold immense power in organizing American life. Like the careful narrative evolution from Malcolm Little to Detroit Red to Malcolm X to El-Hajj Malik El-Shabazz in the *Autobiography*, the Sammy Davis Jr. of *Yes I Can* moves through distinct stages of challenge and understanding on his way to explicating a particular theory of racialized relations in the United States. But this time in sharp contrast to Malcolm, Davis argues for the individual's power to overcome bigotry.

Part I records the "before" and "after" of Davis's awareness of racism as a system, from his highly protected travels as a child along the vaudeville circuits with Davis Sr. and "Uncle" Will Mastin, to his rude awakening as the full force of racist hatred and violence were revealed to him as a young army conscript. The fundamental elements of this section begin with the dim reflections of Jim Crow as refracted through the consciousness of a child. Davis's recognition of racism then hits with full force once the mask is torn off at Fort Warren. Here Davis reassesses his entire Jim-Crowed vaudeville past in the light of this new information, recognizing for the first time what Will Mastin had meant when he said, "someday you'll understand." "Overnight the world looked different," Davis recalls, for the first time fully appreciating the protection that his father and Mastin had always given him as the three navigated the Jim Crow world. The dynamics of racial bullying were relentless at Fort Warren, where a small group of committed racists, whose unity "would intimidate anybody," was able to dictate the texture and rhythm of daily life in the barracks, notwithstanding the better angels of a significant contingent of would-be white allies who were intimidated into silence (50, 51, 62, 56, 54–55). Along with the harsh lesson of racism unveiled came the beginnings of a lesson in the dignity of African Americans' response. Edward Robbins, the other black recruit in the barracks, remained compliant with Jim Crow practices, agreeing to shine white soldiers' shoes, for example. "Glad somebody around here knows his place," was the affirming white judgment. Davis concluded that Robbins's "fear of trouble was greater than his need for dignity," an object lesson going forward for Davis himself, who would try "to keep peace with [ring leader] Jennings without Tom-ing him as Edward was doing" (54–55). (This is one of those places where a wary reader might pause over the lived moment of the 1940s versus the act of narration in the 1960s.)

Amid the newly exposed racist dangers of Fort Warren, Davis discovers the significance of the white ally. In time this roster would come to include Mickey Rooney, Eddie Cantor, Milton Berle, Jerry Lewis, Frank Sinatra and the Rat Pack, Mel Tormé, Morty Stevens, and many others. At Fort Warren, it was one Sergeant Gene Williams who emerged as a force for even-handed meritocracy against the racialized tensions of the barracks. Williams not only assigns the racist Private Jennings to KP duty when needed, but fully takes Davis under his wing, serving as an advisor and an important mentor to the young man. He gives Davis copies of *The Picture of Dorian Gray,* Carl Sandburg's *Lincoln,* books by Dickens, Poe, Mark Twain, and Edmond Rostand's *Cyrano de Bergerac,* beginning what will become an intense period of self-education for the unschooled entertainer.[18] The sergeant also mentors Davis in a philosophical orientation toward his racist enemies among the troops. "You can't beat people into liking you," he tells Davis after another round of racially charged fisticuffs. "You can't hope to change a man's ideas except with another, better idea. You've got to fight with your brain, Sammy, not your fists" (62). The figure of Williams thus establishes one of the running themes of *Yes I Can,* and a central pillar of Davis's racial thought. "I've been knocked down by white people," he later writes, "—but I'm not about to forget that every time it happened the hand that was reaching out to help me up again was white" (316).

It was also Sergeant Williams who invited Davis to join the Friday night shows at the service club, which leads to Davis's identification of *performance* as the best weapon against racial hatred, one of those "better ideas" that will change people's minds. After one of his early shows on the base, and against the advice of a comrade who thought they should stick to the "colored" club to avoid trouble, Davis insists on joining the white soldiers in the audience up front, collecting his due as a talent who has just won them over. "Trouble?" he scoffs, "I just entertained them for an hour. They cheered me. . . . God knows I don't want trouble but there's gotta be a point where you draw the line." Sitting in the mixed-race setting of the club "was the happiest hour I'd spent in the army. I luxuriated in it. I had earned their respect; they were offering their friendship and I was grabbing for it" (56–57). Later, after his first Special Services show, as he takes his bows he catches the eye of one of his earlier tormentors, a Texan in the third row, and offers the reflection we have seen before.

> He was trying to show no recognition at all. At that moment, I knew that because of what I could do on a stage he could never again think, 'But you're still a nigger.' Somehow I'd gotten to him. He'd found something of me in six minutes of my performance which he hadn't seen in the barracks in all those months. My talent was the weapon, the power. . . . I was dancing down the barriers between us (72–73).

Davis's version of "dancing down the barriers" is not only an intensely personal one, but an intensely individualized one as well. His was less a fight against Jim Crow's injustices than it was a battle to heal his own sense of insult. Racism as a broad social phenomenon, in fact, boiled down for Davis to a struggle for "the joys of being *liked*." "I couldn't believe I was going to spend the rest of my life fighting with people who hate me when they don't even know me" (60). We will return to this later, but this hyper-individualized, almost *anti-structural* understanding of racism is pronounced and important throughout *Yes I Can*. "I'd weighed it all, over and over again," he writes,

> What have I got? No looks, no money, no education. Just talent. Where do I want to go? I want to be treated well. I want people to like me. How do I get there? There's only one way I can do it with what I have to work with. I've got to be a star! I have to be a star like another man has to breathe (74).

Reflecting on the odd oasis of adulation that his own fame provided him amid a wider, uglier world of racism, harassment, and danger, pitcher Bob Gibson once told baseball writer Roger Angell, "It's nice to get attention and favors . . . but I can never forget the fact that if I were an ordinary black person I'd be in the shithouse, like millions of others."[19] Davis's "I have to be a star" is the precise inverse of Gibson's notion of collectivity. Where Gibson can never forget, Davis is consumed with never having to remember.

But finally and most importantly, Davis's thesis that his talent will overcome bigotry is shown to be flat wrong. Davis and the Boyars will never say this outright, but their narrative demonstrates it again and again. It is directly after he was basking in the acceptance of his comrades at the Fort Warren nightclub—"the spotlight erased all color," "my talent was giving me a pass"—that his most brutal encounters with racism will come. His nemesis Private Jennings serves him a beer bottle filled with urine, eventually pouring it over Davis, thereby disproving the notion that "I had earned their respect." This confrontation ends with an all-out racial donnybrook (57–60). The story of the white WAC captain and the bullet dance also follows upon Davis's nightclub triumph. These opening chapters may establish racial triumph through talent as Davis's stated personal and political principle, but they also quietly establish persistent disappointment and injury as his biography's nagging subtext.

Part II charts Davis's rise, from the Will Mastin Trio's early postwar successes—"the kid in the middle is funny!"—to Davis's triumphal return to Ciro's after healing from his accident. The narrative throughout is suspended between the certainty that talent will overcome racism on the one hand, and the continual proof that it will not on the other. In this section the *Yes I Can* and *No You Can't* clock Davis's life like a metronome. The Trio gets a series of good gigs, on the road or in Vegas. The Trio gets Jim Crowed from the decent hotels—"nervy nigger wanted a room"; "We can't let you have rooms here. House rules. You'll have to find a place in the—uh, on the other side of town" (86, 88). Davis absolutely kills it on stage with his novel impressions, but discovers that once the show is over, "I was a Negro in a Jim Crow town" (90). He gets an important introduction to Mickey Rooney, who tries to help him land a role in a film. But then, "I don't think they want a colored fellow. They told me, 'Use a Mexican kid, it's less problems'" (101). He gets a plum gig opening for Frank Sinatra at the Capitol Theater in New York. He is turned away from Lindy's by a doorman waving him away from a clearly bustling establishment: "We're closed" (106, 113). He is invited to the

FIG. 15. The Will Mastin Trio. Photo: George Rinhart/Corbis via Getty Images.

Copacabana as Sinatra's special guest, but then "I felt as if I were a bundle of dirty laundry being taken through the dining room. . . . The stares, like countless jabs against my skin" (118). The Will Mastin Trio slays at Ciro's while opening for Janis Paige, to the extent that the owner puts them at the top of the bill. Davis is at the top of the world, with bookings rolling in from the Chez Paree, the Riviera, *The Colgate Comedy Hour*. He is sharing spaces and drinks with the likes of Jerry Lewis, Ed Sullivan, Red Buttons, and Jack

Benny. But then he receives a hate letter—"Dear lousy nigger, keep your filthy paws off Eddie Cantor"—or is greeted by a sign at a Miami Beach hotel, "No Niggers—No Dogs" (151, 153). He opens at the Copa; but when he is house-hunting, the broker drives him straight to the black part of town. "Obviously I wasn't big enough yet" (185).

The section ends on a high, a contract to play the Old Frontier in Vegas that includes accommodations in the hotel. "If Vegas could open up to us like that then it was just a matter of time until the whole country would open up," Davis claims. This is followed by the epic comeback performance at Ciro's after the accident (187). But the downdraft has been significant throughout. At one point following an unabashed piece of Jim Crowing in a Manhattan restaurant, Davis has an exchange with a shocked Marty Mills.

MILLS: I knew it went on, but I never figured New York. . . .

DAVIS [SARDONICALLY]: Baby, keeping us out of restaurants and hotels is the national pastime. It's bigger than baseball.

MILLS: Is it always like this?

DAVIS: Only when I'm colored (114).

In fact, it is in Part II that Davis comes as close as he ever will to countering his own theory of performance as an effective weapon against racism.

I could never satisfy the people I was trying to appease. How could I not offend them by what I do when my very existence was offensive to them? There could be no end to it. Don't be seen at the same tables with white people. Stay away from white women. Don't touch Eddie Cantor. What next? I wanted to make it, but if that was the price, it was too high (151–52).

As this pendulum continues to swing between the poles of hope and despair, confidence and rage, two intertwined subthemes emerge. One is the generational friction within the Will Mastin Trio, and especially between Davis and Mastin, over the proper way to navigate Jim Crow, and over broader questions of racism and "the race." "Colored rooming house, colored hotels?" Davis chafes, when the Trio settles into a fleabag hotel on the colored side of the tracks in Spokane. "Colored, colored, colored! And the way they were accepting it, so matter of factly." But accept it Mastin and Senior did: "that's how it is," says Davis Sr., "and there ain't no use fightin' it. That's how people are." "Why do we have to live *colored* lives?" is a question Davis cannot stop asking, a question that in fact drives much of the narrative. It is also a question that will never make sense to Mastin and to Sr., for whom the *avoidance* of such questions has become essential equipment for living (85). Sensibilities clashed not only around questions of what and what not to "accept," but around questions of performance and style as well. Recall Mastin's shock at Davis's plan to do impressions of white people. Later the two have a similar confrontation when Davis wants to hire a white conductor, Morty Stevens, to run the band. "He ain't no conductor," storms Mastin. "Anyway, this is a colored act. We don't need no white people in it."

> I jumped out of my chair. 'Whattya mean this is a colored act? It's not a colored act or a white act. It's just a plain act.'
> Will was out of his chair, too. 'I'm the boss of this act and what I say goes and don't you forget it! This is a colored act and it's gonna stay a colored act until I die' (144).

The dynamics here are complicated and layered. Mastin's career was reaching its end by this point, just as Davis's star was rising. This could not have been easy, especially as the Trio's contemporary success so obviously hinged upon "the kid in the middle," whom Mastin had mentored since Sammy was in knee pants. But the flashpoint was also generational and political. Mastin had made his peace with the cosmos of "colored" performance—its racially coded styles and patterns of deference, its Jim Crowed circuits and venues, its racialized pay scales—whereas for Davis, "success" itself meant escape into a world where there were no Jim Crow humiliations because color itself had ceased to matter. No "colored lives," no "colored rooming houses," no "colored act."

A related subtheme here is Davis's dawning awareness that, in their embrace of the idea of a "colored" act, his elders were perpetuating some of the old-timey minstrel moves of an earlier era. By a lifetime of habit, he reflects, "by *tradition* . . . we were still doing *Holiday in Dixieland*" (104–5). This was in part a matter of *address*. Davis wanted to remove the veil of minstrelsy that continued to cloak black performance practices, feeling that to defer to conventions that forbade direct address between black performers and white audiences was to concede too much. "I don't want to come on with panting and puffing and fighting for my life like 'Is this good enough, folks?'" he wrote, of one appearance at the Copa as he adjusted his act. "I want to do something that no Negro dance act has ever done before. From now on I'm going to *walk* onto the stage . . . with dignity. I'm a headliner. I want to walk on like a gentleman" (166). Talking this over with comic Nipsey Russell one night in Harlem, the two agree that the old song-and-dance routine was encrusted in a form of racial deference whose day was over. "We came in dancing. Without planning it that way we offered something they would accept from a Negro. . . ." But stand-up comedy was different; white audiences "weren't ready for an articulate man who could face them on their own level and offer ideas" (125, 182–83).

Both his disagreements with Mastin and his own efforts to adjust his affect elaborate the working subtitle *The Story of a Negro in a White World*. Davis's story has to do with black performance practices and white spectatorship, and with the white-controlled spaces of American entertainment. "When we were starving from one town to another I wasn't thinking, 'Someday I'll have a pile of money,'" Davis writes. "I was thinking, 'Someday we'll make it and I'll live like a human being. I'll go where I want to go and I'll be able to do anything I want to do'" (182). "Making it" here, like the more foundational idea of "living like a human being," means forging a new set of practices and challenging an old geography of social inequality. This is precisely where Davis feels like a pioneer and many of his African American compatriots see him in terms of betrayal, of wanting to "be white." This will be the major theme of Part III. In the meantime, a fleeting reference to code-switching is an important piece of ethnography in this context, at once an observation on what is required as one traverses "black" and "white" spaces, *and* a peeling back the curtain—if only momentarily—for a presumed white readership who are otherwise being encouraged by the book's rhetorical strategy to see "dignity" and "indignity" as unraced. Before their important make-or-break moment at Ciro's, the Will Mastin Trio is preparing backstage. "We were lapsing into the deepest Amos 'n' Andy talk, something Negroes do among themselves when they're nervous but happy. . . . perhaps it makes us feel safe, closer to our roots. I don't know. But there are times when 'colored talk' serves the moment as nothing else can" (126). It is a rare admission, for Davis, not only of what was being left behind in his version of "making it," but that there even *is* a behind to be left.

The next segment continues the theme of perpetual racial insult, even while charting Davis's meteoric rise through the New York, Vegas, and Miami Beach nightclub circuit and his Broadway success with *Mr. Wonderful*. Part III opens with Davis's rejection for a hotel reservation in Chicago, and the two-hundred-page stretch is punctuated by unending vicissitudes of greater and lesser insults, some nakedly violent and others more subtle or "refined," as Davis puts it, by "time and sophistication." He is turned down for a room at the Desert Inn; he overhears someone calling him a *schwartza* at a toney Upper East Side supper club; he endures platters of fried chicken and white repartee about "colored people having rhythm" or "the background of jungle life" at a liberal New York cocktail party. The words "colored" and "Negro" are intoned in whispers in this setting, even when spoken to Davis himself. One "phoney all-too-liberal" tells him that he is "a credit to your race." In effect, as Davis understands, this means "telling me colored people are rotten but *I'm* okay and he's waiting for me to say thank you." He reflects, "The worst thing in the world is when you're up against people *who don't even know they're prejudiced*" (400, 233–234, 240–241, 278, 312–313, 357–361). At one point Davis's party is denied a reservation at the El Morocco. A host comments to Burt Boyar on Davis's being "very black" even while "the dance band was playing 'Mr. Wonderful'" audibly in the background in the dining room. This fleetingly dents his "incredibly naïve optimism" ("Yeah, baby, being a star has made it possible for me to get insulted in places where the average Negro could never *hope* to go and get insulted.") But for the most part Davis responds to these injuries as he always had: "I'm a star. This isn't supposed to happen any more"; "I had to get bigger, that's all. I just had to get bigger"; "I've got to get so big, so powerful, so famous, that the day will come when they look at me and see a man—and then somewhere along the way they'll notice he's a Negro" (366, 371, 234, 241, 254).

The generational and philosophical tensions within the Trio continue to intensify as Davis's star rises. "You can't get happiness out of forcing yourself on people," Mastin tells Davis, as they debate whether or not to insist on the right to stay at San Francisco's Fairmont Hotel while performing there. "If I stay away from where I want to be and where I've got a right to be," Davis counters, "then I'm as much as saying, 'Yeah, I agree with you. Colored people shouldn't be here.' . . . I'm too big for that jazz." "You ain't too big for 'em to break your heart," Mastin cautions (235). Similarly, when Davis fights for his grandmother's right to sit ringside for the Trio's Vegas show, Senior reins him in: "you sure you're not pushin' the horse a little faster'n he can run? Colored people sittin' out front in Vegas?" (239). When Milton Berle invites Davis to the Friars' Club "to get some steam," Mastin unloads the skepticism of a generation's worth of exclusion. "They never had a colored member before, and if they wouldn't have Bill Robinson and Bert Williams, then where do you get off thinking they'll have you?" (247).

Much of Mastin and Senior's commentary on such subjects emanates from their own deeply rooted sense of racial decorum, and Senior is clearly

FIG. 16. Davis with Olga James in *Mr. Wonderful*, 1956. Photo: Friedman-Abeles © The New York Public Library for the Performing Arts.

protective of the young, impatient Davis, as well. But a second concern occasionally surfaces: their worry for Davis's reputation in the black community, and the *appearance* of his preference for white spaces and white comrades over black ones. One night in Vegas, Senior warns Davis about his "white" social life and the unfavorable coverage Davis is beginning to garner in the black press. "Just look who you got around you," his father says. "There ain't nothin' but ofays. Now if one of them writers was to walk in here. . . ." "Dad," Davis answers, "where in the goddamned hell am I going to find colored people in Vegas?" As for coverage in the black press, Davis bristles that they never mention that "because of me, colored people sat out front in a Las Vegas hotel for the first time in history." His resentment crackles. "I've worked all my life toward the day when no white man could tell me how to live—now the colored people are trying to do it" (244–45).

But Senior and Mastin are right. The black press's harsh judgments of Davis as a race traitor become a major thread through the latter 1950s, a stretch that includes the false stories about Marilyn Monroe and Ava Gardner, and the accurate ones about Kim Novak and Joan Stuart. A joke is circulating, Mastin tells Davis, "about you sitting in Danny's Hideaway in New York when some guy looks at you and calls out: 'Nigger, nigger, nigger!' and you jump up and yell: 'Where? Where? Where?'" (259). The whipsaw paradox for Davis in the 1950s was that what felt like straight up *resistance* to Jim Crow on his part was interpreted by others as some sort of white wanna-be-ism. African Americans "figure you're living over here with the ofays, when you oughtta be over there [with them] instead," song-and-dance man Finis Henderson tells him. "They think maybe you've gotten a little snow-blind." Davis shoots back, "I've had my nose broken too many times to hear I'm an Uncle Tom."

> Boy, that's beautiful. Wouldn't you think they'd say, 'Go, man! And you've got the strength swingin' for you so *live like you wanta live! Fight it for the rest of us!*' But instead, the immediate reaction is 'Hey, whattya think about Sammy livin' white?' Instead of sayin' here's a cat who might make it a little better for all of us, they turn against me and I become an outcast. I don't hear, 'Hey, crazy! Maybe I can follow him through that door.' All they want is to drag me back to the gutter with them. Well, man, I ain't comin' back! (268).

The black press could be quite acid on this subject. One ran the headline "Sammy Davis Jr. Starring in 'I'd Rather Be White.'" Another announced, "Sammy Davis Jr., once a source of pride to all Negroes, has become a never-ending source of embarrassment." *The Amsterdam News* criticized him for eating downtown instead of in Harlem. When Davis arranged an ill-advised and clumsily-executed presser to address these questions—and then once again got scorched in the black press—Evelyn Cunningham of the *Pittsburgh Courier* wrote an open letter, ending with the postscript, "Ain't it rough being cullud?" Davis called a meeting with John H. Johnson, of the Chicago publishing empire that put out both *Ebony* and *Jet,* to ask point-blank why Johnson was "turning my people against me?" "I've been convicted of taking turn-white pills," he complains. "You've been holding America's first all-colored lynching." Johnson was direct and unsparing in his reply: "the impression which the average Negro has, [is] that you have removed yourself from Negro life and have turned away from him" (271–73). Davis did himself some real disfavors in this regard, it should be said. When contemplating his marriage to Loray White after his many controversies with white women, he remarks that "the Negro press'll go outta their minds; they'll eat it up like a hundred yards of chit'lins" (444).

But for Davis it was as if "the whole world split in half, with me standing in the middle, the Negroes on one side glaring at me and the whites on the other side, laughing" (287). Later, he comments, "It's like I'm the man without a country" (329). His feeling of uncomfortable suspension between two worlds, or exclusion from both, leads Davis to the sharpest anti-racist critiques of *Yes I Can,* an exasperation that even the Boyars cannot render as a brand of indignity "beyond race." As Davis's frustrations mount, his efforts on the white side of town intensify, as does his desire to crack Jim Crow. Much of the text highlights his personal resentment of racial barriers, as when he is told, "if you were white you'd have been in pictures years ago," or an agent tells him that "on certain networks Negroes are banned except if they appear as servants" (255, 257). But what is more striking in this section of *Yes I Can* is some of the subtlety of Davis's analysis. It is in this section that, as noted earlier, Davis critiques the casting practices that disallow black actors from playing parts that are not marked by the scriptwriter as raced in any way. It is also here that he sets the record straight on black cowboys in the historical West and levels a critique of the all-white Hollywood western. During a radio interview, Davis offers a subtle observation about reflexive conceptual understandings of race and about the workings of "difference" in the industry. Though he and Bill Robinson are often compared, he notes, "we are not the same kind of performers. . . . So if you're talking *performance* it would be much more logical to compare Fred Astaire to Bill Robinson, but I never heard *that* done" (252–53). In an interview with Mike Wallace, Davis even offers an analysis of northern racism, at the time nearly unheard of on network television.

Mike, let's not kid ourselves that prejudice is geographic. Down South they lynch you and kill you—up North most Negroes die before they ever really lived at all. . . . If you steal a man's dignity, does it matter if you rob it or embezzle it? . . . Down South they do it openly; the restaurant puts up a sign 'No colored people allowed.' Up here they use raised eyebrows to accomplish the same thing. You don't see many or *any* Negroes lunching or having dinner in ninety percent of the good restaurants below 125th Street (380–81).

Similarly, Davis offers a cultural analysis of race and racism that would be far more common decades on than it was when the book appeared in 1965. On one of the many racial jokes circulating at his expense, he observes, "Charley joke-teller doesn't understand that violence is the smallest part of prejudice." It's the "little jokes, thoughtlessly assuring people that we all carry knives and steal and lie" that will assure "when we try going to school with you, some guy who's been convinced is ready to crack open our skulls to prevent it." "You can pass legislation for desegregation," says Davis, "but you can't legislate people's minds *and that's where progress must finally be made* (316, emphasis added). It is a rare moment in *Yes I Can,* but an important one, where Davis's hyper-individualized or personalized take yields to a more thorough structural understanding of race, not as bigotry merely, but as systemic and as expressive, in its supposedly minor as much as in its major instances, of naked power.

All of this is to say, the reigning rhetorical device of *Yes I Can*—its *racelessness* as a modality of garnering white empathy—is insufficient to contain all that tumbles forth from the Davis biography. These moments of insight and anti-*racist* (as opposed to anti-*bigotry*) critique are fleeting. This is why the book reads like such a pre-Civil Rights fossil, when compared to more radical writings of the period, as we will see—not just from Malcolm X, Stokely Carmichael, or H. Rap Brown, but from Dick Gregory as well. Davis always quickly retreats to his more accustomed style of highly personalized rather than structural struggle. "You want people to like you," Mike Wallace observes. "In its simplest form: I don't want people to *dis*like me before I've earned it" (381, 383).

But throughout this segment of the narrative, as Davis contends with both his black critics and with random white bigots and systemic Jim Crow barriers, the psychic toll mounts. He first suffers a somatic scare that will be recalled a year later in one of the final scenes of *A Man Called Adam:* "As I reached for the big note a searing pain cut across my torso, like a hot wire suddenly drawn tightly around my back and my chest and I knew I was having a heart attack" (416). Part III ends with an attempted suicide, as Davis aims to drive his car off a cliff, seeking "an end to so many years of disastrous self-deception" (458). He is saved only by the fluke of the car's transmission and undercarriage getting hung up on the rocks, leaving the car teetering on the ledge rather than plunging off. In one sense the suicide attempt comes out of nowhere in this narrative. There have been no hints of depression, though Arthur Silber Jr. has written of another suicide attempt on Davis's part. In fact there has been precious little in this narrative of what you might call introspection or even *interiority*. It is rather a cavalcade of events, circumstances, and complaints. As Duberman wrote, Davis seems "unable to make his story a depth analysis of self." Nonetheless, between the tensions within the Will Mastin Trio, Davis's endless disappointments at the hands of white supremacy, and his travails in and against the black press, the desperation has been mounting throughout this section, despite his steady rise in the profession.

Part IV, in contrast, winds miraculously—and perhaps artificially—toward some kind of optimistic note of accomplishment and futurity. Mastin will continue to criticize Davis's stage choices ("You tryin' to get yourself lynched? I never heard a colored man stand in front of a white audience and do *those* kinds of jokes. . . . And in *Florida?*") (466) Davis will be confronted by the Nazi Party in both Britain and the United States, and he will have to hire a security detail. He will navigate the Jim Crow laws of Miami Beach and the long tail of overt discrimination at the Fontainebleau Hotel. He will be widely condemned on both sides of the color line for his marriage to May Britt. He will get booed at the Democratic convention and he will be disinvited from the Kennedy inauguration. But he will also have great successes with *Porgy and Bess,* the Rat Pack, and *Ocean's Eleven* during these years, and he will hit the *Billboard* charts with "What Kind of Fool Am I," "Me and My Shadow" (with Sinatra), and "Sam's Song" (with Dean Martin).

The final inching toward optimism in *Yes I Can* has as much to do with a philosophical turn toward some kind of inner contentment on Davis's part, and an acceptance of where he finds himself towards middle age, as it does with his stage, screen, and recording triumphs, even if this six-hundred-page epic of "making it" has led us to focus on such successes. There is a fleeting moment, while Davis is in Europe, when the moral of the story seems like it might reside in the contrasting racial climates of the United Kingdom and the United States. "I had stopped thinking of myself as a Negro," he writes of his experience in London. "There were no El Moroccos I couldn't go to; I wasn't invited to 'the best private clubs that accept Negroes,' I was invited to the best private clubs, period" (532). Here Davis gives name to the inner emptiness that has nagged his narrative all along—a selfhood that is defined by others' approval as much as it is by a sharp sense of justice. This respite in England also echoes

African American luminaries like Josephine Baker and James Baldwin, and the unnamed thousands of US soldiers during both World Wars, who glimpsed in Europe a brand of racial egalitarianism unknown to them at "home." But in an epiphany, Davis turns away from this interpretation and from this theme of *national* critique. "The colored cat who goes there thinking he's walking into heaven is going to be disappointed," he concludes.

> It could never have happened for me in England. I don't know of any Negro who started with nothing and made it there. Social equality is all they have for the Negro there. In America, although we have far less social equality, we have constantly expanding *opportunity*. . . . Social acceptance is delightful, but it's only ice cream and cake—opportunity is the meat and vegetables (533).

Social equality *is all they have*. This is an astonishing statement, and especially so at the very moment when a generation of sacrifice and courage had exacted the Civil Rights Act from a political culture steeped in white supremacy. But it also represents a significant readjustment on Davis's part, now that he has "made it."

There is a backward glance in this latter segment of the narrative that articulates a new optimism. It perhaps rings hollow, however, in that the terms of engagement have changed somewhat after his decades of feverish chafing to achieve "social equality." "There's no glory attached to being born in a tenement," he writes, in a passage that recalls the *Golden Boy* song "Don't Forget 127th Street." "Not while you're living there. Only when you can look back on it from a penthouse. When I lived up here [in Harlem] I hated it. But I don't mind talking about it now. It glorifies me to say, 'That's where I started, but look where I am." (594). Davis here embraces a kind of Civil Rights optimism that expresses a different kind of being at home in (or with) America. He hitches his narrative to a Civil Rights logic in a few different moments, now returning—really for the first time—to the frank Civil Rights theme announced in the Martin Luther King epigraph on the book's frontispiece. "Can't you see that Martin Luther King is to us what Moses was to the Jews?" he asks. "Whenever we have problems with the racial thing and we wonder if it'll ever change," he writes of Copacabana owner Jules Podell's financial contributions to Civil Rights causes, "we should remember this is the same man whose policy wouldn't let me into his club." The past tense is critical here, as is Davis's attachment of this change to a broader Civil Rights struggle. "Losing gets to be a habit, baby," but "every lunch counter and bus stop was arguing that there *can* be light where thirty million people had come to believe only in the certainty of darkness. The day was coming when we'd no longer be strangers to hope, when there would be no shame in having been the laborers of yesterday because we'd be the architects of our own tomorrow" (591, 588, 595).

If grafting this language to the narrative's end is a way of articulating a racial optimism in *national* terms, it is also a partial rewriting of much of what has come before. There may indeed be a throughline here in Davis's overall philosophy of entertainment and performance as weapons in a wider war. Audiences

> hear me sing and watch me dance and they think 'Isn't he adorable!' and that's my moment—and I have to *do* something with it, I can't waste it—that's when I have to show them: But remember, I'm colored. I *must*. I want to make them equate 'colored people' with *me,* an individual they know and maybe understand, instead of with a formless, mysterious mass they instinctively fear and hate (467).

But formulations such as what "every lunch counter and bus stop" teaches were likely formal additions as the manuscript was under revision between 1962 and 1965, rather than organic features of the raw interview material generated between Davis and the Boyars. These late narrative gestures toward a broader Civil Rights politics perform a kind of narrative reframing, a telescoping of one period into another—the nobler, distinctly 1960s intention of overcoming Jim Crow for the benefit of "the folk" collapses back into the period when, as he admitted to Wallace, "what I do is for me."

As a rhetorical device, *Yes I Can* comes to rest in its final pages on the birth of Davis and Britt's daughter Tracey, and a version of futurity that might encompass both the personal and the political. When they were courting, Britt had asked Davis, "Won't it be great when we're married and have lots of little brown babies?" "I'd love to," is Davis's reply (486). After all the traumas of bomb threats and Nazi protesters, Davis's narrative delivers us to the hospital room where Britt has just given birth. The infant herself becomes a symbol of social change and of all that might be possible. Interestingly, Lena Horne's autobiography of the same year also ends on this chord of procreation and futurity. In her case, it is a tranquil scene where she rocks her mixed-race granddaughter in the nursery. "Tiny as she is, I look for a sign. I know the times are better than they were for me."[20] Davis's passage might also be read in the key of patriarchy. As bell hooks notes, many black men reaching all the way back to Frederick Douglass and Henry "Box" Brown had defined "'freedom' as that change of status that would enable them to fulfill the role of chivalric benevolent patriarch."[21] The happy ending of *Yes I Can*, then, marks not only the arc of Davis's life toward a rare moment of contentment, but also the attainment of his assimilationist dream, and equity itself, by way of the Davis-Britt household. The wish to settle down has not been pronounced throughout *Yes I Can*. But trading the role of playboy for establishing a household with his wife and child provides readers a legible emblem of the assimilationist's having "made it"—not only as a star, but as a man.

Davis and Britt are "ready to impart" to Tracey "everything we had learned the hard way, able to give her all the love and strength she might need—but I prayed that by the time our baby is grown she would not need all that strength, that she would live in a world of people who would not notice or care about a layer of skin." This is not a statement that brims with confidence. All of the decades of social change that had issued forth in Davis's stardom, in his marriage to May Britt, and in Tracey's birth merely represented "cracks in the wall." These might be "widening," but the question remained: "will it happen fast enough? Are people willing to change?" (611). For the book's "yes I can" reading this is a fitting ending and Davis's is a well-earned optimism. The world he was born into, featuring blackface minstrelsy, Jim Crow lunch counters, stifling cultural conventions, and the crushing poverty of the Chitlin' Circuit, has given way to something much more open and promising, a world capable of *both* the "ice cream and cake" of social equality and the "meat and vegetables" of opportunity. But by another reading, the dream of overcoming American racism has been dashed time and again across these six hundred pages, and another crushing experience surely awaits Davis around the next bend. "No you can't" tells us that it is something of a cheap rhetorical trick, a narrative sleight of hand, to deposit the reader in the maternity ward for the birth of this mixed-race baby as a symbol of more peaceful and just worlds to come. As Davis has shown us again and again, even in spite of himself, America has not warranted such optimism. Even his epigraph, King's "We ain't what we oughta be / We ain't what we wanta be," has positioned us to be somewhat skeptical of this text's rosy certainties.

THE SHIFTING LOGIC OF
THE AMERICAN "RACE BOOK"

In December of 1966, about a year after the publication of *Yes I Can*, Alex Haley interviewed Davis for *Playboy*. Now most famous for *Roots: The Saga of an American Family,* Haley had already established himself in black intellectual circles, having done *Playboy* interviews of Miles Davis in 1962 and Cassius Clay and Martin Luther King Jr. in 1964, before finishing work on *The Autobiography of Malcolm X* in 1965. Haley's interview pushed Davis in some unaccustomed directions, revealing occluded elements of *Yes I Can.* More importantly, it situated the entertainer squarely within a Civil Rights discourse that was growing louder, more urgent, and more radical precisely in the post-Civil Rights Act, post-Watts moment of *Yes I Can's* release. Reflecting on the Will Mastin Trio's experience in a racist industry, Davis told Haley that, despite his own ambitions, Mastin kept saying, "'White folks ain't gonna let you get but so far.' But I kept insisting, 'Yes, I can!'—say, there's a good title for a book—and I kept believing that somehow, someday we'd be able to break down the wall of prejudice that was blocking us."[22] One can see here that the political ground is shifting beneath Davis's feet. The meaning of "the wall of prejudice that was blocking us" is plainly evolving in retrospect for Davis, from an intensely personal to a global Civil Rights question.

Haley gave Davis a pretty rough ride. If not fully combative, he was at least unremittingly direct. He wondered about the "many problems—bad reviews, script changes, firings, frictions, accidents, injuries" that had plagued *Golden Boy,* and he remarked that *A Man Called Adam* "didn't fare much better than your TV series." He went at Davis's character, asking point blank about the entertainer's "fanatical desire for approval." In response to Davis's brag that he had done more than anyone for Civil Rights causes, Haley pressed, "How about Harry Belafonte and Sidney Poitier? Do you contribute more than they do to the cause?" And on Davis's social bearing and comportment, he questioned Davis's continued practice of conking his hair. "Have you ever wished that you weren't a Negro?"[23] What he pushed Davis into was not the kind of defensiveness that one might expect in response to these questions, but an honest, reflective, and roving set of comments on—as the Boyars would have put it—*The Story of a Negro in a White World.*

As they pertain to his then-recent autobiography, the revelations in the *Playboy* interview roll out along two axes. The first—tacitly—has to do with aspects that had been muddied or hidden in the book itself. This is not to say that there is always a huge distance between *Yes I Can* and the Haley interview. At certain points Davis drops huge chunks of direct *Yes I Can* prose into his conversation with Haley.[24] This is likely an example of folklorists' common observation that once a story has been told, it has been laid into narrative grooves that will tend not to vary in ensuing retellings. But in other respects, Davis's story here varied quite a lot. Looking back on his early days, Davis tells Haley,

> I wasn't thinking about nothing but *making* it, and then having a ball; wasn't thinking about *nothing* else. I didn't give a damn about no race cause. . . . I knew about the problems, but I just didn't care. I didn't care about nobody but me. I can't tell you the truth more honest than that.[25]

With some work, one might be able to dig this out from the final narrative of *Yes I Can*. But as the book collapses Davis's dawning 1960s consciousness of *injustice* (upon the preparation of the manuscript) with his earlier chafing against *personal injury* (in the Jim Crow period that is narrated), what a reader never quite hears is, "I didn't care about nobody but me." As Davis and the Boyars had worked to elaborate Davis's originary idea for *Yes I Can*—"If people could just know what it's like!"—their articulations of a Jim Crow world folded into a Civil Rights consciousness that partially concealed Davis's earlier outlook, even if the hyperindividuality of Davis's racial injury peeks through. The Haley interview clears these clouds away.

But the second, more significant axis has to do with Davis's political thinking, prodded by the urgency of the moment, by the shifting public language of race in 1966, and by Haley's insistent questioning. First, Davis offers something new for him, an expression of black *pride*. He had always cast his racial aspirations in terms of personal inclusion rather than in the collective principle denoted by the word "pride," and certainly not "power." In the late 1950s, Davis told Haley, he was

> confused and angry, and maybe a little guilty. . . . I wanted to commit myself, but I didn't know how or to what. So I talked to Harry and Sidney and Ossie, and finally I knew: I wanted to help my people. . . . And it's been a gas! This is a glorious time to be alive.
>
> HALEY: And to be a Negro?
> DAVIS: Right! That's something I never felt before; pride in our color and in our cause.[26]

Davis now describes "the obligation of being a Negro" as carrying "the banner of being proud."[27]

Injury and pride are two very different motivators, and in a general way they mark the outgoing and the incoming epochs in African American political life. Haley and Davis were taking up these questions in the shadow of the Civil Rights Act, in the wake of Watts, and at the dawn of Black Power. One faultline in the emergent politics of the mid-1960s is the philosophical rift between a continuing commitment to nonviolence and the more radical or revolutionary stance of the Nation of Islam or the Black Panther Party. Haley elicits from Davis the predictable defense of King: "I would give him my good eye. That's what I think of Dr. King." Then he asks about the revolutionaries who, in Haley's formulation, are "dedicated to 'getting whitey' and sabotaging 'the white power structure.'"[28]

Davis's take on this group begins as an equally predictable condemnation.

> They're living in a dreamworld. They think they're going to 'get Whitey' and take over the country. Well, I got news for them: They ain't going to get nobody or take over nothing! 'Cause whenever they get ready, right there is going to be the end of it. The Man will just open one eye and swat them like a gnat, and that will be that. They ain't made no razor *yet* that will stop an atomic bomb.[29]

Davis then—remarkably—launches into a brief discussion of black retaliation. He backs off very quickly upon Haley's questioning, but not before asserting, "You know what them cats should do who are so mad? Go down to Mississippi and kill them cats that killed them three civil rights workers [James Chaney, Michael Schwerner, and Andrew Goodman]." They should avenge the Birmingham church bombing, he argues, and avenge Viola Liuzzo, the white Civil Rights worker murdered in Selma. "Destroy the guy who has already proven to be your enemy. You know who it was that murdered Mrs. Liuzzo down in Alabama; they're out walking around. Go down there and wipe them out, you're so brave. When they bomb your church, bomb *their* church."[30]

Haley, unsure of how literally to take this, is incredulous: "Are you serious about bombing white churches?" "What I really mean," Davis replies, with a dose more caution but still very directly, "is take care of the bombers themselves . . . all those known murderers, the bombers and others, who are walking around free because segregationist juries wouldn't convict them." When Haley presses him on whether or not he is comfortable "taking the law into your own hands," Davis answers, "Yes . . . I'm for any kind of protest— including retaliatory violence against known killers who get off—as long as Negroes are denied the full rights that any other American enjoys.[31] "Are you predicting more riots like the one in Watts?," Haley asks. Anticipating the

Kerner Commission report that will come down the pike two years later, Davis unflinchingly replies,

> I'm predicting riots that would make Watts look like a Sunday-school picnic—unless we get to work fixing what *causes* them.... Riots are simply *violent* manifestations of what Martin Luther King is protesting *non-violently,* of what every black man in America is protesting.... Rioters are people who have no stake in their country, no stake in their city, no stake in their homes, no stake even in their own survival.[32]

While it is the question of nonviolence vs. revolutionary self-defense that will likely arrest one's attention here, this last comment points to a second, philosophical strand that runs deeper in American thought, that traces a longer arc in US political culture, and that will endure long into the post-Civil Rights years. This is a spectrum of interpretation that privileges individualized bigotry at one pole and systemic racism at the other. *Yes I Can* foregrounds isolated, transactional, anecdotal encounters with various "indignities" inflicted by doormen, hotel clerks, or sneering audience members rather than systemic relations of racialized power. With Haley, Davis thinks more broadly about black collectivity in relation to American democracy. Asked whether "enough is being done in Negro ghettos" to alleviate the kinds of conditions that lead to rioting, Davis scoffs,

> Baby, you got to be putting me on! They ain't even scratched the surface.... You know what always seems to happen after every riot? Immediately, committees are formed to find out why it happened, and they investigate, and they study, and finally they turn in a fat, reassuring report—full of all the standard sociological platitudes—recommending *further* study and investigation and urging 'better understanding between the white and black communities.'

He goes on to quote Malcolm X on the subject of a national system of oppression that he had left untouched and even unnamed in *Yes I Can* the year before: "The Negro's destiny is America's destiny as democracy. Malcolm X said it: 'As the black man walks, so shall all men walk.' Well, if the Negro falls, American democracy will fall, because all of the things it stands for will have been betrayed."[33] By 1966 *even Sammy Davis Jr.* was thinking in terms of systemic racism rather than the individualized prejudice and bigotry emphasized in texts like *An American Dilemma, To Secure These Rights, The Nature of Prejudice*—and *Yes I Can.*

Although he did not invent this perspective, in *An American Dilemma* (1944) Swedish sociologist Gunnar Myrdal had made himself the poster boy for a very particular brand of mid-century analysis that favored individualized "prejudice" over the broader structural, juridical, institutional, and historical elements of racism. The rise of European fascism and the later imperatives of the Cold War made the 1940s and 1950s a tough time for advancing an argument that *American democracy itself* was founded in racism, or that white supremacy undergirded the humanist project of the European Enlightenment. Diasporic writers like C. L. R. James and Frantz Fanon were making such arguments, of course, as had earlier American writers like W. E. B. Du Bois. But in mainstream American discourse—Hollywood, network television, glossy magazines—such arguments would have to wait. In the meantime, Myrdal and others would identify the misguided *individual* as the locus of unfortunate racism."[34] In popular white philosophy "this is a white man's country," Myrdal admitted, and the tentacles of this racialized thinking stretched broadly into economics, policy, and law.[35] But despite the structural breadth of racism's reach, "The American Negro problem is a problem in the heart of the American. It is there that the interracial tension has its focus. . . ." What Myrdal called the "American Dilemma" amounted to an "ever-raging conflict between, on the one hand, the valuations preserved on the general plane which we shall call the 'American Creed,' where the American thinks, talks, and acts under the influence of high national and Christian precepts, and, on the other hand, the valuations on specific planes of individual and group living, where personal and local interests [dominate]," along with specific "jealousies," considerations of "prestige and conformity," and miscellaneous "wants, impulses, and habits." The status of the Negro represented "the most glaring conflict in American conscience and the greatest unsolved task for American democracy."[36]

Myrdal thought the tenets of egalitarianism and democracy at the core of the "American Creed" to be extraordinarily deeply held. They were "conscious to everyone in American society," and all Americans, black and white, lived "under the spell of the great national suggestion" of equality.[37] Deviation from the ideal, then—the "Negro problem"—was "primarily a moral issue," a matter of confusion and misguidance, a question of "attitudes," never of power, oppression, or vested self-interest. What was needed was education and adjustment, not liberation. The "dilemma" itself was a result of cognitive dissonance, a "contradiction" in American attitudes, "a century-long lag of public morals," a grating at the daily violation of the "moralism and rationalism" of the

"American Creed."[38] While it may be the case that sometimes "mental contradictions are elaborated into theories and find their way into learned treatises and documents of state policy," still even the Jim Crow doctrine of separate but equal "belongs to the same category of systematized intellectual and moral *inconsistency.*"[39] "The Negro problem" is not properly the *Negro's* problem, but rather resides "in the minds of white Americans," and the nation's racial tensions represent a "moral struggle [that] goes on within people and not only between them."[40] As such, education is the key; and, crucially, "*an educational offensive against racial intolerance . . . has never seriously been attempted in America.*"[41]

A corollary to this understanding of prejudice in midcentury thought was the proposition that, if the fault lies with individuals, then the solution is to be found in institutions—the same institutions that Stokely Carmichael or H. Rap Brown would later identify as the very culprits. "Huge institutional structures like the church, the school, the university, the foundation, the trade union, the association generally, and, of course, the state," would be palliative, wrote Myrdal.

> It is true, as we shall find, that these institutional structures in their operation show an accommodation to local and temporary interests and prejudices— they could not be expected to do otherwise as they are made up of individuals with all their local and temporary characteristics. As institutions they are, however, devoted to certain broad ideals. It is in these institutions that the American Creed has its instruments: it plays upon them as on mighty organs. . . .

Myrdal highlighted *institutions* as the instruments through which "a constant pressure is brought to bear on race prejudice." Individuals have placed in institutions "their ideals of how the world rightly ought to be," he concluded. "The ideals thereby gain fortifications of power and influence in society. This is a theory of social self-healing that applies to the type of society we call democracy."[42]

While *An American Dilemma* is a book about contradiction, some uncomfortable contradictions are evident in Myrdal's own thinking. His analysis, not unlike Davis's in *Yes I Can* some twenty years later, contains signficant evidence of the very thing it is largely meant to deny. His use of phrases like "the average American" or "ordinary Americans," tacitly marked as *white,* carry the rebuttal to Myrdal's own argument, contrasting as they do with "the Negro." Such acknowledgments that whiteness is written deeply into the political culture at the basic level of the normative citizen raise questions about his central premise that individuals are prone to racism but institutions are not. Similarly, when Myrdal writes of "the failure of Reconstruction" rather than the *defeat* or *destruction* or *decimation* of Reconstruction, he replicates a longstanding white supremacist trope. Concealing white agency in the 1870s, it implies instead that the project of black governance was somehow inherently untenable. Such formulations—easily upended by a reading of Du Bois's *Black Reconstruction* (1935)—are symptomatic of a more general tendency on Myrdal's part to submerge white agency in *all* its forms, when it comes to black subjugation.[43] What he calls "prejudice" is not a question of power maintenance, but of error. The vocabulary that will later animate a book like Carmichael and Hamilton's *Black Power* is nowhere to be found in *An American Dilemma,* bereft of words like "oppression," "co-optation," "subordination," "authority," "policy," "system," "colony" or "colonialism," and also like "freedom," "liberation," and "struggle."

Myrdal's interpretation of the individualized core of "prejudice" was widely shared. It is a premise everywhere to be found in white writers' postwar commentary. Even *To Secure These Rights,* the report on racial injustice commissioned by Harry Truman in 1947, carries heavy traces of this kind of thinking. Since the report is concerned with national questions of legislation, policy, legal precepts and court rulings, and governance, its natural bias is toward the systemic rather than the singular in a way that is unusual for its moment. But although the report is painstaking in its delineation of oppressive legal regimes from housing to lynching, as a matter of fundamental philosophy *To Secure These Rights* falls back on the individual bigot as the basic unit of analysis and intervention. Commissioners articulated a broad aspiration "to strengthen the federal civil rights enforcement machinery" and to wage a national battle against prejudice on "legislative, executive, and judicial" fronts.[44] But even so, amid their fundamentally structural and historical accounting of racism in America, like Myrdal before them, the commission viewed racial injustices of all sorts primarily as "symptoms" that reflect "the ignorance and moral weaknesses of some of our people."[45] *To Secure These Rights* defines "discrimination" itself as "prejudice come to life"—not a *herrenvolk* or caste system of power relations, but a set of "individual abridgements," "foolish generalizations," "secret feelings of the social snob," "murderous impulses of the insanely prejudiced," stirred by fear, perhaps, but "sustained" chiefly by ignorance and therefore chiefly to be fought by education.[46] Here one might also think of the psychologized terms of

Kenneth and Mamie Clark's brief in *Brown v. Board of Education,* which became incorporated into the ruling itself: school segregation generates in African American children "a feeling of inferiority as to their status in the community that may affect their hearts and minds in a way unlikely ever to be undone."[47] Though a powerful plea for justice in its own right, the Clarks' "hearts and minds" formulation was well suited to a dominant discourse that favored the individual over the collective, psychology over structure.

It is no simple thing to pinpoint the timing of the shift in mainstream public discourse from the "bigotry-and-prejudice" model to the "power-and-oppression" model for understanding racialized relations, with its attendant assumptions about white agency in oppression and black agency in liberation. The retreat of the one argument and the advance of the other were halting and uneven. Today one still hears versions of the absolving argument that isolated bigots are the real problem. And conversely, the tenets of the structural interpretation, which focuses on white agency and vested interest in oppression, were nothing *new.* They can be traced backward in time from Carmichael and Malcolm, to Du Bois, to Ida B. Wells, to Frederick Douglass, and beyond. David Walker's *Appeal to the Colored Citizens of the World* had forcefully advanced the case as early as 1829:

> We, (coloured people) and our children are *brutes!!* and of course are, and *ought to be* SLAVES to the American people and their children forever!! to dig their mines and work their farms; and thus go on enriching them, from one generation to another with our *blood* and our *tears!!!!*[48]

If the ideas were longstanding, in mid-twentieth-century American discourse it was the words "black power" that threatened to destabilize and make obsolete any mainstream insistence that isolated ignoramuses posed the greatest danger or that education alone would prove the solution. This was so both because of popular attention to the phrase itself and to the emergent groups that used it, like the Black Panther Party. In a 1966 essay widely disseminated in pamphlet form by the A. Philip Randolph Institute and titled "Black Power and Coalition Politics," Bayard Rustin noted that the concept had already caused some serious rifts among Civil Rights leadership. "'Black power' is, of course, a somewhat nationalistic slogan," Rustin pointed out, "and its sudden rise to popularity among Negroes signifies a concomitant rise in nationalist sentiment (Malcolm X's autobiography is quoted nowadays in Grenada, Mississippi as well as in Harlem.)"[49] Carmichael and Charles V. Hamilton's *Black Power* (1967) presented the case in its most elaborate form.

It may well be that "individual whites acting against individual blacks" are part of the problem, Carmichael and Hamilton argued. But there are also "acts by the total white community against the total black community." The latter they termed "institutional racism," another name for "colonialism." "'Respectable' individuals can absolve themselves from individual blame," the pair wrote. "*They* would never plant a bomb in a church; *they* would never stone a black family." But when all is said and done, "there is no 'American dilemma' because black people in this country form a colony, and it is not in the interest of the colonial power to liberate them."[50] As for the promise of education, "the American educational system continues to reinforce the entrenched values of society," not redressing but actually exacerbating the extent to which "black people have been saddled with epithets."[51]

Rustin's passing reference to the bestselling *Autobiography of Malcolm X* is significant here. Although there were some important academic voices in the mix as the old liberal paradigm came under siege (Hamilton held a Ph.D. in political science from Chicago), for the most part the information industries preceded the knowledge industries onto this terrain. Black Studies had yet to be institutionalized and the curriculum was not only unapologetically but *unselfconsciously* white. In this moment Alex Haley's public intellectual work, not only the *Autobiography* but his *Playboy* interviews, was significant.[52] Mamie Till Bradley's insistence that the world see her son's brutalized corpse, and the coverage of the murder in *Look* and *Life;* coverage of the Woolworth sit-ins and the Freedom Rides by the growing "race beat" of the Associated Press; King's media strategy in Birmingham and Selma, and the nation's firsthand look at the snarling dogs of Southern law enforcement institutions on network television; serious, race-themed productions like Lorraine Hansberry's *A Raisin in the Sun;* and a raft of widely read books on race, including John Howard Griffin's *Black Like Me* (1961); James Baldwin's *The Fire Next Time* and LeRoi Jones's *Blues People* (1963); Charles Silberman's *Crisis in Black and White,* John Williams's *This Is My Country Too,* Martin Duberman's *In White America,* and Charles Grigg and Lewis Killian's *Racial Crisis in America* (1964); Kenneth Clark's *Dark Ghetto,* Claude Brown's *Manchild in the Promised Land,* and, as Rustin noted, *The Autobiography of Malcolm X* (all 1965)—this massive and multi-vocal output at once drew upon and added to a burgeoning Civil Rights "public" in the decade after *Brown.*

Texts and articulations like these helped to prepare the ground, if not for "black power" in every instance, at least for a structural, institutional analysis of racism's operations in the American setting. Even Claude Brown's *Manchild,* the highly idiosyncratic story of Brown's escape from two-bit hustling, violence, and the "shit plague" of drugs in Harlem, is cast as a *collective* portrait of "the first Northern urban generation of Negroes." It promised to study "their searching, their dreams, their sorrows, their small and futile rebellions, and their endless battle to establish their own place in America's greatest metropolis—and in America itself." As such, Brown's narrative remains keenly alive not only to the transactional prejudices of individual white people, but to the structural features of racism and the generalized "condition" of being black in America. When a kindly judge decides to give Brown and his wayward teenage friends a second chance after they have been caught breaking into an A&P, with a dead sociological eye the young man counters, "Man, you not givin' us another chance. You givin' us the same chance we had before."[53]

Mid-sixties ideas of structure and collectivity generated a truly withering heat in public discourse that the older prejudice-and-bigotry model could not fully withstand. Where Gunnar Myrdal had located a profound anti-racist *hope* in "institutional structures" like schools, the national labor assembly, and the legislature, such structures and collectivities were now highly suspect by definition. The most powerful and influential articulations of the emergent, more radical view were the already-mentioned *Autobiography* and *Black Power.* The *Autobiography* was something of a tug o' war between Malcolm X the black nationalist and his integrationist co-writer Alex Haley. Malcolm wanted his criminal past to be as spectacular as possible, as a way of highlighting the significance of his "rescue" by Elijah Muhammad and the Nation of Islam. Haley, for his part, wanted to highlight Malcolm's integrationist turn after the trip to Mecca, which he may have in fact have played up in the final revisions of the manuscript after Malcolm's death. But Malcolm's analysis and his ideas about collectivity shone through nonetheless. On his controversial (among whites) usage of the phrase "white devils," for instance, the *Autobiography* explains,

> Unless we call one white man, by name, a 'devil,' we are not speaking of any *individual* white man. We are speaking of the *collective* white man's *historical* record. We are speaking of the collective white man's cruelties, and evils, and greeds, that have seen him *act* like a devil toward the non-white man. Any intelligent, honest, objective person cannot fail to realize that this white man's slave trade, and his subsequent devilish actions are directly *responsible* for not only the *presence* of this black man in America, but also for the *condi-*

tion in which we find this black man here. You cannot find *one* black man, I do not care who he is, who has not been personally damaged in some way by the devilish acts of the collective white man.[54]

Likewise, Carmichael and Hamilton explicated "black power" as "a call for black people in this country to unite, to recognize their heritage, to build a sense of community. It is a call for black people to begin to define their own goals, to lead their own organizations and to support those organizations. It is a call to reject the racist institutions and values of this society."[55] The black power program that originated within SNCC "affirms that helping *individual* black people to solve their problems on an *individual* basis does little to alleviate the mass of black people." In a discussion of the 1966 housing wars in Cicero, Illinois, meanwhile, *Black Power* identified "white backlash" itself as "the embedded traditions of institutional racism being brought into the open and calling forth overt manifestations of individual racism." Cutting against the grain of a political culture that had long celebrated American genius in the realm of individual liberties, and perhaps never more so than during the Cold War, *Black Power* urged a recognition of "the ethnic basis of American politics as well as the power-oriented nature of American politics."[56] Say what you will about "individual liberties," the fact remains that Africans were enslaved, emancipated, and Jim Crowed *as a group*. True justice would not be brought by a politics that was not attuned to this.

By the end of the decade these ideas were everywhere. Dick Gregory even rendered this mode of analysis the stuff of stand-up comedy. "We don't dislike you," he told a mostly white audience,

> we hate your stinking white racist institutions. . . . We uptight with you because you're responsible for it. Not directly. Let me give you a better example: if you came by my house, and we was good friends, and you brought your little daughter with you, and my dog attacked your daughter, who you going to sue, my dog or me? Although I didn't bite her, right? But I'm responsible for that dog; you're responsible for this white racist system. Not that you're all racists, but you're responsible for the system because it's yours. . . . That's what we're saying, we're very uptight about your dog biting us, and we're going to stay uptight until either you change the dog or get into a position where he's going to bite you, too.[57]

And then there is Sammy Davis Jr. in his interview with Alex Haley— quoting Malcolm X, sweet as you please: "The Negro's destiny is America's destiny as democracy. Malcolm X said it: 'As the black man walks, so shall all men walk.' Well, if the Negro falls, American democracy will fall, because all of the things it stands for will have been betrayed."[58]

. . .

When it comes to the general understanding of racism and its workings in the United States, the before and after of 1966 marked a significant dividing line. Black Power was not synonymous or coeval with the structural, institutional mode of analysis. It was just one of the vehicles by which that analysis traveled. But travel it did, on both sides of the color line. Reporting for *New York Times Magazine* in August of 1967 Sol Stern warned, "What matters is that there are a thousand black people in the ghetto thinking privately what any Panther says out loud."[59] In the Kerner Commission Report, the federal government itself gave its imprimatur to this kind of structural analysis, not only in the famous warning that the nation was "moving toward two societies, one black, one white—separate and unequal," but in the fairly sympathetic reading it gave black radicalism. While white people might wish to seize on emancipation, advances in black literacy rates, the legal protections of constitutional amendments and Civil Rights legislation, and the growing black middle class as signs of "progress," the Commissioners warned,

> Negroes could point to the doctrine of white supremacy, its persistence after emancipation, and its influence on the definition of the place of Negroes in American life. They could point to their long fight for full citizenship when they had active opposition from most of the white population and little or no support from the government. They could see progress toward equality accompanied by bitter resistance. Perhaps most of all, they could feel the persistent, pervasive racism that kept them in inferior segregated schools, restricted them to ghettos, barred them from employment, provided double standards in courts of justice, inflicted bodily harm on their children, and blighted their lives with a sense of hopelessness and despair.[60]

Myrdal's "American Creed" sounded downright quaint after S.W.A.T. teams had deployed in response to the Black Panthers in Los Angeles, or amid the long hot summers of the later 1960s, as tanks prowled the streets of Newark and Detroit. The waning of the "prejudice" model and the ascendence of "institutional racism" as a mode of analysis did not signify consensus, certainly. Daniel Moynihan's screed against the "tangle of pathology" that was the African American family and his ancillary politics of personal responsibility would carry into American conservatism for decades to come, perhaps even defining the Reagan era.[61] And all sorts of faultlines split the engaged black public of the Freedom Struggle—integrationism vs. separatism, non-violence vs. militant and armed self-defense, strategic blueprints that prioritized the courts vs. those that took to the streets on behalf of economic justice and community control, black pride vs. assimilationism, North vs. South, and country vs. city. None of this is even to mention the generational, class, and gender outlooks that oriented African Americans so differently on questions of what justice could or should look like. But the general shift described here, from a 1940s rendition of the individual bigot as the main culprit to a late-1960s understanding of racism as entrenched *power* and as the work of institutions was not among these. This shift aptly describes an overall direction in mainstream *white* discourse—from Myrdal to Kerner— but not necessarily in African American discourse, which of course had noted the behavior and the power of collective whiteness and of white institutions all along.

But this faultline in the political culture is precisely where *Yes I Can* landed. The rhetorical and conceptual earthquake of "Black Power" is what separates *Yes I Can* from Davis's *Playboy* interview with Alex Haley a year later. The interpretive kernel of the debate was: do "attitudes" sustain the structures of white supremacy, or do structures sustain the attitudes? Indeed, do the institutional structures of racism render more or less inconsequential the mere "attitudes" of the individual bigot? Black radicals like Matthew Stelly were probably right that Black Power is what made *Yes I Can* so popular among white readers, promoting as it did an individualized, transactional account of the injuries of racism and of their selves, too. It is certainly its faith in something like an "American Creed" that makes the book read like such a bygone relic in the African American canon. As an accounting of race in America, *Yes I Can* was eclipsed almost the moment it appeared.

Ironically, of the entire trove of "race" books published in the United States in the decade between, say, *A Raisin in the Sun* and the *Kerner Commission Report*, the one that *Yes I Can* most resembles is *Black Like Me,* white writer John Howard Griffin's racial cross-dressing account of traveling the South as a black man. Both narratives locate racism in street-level interactions rather than systemic power relations. Both are aimed at jarring *white* readers out of their complacencies. And both authors rely rhetorically on their own exceptionalism as the key to accessing the reader's sense of outrage. Underneath the racial masquerade that is its method, *Black Like Me* is a tale of aggrieved *whiteness,* Griffin's outrage at his *own* treatment.[62] Just so, *Yes I*

Can bristles at the indignities dished out to someone who, in his star potential, is rhetorically positioned as deserving better. In this, both books strangely echo Solomon Northrop's *Twelve Years a Slave* (1853), an abolitionist narrative that relies for its sense of outrage upon the fact that Northrop was properly a *free-born* man from the North who had been kidnapped and unjustly pressed into slavery, and was therefore singularly undeserving of this cruel lot.

As the emergent political universe of Black Power altered the context of *Yes I Can* between 1965 and 1967, it lent it new meaning to that text and reestablished how Sammy Davis Jr. was widely *figured* as a public icon. By 1967 Davis seemed to many like one of "those token Negroes—absorbed into a white mass" that Carmichael wrote about, "of no value to the remaining black masses. They become meaningless show-pieces for a conscience-soothed white society."[63] Neither the turn in Davis's thinking—as evidenced in the Haley interview—nor his turn toward a black aesthetic in hairstyle and dress in the later 1960s could entirely dislodge that common perception. In a 1969 interview with Muhammad Ali, when Davis was guesting for a week on *The Mike Douglas Show,* the two got into a conversation about black separatism. After laying out the basis of his thinking, Ali observed, "You have the dashiki on and the African beads and a nice beautiful Afro—you must have to admit, and I know you're an intelligent man, well loved by people—all people—you have to admit that you yourself wasn't always thinking like this." As Davis struggled to get his head around the separatist argument—"I'm not for it, but I'm not opposed"—Ali only offered, with a wry smile, "You waiting to see which side wins."[64] Davis's personal revolution, the one that had absorbed him for six hundred pages in *Yes I Can,* may have been won. But as Ali acknowledged, another, very different revolution was underway.

SEVEN

"The Skin Commits You"

CIVIL RIGHTS ITINERARY

JOEY BISHOP: Okay, Sam, you're free now to do anything you like.

SAMMY DAVIS JR.: What do you mean, I'm free? All of a sudden *you're* gonna do it? Lincoln freed me.

—RAT PACK PERFORMANCE, C. 1960

Look at what CBS TV did recently! They put on some old Fred Astaire reruns rather than a new network special featuring someone such as Harry Belafonte or Lena Horne. I guess they were worried about Southern objections if they headlined a Negro. I don't know why. The Negro, after all, is part of America.

—SAMMY DAVIS JR.

DAVIS'S TORTURED PATH THROUGH THE CIVIL RIGHTS era is evocatively conveyed in a pair of competing assessments. One, written over a period of years following Davis's death, comes from Matthew Stelly, a self-described Pan-Africanist and radical sociologist, whose *Feets, Don't Fail Me Now: Sammy Davis, Jr. and the Issue of "Role Conflict"* castigated Davis as a "house negro" and "King of the Minstrels." In the other corner is a wary FBI file, whose field notes tracked Davis from SCLC and NAACP events in the 1950s, to Selma, to the Poor People's Campaign, to the pages of *Muhammad Speaks* and *The Daily Worker,* ever fretting about the entertainer's sympathy toward black radicals, including the Black Panther Party and Angela Davis. The contradiction *itself* is the compelling object of study here. It illuminates how Davis navigated the politics of blackness across the Civil Rights years, and how the fraught racial discourse of the time rendered him a text to be closely read and deciphered on all sides, everywhere he went.

Stelly's book purports to be a sociological study of "role conflict," internalized pressures caused by the "incompatible demands placed on a person"—in this instance, the black psychic economy as it is buffeted by the racialized demands of America's white culture industries. Finally, however, *Feets, Don't Fail Me Now* reads as an unfiltered anti-Davis screed from the standpoint of black separatism and pride.[1] Stelly critiques virtually every dimension of Davis's biography and comportment, from his assimilationist manner, to his choice of white lovers, to his "white"-styled patterns of conspicuous consumption, to the old-school "coon," "minstrel," "house Negro," and "Oreo" elements of his stage act, to the servile bow and scrape of the Hollywood roles he accepted. *Yes I Can,* Stelly snipes, is "Sammy's answer to the question, 'can you kiss the white man's ass no matter what he asks you to do?'" (14) Stelly follows the *Yes I Can* narrative fairly closely, annotating and offering commentary along the way. He nurses a very special brand of contempt for Davis's conversion to Judaism, a capitulation to a sworn white enemy who had long "controlled" the culture industries. "Had Sammy been in tune with his own Africanity, he would have had all the things that he was looking for Judaism to provide him." Worse still, to Stelly, "a lot of Hebrews made money off of Sammy's self-hate" (78). Stelly does acknowledge Davis's once-in-a-generation level of raw talent, but ultimately this only makes the case all the more damning, as Davis's undeniable industry value and success both denote the element of missed political opportunity and unrealized *power* that characterized his rise to the heights of the entertainment world. The entertainer, Stelly writes unsparingly, "apparently thought that if you worked hard and pleased the white men, you became LESS of a nigger as time passed. But that ain't how it works. Not in America, at least." (142)

Matthew Stelly was a singular sort of figure—an organizer who founded a Pan-African Congress chapter in Omaha, Nebraska; a journalist and radical sociologist who claimed to have written over 2,500 articles—but every facet of his critique of Davis as an Uncle Tom engaged with a lexicon, a logic, and a set of idioms from the culture at large, anti-Semitism included. His brief against Davis, if not necessarily "representative" of anything in particular, does speak to a common currency of racial ideas. As one activist, identified by Davis as a "lieutenant" of Maulana Karenga, had told Davis when the two met in the late 1960s, "you *is* black, but you don't *be* black."[2]

This is not exactly how J. Edgar Hoover was looking at things, meanwhile. That the FBI looked upon Martin Luther King Jr. as "the most dangerous Negro" in America is well known, but *Sammy Davis Jr.?* Heavily redacted FBI field notes and Bureau forms and summaries place Davis in proximity to the Congress of Racial Equality, the NAACP, and the SCLC. They note his participation in the "Pilgrimage for Prayer" and the "special freedom train to attend the ceremonies for civil rights legislation"—of particular interest, perhaps, because this had been written up in the *New York Post* by Barry Gray, a longtime foe of McCarthyism. They mark his work among "Noted Californians" supporting the "Southern Conference Educational Fund." They follow his invitation to participate in a CBS television discussion of "Social Problems of Our Time" in 1960, and also his disinvitation for "questionable morals" (undoubtedly the May Britt marriage). They place him at the "rally for freedom" in support of the Birmingham movement and at the March on Washington in 1963. They establish his signature on a "two-page resolution captioned 'The Time Is Now,'" calling for an industry-wide crusade against discrimination in entertainment; they check the NAACP announcement that Davis, Lena Horne, and Steve Allen would co-chair "a special civil rights television program to be aired nationwide on 5/14/64"; they track his movements between March 21 and 24, 1965, as he joined "other entertainers at the conclusion of the march at Montgomery." They verify that "as of 8/25/65, 'Golden Boy,' a musical comedy [sic] starring Sammy Davis Jr. was billed at the Majestic Theater." They document his involvement in "Christmas for Mississippi" and in the protests against the shooting of James Meredith. In a file on "Communist Infiltration of the SCLC," they (comically) write up Davis's role as "Vice President and Treasurer of the Will Master Trio," and his funneling of $16,900 to the SCLC. They monitor his remarks at a benefit in Oakland, that "all races must learn to live together in a peaceful manner"; they record his visit to Resurrection City, and his delivering a check to Ralph Abernathy representing "the proceeds of a benefit performance of 'Golden Boy' given by Davis in Chicago, Ill."; they substantiate his funding of a film about the Black Panthers, as he was "reportedly very sympathetic toward the BPP as he had been very impressed with the film concerning one Fred, believed to be Fred Hampton."[3]

In the course of their monitoring of King, the FBI discovered that he had "discussed the financial status of the SCLC and a means by which additional funds could be obtained. King indicated that he wanted a benefit to be held at Madison Square Garden in NYC, and that he would contact Sammy Davis, Jr...."[4] One detailed summary, dated August 10, 1972, cites "'The Daily World,' a communist publication," reporting that "an all-star show had raised $38,000 for the Angela Davis defense fund. It noted that Sammy Davis, Jr., told the crowd of 6,500 that he wears a 'Free Angela' button because he shares 'her blackness.'" The summary report goes on to note that "while he does not necessarily share the political convictions of Angela Davis, he supports her because she is a black woman."[5]

For the most part these notes say more about the Hoover FBI and the organization's own outlook on race in general and Civil Rights in particular than they do about the subject of their inquiries. But their Davis file does also document the Nazis, "Storm Troopers," and others who "objected to the forthcoming marriage of caucasian [sic] May Britt and Negro entertainer Sammy Davis, Jr." It also includes white supremacist oratory and reportage indicating that Davis's conversion to Judaism was "a publicity stunt, as a Negro could not belong to any social group of Jews."[6] Clippings gathered in the file include an article on Davis's contribution to a Black Cultural Center in Chicago, and an account of his "kidnapping" in Las Vegas by "a pair of tough Chicago gangsters" in relation to the effort to warn Davis away from "the blonde actress" Kim Novak.[7]

One especially tantalizing memorandum in the file, a communication to the Johnson White House dated October 17, 1966, looks like this:

Honorable Melvin Watson
Special Assistant to the President
The White House
Washington, D.C.

Dear Mr. Watson,

███████████████████ has requested an FBI name check concerning Sammy Davis, Jr. the noted Negro singer. Mr. Davis has not been the subject of an investigation by the FBI. However, our files reveal the following information concerning him.

███
██
██
███
██
██
███
██
███

The fingerprint files of the Identification Division of the FBI contain no arrest data identifiable with Mr. Davis. . . .

Whatever lies underneath the heavy black masking of the extensive redactions, it likely did not match Matthew Stelly's or Maulana Karenga's conclusions.[8]

From Davis's rise to national stardom in the early 1950s up to his famed appearances on *All in the Family* and at the Republican National Convention in the early 1970s, both his work and his image were subject to a complicated series of historical undertows and riptides. As we have seen, *Yes I Can* articulated a brand of black cultural politics that was to be submerged almost immediately by Black Power and its correlates. But just so, Davis's entire career as a performer sat astride an immense tectonic divide in the nation's social and cultural history. The practices and conditions characterizing the cultural industries were in flux. Public assumptions regarding "respectability," racial "dignity," and comportment were contested and rapidly changing. The landscape of opportunity and representation for black entertainers was expanding, as was the range of cultural imagery. And the kinds of political battles that represented the real fray in the broadcast industries and in Hollywood were gradually shifting from a politics of mere inclusion to a more varied, truthful, and honorable representation. One thinks here of Diahann Carroll's off-camera battles with NBC over the *framing* of race and racism in *Julia* (1968–1971), for instance. This would have been unthinkable just a decade earlier, when Harry Belafonte and others were fighting just to get some black talent onto the screen.[9] This was all in a context, too, as noted in the previous chapter, when national discourse was shifting its attentions from "bigotry" to "racism." Americans were slowly pivoting away from the most overt and individualized acts of discrimination or hatred to a more systemic understanding that *institutions* reproduce and sustain inequalities, that even well-intentioned people may advance harmful or degrading ideas, that there is such a thing as *slow* or *quiet* or *subtle violence*.

Davis's vulnerabilities in this were many. Some had to do with his vaudeville background and the simple passage of time, which is to say they were generational in the broadest sense. That he was a tap dancer, for instance, carried a completely different meaning in 1966 than it had in 1946. So did his hitching his star to Sinatra and the American standard rather than to rhythm and blues and its derivative, rock and roll. His songbook made a different kind of sense after Chuck Berry's "Maybellene" (1955), Little Richard's "Tutti Frutti" (1956), or the Impressions' "People Get Ready" (1965) than it had before them. But he also carried vulnerabilities into the Civil Rights era that were generational in a more narrowly African American sense.

Davis's assimilationism was certainly not the only path in the business. Paul Robeson had lit a different way in the Popular Front era of the 1930s, and even some of Davis's rough contemporaries like Hazel Scott, Ossie Davis, Ruby Dee, and Harry Belafonte were finding politically alert ways to follow. But neither was Davis altogether unusual among his generation for the kinds of accommodations he made with certain aspects of a blatantly racist culture. Such a separate peace would sit less and less well with younger African Americans, as the SCLC and the NAACP's brand of protest gave way to an increasingly radical SNCC and the Black Panthers. Many of Davis's practices as an entertainer were aging poorly, coming to seem relics of a bygone era. But the cultural conversation around those practices was also evolving very dramatically. As Sidney Poitier wrote,

> Sammy Davis Jr., Duke Ellington, Count Basie, Lena Horne, Sidney Poitier—we weren't leading the charge. We weren't at the forefront, getting our heads cracked open, though our careers were a reflection of what was possible when attention *was* paid. Twenty-five years earlier it hadn't been widely expected, with opportunities so meager, that blacks could be scientists, statesmen, artists. Every time I stepped out, I felt the responsibility to do whatever I could to make pending success seem a natural expectation.[10]

Davis had argued exactly this in *Yes I Can*. But this brand of "struggle" was counting for less and less as time passed and as heads *were* getting cracked open. And this elder generation's version of "what was possible" was passed by in emergent codes of political conduct, social analysis, and cultural interpretation. As Lena Horne acknowledged in 1965, "A new generation was taking over. And they were not interested in symbols." All of the black "firsts" of her generation—"first glamor girl, first baseball player, first this-and-that-and-the-other"—had "reached the end of our usefulness. We were not symbols of the approaching rapprochement between the races. We were sops, tokens, buy-offs for the white race's conscience."[11] To a generation that had begun sitting in for equal rights, Davis's politics would always seem a little hat-in-hand. Even if he did arouse the suspicions of the FBI.

CELEBRITY AS MOVEMENT CAPITAL

"You'll never know what you and Jackie [Robinson] and Roy [Campanella] did to make it possible to do my job," Martin Luther King Jr. once told Dodger pitcher Don Newcomb.[12] A media theorist in his own right, King recognized the power of sports, the arts, and other popular cultural forms to win hearts and minds in the long struggle to bend the arc of history toward justice. In a letter to Davis in 1961, upon the launch of Oscar Brown Jr.'s (unsuccessful) bid to gain backing for his play *Kicks and Co.,* King wrote, "rarely has there come upon the American scene a work which so perceptively mirrors the conflict of soul, the moral choices that confront our people, both Negro and white, in these fateful times. And yet a work which is at the same time, so light of touch, entertaining—and thereby all the more persuasive." *Kicks* told the story of a college student named Ernest Black, and his dueling with an envoy of Satan (Mr. Kicks) over the politics of desegregation. "Art can move and alter people in subtle ways," King wrote to Davis,

> because, like love, it speaks through and to the heart. This young man's work will . . . affect the conscience of vast numbers with the moral force and vigor of our young people. And coming as it does from a source so eminently influential, the Broadway theatre, and an actor of such stature as yourself, it will be both an inspiration and sustenance to us all.[13]

The record of a politicized art on behalf of Civil Rights was long established, even if a Broadway run of *Kicks and Co.* never did pan out. Billie

Holiday's recording of "Strange Fruit," Paul Robeson's "What Is America to Me?," and Josh White's folk rendition of the Langston Hughes poem "Freedom's Road" had all lifted a radical artistic voice on behalf of racial justice. Prewar activists like Robeson and actor Canada Lee passed the mantel to Harry Belafonte and others, even as the Cold War and McCarthyism scorched the old, Popular Front left. But a rising generation was reforging a Civil Rights public, and the 1960s saw a veritable explosion of politically charged, freedom-themed cultural work. These included Sam Cooke's ballad of promise, "A Change Is Gonna Come"; Nina Simone's haunting cabaret epic "Mississippi Goddam"; Odetta's repurposing of the folk repertoire—field hollers, slave songs, work songs—as instruments of education in pre-Black Studies years; and sacred and secular anthems like the Impressions' "Move On Up," James Brown's "Say It Loud—I'm Black and I'm Proud," or Aretha Franklin's "Respect." Hollywood, though problematic even on its best days, as James Baldwin constantly pointed out, was changing the face of American empathy and understanding in films like *The Defiant Ones, Lilies of the Field, Nothing But a Man,* or *In the Heat of the Night.* And network television— with plenty of prodding on the part of stars like Belafonte and Carroll—was making some room for African American actors, including starring roles in primetime series like *I Spy* and *Julia.* And then of course there was the more radical work of the Umbra Workshop, the Harlem Writers Guild, LeRoi Jones (Amiri Baraka), Nikki Giovanni, or the Last Poets.

Davis's artistic work is rarely thought of in quite these terms, even though he held some elaborate theories about how to crack the codes of racial casting in TV and film and despite some of the projects examined earlier. He had worked too hard making himself "safe" to white audiences to be thought of as an oppositional force, either by his own peers or by the generation coming up. It is also true, however, that because of his longevity as a performer in the public eye and because of his ubiquity as he crossed from night clubs, to recording, to Broadway, and to Hollywood and network TV, he was among the most famous African Americans in the world. And so he was an indispensable ally to King and the SCLC, to the Urban League, to the NAACP, and even to SNCC, who all recognized the power and potential of sheer *celebrity* as an asset to the movement, quite aside from artistic messaging.

"Not very long ago," King wrote to Davis after a Carnegie Hall benefit in 1961, "it was customary for Negro artists to hold themselves aloof from the struggle for equality, in the belief that the example of this personal success was in itself a contribution, in that it helped to disprove the myth of Negro inferiority—which indeed it did." King commended Davis, along with "giants like Harry Belafonte, Sidney Poitier, [and] Mahalia Jackson," as people who were not "content to merely identify with the struggle," but actively participated "as artists and as citizens, adding the weight of their enormous prestige and thus helping to move the struggle forward." Who can "measure the impact, the inspirational effect upon the millions of Negroes" after learning of such involvement by "one of their idols . . .?" The impact on white viewers and bystanders was invaluable, too.[14] As Davis himself put it to Alex Haley, "if you're privileged to be a personality, there's the responsibility of what new image of the Negro do you project when you're reaching all them mass audiences in movie theaters and on national television. . . . Every night I do my act, I like to think I change at least a few more white people's way of thinking about Negro people."[15] In this sense, the image of "safeness" that Davis had cultivated was an asset to the very movement that often derided it. Over time, King's command to Belafonte, "Get Sammy," became a familiar refrain whenever the SCLC needed to raise money in a hurry. After Davis's immensely successful benefit at Carnegie Hall with Sinatra, Dr. King paid Davis a visit to talk about future events for the SCLC. "I'm gonna call on you again," he promised, to which Davis replied, "If you need me, you've got me. Only I ain't comin' down South. I'll do all the benefits you want—in the North."[16]

Davis's direct work on behalf of Civil Rights causes and organizations began as early as 1957, when he participated in the "Prayer Pilgrimage to Freedom" and, along with *Mr. Wonderful* cast members, attended a "Stars for Freedom" rally at Madison Square Garden. Ruby Dee misremembers the train ride to the March on Washington as "the first time that Sammy Davis Jr. was among us." The historical record places Davis at Civil Rights events years before that, including events that Dee attended alongside him. But she does recall that on that occasion, "we got a chance to talk about why it was so important for people like us in show business to take part in demonstrations and so forth. He was well informed and genuinely concerned."[17] "Do we want to keep on living in a 'snake pit' for the rest of our lives?" Davis asked in a 1957 promotional flyer, "Why I'm Backing the Chicago Urban League," in advance of a Civic Opera event. "I take my responsibility as a Negro and as a citizen very seriously. I believe in fighting for what is right, for all men, everywhere."[18]

It was also during these early years of mobilization, just as the Montgomery Bus Boycott was making a national figure of a young Martin Luther King Jr., that Davis himself began to be covered in the press in something like a Civil

Rights frame. "There's a tremendous pressure on a Negro entertainer who makes it," he told the *New York Post* in a March 1956 conversation about segregation. "The public is split down the middle—part black, part white. You have to walk a tightrope." The *Post's* biographical sketch for the piece noted that when he was in his teens, Davis had his nose "permanently reshaped by a gang of New York toughs who beat and kicked him because he had dated a girl 'out of his territory.'"[19] (We know what is meant by this.) The following year, progressive writer Barry Gray reported for the *Post* on "several bigoted hotel operators" in a Long Island resort town, who "gave lame excuses about being 'fully booked' when they learned Sammy wanted to stay overnight. Until now, this story has never been told." The news here, of course, is that this sort of thing was *becoming* news. "Sammy had no desire to become a martyr, or singled out," Gray wrote. "He made the long trip home with me, his humor never leaving him, fully cognizant of what had happened, yet urging all about him to never lose heart.... Sammy led the way and proved that being human was a quality one felt across the footlights."[20]

Later that year, days after police had escorted the Little Rock Nine into Central High against the wishes of the segregation-forever crowd, Arkansas Governor Orval Faubus included, Davis got into a well-publicized scrap with Louis Armstrong over Armstrong's continued use of the word "darky" in the song "Mississippi Mud," and for performing before segregated audiences. Challenging Armstrong's credentials as a spokesperson for "the Negro people in the Little Rock integration struggle," Davis insisted, "You cannot voice an opinion about a situation which is basically discrimination, integration, etc. and then go out and appear before segregated audiences."[21] Asked whether he had played before segregated audiences himself, Davis drew a distinction: "Yes, before I became a headliner. Yes, I had no choice. It was a financial situation where if you wanted to eat you had to perform before segregated audiences." But once he commanded a headliner's salary, "I decided then and there ... that I would not ever perform in an audience where my people could not come and see me."[22] Davis—like Armstrong, ironically—would long struggle to establish his own Civil Rights credentials in certain circles. But these early mentions are significant in a press context where, amid events in Montgomery and Little Rock, Civil Rights activism was just beginning to emerge as a cohesive national story.

Davis's own activism begins here, capitalizing on his *Mr. Wonderful* fame. Historian Emilie Raymond numbers Davis among the "leading six" celebrities—with Belafonte, Poitier, Ossie Davis, Ruby Dee, and Dick

Gregory—who contributed to the movement's popular mobilization and financial infrastructure, and to the building of an interracial coalition. These stars circulated generative "Dear Friend" letters and arranged myriad special screenings, concerts, house parties, and VIP parties, not to mention straight-up check-writing, which Davis in fact did more of than any other single individual. Davis raised an estimated $750,000 for the movement (nearly $6.5 million in today's dollars).[23] With or without a credit like *Kicks and Co.,* Davis had extraordinary reach in the culture: in addition to his best-selling book and his popularity on stage and screen, he owned the film company Trace-Mark Productions, two music publishing firms, a recording company that released through Reprise Records (Sinatra's label), and a management company. By the height of the Movement years Davis was not merely a star, in other words, he ran an entertainment empire. And though he became legendary in later years for financial woes born of his own extravagance and some mismanagement and outright theft on the part of his team, he had a lot more than just his celebrity to put on the line. "A man don't just lay around and not contribute something to the society he lives in," Davis told Alex Haley, noting that "maybe half or more" of his significant charitable contri-butions went to Civil Rights groups. As far as Belafonte was concerned, "People tuned in to Sammy. If you told people, 'Sammy Davis Jr., will be at this or that benefit,' you got more people coming."[24]

Within a few years after the Montgomery bus boycott, a piece in the *Pittsburgh Courier* credited Davis with "more than 200 benefits a year, aside from his almost impossible professional schedule," applauding Davis's ability to keep an audience "enthralled" with a ninety-minute act even after a long night of speeches at an NAACP event in Detroit.[25] The numerical claim might not withstand full scrutiny, but the basic principle was important and widely noted. The 1957 "Prayer Pilgrimage" drew over 30,000 people, and according to Belafonte it was here that King first recognized Davis's rapport with whites as an asset for the movement. Immediately after, the NAACP, too, approached Davis to lead a life membership drive on the organization's behalf. "We artists have set an inspiring example of tearing down race barri-ers in our own field," Davis commented. "We must put our time, our money, our whole-hearted efforts on the line with our conscience." The following year he did seven nights at the Apollo Theater to benefit the NAACP, for which the *Chicago Defender* gave him a "public salute" as "the top of the stars" aiding the cause.[26] Ensuing years found Davis traveling from Urban League galas in Chicago to Freedom Ride rallies in Los Angeles to

Rat Pack-sponsored benefits at Carnegie Hall to membership drives in Beverly Hills. "I'll work for the NAACP any time, any place," he told the *Courier*. Through the early Civil Rights years Davis appeared alongside an endless and varied group of celebrities at political benefits: Dizzy Gillespie, Cannonball Adderly, Frank Sinatra and Peter Lawford, Dick Gregory, Nipsey Russell, Mahalia Jackson, the Count Basie Orchestra, Tony Bennett, Carmen McRae, Charlton Heston, and Johnny Mathis, among others.[27]

The movement gathered momentum and won new adherents as events rolled on from Montgomery to Little Rock to Greensboro to Birmingham, from local boycotts to national sit-ins and inter-state Freedom Rides, and from black churches to college campuses. But 1963 marked an inflection point. "Almost one thousand cities were engulfed in civil turmoil," as King himself wrote in "The Negro Revolution—Why 1963?"[28] In addressing the question, "why did a thousand cities shudder?" King explicated the revolutionary compound of raised expectations and dashed hopes that had characterized the post-*Brown* years. The phrase "'with all deliberate speed' did not mean that another century would be allowed to unfold before we released Negro children from the narrow pigeonhole of the segregated schools," he wrote, and yet "statistics make it abundantly clear that the segregationists of the South remained undefeated by the [*Brown*] decision." African Americans' "deep disillusion" was located in the "contrasting emotions at the time of the decision and during the nine years that followed"—the "elation" and "despair" packed into the dashed promise of desegregation after *Brown*. Add to this the bracing global example of decolonization and the broad "recognition that one hundred years had passed since emancipation." Black America was a tinderbox by the time of the Birmingham campaign, when King made his famous moral call to action from jail: "We know through painful experience that freedom is never voluntarily given by the oppressor; it must be demanded by the oppressed. . . . We have waited for more than 340 years for our constitutional and God-given rights."[29]

Washington, wrote King, "is a city of spectacles"; and 1963 was chosen to witness the greatest spectacle of them all.[30] By the time the March on Washington for Jobs and Freedom was being planned in 1963, Davis was all in. He famously cut a check for $20,000 at a fundraising reception held by Burt and Norma Lancaster, matching the reception total. He later pledged one week's salary from the Sands. Amid the continuing popular perception that he had abandoned the black community, *Jet* quoted Davis in his own defense: "This should prove once and for all that my leader is your leader."[31] Davis also headlined fundraisers for the March, helping to gather star power like Marian Anderson, Joe Louis, James Baldwin, Ray Charles, Gene Kelly, Jerry Lewis, Johnny Carson, and the Rat Pack. Although it never fully panned out, the "Salute to Freedom," an "integrated variety show before a non-segregated audience" at the Birmingham Civic Auditorium, was meant to kick off a series of similar events in twenty-one cities across the South. Planned for the run-up to the March on Washington and bringing together a wide range of Civil Rights groups, the "Salute to Freedom" was conceived not only as a fundraiser, but as a Civil Rights *action*. The hope in Birmingham, said Reverend A. D. King, Martin's brother, was to "set the pattern for other cities; if Birmingham breaks the segregation barrier, others will fall."[32]

In August, Davis attended the March itself as a member of the Arts Group anointed by King, an interracial assemblage that included white stars like Burt Lancaster, Marlon Brando, Tony Curtis, and Charlton Heston alongside Belafonte, Davis, Eartha Kitt, Lena Horne, and Ruby Dee. The high-profile participation of entertainers, and especially of movie stars, was a key part of his overall media strategy. According to one of his aides, Clarence Jones, King felt that motion picture personalities "could give his moral crusade a certain degree of authenticity and support from the mainstream media."[33] The idea was not only to harness the white public's adoration of these figures on behalf of the cause, but to create a social portrait of civic engagement around racial justice issues that would be made legible in the very familiarity of its participants. Lena Horne's recording of "Now" soon after the march was a poignant embodiment of precisely this principle, and a nice analogue to Davis's own cross-over appeal in Civil Rights contexts. Set to the traditional Jewish tune of "Hava Nagilah," "Now" is an anthem of political urgency sung both *from* and *to* a multiracial Civil Rights public.

> Now is the moment . . .
> call me naïve
> still I believe
> We're created free and equal[34]

There are reasons to be wary of our standard, retrospective March on Washington narratives. For one thing, in memory where are all the racist nay-sayers? The iconicity of this extraordinary day pulls Americans to misremember the temper of the time. If King appears on the side of "the good" in our national memory, in August 1963 he was still maligned and feared as a menacing outlaw in some quarters. An FBI field operative wrote on that very day that King was "the most dangerous Negro in America." Davis's own experience reveals as much: Robert Kennedy had tried to warn Davis away from the March for his own safety. Because of the ongoing controversies around his interracial marriage, the Attorney General had discovered Davis's name on the White Citizens Council's "Ten Most Wanted" list and was unsure of the DOJ's ability to protect him.[35] If the March has become in collective memory an emblem of national consensus on racial justice, it certainly was not that at the time.

The centrality of the March to the Civil Rights imaginary also tends to suggest a Great Man theory of the movement, enshrining King on the steps of the Lincoln Memorial in a way that occludes the many nameless activists, especially women, who saw to the logistics of this momentous mass enterprise just as they saw to the street-level tactics of the liberation struggle. Overemphasis on a few lines from the day's most famous speech draws us away from the *local*, which is precisely where we need to be in understanding the mass mobilization. The March, and the Movement, were not mobilized on the National Mall, but in barbershops, beauty parlors, pool halls, union halls and organization field offices, in clapboard churches with ministers whose names we do not know and whose congregants were often moved by the women of the church anyway.[36] And besides, as Jeanne Theoharis reminds, in remembering the March we tend to misremember King himself. The "I have a dream" moment—"the content of our character"—not only eclipses in national memory the far more radical positions that King took up in ensuing years, but even those that he had articulated on the very day of the March itself. The speech, "one of the most celebrated in American history," writes Theoharis,

> is largely known for its ending. Forgotten is the beginning, where King laid out how America had given Black people a 'bad check.' The country had 'defaulted on this promissory note insofar as her citizens of color are concerned,' and so they had come to Washington to collect on a debt stemming from generations of economic exploitation and rights abridgement. Crucial to King's vision at the march was the idea that Black people were owed restitution by the nation and had come to claim their rightful payment.[37]

In enshrining "I have a dream" in our now annual celebrations, we have smoothed the jagged edges and the sharpest critical pronouncements of the moment.

These caveats notwithstanding, however, King was not wrong in his assessment of the March's extraordinary accomplishment. "Normally Negro activities are the object of attention in the press only when they are likely to lead to some dramatic outbreak," he wrote. "The March was the first organized Negro operation which was accorded respect and coverage commensurate with its importance. . . . Millions of white Americans, for the first time, had a clear, long look at Negroes engaged in serious occupation."[38] For Davis, whose Movement assignment was to reach moderates on the other side of the color line, the March marked something of a turning point. Looking back in *Hollywood in a Suitcase* (1980), Davis recounted the significance of the day this way:

> It was an exercise in solidarity which was not trying to push the President into anything but to back him in the type of reforms and changes he had in mind. We all felt confident that, for perhaps the first time, it was really worth putting ourselves on the line. The march came just about a hundred years after the emancipation proclamation, and Kennedy said, 'These recent months . . . have seen the decisive recognition by a major part of our society that all our citizens are entitled to full membership in the national community.' It was strange that, a century after the proclamation itself, this kind of thing still needed to be said. But it did, and it was, and we were very happy to hear it.

The celebrities of the Arts Group issued their own statement: "All forms of racial segregation are injurious to the arts of the nation." As Davis recalled, "It seems obvious now, but then it was rather daring."[39]

Davis places a good deal more emphasis on President Kennedy here than most recollections of the March on Washington do. Kennedy had of course announced himself an ally in the fight, arguing before Congress earlier in the summer that, "In this year of the Emancipation Centennial, justice requires us to insure [sic] the blessings of liberty for all Americans and their posterity—not merely for reasons of economic efficiency, world diplomacy and domestic tranquility—but, above all, because it is right."[40] But the president was not an unalloyed fan of the March. He had attempted to dissuade King in June, complaining that the proposed March was "ill-timed" (to which King replied that, in his experience, all direct action was "ill-timed").[41] Davis's foregrounding of Kennedy in his own recollection may have had to do with his complicated feelings about the president, now tangled up in emotions around the assassination. Kennedy had of course snubbed him and Britt by disinviting them to the inaugural. This wound was reopened in early

1963 when Kennedy tried to keep the interracial couple out of all photographs at a Lincoln's Birthday event. (Commented *Jet:* "To Sammy and May Britt—no pics of you, but everybody knew you were there. Great show and you all have so much charm and dignity.")[42] There was never an opportunity to mend fences on this, as Kennedy was assassinated just three months after the March. Davis's big "Stars for Freedom" spectacular in Santa Monica had to be postponed for the funeral.[43] In honoring Kennedy in his rendition of the March, then, Davis may have been doing some of his own emotional housekeeping. But in characterizing the motives of the multitudes at the March as "not trying to push the President . . . but to back him," Davis was also expressing something important in his own politics, as we have seen. To be "bigger than Jim Crow," in his formulation, was to earn an invitation— not to *take* liberation, but indeed to be granted it. In *Hollywood in a Suitcase* Kennedy becomes the great giver of liberation, a view that King himself certainly did not share.

Davis's work on behalf of Civil Rights accelerated in the wake of the March, and he assumed a heightened political profile. His solo stage act at the Copa and elsewhere still retained some of the cringeworthy ethnic humor that had been the trademark of the Rat Pack, but he was now quicker to go on the record with serious, race-themed commentary. "You know these people," he told Robert Alden of the *New York Times,* "they want to send us back to Africa. I'm telling you I'm not going back to Africa. It took me long enough to get to Beverly Hills. No, I'm not going to go back to Africa."[44] In the year after the March on Washington Davis created the "Stars for Freedom" along with Sinatra, Dean Martin, and Count Basie. He hosted a tenth anniversary event honoring *Brown v. Board of Education* at Madison Square Garden, alongside Belafonte and Poitier. With Lena Horne he co-chaired a "Freedom TV Spectacular" that garnered over 150,000 closed circuit viewers to benefit the NAACP. Participants included Poitier, Brando, Ossie Davis, and actress Gloria Foster, who was then starring off-Broadway in Martin Duberman's *In White America.*[45]

Davis closed out 1964 as a member of the "Christmas for Mississippi Committee," a benefit project headed by Dick Gregory. "Before I could say 'We Shall Overcome,'" wrote Gregory, "Sammy agreed to appear" at the inaugural event in Chicago.[46] As Gregory and Davis discussed the possibility of actually visiting Mississippi, a new dimension of Davis's activism opened before him, and also a new test of his commitment. "Some people up North said that Sammy Davis would do a benefit in Chicago, but he was scared

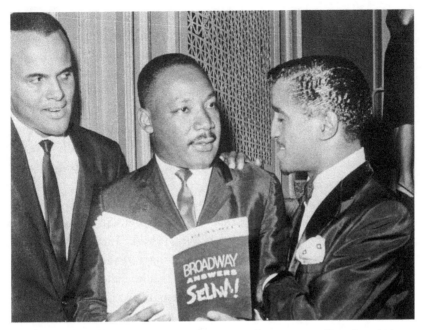

FIG. 17. Davis with Harry Belafonte and Martin Luther King Jr. at "Broadway Answers Selma," 1965. Photo: Bettmann via Getty Images.

to come to Mississippi," Gregory recalled. "Well, he probably is! . . . White folks praise Bob Hope for going to Vietnam and criticize me for going to Mississippi. Well, it's safer in Vietnam."[47] This was on the heels of Robert Kennedy's warning to Davis about the White Citizens Council's "Ten Most Wanted" list, and it was also amid the constant threats and bomb scares associated with *Golden Boy*. Gregory, for one, was forgiving. But the question of going South for Civil Rights agitation would be a persistent one.

That trip down South was going to get harder and harder for Davis to avoid. As tensions rose in Selma, Alabama in early 1965 after incidents of police violence in response to a SNCC drive for voter registration, then the murder of Jimmie Lee Jackson by a state trooper in nearby Perry County, among King's instructions to SCLC executive director Andrew Young was to call up Sammy Davis Jr. and have him do a benefit in Atlanta in the spring.[48] But before those plans were in place, conditions on the ground in Selma spiraled toward confrontation and the famous SCLC/SNCC march from Selma to Montgomery. The violent response of segregationist Governor George Wallace and Sherriff Jim Clark at once heightened the stakes and complicated the logistics of the march, leading up to the violent attack at the

Edmund Pettus Bridge on what became known as Bloody Sunday. King wanted media on hand for the fifty-mile march, which meant that he wanted celebrities on hand as well. Harry Belafonte was quick to respond, chartering a plane for a group of "Stars for Selma," including usual suspects Davis, Poitier, Odetta, Gregory, Dee, Ossie Davis, and others.[49] By all accounts, including his own, Davis balked at making this trip. "I was scared—I was petrified," he later told a British talk show host. "Because first of all they didn't like me—they didn't like me because I was black; they didn't like me because I was a black Jew; and they didn't like a black Jew who was also at that time married to a white lady."[50]

Hillard Elkins recalls going backstage to Davis's *Golden Boy* dressing room at the Majestic to tell him that King wanted him in Selma. "Sammy said, 'I ain't going to Selma.' I said, 'Why?' He said, 'They're going to kill me.'"[51] Davis tried to beg off, telling Belafonte that he had responsibilities to his audience and to his financial backers, and that he could not cancel a performance of his Broadway play. Belafonte's response was bold and brilliant: he bought out the house to pay for the missed performances. "Stars Converge on Alabama," read the headlines, and Davis was among them, just as King had wished.[52]

> As we drove toward Selma the radio was on and we listened to the news of our arrival. The broadcast signed off: 'This is ABC, the *white* news.' A bus took us to where the march was to begin. The streets were barricaded with wooden horses. We walked. Not aggressively. Solemnly. Martin Luther King, Bob Abernathy, Harry [Belafonte], Shelley [Winters], Leonard Bernstein, Hilly [Hilliard Elkins], his girl. Whites, blacks. Three thousand of us. On both sides of the small-town-looking street stood the local people glaring at us, resenting us, angry, fear in their eyes. There were no jeers, no insults, they watched us in silence, despising us. The National Guardsmen, local boys, there to protect us, were little comfort. My stomach, my arms, trembled. My legs were weakened and I walked heavily. But I was glad I was there. Those who watched us walking across their city recognized that our presence was causing cameras and printing presses to record what was happening, to bring our protest to tens of millions of other Americans. And they saw an era fading, a way of life coming to a close.[53]

For lack of a proper, desegregated venue, the night before the last leg of the march entertainers took the stage on "stacked metal casket cases donated by a local Negro undertaker," arranged on an athletic field behind the City of

FIG. 18. Davis performs at a voting rights rally, Selma, Alabama, 1965. Photo: William Lovelace/Daily Express/Hulton Archive/Getty Images.

Jude, "a group of Roman Catholic schools and hospitals operated for Negroes."[54]

Following the dramatic events in Selma, Davis fielded at least one complaint about his cancelled performances of *Golden Boy*. In a letter to the editor of the *New York Times,* he responded to the criticism, garnering exactly the sort of attention and exerting precisely the kind of moral force that, for King and others at the SCLC, was the real point of celebrity involvement in the first place. "Though I have dedicated my life to show business (happily)," Davis wrote, "I am first an American citizen who believes in the dignity and the freedom of man. If any visitors were upset by my missing a performance I have not been made aware of it. If they were, then I leave them with one thought—humbly, what matter if a man gains all the world and loses his soul?"[55] In the month after the march, Davis also led a "Broadway Answers Selma" event to benefit the families of Jimmie Lee Jackson and James Reeb, a white Unitarian Universalist minister from Boston who had been murdered during the Selma protest itself. The event, held at the Majestic Theater with the help of Elkins, raised some $24,000 (the equivalent of over $200,000 today) and enlisted sixty performers, including Robert Preston,

Steve Lawrence, Carol Burnett, Carol Channing, John Gielgud, Chita Rivera, and Barbra Streisand. This had all been planned while Davis was expecting to stay home for the march.[56] Davis also reached out to the Jewish community, speaking after the march to a group from Temple Emanu-El on the parallels between the condition of African Americans in the South and Jews in Nazi Germany.[57]

Davis returned to the South twice more for Civil Rights events. The fear, the death threats, and the warnings from the Attorney General were in play each time. Actor Tony Franciosa, who led a celebrity trip to Gaston, Alabama, recalled, "My sense was that Sammy felt he was walking into a war zone—and as a rookie infantryman, he was scared stiff . . . that he was going to be physically assaulted."[58] Davis also headlined a Hollywood troupe at a rally in Tougaloo, Mississippi for James Meredith, weeks after Meredith had been shot on his March Against Fear in 1966. Robert Kennedy told Davis not to go, warning "the word is out: 'Get Sammy Davis Jr.'" "I'm not going down there to get shot," Davis said, "but we can't all sit around Beverly Hills talking about it. Marlon [Brando] and I and Burt Lancaster are going to Mississippi to show the Negroes there that other[s] . . . aren't afraid to give them moral and spiritual support to get out and vote." Belafonte and Poitier were Davis's "great black knights," by his account, telling him, "'Don't worry about anything, Sam, we're here, we'll protect you.' . . . I said, 'You fuckin' crazy! They could kill you too.'" King himself later joked with Davis, "I got you to Mississippi, Sam, I knew I'd get you down here."[59]

DAVIS, BLACK POWER, AND THE
LANGUAGE OF THE UNHEARD

"In the final analysis, a riot is the language of the unheard," said Dr. King in a 1967 speech called "The Other America."[60] Whether this language could be deciphered by an unresponsive government—by turns callous, uncaring, glacially "deliberate," or monumentally tone-deaf—was tested in the wake of King's own assassination on April 4, 1968. Fury was unleashed in cities across America. The greatest uprisings unfolded across four days in Washington, DC, Baltimore, Chicago, and Kansas City, but overall the unrest eclipsed even the Long Hot Summer of 1967. Spasms of violence in well over a hundred cities resulted in thirty-nine deaths, millions of dollars in damage, and in over a thousand fires in DC alone.[61] That a political era had come to an end with the passing of King was obvious overnight, though what the next era would look like was unclear. When "white America killed Dr. King," said Stokely Carmichael the next morning, "She made it a whole lot easier for a whole lot of black people today. There no longer needs to be intellectual discussions, black people know that they have to get guns." The King assassination, Eldridge Cleaver concurred in "Requiem for Nonviolence," was "a final repudiation by white America of any hope of reconciliation, of any hope of change by peaceful and nonviolent means."[62]

As the unheard raged in America's streets, the more frequently "heard" among African American celebrities and others with a public platform felt an especially keen responsibility. Davis was among them. James Brown's April 5 "Keep Cool" concert, televised from Boston Garden, is the most famous among cultural workers' responses to the assassination and the ensuing urban rebellion. In his efforts to keep the peace, Mayor Kevin White had initially wanted to cancel the concert, along with all other public events. But when the city's black leaders convinced him that the cancellation might be more dangerous than the gathering itself, White prevailed upon local station WGBH to televise Brown's performance in the hopes of keeping Bostonians at home. Standing on stage alongside city councilor Tom Atkins, Brown articulated a brand of black pride and black solidarity meant to turn people away from violent responses to the crisis. Recounting his rise from shoeshine boy to the owner of WRDW in Augusta, Georgia, he told the crowd, "You know what that is? *That's* Black Power."[63]

The Jimi Hendrix Experience was likewise persuaded by civic leaders to keep a date in Newark on April 5. The band had flown up to New York from Virginia Beach, where Hendrix had endured a gang of white toughs taunting him by toasting and celebrating King's death. But they had expected to shelter in the city rather than venturing down to keep their booking. The last time he had been in Newark, Hendrix told his bandmates, there were tanks in the streets. But as with James Brown in Boston, leaders felt the concert's cancellation would be a greater risk. Glasgow-born stagehand Mark Boyle recalled that, at their black driver's insistence, their limo made its way through Newark with Hendrix sitting up front while the Experience's white members, Noel Redding and Mitch Mitchell, slumped in the back along with other white crewmen. When they arrived, the crowd at Symphony Hall was immense. The band took the stage, as advertised, even despite rumors that there was a conspiracy on the right to murder Hendrix and others like him. "This number is for a friend of mine," Hendrix said, in his soft voice. He then "began an improvisation that had a beauty that was simply appalling," Boyle remembers.

> Immediately everyone knew that the friend was Martin Luther King Jr., and this music somehow seemed to convey all the agony of the black people. The whole audience was weeping. Even the stagehands just stood there with tears streaming down their faces. It was a lament for a great man, but it was the most harrowing lament, beyond anyone's imagining. When he finished there was no applause. Everyone in this vast crowd just sat or stood sobbing, and Jimi laid his guitar down and walked quietly off the stage.[64]

A couple days later, Belafonte, Clarence Jones, Berry Gordy, and about a dozen others worked on a plan—failed, as it turned out—to stage a celebrity vigil for King "to provide a focus for all that rage and sorrow, to send a message and set a tone."[65] At the Westbury Music Fair, meanwhile, Nina Simone performed what remains one of the most affecting tributes to King recorded that week. "Why? (The King of Love Is Dead)" was written on April 5 and 6 by bassist Gene Taylor:

> Will my country fall, stand or fall?
> Is it too late for us all?
> And did Martin Luther King just die in vain?
> Folks you'd better stop and think . . . and feel again,
> For we're heading for the brink.
> What's gonna happen now that the king of love is dead?

Simone paused between verses to address the audience, fully keening at moments, as citizens of a nation in mourning.

> Last year, a year ago—maybe it was longer now—Lorraine Hansberry left us, she was a dear friend. . . . Langston Hughes left us, Coltrane left us, Otis Redding left us. Who can go on? . . . And of course for those that we have left, we're thankful. But we can't afford any more losses. [Overcome] Oh no, oh my God, they're shooting us down one by one. [sober] Don't forget that. Because they are. Killing us one by one. Well, all I have to say is that, those of us who know how to protect those of us that we love, stand by them and stay close to them, and I say, if there had been a couple more a little closer to Dr. King, he wouldn't have got it, you know, really. Just a little closer to him, stay there, stay there, we can't afford any more losses.[66]

Throughout these days, Davis, too, made TV appearances in which he pleaded, "We can't answer King's assassination with violence. That would be the worst tribute we could pay him." Davis was working on a trial run for a tour of *Golden Boy* when the news of the assassination came down. He recalls one of the younger black actors in the cast commenting in anger and disgust, "we should kill all the white people." "I snapped, 'Who are you going to start with, the kids in the show?'" Davis himself came close to losing faith in the work they were all doing: "While the ghetto was burning we were fiddling with an interracial musical." But he held to his conviction that the show "was a bridge between two extremes of human non-understanding."[67] Like other culture workers, Davis sought to use his platform to bring peace to the nation's erupting cities. He visited several studios to make public statements. "We don't want every young black person to take the rap for a few," he warned, making what by now has become a familiar distinction at times like these between legitimate and illegitimate brands of protest. Davis deplored the violence and critiqued those who were in open rebellion in American cities.

> I would simply say to all young people, particularly my black brothers and sisters, that the man stood for something very special in a world of violence; he was struck down by violence. Our adding to it, no matter what our frustrations, what our anger, what our justifications might be.... It becomes thievery when the carnival atmosphere ... does prevail. I don't see sad faces mourning the tragic loss of this great American, I see people laughing and giggling. I somehow want to disown those people; I don't want to call those people, who are laughing less than forty-eight hours after our leader died, and stealing—those are not really 'brothers,' those cannot be the people who are striving for the dignity that we should have at this point.[68]

Matthew Stelly later commented that Davis did not necessarily carry the weight of a James Brown in his calls for "cool," because "Sammy had no credibility, except with his generation, and it wasn't his generation that was getting ready to set shit on fire."[69] It was not an easy time to be an elder, as Davis was finding.

There seems as little consensus in retrospect on how to spin a cohesive narrative out of the whirlwind of the post-1968 movement as there was at the time on how justice might be achieved. The year was another turning point, not because Civil Rights was coeval with King's leadership, nor even because his death accelerated a generational passing of the torch and a national shift toward Black Power and militant self-defense. The nature of Richard Nixon's "law and order" policing and the FBI's tactics in COINTELPRO altered the nature of the opposition and the terrain, first of all. It is "time for some honest talk about the problem of order in the United States," Nixon said, as he accepted the Republican nomination. "Let those who have the responsibility to enforce our laws and our judges who have the responsibility to interpret them be dedicated to the great principles of civil rights. But let them also recognize that the first civil right of every American is to be free from domestic violence, and that right must be guaranteed in this country."[70] Under the incoming administration Americans' *first* civil right, in other words, was to be free from the upheavals of the Civil Rights Movement.

J. Edgar Hoover, meanwhile, had famously declared, "justice is incidental to law and order," and his FBI approached the black freedom struggle precisely according to that logic. A Senate Select Committee (known as the Church Committee) later concluded what African Americans had known about the Nixon years all along.

> Domestic activities of the intelligence community at times violated specific statutory prohibitions and infringed the constitutional rights of American citizens. The legal questions involved in intelligence programs were often not considered. On other occasions, they were intentionally disregarded in the belief that because the programs served the 'national security' the law did not apply.

The committee went on to charge the FBI with conducting "a sophisticated vigilante operation aimed squarely at preventing the exercise of First Amendment rights of speech and association."[71] Under this brutal and corrosive regime black leadership became sharply divided, and key leaders were jailed (Bobby Seale, Geronimo Ji-Jaga Pratt, Angela Davis), self-exiled (Eldridge and Kathleen Cleaver, Assata Olugbala Shakur, Pete O'Neal), or killed (Fred Hampton, Mark Clark, Zayd Shakur, John Huggins).

In addition to the heavy toll paid in its battles with criminal justice, both in the courts and in the streets, the freedom struggle in the post-1968 period also splintered along lines that could be strategic, tactical, ideological, or simply practical. As leaders among the clergy like Ralph Abernathy and Jesse Jackson vied for King's mantle, nodes of leadership and social justice activism developed in wholly new places. Many of these were dependent upon earlier Civil Rights victories like anti-discrimination law and voting rights. The Democratic Select Committee in Congress (later the Congressional Black Caucus) was established in 1969 by Shirley Chisholm, Louis Stokes, and William Clay to pursue a legislative agenda from within, quickly earning them a place on Nixon's enemies list. New organizations like Morris Dees and Julian Bond's Southern Poverty Law Center (1971) joined older ones like the Urban League and the NAACP in continued Civil Rights work at the national level, while the local was tended to by community organizers in housing and welfare rights groups, and by a rising generation of African American mayors in cities large and small across the country. Over twenty were elected between 1966 and 1979, North and South, including Carl Stokes (Cleveland), Walter Washington (Washington, DC), Charles Evers (Fayette, Mississippi), Kenneth Gibson (Newark), Maynard Jackson (Atlanta), Tom Bradley (Los Angeles), Henry Marsh (Richmond), Lionel Wilson (Oakland), Ernest Morial (New Orleans), and Richard Arrington Jr. (Birmingham).

These campaigns and administrations became an important training ground in politics for an entire generation of rising black leaders whose way had been cleared by the Civil Rights victories of the previous decade. Similarly, the important work at once consolidated and carried forward in professional organizations like the National Association of Blacks in Criminal Justice (1974), the National Association of Black Journalists (1975), the National Association for Black Law Enforcement Executives (1976), or Association of Black Women in Higher Education (1978), along with the emergence of Black Studies in universities, all built on the anti-discrimination legislation of 1964 and carried the fight into new arenas, whether the classroom, the newsroom, or the stationhouse. Success itself altered the trajectory and clarity of aims within the movement. Expanded opportunity multiplied the sites of struggle, but also proved a cause of fragmentation.

Davis's own political path becomes equally difficult to chart after the King assassination. If his comments in the 1966 *Playboy* interview marked a distance from the asystemic, individualized chafing of *Yes I Can,* the trajectory in his thinking did not necessarily indicate anything like a straight line. After 1968 Davis could be found at many different points along the political spectrum. "He'd give you the peace sign and the black Power sign in one," recalled screenwriter Carl Gottlieb. "And you'd go, 'Excuse me, Sammy, but those are like very different cultures and symbols.' But not in his mind. He'd go, 'Peace, love, and togetherness.' And on togetherness, he would clench his fist." (Gottlieb also recalls hearing Davis sing a version of Randy Newman's "Sail Away" without a hint of irony, though the song is based on a slaver's promises of "sweet watermelon and buckwheat cake" as he attempts to lure his African listeners to the slave ship.) "If it had hostility in it and new revolution," said Gottlieb, "I don't think he could understand that."[72] Many of Davis's movements were more recognizably liberal than radical. He met with

Robert Kennedy after King's funeral, along with Nancy Wilson, Bill Cosby, Eartha Kitt, and others. Davis emerged from that meeting warmly endorsing Kennedy for president: "He is my personal choice and I feel he is the candidate who communicates most fully with the black man."[73] In the short weeks between the King and Kennedy assassinations, Davis was consumed in the progressive but nonetheless mainstream politics of the Democratic Party. Throughout 1968 and beyond, he also continued to do the same kind of fundraising and membership work for the NAACP and the SCLC that he had been doing since Montgomery, including a typical Rat-Pack themed benefit for the SCLC with Sinatra at the Cocoanut Grove in 1969. That year he was also awarded the NAACP's prestigious Springarn Award for his Civil Rights work.[74] "I'm sick of the NAACP being called 'Uncle Tom,'" he said in a 1972 address. As the *San Francisco Sun Reporter* recounted, "Mr. Davis admonished the 'angry young Brothers'. . . . 'I'd much rather have a man go up against the Supreme Court and win than to go up against the First Army with a Coca-Cola bottle and a rag.'"[75] In a street corner conversation with a group of younger black radicals in Chicago, Davis explained himself, "Listen, I marched in *Mississippi* in '66, *Alabama* in '65." Which only fetched the cool reply, "Don't mean shit today. This is '68. . . . We don't need no nigguh lives with whitey. . . ."[76]

And yet, Davis would also befriend Jean Seberg, a supporter of the Black Panther Party and among the most notorious white targets of the COINTELPRO effort to "neutralize" anti-racist activism. It was his relationship with Seberg that brought Davis into the room with figures like Maulana Karenga and others, though perhaps more to debate them than to join them.[77] While in London for *Golden Boy,* Davis met black revolutionary Michael X (Michael de Freitas). Soon after, he announced on the BBC, "I was thinking of giving up my so far moderate stand on Civil Rights in favour of the Black Power Movement. I declared: 'I am not a negro—I'm a black man.' It seems strangely subdued these days, but then it was considered a highly controversial statement."[78] In a 1971 appearance on *Black Journal,* a race-themed PBS program hosted by Tony Brown and funded according to a recommendation in the *Kerner Commission Report,* Brown took note of the "Free Angela" button that Davis was wearing. At the time "the dangerous terrorist Angela Davis" (in Nixon's words) was imprisoned, awaiting trial on charges of aggravated kidnapping and murder for purchasing the guns used in a hostage-taking in Marin County. Many "have an image of me, I guess, of another kind," Davis told Brown.

My involvement with Angela is, again, the injustice of it all. Her political beliefs are her own—I don't share her political beliefs, [but] I share her blackness, and I share the injustice to any black person. There's no way she's gonna get the right kind of trial, we know that, it's stacked against her; they made her the most 'wanted' woman since Bonnie of Bonnie and Clyde, and I think that if a guy like myself wears a button, that's letting somebody in the crowd that I run around with know where my head's at.[79]

Davis's artistic output, meanwhile, stayed right down the middle and never reflected the kind of anti-racist trajectory that seemed to be promised in *A Man Called Adam.* He acquired the film rights to *The Man,* Irving Wallace's 1964 best seller about an African American senator who ascends to the White House through a flukish series of accidents. But he dropped the project when his partnering producer, Irving Stein, died in a car accident in 1969.[80] He recorded but never released a cover of the Mac Davis song "In the Ghetto," a cycle-of-poverty ballad that became a comeback hit for Elvis Presley. Davis's own hit song "I've Gotta Be Me," which charted at number 11 in 1968, had been plucked from the Broadway musical *Golden Rainbow* and had no Civil Rights pedigree, even if it may have read that way amid the smoldering ruins of the 1968 rebellions.

> I want to live, not merely survive
> And I won't give up this dream
> Of life that keeps me alive
> I gotta be me, I gotta be me

Asked in a 1963 interview why he was such a non-conformist, Davis replied that he was "sick of the way society was being run."[81] "I've Gotta Be Me" can certainly be read along those vaguely political lines. The tell, however, is in the concluding verse, a paean not to the kind of collectivity that was the very point of the Freedom Struggle, but rather to the atomization earlier showcased in *Yes I Can:*

> I'll go it alone, that's how it must be
> I can't be right for somebody else
> If I'm not right for me
> I gotta be free, I just gotta be free
> Daring to try, to do it or die
> I gotta be me

Stylistically, too, the song registers as the kind of pop standard that marked Davis as an artist who, as Stelly put it, "had no credibility." There is just a whiff of rhythm and blues in the staccato of the string section laying atop the beat in the opening bars. This is much more pronounced in later versions by the Temptations and the Crickets, but in Davis's arrangement ultimately the feel is closer to the anthemesque character of the patriotic "Ballad of the Green Berets," a 1966 hit that was just then being granted a second life in the summer of '68 through the release of John Wayne's *Green Berets*. The *me* of the song was likely taken by disparate listeners as either Davis the fierce integrationist, so beloved of white liberals since the early Vegas or *Colgate Comedy Hour* days, *or* the Davis who had "forgotten 127th Street," so distrusted and disparaged among younger African Americans. "I've Gotta Be Me"—like "The Impossible Dream," another showtune from *Man of La Mancha* that Davis recorded in 1969, and the Sinatra hit, "My Way," too, for that matter, which he covered in 1970—likely seemed to Davis himself to speak directly to struggles that were inseparable from matters of race. But few even among his own generation would group these songs with Civil Rights anthems like Martha and the Vandellas' "Dancing in the Street," James Brown's "Say It Loud—I'm Black I'm Proud," or Aretha Franklin's cover of "Respect."

But notwithstanding the unappealing racial politics of these Broadway covers and of his two widely misunderstood hits, "Mr. Bojangles" (which was *not* about Bojangles Robinson, nor even about a black figure at all) and "The Candy Man" (which was *not* about a drug pusher), by the early 1970s Davis had become far more outspoken on matters of race than his former self. Certainly, he was bolder than the Rat Pack "mascot" who sucked it up before Sinatra or Martin's racist ribbing at the Sands. In the 1971 *Black Journal* interview, Davis spoke frankly about the nature of his commitment. "There are many who say, 'I don't want to get involved in it [anti-racism],'" he said. "But I don't know how you can *not* get involved in it. Because they are first of all black, and they are committed, whether they want to be committed or not. The very nature of the skin commits you."

In this wide-ranging conversation with one of the nation's premiere black journalists, Davis discussed some of the familiar aspects of his biography, but also broke plenty of less familiar ground. He recalled the "mistake" of emulating white stars, "not trying to get my own identity. . . . I was becoming a black Donald O'Connor, a black Mickey Rooney, instead of becoming a black Sammy Davis." He discussed the ways in which the Rat Pack years were "submerging me as a human being, I think, as I analyze it now." He advanced the theory that Malcolm X had been killed by three black tools ("three *niggers*") working on behalf of a white establishment that saw him as newly dangerous after he came back from Mecca preaching cross-racial solidarity. He discussed the black performer's obligation to weigh and challenge scripts on grounds of representation and racial dignity, but also chastised black audiences for going hard on comedian Flip Wilson for bits that were actually deeply rooted in black culture. He lambasted the staffing policies at NBC: "I walked into the publicity office one day and I didn't see any black people and I said, 'I don't understand this, it looks like the lilies of the white fields' . . . and the guy went, 'Oh, he's very bitter'; and I went, 'Well the hell with it. I *am* very bitter. . . . '" And he again offered a critique of violent means in the movement that was more tactical than philosophical: "There ain't no way you can put . . . a flamethrower against a bottle of Coca Cola with a rag in it— ain't no way you can do that." Finally, he came to rest on a powerful statement on the nature of the society itself:

> When I say 'This is a racist society in which we're living,' *everybody* knows it is. That ain't no big statement to make. Maybe it's shocking from someone you just watched the night before on *Laugh-In,* but it *is,* man. . . . I've got the house, I've got a wife, I have children, I've got success, and now it is time for me to try in every way feasible to help the plight of my people, and to gain our freedom. . . . Money don't make you free. Popularity don't make you free. Don't you know that? Sure I live in Beverly Hills, but I'm shackled by the same thing that happened to the brother in Watts. . . . Our real religion and the thing that connects us all, is our blackness. The religion of blackness.[82]

. . .

Davis's convoluted trajectory through the Civil Rights years—at once impressing Martin Luther King Jr., riling J. Edgar Hoover and countless garden-variety white supremacists, and disappointing black radicals like Maulana Karenga—has much to suggest about race and American public life. "I now have the respect of my people, which I'm proud of, because it's hard earned," Davis told Muhammad Ali in 1969. "There was a time in my life when I didn't have it, when they would put me down, and rightly so, because you cannot be anything without giving back something to your people. It's your obligation, your commitment."[83] It is not Davis's politics themselves that are the chief object of study here, but rather the nature of that obligation—the ways in which, as a public figure, he was interpellated, enlisted, constantly read and misread, judged and misjudged against a backdrop of hotly contested social conditions and political realities. Every move a fulfillment, every move a betrayal—there was no such thing as neutrality, even if Davis might have at times wished it were so. Race politics was the inescapable context within which he operated as a performer, as a public figure, as a private citizen, and as an aspirant to success across a number of platforms and genres while the Freedom Struggle rumbled all about him. And so Davis himself, as I said in the chapter's introduction, became a *text*, for some an emblem of accommodations past and for others, of barriers soon to fall.

Whatever else one wants to say about Davis's politics, he instinctively understood the work that *culture* does. If racism is in part a mode of thinking and the work of anti-racism represents a vast *changing of minds*, then disrupting white habits of interpretation or expectation was as important as rewriting laws and challenging naked power. "I want to talk to people," he told *Ebony* in 1966.

> I want to talk to them through the media in which I work and to say something meaningful.... It's like being invited to that party where you're the only Negro there and at the end of the evening the Man says to you, 'Jesus Christ! It sure was a nice pleasure. You're just like Charlie next door.' And you don't know what to really say, and you know that he's giving you the highest compliment 'cause he's suddenly discovered we are no different. We have our failings. We have our good points, everything else. We just happen to be a little different color.[84]

There are myriad examples of the crucial work performed by artists, entertainers, and other cultural workers during these years. I have already mentioned work by Odetta, Aretha Franklin, Nina Simone, Sidney Poitier, and Dick Gregory, for example. We could add many others: for example, Jim Brown's anti-racist workshops, beginning with the Cleveland Browns, which took political work from the locker room out into the communities of NFL cities across the country. There was Muhammad Ali's unapologetic racial pride, in the ring, in his poetry, and in the public square of anti-racist and anti-war comment. Even network TV took down segregationist norms in the kiss between Captain Kirk and Lieutenant Uhura. Or we could recall the discipline and joy of the 1971 Pittsburgh Pirates, who fielded an all-black starting nine one afternoon on their way to the National League pennant. In sports we could also name Curt Flood's fight against the peonage-like contractual practices of Major League Baseball, a fight which in his view could only be fully understood by reading Frederick Douglass. ("Another happy family sold," read the wry, slavery-themed commentary on Bob Gibson's locker after Flood was figuratively sold downriver to Philadelphia.)[85] A society does not dismantle *de jure* segregation without the work that culture does. Nor, we might add, could that same society travel from Nixon to Barack Obama without that cultural work, either—Toni Morrison, Spike Lee, Oprah Winfrey, August Wilson, Lauryn Hill, Derek Jeter, or (sigh) Bill Cosby.

But what Davis's career illuminates most brightly is not the creativity of anti-racist artistic work in these years, nor its courage. Rather, his movements through the era throw a light on subtler compositions and structures of collective racial thinking and the relentless pressures generated by the era's contending forces. First is the media politics. Once the Movement's direct-action strategy had become in large part a media strategy, in Birmingham and many other places, Civil Rights concerns completely engulfed mass-mediated exchange when it came to the words and images of African Americans in the public eye. There was no utterance or gesture that was *not* political, or that was not interpreted (if variously) *as* political. Next is the related politics of style. As "Negro" became "black" and the conk gave way to the Afro, a politics of sameness and difference—of assimilation versus pluralism—played out on screens and broadcast airwaves every moment. The common charge against someone like Davis may have been "self-hatred," but this was a politics fundamentally composed by the inclusions and exclusions of American political culture from the outset, the narrow, routinary conception of "We the People," and the choices left to those who had been excluded. Davis, Nat King Cole, Poitier, Duke Ellington, and others were middlebrow culture's symbols of a dignified, unthreatening masculinity that appealed to a middle-class white audience and so authenticated the claims of liberal democracy.[86]

This brand of inclusion, of fighting one's way in, was like threading a needle—being "black but not *too* black," as Belafonte once said of his own public image. The period's currents and crosscurrents, as we saw in *Yes I Can,* left Davis at odds with the black community in various ways. "I'm often accused of being anti-Negro," he told Pete Martin of the *Saturday Evening Post.* "The charge most frequently made against me is that I want to be white. That accusation hurts."[87] Such judgments reflected both a generational politics and a politics of style, in some instances, a disdain for what Donna Britt called "the straightest, greasiest conk money could buy" at a time when the Afro was coming into style.[88] But it also had to do with the frequent instances of Davis launching critiques of the black community in a context where the broad expectation was that his most vociferous criticisms would be of whites.

In *Yes I Can,* for instance, he complained bitterly of his troubles raising money for Dr. King up in Harlem. A black bakery owner challenges him, "How can you hope for human rights when you know they don't figure us as human? ... You're counting on people feeling bad when they see what's happening to us, people whose ancestors came over here looking for freedom and the first thing they did was go out and get themselves slaves." A black butcher declines: "You want money from me? Then come up here some day and tell me you're putting together a black army to fight for what's *ours.* ..."[89]

Davis, as the bakery owner's comment implies, could also fall into the trap of a popular "bootstraps" ideology that celebrated the romantic rise of the white ethnics at the expense of African Americans. This Ellis Island romance, a massive disavowal of the white privileges that had come with Jim Crow unions or New Deal-era housing and banking policies, received its first full airing in Daniel Patrick Moynihan and Nathan Glazer's *Beyond the Melting Pot* (1963), reaching its apotheosis in the Moynihan Report two years later and in Glazer's *Affirmative Discrimination* a decade after that. Citing working-class philosopher Eric Hoffer, a *New York Post* interviewer challenged Davis in 1965. "The Negro does need so much help," he asserted; "... the Jews or the Greek-Americans, the Italian-Americans, or something like that—were able largely by themselves to get themselves going up that escalator." Davis perhaps too easily took the bait: "You know, our whole history is, 'Well, you all help us.' Well, if the master doesn't give us food, we could still be standing there. Our history is, 'We won't do it unless he tells us.' It takes years to break and wash that out." This was the kind of comment that infuriated his black compatriots at the height of the struggle, though in this instance Davis did come back at the interviewer. "I've heard it," he objected. "'Sam, what's happening with the civil rights thing? Already they're causing too much of a turmoil.' And you hear it and you say, 'But don't you understand? There are still things to be done.'"[90]

Finally, Davis sought something of a do-over in his own presentation of his politics and his struggles. "Nowadays I've cooled down politically," he wrote in 1980, even if there were many who critiqued him for never having fully heated up.

> I used to be very frustrated, angry and impatient about what was going on. I wanted things to change fast. Maybe I was an optimist. You can heal such sores as violence politically, but it's difficult to change bigotry and intolerance by Washington decrees. I didn't feel I should keep quiet about my ideals. I

used to shout my mouth off about all sorts of things, both privately to anyone who would listen and publicly on any platform I could find. . . . My generation of blacks moved mountains, although many times it didn't seem like it. We've broken down many taboos, now it is up to the younger generation of all colours and creeds, to build on the foundations we have laid.[91]

Davis's second autobiography, *Why Me?* (1989), again written in collaboration with Burt and Jane Boyar, repeated verbatim many of the vaudeville and Vegas scenes from *Yes I Can* before picking up the story where the first book left off, in the early 1960s. In addition to simply finishing out the chronological saga, *Why Me?* embraces the opportunity to narrate Civil Rights issues more frankly than the earlier volume had, with both a clarifying hindsight and often a renewed brief in defense of Davis's stance toward blackness and toward political issues as well. Here he tells the full—and fully charged—story of his disinvitation to the Kennedy inaugural on account of his interracial marriage, for instance. But he also puts a higher Civil Rights gloss on his own rise through the entertainment industries than he had in *Yes I Can*. "I had done a lot," he says, recounting the eve of the Selma march.

> I had been marching since I was seventeen. Long before there was a civil rights movement I was marching through the lobby of the Waldorf-Astoria, of the Sands, the Fontainebleau, to a table at the Copa. And I'd marched alone. Worse. Often to black derision. But had I done 'enough'?[92]

Why Me? may be in some places a productive retelling; but there is a bit of wounded self-righteousness and score-settling as well. *Yes I Can* was meant to pull back the curtain on American racial realities for the benefit of a white readership who still enjoyed the luxury of not knowing. *Why Me?*, by contrast, appeared at a moment when race and racism had been central to American public discourse for decades, and when the brief for a book like this from a figure like Sammy Davis Jr. was much less clear. "It was a strange time, the sixties," he wrote, "a strange feeling suddenly being 'black.' Yet overnight thirty million 'colored people' and 'Negroes' had become 'blacks.'" On the former harshness of the word *black,* he observed, in the era of *black is beautiful* "it was no longer a sneer, but an anthem. 'Say it loud, I'm black and I'm proud. . . .' One song found the pride of a scattered people, one song straightened our backs and raised our heads. . . ."[93]

Why Me? goes back over much of the familiar ground of the Davis story, but this time with the retrospective and self-justifying frame of a purposeful *straightened back* and *raised head*.[94] In response to Karenga's tactical judgment that "Fear is a necessary commodity [in the struggle], Mr. Davis," Davis had objected, "'But why intimidate *me?*' I rubbed my face with my hand. 'This don't exactly come off, y'know. I'm not Al Jolson.'" (It was here that Karenga's right hand observed, "But you ain't black either . . . you *is* black, but you don't *be* black.")[95] Nonetheless, the underlying philosophy of *Why Me?* is not a rejection of the appellation "black performer" in favor simply of "performer," as in *Yes I Can,* but rather the more race-conscious observation, *the skin commits you.* It is a commitment that had taken on many different shades across the decades of his career—not only in how disparate observers like Matthew Stelly and J. Edgar Hoover tended to read him, but in how Davis read himself.

Coda

WHAT IS THE "POST" OF "POST-CIVIL RIGHTS"?

Q: Are you still Jewish?
A: Yes, lady, I have been a black Jew for eighteen years. I have
been black for seven years, and before that I was colored.

SAMMY DAVIS JR. DIED OF CANCER at sixty-four in 1990, and—true to
form—he never completely stopped working until the very end. His credits
in the last decades of his life would include a variety/talk-show, *Sammy and
Company* (1975–1977); a third Broadway show, *Stop the World—I Want to
Get Off* (1978); films like *Cannonball Run* (1981); an old-school Vegas revue
with Jerry Lewis at Bally's (1988); and guest appearances on *The Cosby Show*
and *The Arsenio Hall Show* (1989). In *Tap* (1989) he played one of the old-
timers whose tap dance traditions the young Gregory Hines character
wished to honor but also to update and *redeem* with an edgy, urban sensibility that spoke to contemporary black identity. But as a public figure Davis
remained strangely frozen in time, fixed in the popular imagination in two
contending, seemingly contradictory, and iconic moments from 1972. The
first was the "Sammy's Visit" episode of *All in the Family,* which aired on
February 19. The second was Davis's controversial appearance at the
Republican National Convention in Miami six months later, in August.
One moment was a world-changing kiss, a comic take-down of America's
favorite bigot, Archie Bunker. The other was an ill-advised hug, a cozying
up—literally—to Richard Nixon, the "law and order" president who was
much despised among progressives in general and the African American
community in particular. These two moments, the kiss and the hug, arrested
the Sammy Davis Jr. image in the public mind for years after (the hug more
than the kiss, frankly).

FIG. 19. The kiss. Davis with Carroll O'Connor in *All in the Family*, 1973. Photo: CBS via Getty Images.

But in memory they also convey a central paradox in US culture more generally, as the nation has struggled to establish just what the "post" of "post-Civil Rights" might mean. Any society that can elect Barack Obama on one cycle and Donald Trump on the next is obviously unsettled on some basic questions. From the Nixon inaugural onward, there have been those (like Nixon himself) for whom "post-Civil Rights" meant *it's over—the black community loses.* This was the message of Nixon's "first civil right" speech. Progressive commentary in this vein has not been sparse, either. Among these early reckonings, in 1978 Michele Wallace wrote, "Under pressure the white man wrote meaningless legislation. He continued to debate the inferiority of the black race. He gave blacks the right to vote and nothing to vote for, the

FIG. 20. The hug. Davis with Richard Nixon, 1973. Photo: Associated Press.

right to buy but no money to buy with, the right to go wherever they wanted but no transportation to get there."[1] Over four decades later abolitionist Dylan Rodriguez finds that our post-Civil Rights politics had merely been tasked with "cultivating a desegregated American Dream that was ideologically inclusive of the Black and nonwhite masses while simultaneously rearticulating, diversifying, and strengthening the logics of anti-Blackness and racial-colonial dominance on which that dream was/is based." For

Rodriguez we have entered an era of "multiculturalist white supremacy." Look no further than the state penitentiary.[2]

Meanwhile, there have been others (from Bill Clinton to Bill Cosby) for whom it meant *it's over—and we won.* For still others (one thinks of figures as diverse as John Lewis, Audre Lorde, the Combahee River Collective, Spike Lee, Toni Morrison, or Maxine Waters) "post-Civil Rights" has meant a new phase of an old, ongoing struggle, the continuing relevance of Lewis's "good trouble." Historian Elizabeth Hinton urges that we expand our scope of the cycles of black rebellion and police violence in the years after 1968— literally hundreds of instances from Omaha to Denver to Battle Creek to Miami—as a way of redefining both the limits of the Movement and the meanings attaching to the "post."[3] But the hug and the kiss, Davis's almost contemporaneous takedown of Archie Bunker and propping up of Richard Nixon, embody a central dynamic of American political culture for the decades to come, that peculiar bargain by which the Left took the culture and the Right took the White House.[4] It was no small thing in 1972 for an African American to render a white person the butt of a joke on national television, as Davis did on *All in the Family.* But our *political* life has never been as fixed, when it comes to progressive or anti-racist principle. Even Bill Clinton built out the carceral state; even Barack Obama broke the charts on immigrant deportations and African drone strikes.

The plotline of the "Sammy's Visit" episode was a pretty thin device to bring Davis ("as himself") into the household of the racist Archie Bunker. Archie is moonlighting as a cabdriver, and his passenger has accidentally left a briefcase in his cab and will now drop by the Bunkers' Queens neighborhood to pick it up on his way to the airport.[5] There is much excitement around this celebrity visit, even though certain members of the Bunker family, ahem, might not typically be so eager to entertain a black guest. At the end of Davis's brief call, Munson asks whether he can take a picture of the star with Archie. Davis instructs him to snap the shot on the count of three—at which point he surprises Bunker with a kiss on the cheek, to be captured for posterity on Edith's camera. The show's creator, Norman Lear, recalls the kiss as an ad lib, in which Davis surprised everyone on set and Carroll O'Connor (Archie) managed to react in character; the show's writer Bill Dana swears that he had written the kiss into the script. No matter. The moment immediately became a cultural icon, in that it represented that still-rare phenomenon in 1972, an interracial prime time kiss (with a twist). It was an even rarer instance of a black character's one-upping and getting the best of a white one, not only poking fun at Bunker's racism, but fully playing him for the fool. While some interpreted the kiss as "traitorous," for Lear the Davis episode crystallized precisely what was most radical in the racial humor of *All in the Family,* a piece of ideological and comic labor that was more routinely carried by the characters of the Jefferson family next door.[6]

A few months later, Richard Nixon tapped Davis to serve on his National Advisory Council on Economic Opportunity. Davis answered the call for a number of reasons. One was that he never really had gotten over being snubbed by the Kennedys over his interracial marriage. He was embittered toward the Democrats, and he was easily attracted to a presidential invitation. Politically, Davis was a less committed Democrat than most African Americans in any case, and certainly less so than the other celebrities who surrounded him. Taking a pragmatic view of Nixon on race, Davis remarked that "the Nixon the public knows and the Nixon I know are two different people."[7] Nixon "impressed me," Davis later admitted. "He promised much more funding to black colleges and many new reforms . . . I did not check out all the political affiliations and relied only on what my heart dictated, as I always had. As I now know, that can sometimes lead you into trouble."[8]

The specific "trouble" came at a Republican Youth rally in conjunction with the party's national convention in Miami. Nixon announced Davis's support, and in thanking him for it said a few kind words that caused Davis spontaneously to go over and hug him, warmly if awkwardly. "You aren't going to buy Sammy Davis, Jr. by inviting him to the White House," Nixon said. "You're going to buy him by doing something for America." Davis was accepting the policy promises that the President was touting, and also what he heard as a personal compliment. "That's the first time a President of the United States ever said that about a performer," he remarked. He was "so touched, so overwhelmed by the realization that my problems were on the President's mind."[9] Others were perhaps more taken by the "buying" trope in Nixon's comment—that, whatever else you want to say, he did mean to *buy* Davis, and Davis seemed a little too willing to be bought. Julian Bond thought the hug "unbelievable—an irrational act." "Sammy has the right to make his own decision," Shirley Chisholm said with a wry smile. "Everybody wants a winner. . . ." Newark Mayor Kenneth Gibson reported that, "The feeling in the barbershops and pool halls here is that Sammy was just an inch away from kissing Nixon's tail."[10]

According to his own account, Davis was the one, as late as 1972, who first explained to Nixon, "we say black now. Negro and colored are not in use."

But even so, he would later argue in the President's defense, Nixon had "increased appropriations to black colleges, he's done away with the quota system." "There's an honesty about the man I love," he added in 1972, in a line that rolls pretty deep in irony, knowing what we now know about the Nixon presidency.[11] From his side, the "law and order" president found in Davis the kind of bootstraps racial story that he loved personally and needed politically. At "An Evening at the White House" after Nixon's second inaugural ("This is as far uptown as I'm ever going to get," Davis quipped), Nixon characteristically pressed the Davis biography into the service of conservative argument. "A landing on the moon is pretty hard to beat, as an illustration of American can-do spirit," he said. "But the guest tonight exemplifies that can-do spirit. . . . He began as a relatively poor boy, overcame poverty and prejudice and went to the top because he had that spirit." Can-do spirit, individualism, personal responsibility and initiative—these were inherently anti-Civil Rights rebuttals in the Nixon political lexicon. What African Americans needed was not any sort of policy intervention; they just needed to get their act together. Davis, as we have seen, had not been so terribly far from this argument himself on many occasions.[12]

That hug at the Republican Youth rally became the most famous and iconic eight seconds of Davis's life, fully defining him in the public imagination ever after. "When I saw him kissing Nixon," wrote Truman Capote, "I thought he was the new Checkers"—the spaniel made a household name in the then-Vice President's "Checkers speech" in 1952.[13] If the retribution was swift for Davis, it was also unshakably enduring. In a 1980 appearance on *Midday with Bill Boggs,* Davis turned on Boggs (and by extension, on the wider press) for keeping the issue alive. The controversy of the Nixon hug will "never go away if you keep picking at it," he complained.

> See, my own people, by and large—I explained it in *Ebony,* you can read it in the book [*Hollywood in a Suitcase*]—you would think that I had doped the children. I didn't kidnap nobody. And the only person I hurt was me, and it was an honest hurt. . . . I did hurt myself, because any time you walk down the street in a given period in your life and your own people will not speak to you, and your own people turn you away, then all the money and diamonds, the fame, the fortune mean absolutely nothing. If your own people won't speak to you—thank God that it's not the case today. . . . But it's got to die sometime, meaning, the other side of the color spectrum has got to *let* it die. The press has got to let it die. And stop bringing up things that was back *then.* I can't take it back; and if I was back in 1972 under the same circumstances I would damn well do it again. [applause] *Do you understand me?*[14]

The hug had immediately seemed the kind of thing that might never be forgotten, and it even had its ironic spillover effects. Recalling the acrimony in *The Godfather of Soul* (1986), James Brown wrote, "A lot of the stuff was aimed at me because of a picture of Sammy Davis hugging Mr. Nixon. The picture was in newspapers and in *Jet* and made a lot of black folks mad. But somehow the rumor got started that I was the one hugging the president. That caused more mess, pickets and threats and boycotts...."[15] But most pegged the event to the right name. Almost two decades after it happened, the hug haunted nearly every obituary that was written for Davis. It was the hug, more than any other single thing, that caused writer Margot Jefferson to think on the figure of Davis as a "lurid spectacle of Sambo and Sammy Glick joining hands."[16]

· · ·

Post-Civil Rights. Across recent decades the nation has served up its best and its worst, side by side, two contending sets of tradition and precedent in one troubled body politic. One stream encompasses Nixon's "Southern strategy," as it came to define the Republican Party and so American politics more generally in the decades since the 1960s. This stream includes Ronald Reagan's cynical campaign stop in Neshoba County, Mississippi in 1980, a "states' rights" speech before an all-white rally just sixteen short years after Chaney, Goodman, and Schwerner had been murdered there during the Freedom Summer. It includes Reagan's cuts to the Equal Employment Opportunity Commission (EEOC) and the Civil Rights division of the Justice Department once he had attained office. It includes political dog-whistles like the Willie Horton ad, a "dangerous black renegade" narrative used to tag candidate Michael Dukakis as soft on crime in the 1988 election. It includes gerrymanders and the legal assaults on voting rights, police violence and the rise of a racially skewed carceral state. It runs down through Donald Trump's "fine people on both sides" moment, as neo-Nazis with tiki torches stormed Charlottesville in a frank public display of white nationalism. Trump may be uncommonly boorish, but this stream in the nation's post-Civil Rights politics says that he is anything but an *aberration*.

The other, contrary stream runs forward from Freedom Summer itself. It includes the Shirley Chisholm campaign and the emergence of the Congressional Black Caucus; a generation of black elected officials at every level; significant African American political appointments, even of conservatives like Colin Powell and Condoleezza Rice. It includes street-level radicalism from the Combahee River Collective, the anti-apartheid and divestment movements, and Black Lives Matter. It includes the election of Barack Obama, whose victory in 2008 took most Americans by surprise ("never thought I'd see the day"), but which made a certain kind of sense in retrospect, once one did the work of tracing this anti-racist stream across the topography of post-Civil Rights America. It includes the burgeoning movement for racial justice in the wake of the George Floyd murder in Minneapolis, and the long overdue toppling of monuments to the Confederacy.

One chapter in this history of contending forces was the rising brand of "multiculturalism"—*you take the White House, we'll take Hollywood*—that characterized Davis's last film, *Tap,* during the first Bush administration.[17] The film is a love note to the old-timers who carried tap dance through the twentieth century, but also an unwitting eulogy for the form. In the opening scene, Max Washington (Gregory Hines) tap-dances in the cold blue light of his prison cell in Sing Sing. He dances angry, with edge and fury and percussive violence, in a strange bookend to the old jailhouse softshoe routine that Tom Jones and Davis had staged to "Mr. Bojangles" years before (1970).[18] As the Hines character tries to navigate the choice between his best-seeming options after prison, whether to find work as a dancer, or resume his role as "second-story man" in a burglary ring, the film brings some "street" to the idea of tap for a contemporary audience. But much of the film also captures the dying gasp and the *pastness* of tap as a form that has evidently been tossed on the trash heap. A photo gallery on the wall of Max's father's Sonny's Dance Studio is a kind of black dancers' Hall of Fame, which with a wink includes a shot of Davis and Eartha Kitt in *Anna Lucasta* alongside the likes of Bill Robinson and Bert Williams. But these figures have been eclipsed along with the likes of the Flying Wallendas and the *Ed Sullivan Show* sensation the Italian puppet mouse Topo Gigio, as a distant announcer's voice under the opening titles suggests.

The old-timers in the cast alongside Davis include Bunny Briggs, Arthur Duncan, Jimmy Slyde, Howard "Sandman" Sims, and Harold Nicholas, a group that still enjoys a good cutting session or "hoofers' night," but also comments with some regularity on their approaching death and that of their form. "I'm only good at one thing," Little Mo (Davis) says to Amy Simms (Suzzanne Douglas), who has scolded the old gentleman for over-exerting himself. "I'm a tap dancer . . . If I'm gonna die, I wanna die with my tap shoes on." "It was rock and roll that killed us," Sandman Sims later observes, as the old dancers lament a death that has already occurred. "What'ya gonna do?" Washington's old partner in crime (Joe Morton) asks, with an acid disdain that seems to speak for the younger generation. "Sit around and tell stories about the golden days of *tap dancing*?" Later Max and Amy reminisce about the "black Fred and Ginger" routine they used to do—"about forty years too late."

Tap is a feelgood movie very much on the Hollywood formula. Several formulae, actually, including love story, nostalgic tip of the hat to a passing generation, and gritty crime drama, all wrapped up in the genre of the showbiz triumph narrative. Will Max Washington get the girl? Will he honor his elders by staying true to his gifts as a dancer? Will he resist the life of crime? Will he find a way to make tap *pay*? There is also something of a Prospero motif here. Will the sorcerer renounce his magic, while still at the height of his powers? At one point, frustrated in his brief flirtation with Broadway, Washington casts his tap shoes, like *The Tempest*'s magic books, into the East River. The film embodies at least a philosophical critique of capitalism, if not a sharply political one. It makes a purist's complaint on behalf of people like Little Mo and Max Washington, whose artistry and good work will never be properly repaid in this world. This is a lament that heaps bland Broadway musicals and outright criminal activity into the same tainted bin of "cash money," pursuits that will always hold a greater payoff than the more deserving arts. Little Mo and his circle have been done in by the advent of rock and roll and by the passing of styles. Washington, meanwhile, is nearly done in by a capitulation to the commercialized, inauthentic version of tap that endures on Broadway. His audition before a sneering white director is perhaps the one moment where *Tap* seems to be directly about race. This is a battle of wills between a dancer whose talents far exceed the vision of the show as choreographed, and a stubborn director who claims to better know how a Broadway show must look, and what a Broadway audience will buy. He has therefore buried "real" tap beneath the stylistic trappings of whiteness, what the Davis character later calls "all this Broadway happy feet bullshit." The racial dynamic in this confrontation is impossible to miss. At its core, though, theirs is an argument over what is *salable*.

Ultimately the "post" that marks *Tap* as a post-Civil Rights production is its matter-of-fact concern with a gallery of black characters who are only peripherally concerned about the white world at all. But unlike *Porgy and*

Bess, Tap is not self-absorbed in any kind of epic, Gershwinian portraiture of "the folk." Unlike *Anna Lucasta,* the black cast here is very much embedded in a Harlem community and in generations-old black cultural traditions. And unlike in *A Man Called Adam,* Max Washington's struggle has less to do with his being black than with his being a dancer. Max's demons are all his own; they have not been bequeathed by "the man." *Tap* represents Hollywood multiculturalism right at that moment when on-screen "diversity" was a matter of Hollywood branding, and, consequently, bleached of all politics. Max Washington will endure a hostile white parole officer and knock heads with an arrogant white director. But insofar as the film advances any racial messaging at all, this is conveyed mostly in the rattle and hum of the New York streetscape, sharply dressed black businessmen and women jostling alongside the street vendors and hustlers, a teeming urban backdrop whose race *and class* diversity punctuates Max Washington's own efforts at self-emancipation as he moves about the city. The Civil Rights movement is over, in other words—*we win.*

Futurity, in this formulation, has less to do with racial struggle than it does with God-given talents, personal voice, and available cultural avenues. In proposing a future for tap as a form, the film strangely casts its lot with rock and roll rather than with hip hop. Little Mo's personal dream, and his perpetually extended invitation to Max, is to institute a rock/tap fusion show to be mounted at a local club, Charlie's. Etta James makes a cameo as a rhythm and blues singer, reclaiming the form as *black* tradition in a counterpoint to Sandman Sims's "it was rock that killed us." Futurity is also carried here in the character of Amy's teenaged son Louis (Savion Glover), reared in the tradition amid two prior generations of dancers and now a brilliant dancer in his own right. It is Louis who most proves the *cool* of tap for a post-*Thriller,* post-Moonwalk generation, and it is he more than Max and Amy who promises a legacy for the Little Mos and Harold Nicholases and Jimmy Slydes of the world.

But the futurity of tap also points us back to the deep, west African past from whence the form came. Max Washington speaks of "hearing the combinations" in the ambient sounds at Sing Sing. It was the combinations that urged him to dance, and it was the dance that "pulled him back from the edge" when he threatened to lose himself in rage and despair. It was likewise the "combinations" in the sounds of the street that brought him back from the edge just as he was about to resume his life of crime; the sound and the dance set him free from *that* future and allow him to go straight. As Little Mo tells him, speaking of Max's father:

You thought your father was a failure? Sure they took away the money, the fame, the jobs. But there was one thing they couldn't take away, Max. They couldn't take away his legs. They couldn't take away his pride and his dignity. You know the reason why? Because he knew he was good. That's why he could smile, because he knew he was good, Max.

Both Max's salvation and his father Sonny's liberation in dance point back to Ralph Ellison's "jazzman's academy," that sense that in spite of the negative connotations descending from minstrelsy, tap could be a joyous expression of self-emancipation, "an act of black beauty and power," "a means of survival," as historians of dance have noted.[19] The finale of the film is that tap/rock fusion performance at Charlie's that Little Mo had been dreaming of all along. This triumphal moment in the arc of the entertainment narrative—a convention that runs all the way from Jack Robin's breakout secular performance in *The Jazz Singer* to the climactic lift in *Dirty Dancing*—reintroduces tap as a diasporic form by putting it in conversation with both conga drumming and an electronic, moog-driven post-soul sound. The past and present of tap are sutured and restored when Sandman Sims, watching Max's innovative moves, exclaims, "That's one of *my* steps. You stole my step!" But as all great dancers from Master Juba on down would tell you, not only are all the steps stolen, but all steps *steal*. The form has a certain fugitivity; the steps are designed to steal a measure of freedom for the black body dancing.

In the years after the Black Power movement had crested, Davis felt misunderstood in his politics, and as we have seen he could be quite defensive about his Civil Rights cred. "I wish I had a goddamn film of me marching in Selma, in Tougaloo and Atlanta, just to prove it," he said.

> Once Bull Connor came up to a car I was sitting in and just stared at me. It was like a bad movie.... I didn't march up front because I wasn't one of the organizers. And I don't think performers should be leaders. Also, I was on the Klan's 10-Most-Wanted list. I couldn't stay for the rallies after the marches because I had to fly back someplace and perform. But I was there![20]

For those coming up behind him, he was a figure less like *Tap's* Little Mo than like the Louis Armstrong character in *A Man Called Adam,* an old-timer whose artistic and political style harkened back to a jettisoned past of indignity and racial deference. "Sometimes it hurt a little watching Sammy," wrote journalist Donna Britt, "the way it hurts when someone you respect laughs a little too loudly at the boss's quips." For Britt, Davis represented

America's top 'Negro' star at the precise moment that much of black America discovered itself. Suddenly, certain blacks' quest to assimilate, to ape white folks' hair and mannerisms and values, seemed embarrassing to a culture that was declaring itself beautiful and valid. Davis epitomized everything that many blacks were rejecting. By the time Davis caught on—sporting his own Afro and beautiful black wife—much of the damage had been done.[21]

Davis was intensely self-aware as a figure bobbing amid shifting historical currents. "When I die," he said, a good ten years before playing Little Mo,

> that's the last of a breed. There ain't no more stumping stumpies, there ain't no more bucking bubbles, there ain't no more Nicholas Brothers, and there ain't no more none of them people anymore. I am the last. Do it die with me? That's what frightens me. Is it all gonna be do wop, do wop, do wop from here on out?"[22]

Elsewhere he expressed anxiety that he would end up like the Bojangles figure in the Jerry Jeff Walker song—not Bojangles Robinson, but a sad, washed-up, cast-aside figure who represented an art and a moment no longer valued.

> That culmination of different black performers, minstrels that I've known, performers who got hooked on junk, who got wiped out by alcohol, got wiped out by changing of times. I've seen them disappear—great dancers, great stylists. And when I do that number some nights, I say Oh my God, that's me, that's how I'll be when I'm seventy years old, man, I'll be working little joints and I'll talk about what I used to be, and that'll be the end of it.[23]

The role of Little Mo, and the *Tap* project in general, in a sense saved him from the worst of this. He was also spared by dying relatively young, and he was revered to the very end by people like Gregory Hines. (Hines literally kissed Davis's dancing shoes at a Sixtieth Anniversary Celebration for Davis at Hollywood's Shrine Auditorium, at the end of a cutting session duet that turned out to be Davis's last performance.)

At a Black Film Makers Hall of Fame award ceremony in 1987, Davis was honored alongside Spike Lee, then a twenty-nine-year-old upstart fresh off his first success with the miraculous, shoestring production *She's Gotta Have It*. Davis and Lee covered a good bit of the political spectrum, and end to end their careers would span a century of varied cultural production. Lee's recognition inaugurated a new era in African American arts, just as Davis's marked—as he put it—the end of a breed. Honoring Davis, the Reverend

Cecil Williams said that Sammy had boycotted South Africa's Sun City entertainment center "before it was fashionable" to do so, giving voice to the long-held Movement view of celebrities' anti-racist principle as political capital.[24] But for the other honoree, Spike Lee, and for many others who came up in the later twentieth century, *art itself* could and should speak politics. One thinks of Carrie Mae Weems, Kara Walker, Glenn Ligon, John Singleton, Ice Cube, Ava DuVernay, Barry Jenkins. As Lee explained a few years ago, history shows that "when times have been rough, they've produced some of the greatest music, movies, plays and whatnot from artists who feel that it's their duty to comment or hold up a window to the evil that's going on."[25] It is not just that now "All black art is political," as DuVernay has argued.[26] It's that the politicized arts have gone mainstream and have captured a broad national audience. This is one important element of the "post" of "post-Civil Rights." For Sammy Davis, Jr., by contrast, artistic talent was the ticket to a freedom that he gauged in highly personal terms. It was a weapon in the anti-racist war for hearts and minds, to be sure, and rooted in a deep diasporic history, too—hence the Sun City boycott. But most of all it was a mode of *self*-emancipation encased in worlds of injury and apprehension, a sort of unending bullet dance. Which is why it was often impossible to tell whether Davis was really dancing the barricades down, or merely dancing down them, and to distinguish his political from his personal aspirations across six decades of performance, from the pre- to the post- of Civil Rights history.

NOTES

AUTHOR'S NOTE

1. Pat Parker, "For the White Person Who Wants to Know How to Be My Friend," *Movement in Black* (Oakland, CA: Diana Press, 1978.) Available at https://lithub.com/three-poems-by-pat-parker.

PREFACE. THE LONG CIVIL RIGHTS ERA

Sammy Davis, Jr., Burt Boyar, and Jane Boyar, *Why Me? The Sammy Davis, Jr. Story* (New York: Farrar, Straus, Giroux, 1989), 134.

1. Sammy Davis, Jr., Burt Boyar, and Jane Boyar, *Yes I Can* (New York: Farrar, Straus, Giroux, 1965), 67–68.

2. M. Honey, *Sharecropper's Troubadour: John L. Handcox, the Southern Tenant Farmers' Union, and the African American Song Tradition* (New York: Palgrave, 2013), 11.

3. Frederick Douglass, "If There Is No Struggle, There Is No Progress," 1857, https://www.blackpast.org/african-american-history/1857-frederick-douglass-if-there-no-struggle-there-no-progress. On the "long Civil Rights movement" see Jacquelyn Dowd Hall, "The Long Civil Rights Movement and the Political Uses of the Past," *Journal of American History* 91, no. 4 (2005): 1233–63.

4. James Brown, *The Godfather of Soul: An Autobiography* (New York: MacMillan, 1986), 88, emphasis added.

5. Houston Baker, *Modernism and the Harlem Renaissance* (Chicago: University of Chicago Press, 1989), 50.

6. Carole Pateman, *The Sexual Contract* (Palo Alto: Stanford University Press, 2018 [1988]); bell hooks, *We Real Cool: Black Men and Masculinity* (New York: Routledge, 2004), 67–84; Michele Wallace, *Black Macho and the Myth of the Super Woman* (New York: Verso, 2015 [1978]), xxiii, 33.

7. Burt Boyar, *Photo by Sammy Davis, Jr.* (New York: It Books, 2007), quoted in Tracey Davis and Nina Bunche Pierce, *Sammy Davis, Jr.: A Personal Journey with My Father* (Philadelphia, PA: Running Press, 2014), 165.

8. Cedric Robinson, *Forgeries of Memory and Meaning: Blacks and the Regimes of Race in American Theater and Film before World War II* (Chapel Hill: UNC Press, 2007), 297.

9. Robinson, *Forgeries,* 35.

10. Robinson, *Forgeries,* 126.

11. Robinson, *Forgeries,* 47–48.

12. Robinson, *Forgeries,* 231.

13. Sammy Davis, Jr., BBC interview [c. 1957], in Jacci Parry, dir., *Sammy Davis, Jr.: The Kid in the Middle* (BBC, 2017).

14. Eartha Kitt, *I'm Still Here: Confessions of a Sex Kitten* (New York: Barricade Books, 1989), 132.

15. Gerald Early, *This Is Where I Came In: Black America in the 1960s* (Lincoln: University of Nebraska Press, 2003), 36.

CHAPTER 1. STAR RISING AT TWILIGHT

Davis: *New York World-Telegram,* December 24, 1956. Davis, Sammy Jr., Box 59, Clippings File of the James Weldon Johnson Memorial Collection in the Yale Collection of American Literature, Beinecke Rare Book and Manuscript Library, hereafter Box 59, Clippings File of the JWJ Memorial Collection, Beinecke Library, Yale University. Sanchez: Wil Haygood, *In Black and White: The Life of Sammy Davis, Jr.* (New York: Knopf, 2003), 44.

1. *Late Night with David Letterman,* September 16, 1985, https://www.youtube.com/watch?v=iIZxk4J7mWY.

2. Alain Locke, *The Negro and His Music: Negro Art, Past and Present* (New York: Arno, 1969 [1936]), 87.

3. Locke, *The Negro and His Music,* 72.

4. Constance Valis Hill, *Tap Dancing in America: A Cultural History* (New York: Oxford University Press, 2014), 168, 169, 174, 178–79.

5. Locke, *The Negro and His Music,* 82, 90.

6. Cedric Robinson, *Forgeries of Memory and Meaning: Blacks and the Regimes of Race in American Theater and Film before World War II* (Chapel Hill: UNC Press, 2007), 297.

7. Gerald Early, *This Is Where I Came In: Black America in the 1960s* (Lincoln: University of Nebraska Press, 2003), 42.

8. *New York Post,* March 13, 1956.

9. Marshall Stearns and Jean Stearns, *Jazz Dance: The Story of American Vernacular Dance* (New York: De Capo, 1994), 128.

10. *New York Post,* March 13, 1956, 36; Haygood, *In Black and White,* 56.

11. *People Weekly,* May 28, 1990, 92.

12. John Kassen, *The Little Girl Who Fought the Great Depression: Shirley Temple and 1930s America* (New York: W. W. Norton, 2014), 111.

13. Brian Seibert, *What the Eye Hears: A History of Tap Dancing* (New York: Farrar, Straus, Giroux, 2015), 329.

14. Roy Mack, dir., *Rufus Jones for President* (Vitaphone: 1933). As of summer, 2021, *Rufus Jones for President* was available on YouTube at https://www.youtube.com/watch?v=cos3b3gMGeY.

15. Thomas Cripps, *Slow Fade to Black: The Negro in American Film, 1900–1942* (New York: Oxford Univsersity Press, 1985), 233–35.

16. Valis Hill, *Tap Dancing in America*, 68.

17. Yuval Taylor, "Underneath the Harlem Moon," August 11, 2007, https://fakingit.typepad.com/faking_it/2007/08/underneath-the-.html.

18. Locke, *The Negro and His Music,* 59

19. *The Ed Sullivan Show*, 1964. Clip available at http://www.jewishhumorcentral.com/2020/01/the-great-jewish-comedians-phil-silvers.html.

20. Stearns and Stearns, *Jazz Dance*, 80–81; Valis Hill, *Tap Dancing in America*, 56–57; Seibert, *What the Eye Hears*, 113. See Rusty Frank, *Tap: The Greatest Tap Dance Stars and Their Stories, 1900–1955* (New York: De Capo, 1995).

21. "Bobalition Broadsides," https://www.loc.gov/item/2008661751. See also David Waldstreicher, *In the Midst of Perpetual Fetes: The Making of American Nationalism, 1776–1820* (Chapel Hill: UNC Press, 1997).

22. Valis Hill, *Tap Dancing in America*, 4.

23. Stearns and Stearns, *Jazz Dance*, 17.

24. Brenda Gottschild, *The Black Dancing Body: A Geography from Coon to Cool* (New York: Palgrave, 2005), 113; Jacqui Malone, *Steppin' on the Blues: The Visible Rhythms of African American Dance* (Urbana: University of Illinois Press, 1996), 41.

25. Stearns and Stearns, *Jazz Dance*, 13, 20, 27.

26. Locke, *The Negro and His Music*, 15.

27. Stearns and Stearns, *Jazz Dance*, 15, 32; Malone, *Steppin' on the Blues*, 70–91.

28. Seibert, *What the Eye Hears*, 31–32; Robert Ferris Thompson, *Aesthetic of the Cool: Afro-Atlantic Art and Music* (New York: Periscope, 2011).

29. Gottschild, *The Black Dancing Body*, 113; Valis Hill, *Tap Dancing in America*, 5–6.

30. Gottschild, *The Black Dancing Body*, 114.

31. Valis Hill, *Tap Dancing in America*, 100.

32. Malone, *Steppin' on the Blues*, 5–6; Valis Hill, *Tap Dancing in America*, 17.

33. Ralph Ellison, *Shadow and Act* (New York, Vintage, 1995), 208–9.

34. Robert O'Meally, "Deep jazz: Ralph Ellison's words swing on the page," *CSO Sounds & Stories* [Chicago Symphony Orchestra], February 7, 2019, https://csosoundsandstories.org/deep-jazz-ralph-ellisons-words-swing-on-the-page.

35. Gottschild, *The Black Dancing Body*, 120; Malone, *Steppin' on the Blues*, 7.

36. Malone, *Steppin' on the Blues*, 32–33; Ellison, *Shadow and Act*, 255.

37. Seibert, *What the Eye Hears*, 50.

38. Locke, *The Negro and His Music,* 53; Alain Locke, *The Negro in Art: A Pictorial Record of the Negro Artist and of the Negro Theme in Art* (Associates in Negro Folk Education, 1936), 139; Valis Hill, *Tap Dancing in America,* 24.

39. Gottschild, *The Black Dancing Body,* 110–11.

40. Malone, *Steppin' on the Blues,* 18.

41. Stearns and Stearns, *Jazz Dance,* 22; Valis Hill, *Tap Dancing in America,* 33; Seibert, *What the Eye Hears,* 52.

42. Seibert, *What the Eye Hears,* 60.

43. Thomas Riis, *Just Before Jazz* (Washington, DC: Smithsonian Press, 1989), 5–7.

44. Camille Forbes, *Introducing Bert Williams: Burnt Cork, Broadway, and the Story of America's First Black Star* (New York: Civitas, 2008), 58.

45. Gottschild, *The Black Dancing Body,* 126; Stearns and Stearns, *Jazz Dance,* 39–48 (Walker quoted p. 57).

46. Stearns and Stearns, *Jazz Dance,* 121; Valis Hill, *Tap Dancing in America,* 89.

47. Seibert, *What the Eye Hears,* 33.

48. Malone, *Steppin' on the Blues,* 106.

49. Forbes, *Introducing Bert Williams,* 93, 116; Seibert, *What the Eye Hears,* 107.

50. Forbes, *Introducing Bert Williams,* 64–66, 77.

51. Locke, *The Negro and His Music,* 61.

52. Seibert, *What the Eye Hears,* 106; Daphne Brooks, *Bodies in Dissent: Spectacular Performances of Race and Freedom, 1850–1910* (Durham, NC: Duke University Press, 2006), 220.

53. Brooks, *Bodies in Dissent,* 207, 210; Forbes, *Introducing Bert Williams,* 126–27.

54. Stearns and Stearns, *Jazz Dance,* 131.

55. Malone, *Steppin' on the Blues,* 76.

56. Seibert, *What the Eye Hears,* 152; Jervis Anderson, *This Was Harlem: A Cultural Portrait* (New York: Farrar, Straus, Giroux, 1982); David Levering Lewis, *When Harlem Was in Vogue* (New York: Penguin, 1997).

57. Stearns and Stearns, *Jazz Dance,* 139; Valis Hill, *Tap Dancing in America,* 71; James Haskins and N. R. Mitgang, *Mr. Bojangles: The Biography of Bill Robinson* (New York: William Morrow & Co., 1990), 108–15.

58. Seibert, *What the Eye Hears,* 158, 167; Stearns and Stearns, *Jazz Dance,* 151; Haskins and Mitgang, *Mr. Bojangles,* 115.

59. Valis Hill, *Tap Dancing in America,* 67; Seibert, *What the Eye Hears,* 262.

60. Malone, *Steppin' on the Blues,* 97; Valis Hill, *Tap Dancing in America,* 74.

61. Seibert, *What the Eye Hears,* 23, 26 15.

62. Malone, *Steppin' on the Blues,* 94–95; Valis Hill, *Tap Dancing in America,* 76; Stearns and Stearns, *Jazz Dance,* 151; Seibert, *What the Eye Hears,* 183–86.

63. Jayna Brown, *Babylon Girls: Black Women Performers and the Shaping of the Modern* (Durham, NC: Duke University Press, 2008); Saidiya Hartman, *Wayward*

Lives, Beautiful Experiment: Intimate Histories of Riotous Black Girls, Troublesome Women, and Queer Radicals (New York: W. W. Norton, 2020);

64. Seibert, *What the Eye Hears*, 142; Joel Dinerstein, *Swingin' the Machine: Modernity, Technology, and African American Culture between the World Wars* (Boston: University of Massachusetts Press, 2003).

65. Seibert, *What the Eye Hears*, 173; Dinerstein, *Swinging the Machine*, 3, 105–20. Le Corbusier is quoted in Mabel Wilson, "Black Bodies/White Cities: Le Corbusier in Harlem," *ANY: Architecture in New York* 16, Whiteness: White Forms/Forms of Whiteness (1996): 35–39.

66. Seibert, *What the Eye Hears*, 124; Malone, *Steppin' on the Blues*, 54–58.

67. Malone, *Steppin' on the Blues*, 68, 82; Stearns and Stearns, *Jazz Dance*, 254.

68. Malone, *Steppin' on the Blues*, 68.

69. Stearns and Stearns, *Jazz Dance*, 55; Frank, *Tap!*, 145.

70. Bob and Betty Lewis interview with SDJ, Las Vegas, December 1963, Performing Arts Collection—Recorded Sound—Billy Rose Library, NYPL, LDC 37524.

71. Haygood, *In Black and White*, 68; Sammy Davis Interview [sound recording], produced by WMAQ Radio, Chicago, https://legacycatalogue.nypl.org/record=b11973518-S1, Schomberg Center forResearch in Black Culture, Moving Image and Sound Division.

72. Frank, *Tap*, 227.

73. Frank, *Tap*, 144; Stearns and Stearns, *Jazz Dance*, 140, 149.

74. Stearns and Stearns, *Jazz Dance*, 78–79.

75. Mel Watkins, *On the Real Side: A History of African American Comedy* (Chicago: Lawrence Hill, 1999), 367.

76. Frank, *Tap*, 48–50.

77. Stearns and Stearns, *Jazz Dance*, 90.

78. Frank, *Tap*, 257–58.

79. *Mr. Wonderful: A New Musical Comedy.* Box 59, Clippings File of the JWJ Memorial Collection, Beinecke Library, Yale University.

80. Sammy Davis, Jr., Burt Boyar, and Jane Boyar, *Yes I Can* (New York: Farrar, Straus, Giroux, 1965), 26.

81. Florian Kerz and Ivor Halstvedt, *Beyond Bojangles: The Sammy Davis, Jr. Encyclopedia* (Books on Demand, 2014), 275.

82. Frank, *Tap*, 152; Sammy Davis, Jr., and Gerald Early, *The Sammy Davis, Jr. Reader* (New York: Farrar, Straus, Giroux, 2001), 464; Haygood, *In Black and White*, 72.

83. Davis, *Yes I Can*, 35, 36.

84. Haygood, *In Black and White*, 69.

85. Davis, *Yes I Can*, 25.

86. *Mr. Wonderful: A New Musical Comedy.* Box 59, Clippings File of the JWJ Memorial Collection, Beinecke Library, Yale University.

87. Davis, *Yes I Can,* 40.

88. Mia Bay, *Traveling Black: A Story of Race and Resistance* (Cambridge, MA: Harvard/Belknap, 2021), 138.

89. Davis, *Yes I Can,* 42, 22, 38, 39.

90. "Alex Haley Interviews Sammy Davis, Jr.," *Playboy,* December, 1966, in Davis and Early, *The Sammy Davis, Jr. Reader,* 467.

91. Davis, *Yes I Can,* 45, 46.

92. Davis, *Yes I Can,* 20.

93. Davis, *Yes I Can,* 29, 34.

94. Haygood, *In Black and White,* 70.

95. Seibert, *What the Eye Hears,* 164, 214, 247.

96. Malone, *Steppin' on the Blues,* 115.

97. Valis Hill, *Tap Dancing in America,* 122, 138.

98. Seibert, *What the Eye Hears,* 214–15.

99. Seibert, *What the Eye Hears,* 231, 12.

100. *Christian Science Monitor,* May 23, 1990, 11; *New York Times,* May 19, 1990, 30.

101. *Philadelphia Evening Bulletin,* February 22, 1956, 18. Box 59, Clippings File of the JWJ Memorial Collection, Beinecke Library, Yale University.

102. *Philadelphia Inquirer,* February 22, 1956, 36. Box 59, Clippings File of the JWJ Memorial Collection, Beinecke Library, Yale University.

103. Langston Hughes, "The Influence of Negro Music on American Entertainment," in *Langston Hughes and the Chicago Defender: Essays on Race, Politics, and Culture, 1942–62,* ed. Christopher C. DeSantis (Urbana: University of Illinois Press, 1995), 207.

104. *New York Journal-American,* March 23, 1956, 22. Box 59, Clippings File of the JWJ Memorial Collection, Beinecke Library, Yale University. *Daily News,* March 24, 1956, 20, emphasis added.

105. *Rowan & Martin's Laugh-In,* https://www.youtube.com/watch?v=wn6vl5ymFIM.

106. *Rowan & Martin's Laugh-In,* https://www.youtube.com/watch?v=iMJOdLZaKEo.

107. Davis, *Yes I Can,* 3.

108. Sinatra and Armstrong, "Birth of the Blues," https://www.youtube.com/watch?v=7sYdUGoIqUM.

109. Lena Horne and Richard Schickel, *Lena* (New York: Doubleday, 1965), 112–14.

110. Robert O'Meally, ed., *Living with Music: Ralph Ellison's Jazz Writings* (New York: Modern Library, 2002), 103.

111. LeRoi Jones [Amiri Baraka], *Blues People: Negro Music in White America* (New York: Harper Perennial, 1999 [1962]), 17.

112. Ellis Cashmore, *The Black Culture Industry* (London: Routledge, 1997), 39.

Joe Louis, *Joe Louis: My Life* (New York: Ecco, 1997), 161; Lena Horne and Richard Schickel, *Lena* (New York: Doubleday, 1965), 173; Sammy Davis, Jr., Burt Boyar, and Jane Boyar, *Yes I Can* (New York: Farrar, Straus, Giroux, 1965), 61.

1. Davis, *Yes I Can,* 47–48.

2. "What Makes Sammy, Jr. Run?," *Esquire,* 1973, and "Sammy Davis, Jr.," in Sammy Davis, Jr., and Gerald Early, *The Sammy Davis, Jr. Reader* (New York: Farrar, Straus, Giroux, 2001), 339, 48.

3. James Baldwin, *The Fire Next Time* (New York, Vintage, 1992), 54.

4. Sam Kashner, "The Color of Love," *Vanity Fair,* September 2013, https://www.vanityfair.com/style/1999/03/sammy-davis-kim-novak-dating.

5. James Baldwin, *Nobody Knows My Name* (New York, Vintage, 1992), 156–57; "The Shot That Echoes Still" is available at https://www.esquire.com/news-politics/a14443780/james-baldwin-mlk-funeral.

6. George Orwell, *Coming Up for Air* (New York: Mariner Books, 1969 [1939]), 144.

7. *Los Angeles Times,* May 17, 1990, 1; Brian Seibert, *What the Eye Hears: A History of Tap Dancing* (New York: Farrar, Straus, Giroux, 2015), 93.

8. Willard Gatewood, *Black Americans and the White Man's Burden, 1898–1903* (Urbana: University of Illinois Press, 1975); Willard Gatewood, *"Smoked Yankees" and the Struggle for Empire: Letters from Negro Soldiers, 1898–1902* (Fayetteville: University of Arkansas Press, 1987).

9. David Levering Lewis, *W. E. B. Du Bois: A Biography, 1868–1963* (New York: Holt, 2009), 530.

10. Claude MacKay, "If We Must Die," in Alain Locke, *The New Negro: Voices of the Harlem Renaissance* (New York: Touchstone, 1992 [1925]), 134.

11. Adriane Lentz-Smith, *Freedom Struggles: African Americans and World War I* (Cambridge, MA: Harvard University Press, 2011), 42, 54.

12. Langston Hughes, "Freedom Road," http://pancocojams.blogspot.com/2014/02/freedom-road-poem-by-langston-hughes-as.html; Josh White, "Freedom Road," *Josh White: Vol. 5, 1944* (Document Records, 1997).

13. Kimberly Philips, *War! What Is It Good For?: Black Freedom Struggles and the US Military from World War II to Iraq* (Chapel Hill: UNC Press, 2014), 62.

14. *New York Times,* September 16, 1935, 1.

15. John Dower, *War Without Mercy: Race and Power in the Pacific War* (New York: Pantheon, 1987), 77–93, 182–89.

16. Michi Weglyn, *Years of Infamy: The Untold Story of America's Concentration Camps* (Seattle: University of Washington Press, 1996), 38; David Stafford, *Roosevelt and Churchill: Men of Secrets* (New York: Abrams, 2000), 142.

17. "WWII in American Music," https://www.historyonthenet.com/authentichistory/1939-1945/3-music/04-PH-Reaction.

18. Philips, *War!,* 65.

19. *Fighting Racism in World War II* (New York: Pathfinder, 2001), 20.

20. Ronald Takaki, *Double Victory: A Multicultural History of America in World War II* (Boston: Back Bay, 2001), 23.

21. *Fighting Racism in World War II,* 132, 381–83.

22. Personal conversation with the author, New Haven, CT, December, 1998.

23. Christopher Moore, *Fighting for America: Black Soldiers—the Unsung Heroes of World War II* (New York: One World, 2004), 184.

24. Moore, *Fighting for America,* 204–5.

25. Marshall Stearns and Jean Stearns, *Jazz Dance: The Story of American Vernacular Dance* (New York: De Capo, 1994), 186; Moore, *Fighting for America,* 205; John A. Williams, *This Is My Country Too* (New York: New American, 1965), 14.

26. *Fighting Racism in World War II,* 36; Takaki, *Double Victory,* 22–57.

27. *Fighting Racism in World War II,* 39.

28. *Fighting Racism in World War II,* 57.

29. *Fighting Racism in World War II,* 128–63; Takaki, *Double Victory,* 40–42.

30. Takaki, *Double Victory,* 40.

31. *Pittsburgh Courier,* January 31, 1942. Box 59, Clippings File of the JWJ Memorial Collection, Beinecke Library, Yale University.

32. Takaki, *Double Victory,* 26–28.

33. Takaki, *Double Victory,* 29–30; Herbert Shapiro, *White Violence and Black Response: From Reconstruction to Montgomery* (Boston: University of Massachussetts Press, 1988), 308–9.

34. Gunnar Myrdal, *An American Dilemma: The Negro Problem and Modern Democracy, Volume I* (New York: Routledge, 1995 [1944]), 26.

35. Takaki, *Double Victory,* 50–52.

36. "The Riots," *Crisis,* July 1943, 199.

37. Takaki, *Double Victory,* 55.

38. James Baldwin, *Notes of a Native Son* (Boston: Beacon, 2012 [1955]), 100.

39. Baldwin, *Notes of a Native Son,* 112.

40. Adam Clayton Powell, *Marching Blacks* (New York: Dial, 1946), 171–72.

41. Farah Jasmine Griffin, *Harlem Nocturne: Women Artists and Progressve Politics during World War II* (New York: Civitas, 2013), 120.

42. Martin Luther King, Jr., "The Other America," 1967, https://www.crmvet.org/docs/otheram.htm.

43. Ann Petry, "In Darkness and Confusion," in *Miss Muriel and Other Stories* (Evanston: Nothwestern University Press, 2017), 264.

44. Griffin, *Harlem Nocturne,* 122–24.

45. Petry, "Darkness and Confusion," 262.

46. Petry, "Darkness and Confusion," 266–68.

47. Petry, "Darkness and Confusion," 79–80.

48. Petry, "Darkness and Confusion," 281–82.

49. Petry, "Darkness and Confusion," 287, 289.

50. Petry, "Darkness and Confusion," 256–57.

51. Petry, "Darkness and Confusion," 289–90, 292.

52. *New York Times,* August 3, 1943, 1; Griffin, *Harlem Nocturne,* 125.

53. *New York Post,* March 12–14, 1956; *Saturday Evening Post* May 21, 1960. Box 59, Clippings File of the JWJ Memorial Collection, Beinecke Library, Yale University; Wil Haygood, *In Black and White: The Life of Sammy Davis, Jr.* (New York: Knopf, 2003), 101–4.

54. "Sammy Davis, Jr. in His Own Words," *Black Journal* Episode 31, 1971, PBS, https://www.youtube.com/watch?v=CAk1P4p05Qk.

55. Gary Fishgall, *Gonna Do Great Things: The Life of Sammy Davis, Jr.* (New York: Scribner, 2010), 31. On the travails of the African American soldier traveling to and from wartime assignments, see Mia Bay, *Traveling Black: A Story of Race and Resistance* (Cambridge, MA: Harvard/Belknap, 2021), 240–47.

56. Fishgall, *Gonna Do Great Things,* 29–30; Haygood, *In Black and White,* 101.

57. *New York Post,* March 14, 1956, Box 59, Clippings File of the JWJ Memorial Collection, Beinecke Library, Yale University.

58. "Alex Haley Interviews Sammy Davis, Jr.," in Davis and Early, *The Sammy Davis, Jr. Reader,* 461.

59. Davis, *Yes I Can,* 61.

60. Davis, *Yes I Can,* 51.

61. Davis, *Yes I Can,* 50–72.

62. Davis, *Yes I Can,* 67–68.

63. Davis, *Yes I Can,* 60.

64. *People Weekly,* 1978, in Davis and Early, *The Sammy Davis, Jr. Reader,* 513.

65. "10 Out and Proud Bisexual Celebrities," GCN, September, 2015, https://gcn.ie/10-out-and-proud-bisexual-celebrities.

66. "Early, Sammy Davis, Jr."; *People Weekly,* 1978, in Davis and Early, *The Sammy Davis, Jr. Reader,* 48n57, 515.

67. Sammy Davis, Jr., Burt Boyar, and Jane Boyar, *Why Me?: The Sammy Davis, Jr. Story* (New York: Farrar, Straus, Giroux, 1989), 20.

68. Davis, *Yes I Can,* 65–66.

69. Davis, *Yes I Can,* 72; Fishgall, *Gonna Do Great Things,* 37.

70. Davis, *Yes I Can,* 44.

71. "Alex Haley Interviews," 460–61.

72. *"At Ease," Volume II: Minstrel Shows* (New York: USO-Camp Shows, Inc., 1942), 10–11.

73. James Cooke, *American Girls, Beer, and Glenn Miller: GI Morale in World War II* (Columbia: University of Missouri Press, 2012), 35, 66.

74. *"At Ease," Volume II: Minstrel Shows,* 9–10, 15, 44.

75. *"At Ease," Volume II: Minstrel Shows,* 49–50.

76. Michael Curtis, dir., *This Is the Army* (Warner Bros., 1943).

77. Cooke, *American Girls,* 63.

78. June Cross, dir., *Secret Daughter* (PBS and WGBH, 1996). See also June Cross, *Secret Daughter: A Mixed-Race Daughter and the Mother Who Gave Her Away* (New York: Penguin, 2007).

79. Astaire was willing to spout this racist libel even though he had learned his craft by watching "the black dancers on the bill or in the alley by the theater and ask for a step" (Seibert, *What the Eye Hears,* 223–24).

80. Danielle Fuentes Morgan, *Laughing to Keep from Dying: African American Satire in the Twenty-First Century* (Urbana: University of Illinois Press, 2020), 15. I've had the opportunity on a few occasions to discuss this setpiece with Jimmy Cross's stepson, historian Lary May. In our first conversation, I argued that Cross was hewing to overtly racist direction from the white production team of *This Is the Army,* and May insisted that Cross was undermining their project by playing the minstrel angle over the top. A year or so later we met again; upon further reflection, I had come around to May's position, and he had come around to mine. The indeterminacy is the compelling point here.

81. Seibert, *What the Eye Hears,* 324.

82. Cheryl Mullenbach, *Double Victory: How African American Women Broke Race and Gender Barriers to Help Win World War II* (Chicago: Chicago Review Press, 2013), 205.

83. Mullenbach, *Double Victory,* 206, 207, 215.

84. Mullenbach, *Double Victory,* 196.

85. Mullenbach, *Double Victory,* 204.

86. Mullenbach, *Double Victory,* 232–33.

87. Samantha L. Quigley, "'Mr. Entertainment' Goes to Vietnam," June 11, 2014, https://www.uso.org/stories/1725-mr-entertainment-goes-to-vietnam; George Stephenson, dir., *Peace, Togetherness, and Sammy: Sammy Davis Jr.'s Tour of Vietnam* (Office of Information for the Armed Forces Department of Defense, 1972), https://www.youtube.com/watch?v=gY9un2btpuo.

88. Ray Sprigle, *In the Land of Jim Crow* (New York: Simon & Schuster, 1949), 91–92.

89. Patrick Novotny, *This Georgia Rising: Education, Civil Rights, and the Politics of Change in Georgia in the 1940s* (Macon: Mercer University Press, 2008), 208; Springle, *Land of Jim Crow,* 200–1.

90. Thomas Cripps, *Making Movies Black: The Hollywood Message Movie from World War II to the Civil Rights Era* (New York: Oxford University Press, 1993), 52.

91. Cripps, *Making Movies Black,* 105, 108–10.

92. Cripps, *Making Movies Black,* 101.

93. *Los Angeles Times,* May 17, 1990, 1.

94. *New York Daily News,* March 24, 1956, 20.

CHAPTER 3. THE ALL-NEGRO CAST,
AND OTHER BLACK SPACES

James Baldwin, "On the Horizon, on Catfish Row," *Commentary,* September, 1959, https://www.commentarymagazine.com/articles/james-baldwin/on-the-horizon -on-catfish-row.

1. Langston Hughes, "Key Chains with No Keys" [1943] and "The Influence of Negro Music on American Entertainment" [1953], in *Langston Hughes and the Chicago Defender: Essays on Race, Politics, and Culture, 1942–62,* ed. Christopher C. DeSantis (Urbana: University of Illinois Press, 1995), 122, 207.

2. *New York Times,* January 18, 1959, X1.

3. *New York Times,* January 25, 1959, X7.

4. Thomas Cripps, *Making Movies Black: The Hollywood Message Movie from World War II to the Civil Rights Era* (New York: Oxford University Press, 1993), 180; Thomas Cripps, *Slow Fade to Black: The Negro in American Film, 1900–1942* (New York: Oxford University Press, 1985), 108, 374–76, 387; Lena Horne and Richard Schockel, *Lena* (New York: Doubleday, 1965), 187–88.

5. Cripps, *Slow Fade to Black,* 3–7, 349, 375–76.

6. Cripps, *Slow Fade to Black,* 379–81; Ellen Scott, *Cinema Civil Rights: Regulation, Repression, and Race in the Classical Hollywood Era* (New Brunswick: Rutgers University Press, 2015).

7. Cripps, *Making Movies Black,* 226, 207.

8. Cripps, *Making Movies Black,* 142–45; Cripps, *Slow Fade to Black,* 379.

9. Cripps, *Making Movies Black,* 226.

10. Cripps, *Making Movies Black,* 187.

11. Cripps, *Making Movies Black,* 178; Cripps, *Slow Fade to Black,* 111.

12. Cripps, *Making Movies Black,* 190.

13. Ronald L. Jackson II, *Scripting the Black Masculine Body: Identity, Discourse, and Racial Poliics in Popular Media* (Albany: SUNY Press, 2006), 75.

14. James Baldwin, "Carmen Jones: The Dark is Light Enough," in *Notes of a Native Son* (Boston: Beacon, 2012 [1955]), 76, 74.

15. Baldwin, "Carmen Jones," 75.

16. James Baldwin, "Life Straight in de Eye," *Commentary,* January 1, 1955, 74–77.

17. *Time,* January 26, 1959, 91.

18. *Time,* January 26, 1959, 91; *Los Angeles Times,* May 1, 1958, B9.

19. Wil Haygood, *In Black and White: The Life of Sammy Davis, Jr.* (New York: Knopf, 2003), 274–75.

20. "An accordion was wheezing away happily but faultily," Anna finds upon entering a local bar, "a folk song such as Ma or Otto Strobel might have sung on that boat coming over." See Philip Yordan, *Anna Lucasta* (New York: Dell, 1949 [1945]), 106.

21. Yordan, *Anna Lucasta,* 34, 81; Judith Smith, *Visions of Belonging: Family Stories, Popular Culture, and Postwar Democracy, 1940–1969* (New York: Columbia University Press, 2006), 310–11.

22. Arnold Lavan, dir., *Anna Lucasta* (Samuel Goldwyn Studios, 1958).

23. *Christian Science Monitor,* February 19, 1959, 5; *New York Times,* January 15, 1959, 27; Gary Fishgall, *Gonna Do Great Things: The Life of Sammy Davis, Jr.* (New York: Scribner, 2010), 122; *Los Angeles Times,* June 15, 1958, E1.

24. *Time,* January 26, 1959, 91.

25. Cripps, *Making Movies Black,* 284.

26. Haygood, *In Black and White,* 278; Smith, *Visions of Belonging,* 311.

27. *The Catholic World,* February 1959, 416.

28. *Newsweek,* December 8, 1958, 95.

29. Toni Morrison, *Love* (New York: Vintage, 2005), 75.

30. *Los Angeles Times,* November 9, 1958, E1.

31. Eartha Kitt, *I'm Still Here: Confessions of a Sex Kitten* (Fort Lee: Barricade Books, 1989), 196.

32. *Commonweal,* February 6, 1959, 497; *America,* January 31, 1959, 531.

33. *New York Times,* January 18, 1959, X1.

34. Otto Preminger, dir., *Porgy and Bess* (Samuel Goldwyn, 1959).

35. Sammy Davis, Jr., *Hollywood in a Suitcase* (New York: Star Books, 1981), 39; *New York Times,* February 18, 1958, Box 59, Clippings File of the JWJ Memorial Collection, Beinecke Library, Yale University.

36. Hedda Hopper, *Chicago Tribune,* October 28, 1964, B4; Sammy Davis, Jr., Burt Boyar, and Jane Boyar, *Yes I Can* (New York: Farrar, Straus, Giroux, 1965), 461–62; Emilie Raymond, *Stars for Freedom: Hollywood, Black Celebrities, and the Civil Rights Movement* (Seattle: University of Washington Press, 2015), 20.

37. Sammy Davis, Jr. and Gerald Early, *The Sammy Davis, Jr. Reader* (New York: Farrar, Straus, Giroux, 2001), 44; Haygood, *In Black and White,* 285; Aram Goudsouzian, *Sidney Poitier: Man, Actor, Icon* (Chapel Hill: UNC Press, 2004), 151.

38. *New York Mirror,* June 25, 1959, Box 59, Clippings File of the JWJ Memorial Collection, Beinecke Library, Yale University.

39. Goudsouzian, *Sidney Poitier,* 149.

40. Ellen Noonan, *The Strange Career of Porgy and Bess: Race, Culture, and America's Most Famous Opera* (Chapel Hill: UNC Press, 2012), 264–65; Goudsouzian, *Sidney Poitier,* 150–51.

41. DuBose Heyward, *Porgy* (Jackson: University of Mississippi Press, 2015 [1925]), 13–14.

42. Heyward, *Porgy,* 63.

43. Daphne Brooks, "A Woman Is a Sometime Thing: (Re)Covering Black Womanhood in *Porgy and Bess,*" *Daedalus,* Winter, 2021, https://www.amacad.org/publication/recovering-black-womanhood-porgy-and-bess; Noonan, *Strange Career,* 17, 45.

44. Jeffrey Melnick, *A Right to Sing the Blues: African Americans, Jews, and American Popular Song* (Cambridge, MA: Harvard University Press, 1999), 45–46, 122.

45. Noonan, *Strange Career,* 73, 77.

46. Noonan, *Strange Career,* 92–93.

47. Noonan, *Strange Career,* 85–87, 97–100.

48. Noonan, *Strange Career,* 76.

49. Heyward, *Porgy,* 32.

50. Melnick, *A Right to Sing the Blues,* 74, 123; Noonan, *Strange Career,* 174–75.

51. Melnick, *A Right to Sing the Blues,* 73.

52. Melnick, *A Right to Sing the Blues,* 74.

53. Melnick, *A Right to Sing the Blues,* 123–27; Noonan, *Strange Career,* 176–77.

54. Noonan, *Strange Career,* 179.

55. Noonan, *Strange Career,* 153, 174.

56. Goudsouzian, *Sidney Poitier,* 148.

57. *New York Times,* March 31, 1959, 26; *Los Angeles Times,* May 4, 59, C17; *Chicago Daily Tribune,* June 14, 59, E8; *New York Times,* June 25, 1959, 9.

58. *Los Angeles Times,* July 12, 1959, K85; *New York Times,* May 24, 1959, X15; *Los Angeles Times,* June 17, 1959, A11.

59. Scott, *Cinema Civil Rights,* 185.

60. Noonan, *Strange Career,* 262, 264; Haygood, *In Black and White,* 284.

61. Goudsouzian, *Sidney Poitier,* 159.

62. Haygood, *In Black and White,* 286; Noonan, *Strange Career,* 266–67.

63. Haygood, *In Black and White,* 286–87; Goudsouzian, *Sidney Poitier,* 160.

64. Haygood, *In Black and White,* 285; Davis, *Hollywood in a Suitcase,* 47; Goudsouzian, *Sidney Poitier,* 160–61, 163; Nichelle Nichols, *Beyond Uhura: Star Trek and Other Memories* (New York: Putnam, 1994), 89–90; Raymond, *Stars for Freedom,* 26–34; Goudsouzian, *Sidney Poitier,* 160.

65. Haygood, *In Black and White,* 286–87.

66. Davis, *Hollywood in a Suitcase,* 46.

67. *Esquire* portrait, Davis and Early, *The Sammy Davis, Jr. Reader,* 342; Davis, *Hollywood in a Suitcase,* 40–41.

68. Constance Valis Hill, *Tap Dancing in America: A Cultural History* (New York: Oxford University Press, 2014), 100.

69. Davis, *Hollywood in a Suitcase,* 42–43; Fishgall, *Gonna Do Great Things,* 130; *Dance Magazine,* in Davis and Early, *The Sammy Davis, Jr. Reader,* 243–44.

70. Daphne Brooks, "I Got Plenty O' Nuttin': Blackface, Black Women Vocalists, and the 'Folk Opera' Crisis"; "A Woman Is a Sometime Thing: Black Feminist Sound and Fury in the *Porgy and Bess* Archive," both in "'Lemonade from Lemons': Black Women Artists and the Gershwin Problem, 1935–2020," lecture series at the Hutchins Center for African American Studies, Harvard University, October, 2020.

71. Fishgall, *Gonna Do Great Things,* 130; *Chicago Daily Tribune,* January 22, 1959, C6.

72. *Chicago Daily Tribune,* July 30, 1959, B6; Fishgall, *Gonna Do Great Things,* 131; Haygood, *In Black and White,* 291; *Chicago Daily Tribune,* March 15, 1959, M14.

73. "Sammy Davis, Jr. Dies, 64," *New York* Times, 1990, in Davis and Early, *The Sammy Davis, Jr. Reader,* 395; Haygood, *In Black and White,* 291; *Pittsburgh Courier,* November 7, 1959, 22.

74. Davis, *Hollywood in a Suitcase,* 48; Fishgall, *Gonna Do Great Things,* 130.

75. Haygood, *In Black and White,* 291.

76. Goudsouzian, *Sidney Poitier,* 160, 166, 274–75.

77. Mia Mask, *Divas on Screen: Black Women in American Film* (Urbana: University of Illinois Press, 2009), 52.

78. Baldwin, "On the Horizon," *Commentary,* September 1959, https://www
.commentarymagazine.com/articles/james-baldwin/on-the-horizon-on-catfish
-row.

79. Baldwin, "On the Horizon."

80. *Pittsburgh Courier,* January 2, 60, 4.

81. Noonan, *Strange Career,* 270; Goudsouzian, *Sidney Poitier,* 165.

82. Leo Penn, dir., *A Man Called Adam* (Trace-Mark, 1966).

83. "Alex Haley Interviews Sammy Davis, Jr.," in Davis and Early, *The Sammy
Davis, Jr. Reader,* 459.

84. *New York Times,* November 26, 1965, 44.

85. *Newsweek,* August 8, 1966, 80.

86. *New York Times,* November 26, 1965, 44.

87. *Time,* August 19, 1966, 78.

88. *New York Post,* October 4, 1957, Box 59, Clippings File of the JWJ Memorial
Collection, Beinecke Library, Yale University.

89. *Los Angeles Times,* October 5, 1966, D18; *Chicago Defender,* August 8, 1966,
10; *New York Times,* August 21, 1966, 108.

90. Baldwin, "On the Horizon."

91. Adriane Lentz-Smith, *Freedom Struggles: African Americans and World War
I* (Cambridge, MA: Harvard University Press, 2011), 184.

92. Henry Louis Gates, *Colored People: A Memoir* (New York: Vintage, 1995),
211; *New York Times Magazine,* April 30, 1961, 37.

93. Gates, *Colored People,* 64–65.

94. Ferguson Jenkins, interview with the author, December 20, 2013, Oak
Brook, IL, for Gaspar Gonzalez, dir., *Long Way from Home: The Untold Story of
Baseball's Desegregation* (Hammer and Nail, 2018).

95. Annelise Orleck, *Storming Caesars Palace: How Black Mothers Fought Their
Own War on Poverty* (Boston: Beacon, 2006), 197.

96. Orleck, *Storming Caesars Palace,* 62; Marvin Clemons, "Moulin Rouge
Played Important Role in Las Vegas History," *Las Vegas Review-Journal,* October
24, 2019, https://www.reviewjournal.com/business/casinos-gaming/moulin-rouge-
played-important-role-in-las-vegas-history-1877676.

97. Orleck, *Storming Caesars Palace,* 197, 61.

CHAPTER 4. THE VEGAS STRIP, NETWORK TV, AND
OTHER WHITE SPACES

Prima, quoted in Ted Fox, *Showtime at the Apollo: The Story of Harlem's World
Famous Theater* (New York: Mill Road Enterprises, 2003), 160; Davis: "Sammy
Davis, Jr. in His Own Words," *Black Journal* Episode 31, 1971, PBS, https://www
.youtube.com/watch?v=CAk1P4po5Qk.

1. George Lipsitz, *How Racism Takes Place* (Philadelphia: Temple University
Press, 2011), 40.

2. Rebecca Davis, "These Are a Swinging Bunch of People: Sammy Davis, Jr., Religious Conversion, and the Color of Jewish Ethnicity," *American Jewish History* 100, no. 1 (January, 2016): 41; Craig Werner, *A Change Is Gonna Come: Music, Race & the Soul of America* (Ann Arbor: University of Michigan Press, 2006), 37; Gerald Early, *This Is Where I Came In: Black America in the 1960s* (Lincoln: University of Nebraska Press, 2003), 42–43.

3. Paul Robeson, *Here I Stand* (Boston: Beacon, 1998), 74–75.

4. Lipsitz, *How Racism Takes Place,* 57.

5. Sammy Davis, Jr., Burt Boyar, and Jane Boyar, *Why Me? The Sammy Davis, Jr. Story* (New York: Farrar, Straus, Giroux, 1989), 227.

6. Sammy Davis, Jr., Burt Boyar, and Jane Boyar, *Yes I Can* (New York: Farrar, Straus, Giroux, 1965), 291.

7. Davis, *Yes I Can,* 301–2, 305, 306.

8. *Philadelphia Evening Bulletin,* February 22, 1956, Box 59, Clippings File of the JWJ Memorial Collection, Beinecke Library, Yale University; Thomas Cripps, *Slow Fade to Black: The Negro in American Film, 1900–1942* (New York: Oxford Univsersity Press, 1985), 253; Davis, *Yes I Can,* 301.

9. Jerry Hopper, dir., *Sweet and Low* (Paramount Musical Parade: 1947), https://www.youtube.com/watch?v=GLuYWEuCm2A.

10. Davis, *Yes I Can,* 86; Sam Pollard, dir., *Sammy Davis, Jr.: I've Gotta Be Me* (ARTE American Masters: 2019).

11. Joe Brown, "Larry Storch," *Washington Post,* June 8, 1983, https://www.washingtonpost.com/archive/lifestyle/1983/06/08/larry-storch/f3a50a23-ed3c-4edd-a668-5febadadb45d.

12. *New York Post,* March 14, 1956, Box 59, Clippings File of the JWJ Memorial Collection, Beinecke Library, Yale University.

13. Davis, *Yes I Can,* 128.

14. *Colgate Comedy Hour,* http://sammydavisjr.info/eddie-cantor-sammy.

15. Brian Seibert, *What the Eye Hears: A History of Tap Dancing* (New York, Farrar, Straus, Giroux, 2015), 334–35, 339–40.

16. Davis, *Yes I Can,* 151, 152–53.

17. Arthur Silber, Jr., *Sammy Davis, Jr.: Me and My Shadow* (Los Angeles: Samart Enterprises, 2003), 82.

18. Silber, *Sammy Davis, Jr.,* 82–83; Davis, *Yes I Can,* 148.

19. Silber, *Sammy Davis, Jr.,* 19–21; Davis, *Yes I Can,* 153, 154; James Loewen, *Sundown Towns: A Hidden Dimension of American Racism* (New York: New Press, 2018).

20. Silber, *Sammy Davis, Jr.,* 23; Davis, *Yes I Can,* 153–60.

21. Flash McDonald in Rusty Frank, *Tap! The Greatest Tap Dance Stars and Stories, 1900–1955* (New York: De Capo, 1995), 221; Stefan Al, *The Strip: Las Vegas and the Architecture of the American Dream* (Cambridge: MIT Press, 2017); Geoff Schumacher, *Sun, Sin & Suburbia: The History of Modern Las Vegas* (Reno: University of Nevada Press, 2015), 67–83; Barbara Land and Myrick Land, *A Short History of Las Vegas* (Reno: University of Nevada Press, 2004), 83–91.

22. Annelise Orleck, *Storming Caesars Palace: How Black Mothers Fought Their Own War on Poverty* (Boston: Beacon, 2006), 44, 37, 47–48.

23. Davis, *Yes I Can*, 90, 88.

24. Davis, *Yes I Can*, 120; Davis, *Why Me?*, 35; Land and Land, *Short History of Las Vegas*, 145–46; Al, *The Strip*, 50.

25. Geraldine Branton in Chris Bould and Michael Martin, dirs., *The Nicholas Brothers: We Sing, We Dance* (A&E: 1992); Orleck, *Storming Caesars Palace*, 62; Davis, *Yes I Can*, 240–41.

26. Shawn Levy, *Rat Pack Confidential: Frank, Dean, Sammy, Peter, Joey and the Last Great Show Biz Party* (New York: Crown, 1999), 68; Lawrence Quirk and William Schoell, *The Rat Pack: Neon Nights with the Kings of Cool* (New York: Perenial, 2003), 104–6, 150–2; Joel Dinerstein, *The Origins of Cool in Postwar America* (Chicago: University of Chicago Press, 2017), 298–99.

27. Davis, *Yes I Can*, 187; Levy, *Rat Pack Confidential*, 149.

28. Davis, *Yes I Can*, 192; Pollard, *Sammy Davis, Jr.*

29. Davis, *Why Me*, 117–18; Land and Land, *Short History of Las Vegas*, 148.

30. Orleck, *Storming Caesars Palace*, 209.

31. Wil Haygood, *King of the Cats: The Life and Times of Adam Clayton Powell, Jr.* (New York: Harper, 2006), 232–33; Orleck, *Storming Ceasar's Palace*, 61, 63–64.

32. Orleck, *Storming Caesars Palace*, 59.

33. "Blacks Remember Strip Desegregation," *Las Vegas Sun*, March 21, 1999, https://lasvegassun.com/news/1999/mar/21/blacks-remember-strip-desegregation; Levy, *Rat Pack Confidential*, 146–47.

34. Pollard, *Sammy Davis, Jr.*; Gary Fishgall, *Gonna Do Great Things: The Life of Sammy Davis, Jr.,* (New York: Scribner, 2010), 172.

35. David and Joe Henry, *Furious Cool: Richard Pryor and the World that Made Him* (Chapel Hill, NC: Algonquin, 2014), 68–69.

36. Dinerstein, *Origins of Cool*, 9, 11, 12, 14, 20, 23, 272–74; Ronald L. Jackson II and Mark Hopson, *Masculinity in the Black Imagination: Politics of Communicating Race and Manhood* (New York: Peter Lang, 2011), 169–71.

37. Dinerstein, *Origins of Cool*, 24, 31.

38. bell hooks, *We Real Cool: Black Men and Masculinity* (New York: Routledge, 2004), 147.

39. Pollard, *Sammy Davis, Jr.*; Steven Grandison, dir., *Rat Pack: A Conference of Cool* (BBC: 1999); *Rat Pack: Live at the Sands,* double LP (Capitol Records, 2014).

40. Quirk and Schoell, *Rat Pack*, 61–62.

41. Davis, *Yes I Can*, 482–83.

42. Davis, *Yes I Can*, 468.

43. Davis, *Yes I Can*, 469.

44. Silber, *Sammy Davis, Jr.*, 287.

45. Mel Watkins, *On the Real Side: A History of African American Comedy* (Chicago: Lawrence Hill, 1999), 19.

46. Donna Britt, "Sammy Davis Jr., Showman Symbol," *The Washington Post*, May 17, 1990, E1.

47. Levy, *Rat Pack Confidential,* 113.

48. Silber, *Sammy Davis, Jr.,* 290.

49. Davis, *Yes I Can,* 352, 353.

50. *Time,* April 18, 1955. Box 59, Clippings File of the JWJ Memorial Collection, Beinecke Library, Yale University.

51. Davis, *Yes I Can,* 104–5, 111.

52. Gaspar Gonzalez, dir., *A Long Way from Home: The Untold Story of Baseball's Desegregation* (Hammer and Nail, 2018); Jonathan Holloway, *Jim Crow Wisdom: Memory and Identity in Black America since 1940* (Chapel Hill: UNC Press, 2013).

53. *Tri-State Defender,* September 10, 1955.,Box 59, Clippings File of the JWJ Memorial Collection, Beinecke Library, Yale University; Lena Horne and Richard Schickel, *Lena* (New York: Doubleday, 1965), 178.

54. Barry Gray in the *New York Post,* March 27, 1955, Box 59, Clippings File of the JWJ Memorial Collection, Beinecke Library, Yale University.

55. Davis, *Why Me?,* 74.

56. Ann duCille, *Technicolored: Reflections on Race in the Time of TV* (Durham, NC: Duke University Press, 2018), 81–82; Fred McDonald, *Blacks and White TV: African Americans in Television since 1948* (Belmont, CA: Wadsworth Publishing, 1992), 64; *Nat King Cole Show* archived at Black Media Mine, https://blackmediamine. blogspot.com /2014/03/madison-avenue-is-afraid-of-dark-nat.html.

57. Jan Willis, *Dreaming Me: Black, Baptist, and Buddhist—One Woman's Spiritual Journey* (Somerville, MA: Wisdom, 2008), 70.

58. Alan Nadel, *Television in Black-and-White America: Race and National Identity* (Lawrence: University of Kansas Press, 2005), 3, 7 and Chapter 1 *passim.*

59. Davis, *Yes I Can,* 409–10.

60. Davis, *Yes I Can,* 410.

61. DuCille, *Technicolored,* 3, 59. DuCille cites Peter Stallybrass and Allon White, *The Politics and Poetics of Transgression* (Ithaca, NY: Cornell University Press, 1986); see also Herman Gray, *Watching Race: Television and the Struggle of Blackness* (Minneapolis: University of Minnesota Press, 1995).

62. DuCille, *Technicolored,* 159.

63. Matthew Frye Jacobson, *Roots Too: White Ethnic Revival and Post-Civil Rights America* (Cambridge: Harvard University Press, 2006), 74.

64. Nadel, *Television in Black-and-White America,* 13.

65. Davis, *Yes I Can,* 409–11; Davis, *Hollywood in a Suitcase,* 216; *Baltimore Afro-American,* November 1, 1958, 18.

66. Lillian Schlissel, *Black Frontiers: A History of African American Heroes in the Old West* (New York: Aladdin, 2000); Katie Nodjimbadem, "The Lesser-Known History of African American Cowboys," *Smithsonian Magazine,* February 13, 2017.

67. Miriam Petty, *Stealing the Show: African American Performers and Audiences in 1930s Hollywood* (Oakland: University of California Press, 2016), 98.

68. William Yardley, "Herb Jeffries, 'Bronze Buckaroo' of Song and Screen, Dies at 100 (or So)," *New York Times,* May 26, 2014, https://www.nytimes.com/2014/05 /27/arts/music/herb-jeffries-singing-star-of-black-cowboy-films-dies-at-100.html.

69. Fishgall, *Gonna Do Great Things,* 133; Nadel, *Television in Black-and-White America,* 152–53; Cedric Robinson, *Forgeries of Memory and Meaning: Blacks and the Regimes of Race in American Theater and Film before World War II* (Chapel Hill: UNC Press, 2007), 369–70.

70. Arnold Lavan, dir., "Two Ounces of Tin," *The Rifleman* season 4, episode 21 (Four Star Productions, 1962); Arthur H. Nadel, dir., "The Most Amazing Man," *The Rifleman* season 5, episode 9 (Four Star Productions, 1962).

71. Gerald Early, *This Is Where I Came In: Black America in the 1960s* (Lincoln: University of Nebraska Press, 2003), 37.

72. Henry Louis Gates, "The Chitlin Circuit," *The New Yorker,* February 3, 1997, https://www.newyorker.com/magazine/1997/02/03/the-chitlin-circuit.

73. Steven Classen, *Watching Jim Crow: The Struggles over Mississippi TV, 1955–1969* (Durham, NC: Duke University Press, 2004), 120–21.

74. John Sturges, dir., *Sergeants 3* (Essex Productions, Meadway-Claude Productions: 1962).

75. Matthew Stelly, *Feets Don't Fail Me Now* (CreateSpace, 2018), 12.

76. Nick Estes, *Our History Is the Future: Standing Rock Versus the Dakota Access Pipeline, and the Long Tradition of Indigenous Resistence* (New York: Verso, 2019), 46.

77. Patrick Wolfe, "Settler Colonialism and the Elimination of the Native," *Journal of Genocide Research* 8, no. 4 (2006), doi/full/10.1080/14623520601056240; Patrick Wolfe, *Traces of History: Elementary Structures of Race* (New York: Verso, 2016).

78. Gaspar Gonzalez and Matthew Frye Jacobson, *What Have They Built You to Do? The Manchurian Candidate and Cold War America* (Minneapolis: University of Minnesota Press, 2006), 128–29.

79. *New York Courier,* July 7, 1962, quoted in Fishgall, *Gonna Do Great Things,* 174.

80. Dick Gregory, *Nigger: An Autobiography* (New York: Plume, 2019 [1964]), 42.

81. Earl Bellamy, dir., *The Trackers* (Aaron Spelling Productions, 1971); Norman Jewison, dir., *In the Heat of the Night* (The Mirisch Corporation, 1967).

82. James Baldwin, *The Devil Finds Work* (New York: Vintage, 2011 [1976]), 53, 58–59, 65.

83. Everett Carter quoting Woodrow Wilson in "Cultural History, Written with Lightning: The Significance of *The Birth of a Nation,*" *American Quarterly* 12, no. 3 (1960): 347–57.

84. Davis, *Yes I Can,* 151–52.

85. Thomas Cripps, *Slow Fade to Black: The Negro in American Film, 1900–1942* (New York: Oxford University Press, 1985), 112, 271.

86. *People Weekly,* May 28, 1990, 92.

87. George Stephenson, dir., *Peace, Togetherness, and Sammy: Sammy Davis Jr.'s Tour of Vietnam* (Office of Information for the Armed Forces Department of Defense, 1972), https://www.youtube.com/watch?v=s4ROtjTkb8A.

88. Sammy Davis, Jr., *That's All: Live at the Sands* (Reprise Records, 1967).

89. R. Davis, "These Are a Swinging Bunch of People," 41.

90. Davis, *Why Me?,* 162.

91. Davis, *Yes I Can*, 278–79.

92. Davis, *Yes I Can*, 246.

93. Gerald Nachman, *Seriously Funny: The Rebel Comedians of the 1950s and 1960s* (New York: Pantheon, 2003), 407.

CHAPTER 5. "DIVISION IS NOT OUR DESTINY"

Gunnar Myrdal, *An American Dilemma: The Negro Problem and Modern Democracy, Volume I,* (New York: Routledge, 1995 [1944]), 606; Sammy Davis, Jr., Burt Boyar, and Jane Boyar, *Yes I Can* (New York: Farrar, Straus, Giroux, 1965), 543.

1. Diane McWhorter, *Carry Me Home: Birmingham, Alabama: The Climactic Battle of the Civil Rights Revolution* (New York: Simon and Schuster, 2013), 295; Taylor Branch, *Parting the Waters: America in the King Years, 1954–63* (New York: Simon and Schuster, 1989), 654.

2. Peggy Pascoe, *What Comes Naturally: Miscegenation Law and the Making of Race in America* (New York: Oxford University Press, 2010); Kirsten Fischer, *Suspect Relations: Sex, Race, and Resistence in Colonial North Carolina* (Ithaca, NY: Cornell University Press, 2001); Jennifer Morgan, *Reckoning with Slavery: Gender, Kinship, and Capitalism in the Early Black Atlantic* (Durham, NC: Duke University Press, 2021).

3. Hortense Spillers, "Mama's Baby, Papa's Maybe," *Diacritics* 17, no. 2 (Summer 1987), 74.

4. Pascoe, *What Comes Naturally*, 7, 27.

5. Pascoe, *What Comes Naturally*, 30, 12.

6. Lillian Smith, *Killers of the Dream* (New York, W. W. Norton, 1994 [1949]), 121; Henry Louis Gates, Jr., *Stony the Road: Reconstruction, White Supremacy, and the Rise of Jim Crow* (New York: Penguin, 2020), esp. chapter 3.

7. Crystal Feimster, *Southern Horrors: Women and the Politics of Rape and Lynching* (Cambridge, MA: Harvard University Press, 2011), 37.

8. Werner Sollors, *Interracialism: Black-White Intermarriage in American History, Literature, and Law* (New York: Oxford University Press, 2000), 64, 221.

9. Matthew Frye Jacobson, *Whiteness of a Different Color: European Immigrants and the Alchemy of Race* (Cambridge, MA: Harvard University Press, 1998), 53; Feimster, *Southern Horrors*, 49; Michele Wallace, *Black Macho and the Myth of the Superwoman* (New York: Verso, 2025 [1978]), 23.

10. Ida B. Wells, *The Red Record: Tabulated Statistics and Alleged Causes of Lynching in the United States* (CreateSpace, 2015 [1895]), iv.

11. Smith, *Killers of the Dream*, 78–79.

12. Charles White, *The Life and Times of Little Richard* (Baltimore: Omnibus, 2003), 82.

13. *New York Times,* January 15, 1963, 16.

14. Sollors, *Interracialism*, 28, 135.

15. Pascoe, *What Comes Naturally*, 203, 243.

16. Sollors, *Interracialism,* 33.

17. Ann duCille, *Technicolored: Reflections on Race in the Time of TV* (Durham, NC: Duke University Press, 2018), 94–95.

18. Jacobson, *Whiteness of a Different Color,* 93.

19. Thomas Cripps, *Slow Fade to Black: The Negro in American Film, 1900–1942* (New York: Oxford University Press, 1985), 277.

20. Thomas Cripps, *Making Movies Black: The Hollywood Message Movie from World War II to the Civil Rights Era* (New York: Oxford University Press, 1993), 264–65; Lisa McGill, *Constricting Black Selves: Caribbean American Narratives and the Second Generation* (New York: NYU Press, 2005), 64–65.

21. Frank Tashlin, dir., *The Girl Can't Help It* (Twentieth Century Fox, 1956).

22. Cripps, *Making Movies Black,* 186. On sex and postwar pluralism, see Beth Bailey, *Sex in the Heartland* (Cambridge, MA: Harvard University Press, 2002).

23. White, *The Life and Times of Little Richard,* 81.

24. Elvera Davis interview in Carole Langer, dir., *The Rat Pack* (Praeses Productions, 1999), https://www.youtube.com /watch?v=-b8OfxDfvaA.

25. *New York Post,* March 15, 1956, Box 59, Clippings File of the JWJ Memorial Collection, Beinecke Library, Yale University.

26. Davis, *Yes I Can,* 162, 205–6; *Norfolk Journal and Guide,* July 2, 1955, 10.

27. *New York World,* November 6, 1959; *Pittsburgh Courier,* November 7, 1959, 22, Box 59, Clippings File of the JWJ Memorial Collection, Beinecke Library, Yale University; Davis, *Yes I Can,* 226, 260.

28. Davis, *Yes I Can,* 309, 334, 367; Gary Fishgall, *Gonna Do Great Things: The Life of Sammy Davis, Jr.* (New York: Scribner, 2010), 111; "Alex Haley Interviews Sammy Davis, Jr.," *Playboy,* December 1966, in Sammy Davis, Jr. and Gerald Early, *The Sammy Davis, Jr. Reader* (New York: Farrar, Straus, Giroux, 2001), 474–75.

29. Wil Haygood, *In Black and White: The Life of Sammy Davis, Jr.* (New York: Knopf, 2003), 258, 259.

30. Davis, *Yes I Can,* 420; Fishgall, *Gonna Do Great Things,* 112.

31. Sollors, *Interracialism* 67; Cheryl Harris, "Whiteness as Property," *Harvard Law Review* 106, no. 8 (June 1993).

32. Haygood, *In Black and White,* 263–68; Fishgall, *Gonna Do Great Things,* 112–15; Davis, *Yes I Can,* 420–23.

33. *New York World,* November 6, 1959; *New York Post,* April 4 1960, Box 59, Clippings File of the JWJ Memorial Collection, Beinecke Library, Yale University.

34. Donna Britt, "Sammy Davis Jr., Showman Symbol," *Washington Post,* May 17, 1990, E1.

35. Davis, *Yes I Can,* 528, 543.

36. Davis, *Yes I Can,* 534, 546.

37. Barry Norman, dir., *Hollywood Greats: Sammy Davis, Jr.* (BBC, 2001); Davis, *Yes I Can,* 556, 557, 558–61, 572, 574, 575, 584.

38. *New Pittsburgh Courier,* January 12, 1963, 20.

39. Davis, *Yes I Can,* 548, 551–52.

40. Bill Moyers, *Moyers on America: A Journalist and His Times* (New York: New Press, 2004), 167.

41. Davis, *Yes I Can*, 552–53, 538–39.

42. Davis, *Yes I Can*, 554.

43. Emilie Raymond, *Stars for Freedom: Hollywood, Black Celebrities, and the Civil Rights Movement* (Seattle: University of Washington Press, 2015), 71; Aram Goudsouzian, *Sidney Poitier: Man, Actor, Icon* (Chapel Hill: UNC Press, 2004), 194; Sammy Davis, Jr., Burt Boyar, and Jane Boyar, *Why Me? The Sammy Davis, Jr. Story* (New York: Farrar, Straus, Giroux, 1989), 106–8.

44. Davis, *Why Me?*, 106, 108; Davis, *Yes I Can*, 549.

45. "The Sammy Davis, Jr. Story," *New York Post*, March 12, 1956, Box 59, Clippings File of the JWJ Memorial Collection, Beinecke Library, Yale University.

46. William Gibson, "A Memento," in William Gibson, Clifford Odets, Lee Adams, and Charles Strouse, *Golden Boy: The Book of a Musical* (New York: Atheneum, 1965), 9.

47. Hilliard Elkins, "Last Days of Clifford Odets," *Sammy Davis in the New Musical Smash Golden Boy*, 1964 n. Box 59, Clippings File of the JWJ Memorial Collection, Beinecke Library, Yale University; Davis, *Why Me?*, 119.

48. *New York Times*, October 18, 1964, X3, emphasis added.

49. Clifford Odets, *Golden Boy: Acting Edition* (New York: Dramatists Play Service, Inc., 1998 [1937]) 23.

50. Odets, *Golden Boy*, 75.

51. Odets, *Golden Boy*, 31.

52. Odets, *Golden Boy*, 7.

53. Cripps, *Slow Fade to Black*, 304–5.

54. Gibson, "A Memento," in Gibson, et al., *Golden Boy*, 10.

55. William Gibson, "Afterword," in Gibson, et al., *Golden Boy*, 127–28.

56. *New York Times*, October 18, 1964, X3.

57. Gibson, "A Memento," 11; Haygood, *In Black and White*, 337–39.

58. Gibson, et al., *Golden Boy*, 34, 27, 54.

59. Gibson, et al., *Golden Boy*, 41, 42, 43.

60. Gibson, et al., *Golden Boy*, 63.

61. Gibson, et al., *Golden Boy*, 68, 74.

62. Gibson, et al., *Golden Boy*, 89.

63. Gibson, et al., *Golden Boy*, 98, 104–5.

64. Gibson, et al., *Golden Boy*, 113, 124, 126.

65. Theresa Runstedtler, *Jack Johnson, Rebel Sojourner: Boxing in the Shadow of the Global Color Line* (Berkeley: University of California Press, 2013), 134–35.

66. Fishgall, *Gonna Do Great Things*, 192–96.

67. Davis, *Why Me?*, 127.

68. Davis, *Why Me?*, 127, 178–79.

69. *New York Times*, October 18, 1964, X3.

70. *Los Angeles Times,* August 24, 1965, D11; *Wall Street Journal,* October 22, 1964, 18; *New York World-Telegram and Sun,* October 21, 1964, Box 59, Clippings File of the JWJ Memorial Collection, Beinecke Library, Yale University.

71. *The Washington Post, Times Herald,* November 8, 1964, G2, emphasis added.

72. *New York Times,* October 21, 1964, 56.

73. *New York Times,* May 8, 1965, 21.

74. *Julia,* season 1, episode 1 (20th Century Fox Television, 1968).

75. *New York Times,* October 21, 1964, 56.

76. Davis, *Yes I Can,* 321, 344, 331.

77. Davis, *Yes I Can,* 186.

78. bell hooks, *We Real Cool: Black Men and Maculinity* (New York: Routledge, 2004), 73–74.

79. New York *Herald Tribune,* October 21, 1964, Box 59, Clippings File of the JWJ Memorial Collection, Beinecke Library, Yale University.

80. *New York Times,* March 22, 1965; *Chicago Tribune,* April 12, 1968, 14.

81. Haygood, *In Black and White,* 353.

CHAPTER 6. WRITING WRONGS IN *YES I CAN*

"Alex Haley Interviews Sammy Davis, Jr.," Playboy, 1966, in Sammy Davis, Jr. and Gerald Early, *The Sammy Davis, Jr. Reader* (New York: Farrar, Straus, Giroux, 2001), 460; Sammy Davis Jr., Burt Boyar, and Jane Boyar, *Yes I Can* (New York: Farrar, Straus, Giroux, 1965), 325–26.

1. Davis, Boyar, and Boyar, *Yes I Can,* 3. Hereafter in this chapter, quotes from *Yes I Can* will be noted by page number in the text. All citations refer to the 1965 edition.

2. *New York Post* in 1966, beginning March 21; *Harper's Magazine* in August, 1965, 87–90; *Ebony* in December, 1965, 151–54.

3. *New York Herald Tribune Book Review,* Spring 1966, Box 59, Clippings file of the JWJ Memorial Collection, Beinecke Library, Yale University; *New York Post,* September 19, 1965, 60.

4. *Pittsburgh Courier,* September 18, 1965, 16; "Hazel Garland: Femaile Trailblazer, *Pittsburgh Courier,* January 27, 2011, https://newpittsburghcourier.com/2011/01/27/hazel-garland-female-trailblazer.

5. *Christian Science Monitor,* September 30, 1965, 11; *Chicago Daily Defender,* September 7, 1965, 1.

6. *New York Times,* September 19, 1965, Box 59, Clippings File of the JWJ Memorial Collection, Beinecke Library, Yale University.

7. *New Pittsburgh Courier,* October 16, 1965, 11; Gerald Early, *This Is Where I Came In: Black America in the 1960s* (Lincoln: University of Nebraska Press, 2003), 49–54.

8. Library of Congress, LIC ML31.B68 boxes 8–10.

9. Wil Haygood, *In Black and White: The Life of Sammy Davis, Jr.* (New York: Knopf, 2003), 6.

10. Haygood, *In Black and White,* 6.

11. Haygood, *In Black and White,* 31.

12. Haygood, *In Black and White,* 28.

13. Matthew Stelly, *Feets, Don't Fail Me Now: Sammy Davis, Jr. and the Issue of "Role Conflict"* (CreateSpace, 2018), 89.

14. Haygood, *In Black and White,* 17.

15. *Los Angeles Times,* January 27, 1966, SF5.

16. Saidiya Hartman, *Scenes of Subjection: Terror, Slavery, and Self-Making in Nineteenth-Century America* (New York: Oxford University Press, 1997), 18–19, emphasis added.

17. John Howard Griffin, *Black Like Me* (New York: Berkley, 2021 [1961]), "Preface," np.

18. *New York Post,* March 14, 1956, Box 59, Clippings File of the JWJ Memorial Collection, Beinecke Library, Yale University.

19. Roger Angell, "Distance" [1980], in *Game Time* (New York: Harcourt, 2003), 208.

20. Lena Horne and Richard Schickel, *Lena* (New York: Doubleday, 1965), 300.

21. bell hooks, *We Real Cool: Black Men and Masculinity* (New York: Routledge, 2004), 3.

22. "Alex Haley Interviews Sammy Davis, Jr.," in Sammy Davis, Jr. and Gerald Early, *The Sammy Davis, Jr. Reader* (New York: Farrar, Straus, Giroux, 2001), 484.

23. "Alex Haley Interviews," 458–59, 471, 476, 477; Haygood, *In Black and White,* 375–79.

24. "Alex Haley Interviews," 460.

25. "Alex Haley Interviews," 472–73.

26. "Alex Haley Interviews," 472–73.

27. "Alex Haley Interviews," 477–78.

28. "Alex Haley Interviews," 478.

29. "Alex Haley Interviews," 478–79.

30. "Alex Haley Interviews," 479.

31. "Alex Haley Interviews," 479, 480.

32. "Alex Haley Interviews," 481.

33. "Alex Haley Interviews," 481, 482.

34. Gunnar Myrdal, *An American Dilemma: The Negro Problem and Modern Democracy, Volume I,* (New York: Routledge, 1995 [1944]), 74.

35. Myrdal, *American Dilemma,* lxxxiv.

36. Myrdal, *American Dilemma,* lxxix, 21.

37. Myrdal, *American Dilemma,* 3, 4.

38. Myrdal, *American Dilemma,* lxxxii, xxvii, 24, xxviii.

39. Myrdal, *American Dilemma,* 39, 79.

40. Myrdal, *American Dilemma,* lxxxiii, lxxx.

41. Myrdal, *American Dilemma,* 49, emphasis in original.

42. Myrdal, *American Dilemma,* 80.

43. Myrdal, *American Dilemma,* 19.

44. Steven Lawson, *To Secure These Rights: The Report of President Harry S. Truman's Committee on Civil Rights* (New York: Bedford/St. Martins, 2003), 140, 155.

45. Lawson, *To Secure These Rights,* 155–56.

46. Lawson, *To Secure These Rights,* 156–57.

47. *Brown v. Board of Education,* 1954, text available at https://www.archives.gov/milestone-documents/brown-v-board-of-education.

48. David Walker, *Walker's Appeal in Four Articles; together with a Preamble, to the Colored Citizens of the World,* 1829, https://docsouth.unc.edu/nc/walker/walker.html.

49. Bayard Rustin, "Black Power and Coalition Politics," A. Philip Randolph Institute, 1966, https://www.crmvet.org/info/6609_rustin_blkpwr.pdf.

50. Kwame Ture [Stokely Carmichael] and Charles V. Hamilton, *Black Power: The Politics of Liberation* (New York: Vintage, 1992 [1966]), 4–5.

51. Ture and Hamilton, *Black Power,* 37; compare Michele Wallace, *Black Macho and the Myth of the Superwoman* (New York: Verso, 2015 [1978]), 9.

52. Ture and Hamilton, *Black Power,* 9.

53. Claude Brown, *Manchild in the Promised Land* (New York: Signet, 1965), vii, 123.

54. Malcolm X and Alex Haley, *The Autobiography of Malcolm X* (New York: Grove, 1965), 266; Manning Marable, *Malcolm X: A Life of Reinvention* (New York: Penguin, 2011), 465–67; Robin D. G. Kelley, "The Riddle of the Zoot," in *Race Rebels: Culture, Politics, and the Black Working Class* (New York: Free Press, 1996).

55. Ture and Hamilton, *Black Power,* 44.

56. Ture and Hamilton, *Black Power,* 54, 56, 47.

57. Dick Gregory, "White Racist Institutions," *Light Side-Dark Side* (Poppy, PYS 6001, 1969).

58. "Alex Haley Interviews," 482.

59. Clayborne Carson, et al., eds., *Reporting Civil Rights, Vol. II* (New York: Library of America, 2013), 636.

60. National Advisory Commission on Civil Disorders, *The Kerner Report* (Princeton, NJ: Princeton University Press, 2016 [1968]), 1, 236.

61. Daniel Patrick Moynihan, *The Moynihan Report: The Negro Family—the Case for National Action* (New York: Cosimo Reports, 2018 [1965]), 29.

62. On Griffin's project see Eric Lott, *Black Mirror: The Cultural Contradictions of American Racism* (Cambridge, MA: Belknap/Harvard, 2017), 119–37.

63. *New York Herald Tribune Book Review,* Spring 1966, Box 59, Clippings File of the JWJ Memorial Collection, Beinecke Library, Yale University; Ture and Hamilton, *Black Power,* 53.

64. *The Mike Douglas Show,* 1969, https://www.youtube.com/watch?v=dp3Pbc3NatY.

Undated clipping, Box 59, Clippings File of the JWJ Memorial Collection, Beinecke Library, Yale University; *New York Sunday News*, February 14, 1965, 24.

1. Matthew Stelly, *Feets, Don't Fail Me Now: Sammy Davis, Jr. and the Issue of "Role Conflict"* (CreateSpace, 2018), 4. Page citations in the passage that follows refer to this edition.

2. Sammy Davis, Jr., Burt Boyar, and Jane Boyar, *Why Me? The Sammy Davis, Jr. Story* (New York: Farrar, Straus, Giroux, 1989), 193–194.

3. *Sammy Davis, Jr.—the FBI Files* (Washington, DC: FBI Files, 2009), 3, 5, 10–11, 19, 22, 23, 25, 27, 36.

4. *Sammy Davis, Jr.—the FBI Files*, 21.

5. *Sammy Davis, Jr.—the FBI Files*, n.p.

6. *Sammy Davis, Jr.—the FBI Files*, 6, 12, 16.

7. *Sammy Davis, Jr.—the FBI Files*, n.p.

8. *Sammy Davis, Jr.—the FBI Files*, 43–45.

9. Christine Acham, *Revolution Televised: Prime Time and the Struggle for Black Power* (Minneapolis: University of Minnesota Press, 2004), 114–18.

10. Sidney Poitier, *The Measure of a Man: A Spiritual Autobiography* (New York: Harper, 2000), 140.

11. Lena Horne and Richard Schickel, *Lena* (New York: Doubleday, 1965), 271, 276.

12. Robert Weisbrot, *Freedom Bound: A History of America's Civil Rights Movement* (New York: Plume, 1991), 223.

13. Martin Luther King Jr. to Sammy Davis Jr. December 20, 1960, https://kinginstitute.stanford.edu/king-papers/documents/sammy-davis-jr.

14. Brian Ward, *Just My Soul Responding: Rhythm and Blues, Black Consciousness, and Race Relations* (Berkeley: University of California Press, 1998), 334.

15. "Alex Haley Interviews Sammy Davis, Jr.," in Sammy Davis, Jr., and Gerald Early, *The Sammy Davis, Jr. Reader* (New York: Farrar, Straus, Giroux, 2001), 472.

16. Wil Haygood, *In Black and White: The Life of Sammy Davis, Jr.* (New York: Knopf, 2003), 252; Davis, *Why Me?*, 110–11.

17. Ossie Davis and Ruby Dee, *With Ossie and Ruby: In This Life Together* (New York: It Books, 2000), 306.

18. Urban League flyer, Box 59, Clippings File of the JWJ Memorial Collection, Beinecke Library, Yale University; *Chicago Defender*, November 9, 1957, 18.

19. *New York Post*, March 12, 1956, 31, Box 59, Clippings File of the JWJ Memorial Collection, Beinecke Library, Yale University.

20. *New York Post*, February 21, 1957, F16, Box 59, Clippings File of the JWJ Memorial Collection, Beinecke Library, Yale University.

21. *New York Post*, October 4, 1957, Box 59, Clippings File of the JWJ Memorial Collection, Beinecke Library, Yale University.

22. *New York Post*, October 4, 1957, Box 59, Clippings File of the JWJ Memorial Collection, Beinecke Library, Yale University.

23. Emilie Raymond, *Stars for Freedom: Hollywood, Black Celebrities, and the Civil Rights Movement* (Seattle: University of Washington Press, 2015), ix, xi, 66, 74.

24. "Alex Haley Interviews Sammy Davis, Jr.," in Davis and Early, *The Sammy Davis, Jr. Reader,* 466, 471–72; Matt Birkbeck, *Deconstructing Sammy: Music, Money, Madness, and the Mob* (New York: Amistad, 2008); Raymond, *Stars for Freedom,* 66.

25. *Pittsburgh Courier,* April 22, 1961, 2.

26. Aram Goudsouzian, *Sidney Poitier: Man, Actor, Icon* (Chapel Hill: UNC Press, 2004), 141; Raymond, *Stars for Freedom,* 50–55, 57.

27. *Pittsburgh Courier,* February 23, 1963, 4; *Pittsburgh Courier,* August 4, 1962, 14; Raymond, *Stars for Freedom,* 65, 68–69, 71–72, 74, 100; Gary Fishgall, *Gonna Do Great Things: The Life of Sammy Davis, Jr.,* (New York: Scribner, 2010), 169; *Pittsburgh Courier,* April 22, 1961, 2; *Pittsburgh Courier,* July 28, 1962, 15; *Pittsburgh Courier,* August 4, 1962, 14; *Pittsburgh Courier,* December 22, 1962, 13.

28. Martin Luther King, Jr., *Why We Can't Wait* (Boston: Beacon, 2011 [1964]), 6.

29. King, *Why We Can't Wait,* 8, 9, 10, 14, 91.

30. King, *Why We Can't Wait,* 145.

31. Diane McWhorter, *Carry Me Home: Birmingham, Alabama: The Climactic Battle of the Civil Rights Revolution* (New York: Simon and Schuster, 2013), 478; Taylor Branch, *Parting the Waters: America in the King Years, 1954–63* (New York: Simon and Schuster, 1989), 805; Fishgall, *Gonna Do Great Things,* 179–80; Raymond, *Stars for Freedom,* 119.

32. *New York Times,* July 11, 1963, Box 59, Clippings File of the JWJ Memorial Collection, Beinecke Library, Yale University.

33. Raymond, *Stars for Freedom,* 124.

34. Betty Comden, Adolph Green, A. Z. Idelsohn, and Jule Styne, "Now," https://www.lyricsfreak.com/l/lena+horne/now_20865319.html; Lena Horne and Richard Schickel, *Lena* (New York: Doubleday, 1965), 288–91. I am indebted to Josh Kun for this song and its history. See Josh Kun, "The Time Is Still, Always, Now!" in *Nights of the Dispossessed: Riots Unbound,* ed. Natasha Ginwala, Gal Kirn, and Niloufar Tajeri (New York: Columbia University Press, 2021), 416–28.

35. Fishgall, *Gonna Do Great Things,* 180.

36. Compare Charles Payne, *I've Got the Light of Freedom: The Organizing Tradition and the Mississippi Freedom Struggle* (Berkeley: University of California Press, 1995); Francoise Hamlin, *Crossroads at Clarksdale: The Black Freedom Struggle in the Mississippi Delta Aafter World War II* (Chapel Hill: UNC Press, 2014); Barbara Ransby, *Ella Baker and the Black Freedom Movement: A Radical Democratic Vision* (Chapel Hill: UNC Press, 2003).

37. Jeanne Theoharis, *A More Beautiful and Terrible History: The Uses and Misuses of Civil Rights History* (Boston: Beacon Press, 2019), 131.

38. King, *Why We Can't Wait,* 147; *Pittsburgh Courier,* August 31, 1963, 1; *New York Times,* August 25, 1963, X7.

39. Sammy Davis, Jr., *Hollywood in a Suitcase* (New York: Star Books, 1981), 207.

40. President John F. Kennedy's Message to Congress, June 19, 1963, https://www.archives.gov/legislative/features/march-on-washington/kennedy.html.

41. Haygood, *In Black and White*, 314.

42. Raymond, *Stars for Freedom*, 106.

43. *Los Angeles Times*, October 13, 1963, WS2; November 10 1963 B29; November 24, 1963, B31; December 6, 1963, B10. See *Stars for Freedom*, 139.

44. *New York Times*, May 9, 1964, Box 59, Clippings File of the JWJ Memorial Collection, Beinecke Library, Yale University.

45. Raymond, *Stars for Freedom*, 139; Goudsouzian, *Sidney Poitier*, 221; *Los Angeles Times*, April 2, 1964, C9; *Pittsburgh Courier*, May 9, 1964, 16; *Pittsburgh Courier*, May 16, 1964, 16; *Pittsburgh Courier*, May 23, 1964, 2; *Pittsburgh Courier*, May 23, 1964, 2; *Pittsburgh Courier*, February 29, 1964, 17; *Pittsburgh Courier*, March 21, 1964, 20; *Pittsburgh Courier*, May 9, 1964, 6.

46. *Chicago Defender*, December 7, 1964, Box 59, Clippings File of the JWJ Memorial Collection, Beinecke Library, Yale University. Stars for Freedom, 171; Dick Gregory, *Up from N*gger* (New York: Stein and Day, 1976), 77.

47. Gregory, *Up from N*gger*, 85.

48. David Garrow, *Bearing the Cross: Martin Luther King, Jr., and the Southern Christian Leadrship Conference* (New York: William Morrow, 2004), 384.

49. "Stars for Freedom" reportage, https://uwpressblog. com/2015/02/05/stars-for-selma.

50. Barry Norman, dir., *Hollywood Greats: Sammy Davis, Jr.* (BBC, 2001).

51. Haygood, *In Black and White*, 363.

52. Fishgall, *Gonna Do Great Things*, 201–3; Haygood, *In Black and White*, 363–64; *New York Post*, March 24, 1965, Box 59, Clippings File of the JWJ Memorial Collection, Beinecke Library, Yale University.

53. Davis, *Why Me?*, 135. Belafonte had also enlisted Billy Eckstine, Ella Fitzgerald, Tony Bennett, Mahalia Jackson, Nina Simone, Pete Seeger, Leon Bibb, Peter Paul & Mary, George Kirby, and Nipsey Russell.

54. *New York Post*, March 24, 1965, Box 59, Clippings File of the JWJ Memorial Collection, Beinecke Library, Yale University.

55. *New York Times*, May 9, 1965, X5.

56. Ward, *Just My Soul Responding*, 314–15; Raymond, *Stars for Freedom*, 189–90.

57. Raymond, *Stars for Freedom*, 195; Haygood, *In Black and White*, 366–67.

58. Haygood, *In Black and White*, 386.

59. Raymond, *Stars for Freedom*, 204; Fishgall, *Gonna Do Great Things*, 225; Davis, *Why Me?*, 155–58.

60. Martin Luther King, "The Other America," 1967, https://www.youtube.com/watch?v=dOWDtDUKz-U.

61. Elizabeth Hinton, *America on Fire: The Untold History of Police Violence and Black Rebellion Since 1968* (New York: Liveright, 2021).

62. See UPI coverage of 1968, https://www.history.com/speeches/stokely-carmichael-on-assassination-of-martin-luther-king-jr; Hinton, *America on Fire*, 21–22.

63. "James Brown At The Boston Garden; James Brown Speaks to the Crowd at the Boston Garden," April 5, 1968, WGBH Media Library & Archives, http:// openvault.wgbh.org/catalog/A_15770C18FF5B4F8EA0F6B5FC23218277.

64. Quoted in Sharon Lawrence, *Jimi Hendrix: the Man, the Magic, the Truth* (New York: HarperEntertainment, 2005), 96–97; Johnny Black, *Jimi Hendrix: The Ultimate Experience* (New York: De Capo, 1999), 141–42. Harry Shapiro and Caesar Glebbeek, *Jimi Hendrix: Electric Gypsy* (New York: St. Martins Griffin, 1999), 270–72. Compare John McDermott and Edward Kramer, *Hendrix: Setting the Record Straight* (New York: Grand Central Publishing, 1992), 116. They claim that the second show was cancelled because "the rioting became so bad." But there was in fact no rioting in Newark. See *Newark Star-Ledger,* April 5, 1993, 21.

65. Harry Belafonte, *My Song: A Memoir* (New York: Knopf, 2011), 332–33.

66. Nina Simone, "Why? The King of Love Is Dead," *'Nuff Said!* (RCA Victor, 1968). The performance can be found at https://www.youtube.com/watch?v =Wh6R0BRzjW4. See also Ruth Feldstein, *How It Feels to Be Free: Black Women Entertainers and the Civil Rights Movement* (New York: Oxford University Press, 2017), 111–12.

67. Davis, *Why Me?,* 174, 176.

68. Post-assassination commentary at https://www.legacy.com/news/mlk -memories; https://www.youtube.com/watch?v=JwW71mffOH4; https://www .criticalpast.com/video/65675070921_man_assassination-of-Martin-Luther-King _people-have-no-sorrow_respect-dignitary; Fishgall, *Gonna Do Great Things,* 239.

69. Stelly, *Feets Don't Fail Me Now,* 152–53; Davis, *Why Me?,* 210.

70. Richard Nixon, "The First Civil Right of Every American Is to Be Free from Domestic Violence," August 8, 1968, in *Richard Nixon: Speeches, Writings, Documents,* ed. Rick Perlstein (Princeton, NJ: Princeton University Press, 2008), 145.

71. "United States Senate Select Committee of Study Governmental Operations with Respect to Intelligence Activities" [the Church Commttee Report], https:// www.aarclibrary.org/publib/contents/church/contents_church_reports_book2 .htm.

72. Fishgall, *Gonna Do Great Things,* 284–85.

73. *New York Times,* April 17, 1968, 34.

74. *Los Angeles Times,* November 18, 1969, E20; *Oakland Post,* April 10, 1969, 21; Fishgall, *Gonna Do Great Things,* 250; *Los Angeles Times,* July 24, 1970, 20; *Oakland Post,* March 5, 1970, 10; *Jet,* April 24, 1969, 14–17.

75. *San Francisco Sun Reporter,* March 11, 1972, 9.

76. Davis, *Why Me?,* 178.

77. Davis, *Why Me?,* 160–61.

78. Davis, *Hollywood in a Suitcase,* 225.

79. "Sammy Davis, Jr. in His Own Words," *Black Journal* Episode 31, 1971, PBS, https://www.youtube.com/watch?v=CAk1P4p05Qk; Bettina Aptheker, *The Morning Breaks: The Trial of Angela Davis* (Ithaca, NY: Cornell University Press, 1999); National Advisory Commission on Civil Disorders, *The Kerner Report* (Princeton: Princeton University Press, 2016 [1968]), 385–87.

80. *New York Herald Tribune,* May 26, 1969, Box 59, Clippings File of the JWJ Memorial Collection, Beinecke Library, Yale University.

81. Bob and Betty Lewis interview with Sammy Davis, Jr., Las Vegas, December 1963, Performing Arts Collection—Recorded Sound—Billy Rose Library, NYPL, LDC 37524.

82. "Sammy Davis, Jr. in His Own Words"; Devorah Heitner, *Black Power TV* (Durham, NC: Duke University Press, 2013); Phyllis Rauch Klotman and Janet Cutler, *Struggles for Representation: African American Documentary Film and Video* (Bloomington: Indiana University Press, 2000).

83. *The Mike Douglas Show,* 1969, at https://www.youtube.com/watch?v=dp3Pbc3NatY.

84. *Ebony,* April 1966, 178.

85. Matthew Frye Jacobson, *Odetta's One Grain of Sand* (New York: Bloomsbury, 2019); Jim Brown, *Out of Bounds* (New York: Random House, 1995); Mike Marqusee, *Redemption Song: Muhammad Ali and the Spirit of the Sixties* (New York: Verso, 2017); Nichelle Nichols, *Beyond Uhura: Star Trek and Other Memories* (New York: G. P. Putnam's Sons, 1994); Curt Flood with Richard Carter, *The Way It Is* (New York: Pocket Books, 1972); Gaspar Gonzalez, dir., *A Long Way from Home: The Untold Story of Baseball's Desegregation* (Hammer and Nail, 2018); Matthew Frye Jacobson, "Richie Allen, Whitey's Ways, and Me: A Political Education In the 1960s," in *In the Game: Race, Identity, and Sports n the Twentieth Century,* ed. Amy Bass (New York: Palgrave, 2005).

86. Shane Vogel, *Stolen Time: Black Fad Performance and the Calypso Craze* (Chicago: University of Chicago Press, 2018), 21.

87. Pete Martin, "I Call on Sammy Davis, Jr.," *Saturday Evening Post,* May 21, 1960, 24, 44.

88. Donna Britt, "Sammy Davis Jr., Showman Symbol," *Washington Post,* May 17, 1990, E1.

89. Sammy Davis, Jr., Burt Boyar, and Jane Boyar, *Yes I Can* (New York: Farrar, Straus, Giroux, 1965), 590–93.

90. *New York Post,* February 7, 1965, Magazine 5.

91. Davis, *Hollywood in a Suitcase,* 206.

92. Davis, *Why Me?,* 106, 134.

93. Davis, *Why Me?,* 116.

94. Davis, *Why Me?,* 117–19.

95. Davis, *Why Me?,* 160–61.

CODA. WHAT IS THE "POST" OF "POST-CIVIL RIGHTS"?

New York Post, May 6, 1974, Box 59, Clippings File of the JWJ Memorial Collection, Beinecke Library, Yale University.

1. Michele Wallace, *Black Macho and the Myth of the Super Woman* (New York: Verso, 2015 [1978]), 72.

2. Dylan Rodriguez, *White Reconstruction: Domestic Warfare and the Logics of Genocide* (New York: Fordham University Press, 2021), 6, 12.

3. Elizabeth Hinton, *America on Fire: The Untold History of Police Violence and Black Rebellion Since the 1960s* (New York: Liveright, 2021), 304.

4. In sociologist Todd Gitlin's formulation, "the right marched on Washington and took a great deal of it while the left was marching on the English department." See "A Conversation with Todd Gitlin," *Think Tank with Ben Wattanberg,* https://www.pbs.org/thinktank/transcript235.html; Todd Gitlin, *The Twilight of Common Dreams: Why America Is Wracked by Culture Wars* (New York: Henry Holt & Co., 1995).

5. John Rich, dir., "Sammy's Visit," *All in the Family,* season 2, episode 21 (Tandem Productions, 1972).

6. "Bill Dana discusses the Sammy Davis Jr. episode of 'All in the Family,'" Emmy TV Legends interview clip, https://www.youtube.com/watch?v=JDe-WrwO9m3U; Emilie Raymond, *Stars for Freedom: Hollywood, Black Celebrities, and the Civil Rights Movement* (Seattle: University of Washington Press, 2015), 230–31.

7. Sammy Davis, Jr., Burt Boyar, and Jane Boyar, *Why Me?: The Sammy Davis, Jr. Story* (New York: Farrar, Straus, Giroux, 1989), 208, 215; *New York Sunday News,* July 8, 1973, Section 3 p. 1.

8. Sammy Davis, Jr., *Hollywood in a Suitcase* (New York: Star Books, 1981), 210.

9. *New York Times Magazine,* October 15, 1972, 119; Davis, *Why Me?,* 220.

10. *New York Times Magazine,* October 15, 1972, 112, 117.

11. "We say black now" and "honesty": *New York Times Magazine,* October 15, 1972, 112. Black colleges: Davis, *Why Me?,* 215.

12. *Washington Post, Times Herald,* March 5, 1973, B1.

13. *People Weekly,* May 28, 1990, 92.

14. *Midday with Bill Boggs,* https://www.youtube.com/watch?v=n2wq4hGewA4.

15. James Brown, *The Godfather of Soul: An Autobiography* (New York: MacMillan, 1986), 230–31.

16. *People Weekly,* May 28, 1990, 92.

17. Nick Castle, dir., *Tap* (Beco Films/TriStar Pictures, 1989).

18. Tom Jones and Sammy Davis, Jr. "Mr. Bojangles," *This Is Tom Jones* (Associated Television, 1970), https://www.dailymotion.com/video/x31jh6j.

19. Brenda Gottschild, *The Black Dancing Body: A Geography from Coon to Cool* (New York: Palgrave, 2005), 120; Jacqui Malone, *Steppin' on the Blues: The Visible Rhythms of African American Dance* (Urbana: University of Illinois Press, 1996), 7.

20. *New York Times Magazine,* October 15, 1972, 116.

21. Donna Britt, "Sammy Davis Jr., Showman Symbol," *Washington Post,* May 17, 1990, E1.

22. *New York Amsterdam News,* August 18, 1979, 31.

23. Sam Pollard, dir., *Sammy Davis, Jr.: I've Gotta Be Me* (ARTE/American Masters, 2017).

24. *San Francisco Chronicle,* February 24, 1987, 58.

25. Ann Hornaday, "Spike Lee on his role as an artist in tumultuous times: 'I'm built for this,'" *Washington Post,* June 9, 2020, https://www.washingtonpost.com /lifestyle/style/spike-lee-on-his-role-as-an-artist-in-tumultuous-times-im-built-for -this/2020/06/08/51ef1d74-a98d-11ea-a9d9-a81c1a491c52_story.html.

26. Jesmyn Ward, "Avy Duvernay's Visionary Filmmaking is Reshaping Holly-wood," *Smithsonian Magazine,* December, 2017, https://www.smithsonianmag.com /arts-culture/ava-duvernay-visionary-filmmaking-reshaping-hollywood-180967217.

INDEX

Note: Sammy Davis Jr. may be abbreviated in this index as SDJ. Page numbers in *italics* denote photographs.

all-black films (continued)
See also Anna Lucasta (1958); Man Called Adam, A (1966); Porgy and Bess (1959); racial liberalism in the postwar era

Allen, Steve, 118, 207

All in the Family, "Sammy's Visit" (SDJ kisses Archie Bunker), 239–40, 240, 242–43

Allyson, June, 149

American conservatism: "bootstraps" ideology and disavowal of white privilege, 236, 244; "personal responsibility," 202–3, 244

"American Creed," defined, 195

American Film Center Incorporated, 61

American Nazi Party, triggered by SDJ, 124; Golden Boy, 165; intermarriage of, 141–42, 146, 152, 187, 208

American Negro Theater (ANT), 70, 71

Anderson, Eddie, 68

Anderson, Marian, 59, 217

Angell, Roger, 177

Angelou, Maya, 81

Anka, Paul, 52

Anna Lucasta (1958 film), 74; overview, 65, 89, 98; critical reception of, 65–66, 72, 73–76; history of the property, 70–71; and inclusive hiring, 74–75; photo appearing Tap, 246; plot of, 71–73; and representation, 74, 75

anthropology, and African cultural "survivals" in dance, 11, 12

anti-black violence. See white violence against black people

Antin, Mary, xxiv

anti-racism: politicized art on behalf of, 211–12, 234–35. See also Black Power; Civil Rights Movement; post-Civil Rights era; racial liberalism in the postwar era

anti-Semitism, 105; film treatments of, reflecting the postwar racial liberalism, 68; Germany's Nuremburg Laws, 36, 38–39, 43; of SDJ critic Matthew Stelly, 206

appropriation: George White's Scandals (1926), 32; and Gershwin's Porgy and

Bess, 79–80; of minstrelsy, 29, 34; and white fascination with black culture, 34

Archie Bunker. See All in the Family

Armstrong, Louis: in A Man Called Adam, 90, 92–93, 249; postwar discomfort with persona of, 67, 93; SDJ impression of, 103; SDJ's disagreement with, 93, 214; songs of, 7, 26, 33, 81, 93, 214

Arrington, Richard Jr., 229

The Arsenio Hall Show (TV), 239

assimilation, definition of, xxiii–xxiv

assimilationism of SDJ, 134; and appearing to be a cultural throwback, xxiv; black community scorn for, xxii; claim of "self-hatred" due to, xxiv–xxv, 139–40, 235; as endearing SDJ to white people, xxii; and his meteoric rise, 63; as an integration project, 136; Rat Pack membership and, xxiv; Yes I Can as narrative of, 172–74, 190

Associated Negro Press: as fighting for representation, 67; and the "official" anti-racism forged during World War II, 61

Association of Black Women in Higher Education (1978), 229

Astaire, Fred, 29, 185; songs of, 56

Atkins, Tom, 225

Atlanta, GA, election of black mayor, 229

Atlantic City, NJ, Club Harlem, 20

Attucks, Crispus, 38

Bailey, Pearl, 63, 81, 83, 97

Baker, Houston, xxiii

Baker, Josephine, 13, 17, 110, 187–88

Baldwin, James: Civil Rights benefits and, 217; cynicism about the Heat of the Night, 132–34; and the effects of the Jim Crow military in World War II, 37–38, 46; The Fire Next Time (1963), 168, 199; and funeral of MLK, 38; on Hollywood, 212; No Name in the Street (1972), 38; on the Porgy and Bess film, 64, 86, 87, 95; on postwar all-black films and erasure of blackness, 69–70, 74; and the racial egalitarianism of Europe, 187–88; relationship with SDJ, xxi, 37–38

Baltimore, MD: riots following assassination of MLK, 224; Royal theater, 25

Baraka, Amiri. *See* Jones, LeRoi

Bates, Pegleg, 24–25, 104

Batman (TV), 99, 134

Beaumont, TX, anti-black violence in, 44

bebop, 3, 113

Belafonte, Harry, xxi; after hours at the Moulin Rouge (Las Vegas), 97; and assassination of MLK, 226; on Civil Rights contributions of SDJ, 215; and the Civil Rights Movement, 191, 212, 213, 214–15, 217, 220, *221*, 222, 224; and desegregation of Las Vegas, 110; as fighting for inclusion, 67, 210, 235; in *Island in the Sun*, 146–47; MLK commending, 213; and the postwar "official anti-racism," 63; as refusing *Porgy and Bess*, 76, 81–82, 83; songs of, 81, 136

Ben Casey (TV), 134

Benchly, Robert, 30

Bennett, Lerone, 31

Bennett, Tony, 216

Benny, Jack, 76, 104, 178–79

Berle, Milton, xxi; defends SDJ, 107, 138; as friend and mentor to SDJ, 138, 139, 175, 182; roasting SDJ at Friar's Club, 136, 138; *Texico Star Theater*, 104, 118

Berlin, Irving: "Puttin' on the Ritz," 56–57; "What the Well Dressed Man in Harlem Will Wear," 56, 57, 58; World War II benefit pitch, 55

Bernstein, Leonard, 222

Berry, Chuck, xxvii, 210

Betty Boop, 7

The Beverly Hillbillies (TV), 99

Beverly Hills, CA: Civil Rights benefits in, 216; desegregated by SDJ, 100; SDJ subjected to racist slights in, 139

Beverly Hilton, bomb threat made to SDJ, 152

Birmingham, AL: anti-black violence in, 34, 36; church bombing, 34; election of black mayor, 229; MLK's media strategy in, 199; Nazi attacking MLK for mentioning SDJ, 141–42, 146, 166; rally for freedom (1963), 207, 216; "Salute to Freedom," 217

Birth of a Nation (1915), 6–7, 10, 67, 69, 133–34, 145, 159

Bishop, Joey, *112*, 118, 138. *See also* Rat Pack

Bizet, *Carmen*, 69

black, adoption of term, 235, 237, 243

black audiences: Al Jolson disparaged among, when *Mr. Wonderful* opened, 101; *Porgy and Bess* and, 76–79, 80, 81–83, 86–88

black citizenship: and a changing politics of representation, 16–17; and interracial relationships, white panic about, 143, 144–45; masculinism and soldiering as argument for, 38–39; minstrelsy and disparagement of, 143; as stripped with the end of Reconstruction, 145

black community. *See* African American community, SDJ viewed by; freedom struggle

black dignity: masculinity concerns of SDJ and, 53; *Porgy and Bess* and, 86; SDJ on achievement of, xxviii; SDJ on obligation to consider, in scripts, 233; wartime narrative films and duty to, 67

blackface: child performer SDJ disguised with, 1, *2*, 26, 34; prescribed by the government for World War II troop entertainments, 54, 55, 59; as resurfacing into the twenty-first century, 63; tap dance made familiar by white performers in, 14–15. *See also* Jolson, Al; minstrelsy

Black Film Makers Hall of Fame, 250–51

black is beautiful, xxiv, 237

Black Journal (TV), 49–50, 230–31, 232–33

blacklisted entertainers, 63, 109

Black Lives Matter, 246

black masculinity: dignity/indignity and, 53; minstrelsy as defanging, 143; and sex and sexual healing as freedom, 165; social scripts assigned to, 69; unthreatening, of SDJ's generation, 235

blackness: erasure in film and television, 121, 123, 125; erasure in postwar all-black films, 69–70, 74; minstrelsy and commodification of, 29, 34; of *Porgy and Bess*, as rerouted through white, minstrelized imaginations, 81–82, 85, 87

Brown, Jayna, 19
Brown, Jim, 234
Brown, Joyce, 162
Brown, King Rastus, 19
Brown, Oscar Jr., *Kicks and Co.*, 211
Brown, Tony, *Black Journal*, 49–50, 230–31, 232–33
Brown v. Board of Education (1954 school desegregation), 100, 197–98, 216; Little Rock Nine, 214; tenth anniversary benefit hosted by SDJ, 220; white defense of segregation, 45, 145–46, 148–49
Bruce, Lenny, 139
Bubbles, John (Sublett), 19, 29, 80, 83
Buffalo Soldiers, 38–39, 50, 123
bullet dance, xix–xx, xxviii, 51, 126, 177, 251
Burnett, Carol, 223–24
Burns, George, 76
Buttons, Red, 178–79

Cagney, James, 53, 103, 104
Calloway, Cab, 6, 25, 68, 76, 134
Campanella, Roy, 106, 211
Camp Claiborne (Louisiana), 42–43
Cannonball Run (1981 film), 239
Cantor, Eddie, xxi, xxviii, 1; citing his own Jewishness in rejecting anti-black bigotry, 105–6; as friend and mentor to SDJ, 106, 139, 175; gifting SDJ with Jewish mezuzah, 105–6; hate mail received after SDJ handkerchief incident on *Colgate*, 104, 105, 119, 134, 149, 179. See also *Colgate Comedy Hour, The*
Capote, Truman, 244
Capra, Frank, *Know your Enemy—Japan* (1943), 41
Captured (1957 film short by SDJ and Arthur Silber Jr.), 123
Carmichael, Stokely, xxviii, 196, 198; on the assassination of MLK, 225; *Black Power* (1966, co-author Charles V. Hamilton), 168, 186, 197, 198–99, 201, 204
Carroll, Diahann, 63, 81, 124; and *Julia*, 162, 209–10, 212
Carson, Johnny, 217
Carter, Jack, 21
Carter, Katie, 13

Caruso, Enrico, 155
Cashmore, Ellis, 34
CBS television network: delay of airing show SDJ appears in, 119–20; disinvitation of SDJ to discussion program due to Britt marriage, 207
Chamberlain, Neville, 134
Chamberlain, Wilt, 137
Chaney, James, 34, 193, 245
Channing, Carol, 223–24
Chapel Hill, NC, *Porgy and Bess* pickets in, 88
Charles, Ray, 135, 217
Charlottesville, VA, neo-Nazi demonstration, 245
Cheyenne. *See* Fort Warren (Cheyenne, WY), service of SDJ
Chicago: anti-black violence in, 88; Black Cultural Center, 208; Chez Paree, 104, 178; Civil Rights benefits in, 213, 215, 220–21; Club de Lisa, 20; *Golden Boy* in (1968), 166, 207; March on Washington originating in, 44; Pekin theater, 24; riots following assassination of MLK, 224; Urban League, 213, 215
child performer, SDJ as: overview, xxv, 25–26; in blackface, 1, *2*, 26, 34; childhood as lost to, 1, 3, 25, 28–29; child welfare authorities, evasion of, 1, 26; debut at age two, 5; and racism, 27, 35, 49–50, 174; as regular in the troupe, 5, 26; *Rufus Jones for President* (1933 film), *xxv*, 5–10, *7*, 16, 29; tutored by Bill Robinson, 27, 30; versatility developed as, 26–27. *See also* Mastin, Will, vaudeville troupe of; Will Mastin Trio
Chinese immigrants, xxiii
Chisholm, Shirley, xxviii, 228, 243, 245
Cho, Margaret, 138
Christianity, used to justify racial segregation, 145–46, 152
Church Committee findings on FBI civil rights violations, 228
Cicero, IL, housing wars (1966), 201
Ciro's (Sunset Strip), *102*; as aspiration for Will Mastin Trio, 28, 101; breakthrough at, 103–4, 118, 178, 181; comeback after the car accident, 118, 179

citizenship, 144; normative whiteness of, 196–97. *See also* black citizenship

Civil Rights Act (1964), 36–37, 166, 188, 228, 229

Civil Rights era, defined, xxii, 36

Civil Rights Movement: 1963 as inflection point in, 216, 219; celebrities rallying to, 212–13, 214–15, 216–17, 222, 223–24, 250–51; as context for *Golden Boy* revival, 156–57, 159–64, 165–66; local organizing and, 218, 229; and meaning of *Porgy and Bess,* 81–82, 86–88; platform planks for Civil Rights (1944), 36; politicized art on behalf of, xxvii–xxviii, 211–12, 234–35; sit-ins, xxvii, 96, 111, 118, 199, 216; and the Western genre, 122, 124–25; women in, 44, 218; in *Yes I Can,* 188–89, 192. *See also* Civil Rights Movement, SDJ's participation in; King, Martin Luther Jr.; NAACP; post-Civil Rights era

Civil Rights Movement, SDJ's participation in: benefits attended and organized, 213, 215–17, 220–21, *221,* 222–24, *223,* 230; death threats to SDJ and, 218, 221, 222, 224; defensiveness of SDJ about, 237, 249; earliest involvement, 213; FBI file documenting, 206–8; *Golden Boy* runs interrupted for, 166, 222, 223; March on Washington (1963), 207, 213, 216–17, 218, 219, 220; MLK and, 141–42, 146, 166, 212–13, 221; money raised and given, 215, 216, 223; Selma Voting Rights rally (1965), 166, 222–23, *223,* 237; "Stars for Freedom" events, 213, 220; "Why I'm Backing the Chicago Urban League," 213. *See also* politics of SDJ

Clark, Jim, 221

Clark, Kenneth, *Dark Ghetto,* 199

Clark, Kenneth and Mamie, 197–98

Clark, Mark, 228

Clay, William, 228

Cleaver, Eldridge, 228; "Requiem for Non-violence," 225

Cleaver, Kathleen, 228

Cleveland Browns, 234

Cleveland, OH, election of black mayor, 229

Clinton, Bill, 242

Clooney, Rosemary, 135

codeswitching by SDJ, 85, 181

Cohan, George M. Jr., collaboration with SDJ in the Army, 52–53, 54, 59

Cohan, George M. Sr., 53

Cohn, Harry, 150, 153

COINTELPRO (FBI), 133, 227, 228, 230

Cold War, 4, 115, 195, 212; and racial liberalism in the postwar era, 63, 68, 114; the Western as allegory for, 121, 122

Cole, Nat King, xxi, 97, 109, 235; in *Cat Ballou,* 122; end of the *Nat King Cole Show,* 120

Cole, Robert, 20; *A Trip to Coontown* (1898 theater), 17

Coles, Honi, 13

The Colgate Comedy Hour, 104, 105–6, 119, 134, 149; Will Mastin Trio appearances on, 24, 104, *105,* 123, 178

Collins Park, DE, anti-black violence in, 88

colorism, 5

Coltrane, John, 113, 226

Combahee River Collective, 242, 246

Committee for Mass Education in Race Relations, 61

Committee on Drug Abuse (1970 Nixon appointment of SDJ), 59

Communist Party, 39

Confederate Lost Cause, 68–69

Congressional Black Caucus (1969), 228, 245

Congress of Racial Equality, 206

Connor, Bull, 33, 249

Connor, Edgar, 6

Constitution Hall, black entertainers barred from, 59

Cooke, Sam, 100; "A Change is Gonna Come," 163, 212

Cooke, Will Marion, *Clorindy—The Origin of the Cakewalk* (1897 theater), 17

Cook, Jim, 149

cool: as African dance attitude, 12; in black jazz culture, 112–13; "cool mask," 113; racial humor of the *Dean Martin Celebrity Roast* of SDJ, 137; the Rat Pack and, 111, 112, 113; of tap dancing, 29, 248

Copacabana (New York City), 117–18, 119, 177–78, 220; breaking racial barriers at, xix, 118, 179, 180, 188, 237; and Will Mastin Trio, 28, 101, 104

Corpus Christi, TX, anti-black violence in, 44

Cosby, Bill, 229–30, 235, 242; *Cosby Show,* 239; *I Spy,* 212

Count Basie, 118, 210, 216, 220

The Courtship of Eddie's Father (TV), 134

Covan, DeForest, 21

Crain, Jeanne, 146

Crickets, 232

Cripps, Thomas, 68, 147, 148

Croley, David, 144

Crosby, Bing, songs of, 32–33

Cross, Jimmy "Stump," 24, 55–56, 57–58, 262n80

Crothers, Scatman, 81

Crowther, Bosley: on *Anna Lucasta,* 65–66, 72, 75–76; on SDJ in *Porgy and Bess,* 86; on *Song of the South,* 69

Crystal, Billy, 111, 112

Cuba, xxiii, 39; as heritage of SDJ's mother, 4, 5, 115

Cullen, Countee, 68

culture industries: antidiscrimination petition to, 207; interracial relationships represented in, 146–48; and the invention of the Negro, xxvi, xxvii, 4; politicized art in projects of social justice, xxvii–xxviii, 211–12, 234–35, 251; postwar period, 67; versatility of SDJ in, xx–xxi, xxi, xxvi, 22–23. *See also* Broadway; film industry; music recording; nightclub/casino circuit; television; theater, African American; vaudeville; white-over-black structures of the industry

Cunningham, Evelyn, 184

Curtis, Tony, 75–76, 217

Dana, Bill, 242

dance: African drumming outlawed, 12; African social dance, 10–12, 16; buck dancing (pre-tap), 12–13, 18; cakewalk, 3, 14–15, 17; closure of dance venues, 3; commercialization of, 12–13; and "cool," origins of, 12; European forms, 11; the "jig," 14; masculinism and, 13, 14;

minstrelsy and, 14–16; and polyrhythms, 11–12, 18, 19; Protestant strictures against, 12; slavery and fugitive dance moves, 12, 16; social relations among the dancing ensemble, 12–13, 16. *See also* tap dance

Dandridge, Dorothy, 81, 83, 85

Daughters of the American Revolution, 59

Davis, Altovise (wife of SDJ), 60

Davis, Angela, 228; sympathy of SDJ for, 205, 207–8, 230–31

Davis, David Brion, 42

Davis, Mac, "In the Ghetto," 231

Davis, Miles, xxiii, 81, 93, 113, 191

Davis, Ossie: and alternative paths in culture industries, 210; and *Anna Lucasta,* 71; in the Civil Rights Movement, 89–90, 214–15, 220, 222; as fighting for inclusion, 67; and *A Man Called Adam,* 89–90

Davis, Sammy Jr.: overview of career of, xxv–xxvi, 118; attempted suicides, 186–87; being liked, importance of, 53–54, 176; birth of, xxv, 4, 37; on black, adoption as term, 237, 243; black aesthetic in hairstyle and dress, turn to, xxiv, 204, 250; Black Film Makers Hall of Fame award ceremony (1987), 250–51; conk hairstyle of, 191, 235; Cuban lineage of, 4, 5, 115; on death as the end of tap, 250; death of, 239, 245, 250; entertainment empire of, 215; gun carried for safety, 152; gun-handling expertise of, 123, 124; iconic kiss of Archie Bunker (*All in the Family,* 1972), 239–40, *240,* 242–43; and Judaism, conversion to, xxiv, 83, 105–6, 138–39, 206, 208, 239; marriage to Altovise, 60; marriage to Loray White, 150, 185; mother of (Elvera Sanchez), 4, 5, 25, 148; named *Metronome* magazine's "Outstanding New Personality of 1946," 63; obituaries of, 245; sexuality of, as possibly fluid, 52; silent, exaggerated laugh of, 116–18, *117*; Sinatra-like singing style and repertoire, xxvii, 53, 135, 136, 210, 231–32; as "singing 'white' and dancing 'black'," 5, 135; Sixtieth Anniversary Celebration for

Davis, Sammy Jr. *(continued)*
SDJ, at Shrine Auditorium, 250; tutored by Bill Robinson, 27, 30; versatility of, xx–xxi, xxi, xxvi, 5, 21, *22–23*, 24, 26–27, 102. *See also* African American community, SDJ viewed by; Britt, May (marriage with SDJ); Broadway and SDJ; child performer, SDJ as; films of SDJ; Haley, Alex, interview with SDJ (1964); interracial relationships of SDJ; music recordings by SDJ; nightclub/casino circuit and SDJ; politics of SDJ; Rat Pack; songs; television and SDJ; vaudeville and SDJ; Western genre; Will Mastin Trio; *Yes I Can* (1965 autobiography)
Davis, Sammy Sr. (father): background of, 4; and Elvera Sanchez (mother of SDJ), 4–5; press mention of, 26. *See also* black vaudeville circuit; child performer, SDJ as; Mastin, Will, vaudeville troupe of; vaudeville; Will Mastin Trio
Davis, Tracey (daughter), 189, 190
Dean Martin Celebrity Roast of SDJ, racial humor and, 136–38
death threats. *See* hate mail and death threats
decolonization: and 1963 as inflection point in the Civil Rights Movement, 216; and racial liberalism in the postwar era, 63, 68
Dee, Ruby, 210; and *Anna Lucasta,* 71; in the Civil Rights Movement, 213, 214–15, 217, 222; as fighting for inclusion, 67
Dees, Morris, 228
Del Rio, Dolores, 147
democracy, 194, 195–96, 201–2; jazz and, 13; and the Jim Crow military in World War II, 43–44, 45, 49; representation of African Americans in film and, 64, 66; World War II and new urgency of pushing ideals of, 36
Democratic Party: Civil Rights platform planks (1944), 36; SDJ as embittered toward, 243; SDJ booed of SDJ at convention (1960), 153, 187; SDJ working on behalf of RFK (1968), 230; Southern white supremacists in, and

reaction to Davis-Britt marriage, 152–53, 187. *See also* Kennedy, John F.
desegregation: "all deliberate speed" as more deliberation than speed, 100; Las Vegas, 100, 109–11, 182, 184; Miami Beach, 100; of the military, 36, 60–62, 197–98; World War II newsreels and information, and vision of, 67. See also *Brown v. Board of Education* (1954 school desegregation); culture industries; federal government, official antiracist position of; grassroots movement for desegregation; integration
DeSylva, Buddy, 32, 78
Detroit, MI, 202; anti-black violence during World War II, 36, 45–46; Civil Rights benefits in, 215; Club Plantation, 20; *Golden Boy* opening during race riots of, 159–60; Michigan Theater, 26; riot of 1943, 45–46
DeWitt, John L., 41
Diller, Phyllis, 136
Dinerstein, Joel, 113
discrimination: Civil Rights Act (1964), 36–37, 166, 188, 228, 229; the enforced gradualism following *Brown* as, 100; the Kennedy campaign of 1960 and argument against, 114; miscegenation laws as, 146; prohibition in defense industries, 36, 44; *To Secure These Rights,* 197–98
Disney, *Song of the South* (1946), 68–69
Dorsey, Tommy, 25, 26, 102
Double Victory campaign (victory against fascism abroad and against racism at home), 39–40, 44, 111, 118
Douglass, Frederick, xxii, 189–90, 198, 234
Douglas, Suzzanne, 246
Dred Scott decision (1857), 145
Duberman, Martin, 170–71, 187; *In White America,* 199, 220
Du Bois, W. E. B.: on the arrival of the "New Negro" after WWI, 39; and assimilation vs. pluralism, xxiii; *Black Reconstruction* (1935), 197; on sorrow songs, 34; on systemic racism, 195, 197, 198; on the wage of whiteness, xxvi
duCille, Ann, 121

Dukakis, Michael, 245
Dunbar, Paul Laurence, *Clorindy—The Origin of the Cakewalk* (1897 theater), 17
Duncan, Arthur, 246
Duncan, Ruby, 97–98
Duncan, Todd, 80
DuVernay, Ava, 251

Early, Gerald, xxi, xxviii
Eckstein, Billy, 25, 103, 104
Edison, Thomas, *The Pickanniny Dance* (1894), 10
Ed Sullivan Show (TV), 104, 118, 120, 246
Eisenhower, Dwight D., 36
Elkins, Hillard: and the Civil Rights Movement, 222, 223–24; as producer of *Golden Boy*, 154, 155, 158, 160, 161–62, 166, 222
Ellington, Duke, 25, 79, 210, 235
Ellison, Ralph: on the blues, 33, 34; on "cool," 113; the jazzman's academy, 13–14, 16, 249; on zoot suiters, 47
emancipation: and increased white violence against black people, 45, 143–45; the limitations and false promises of, xx; miscegenation laws (forbidding all interracial relationships) following, 143–44, 145–46. *See also* Jim Crow system of segregation and hierarchy; Reconstruction
empathy: colorblind humanism and, 172; and focus on the (white) witness vs. black suffering, 173; and politicized film on behalf of Civil Rights, 212; racial interchangeability and, 173–74, 186
Entratter, Jack, 110
Equal Employment Opportunity Commission (EEOC), 245
Estes, Nick, 126
Ethiopia, Mussolini's invasion of, 39
eugenics, 144
Europe: dance forms of, 11; racial climate contrasted with the US, 187–88
Evans, Gil, 81
Evers, Charles, 229
Executive Order 8802 (prohibiting discrimination in defense industries), 44

Executive Order 9981, *To Secure These Rights* (1947 desegregation of the military), 36, 60–62, 197–98

Falana, Lola, 166
Fanon, Frantz, 195
Faubus, Orval, 214
Fayette, MS, election of black mayor, 229
FBI: COINTELPRO, 133, 227, 228, 230; file on SDJ, 205, 206–9, 211, 233, 238; and justice as "incidental to law and order," 228; MLK named "the most dangerous Negro in America," 206, 218; Senate (Church Committee) finding of violation of civil rights by, 228
federal government, official anti-racist position of: Civil Rights Act (1964), 36–37, 166, 188, 228, 229; desegregation of the military, 36, 60–63, 197–98; fascism as racism and, 36, 39–40; "modern" Civil Rights era distinguished by, 36; and tactic of street-level agitation, 36–37, 44; Voting Rights Act (1965), 36–37, 228; war industries hiring practices, nondiscriminatory, 36, 44; World War II as inflection point producing, 36–37. *See also* racial liberalism in the postwar era
Feimster, Crystal, 144
film industry: and decline of dance venues and tap dance, 3; and decline of vaudeville, 25, 28; Hollywood formula/triumph narrative, 247–50; Jim Crow dynamics of, 29–30; minstrelsy perpetuated by, 29–30; multiculturalism, 246, 248; "pickaninnies" or "picks," 10; and politicized art on behalf of Civil Rights, 212; Trace-Mark Productions (SDJ owned), 215; wartime rhetoric of anti-Nazism, and the postwar Hollywood liberalism, 61–63. *See also* African Americans hired in film and television; all-black films, postwar racial liberalism and cycle of; films of SDJ; "race" movies; representation of African Americans in film and television; Vitaphone African American shorts; Western genre (film and television)

films of SDJ: *Cannonball Run* (1981), 239; *Captured* (1957 short by SDJ and Arthur Silber Jr.), 123; *Rufus Jones for President* (1933), *xxv*, 5–10, 7, 16, 29; *Sweet and Low* (1947 short), 101–2; *Tap* (1989), 13, 239, 246–50; *The Man* (by Irving Wallace, dropped project), 231. See also *Anna Lucasta* (1958); *Man Called Adam, A* (1966); *Porgy and Bess* (1959); Western genre appearances by SDJ

Fishgall, Gary, 50

Fitzgerald, Ella, 81

Fletcher, Dusty, 6; in *Rufus Jones*, 6, 7

Flood, Curt, 234–35

Floyd, George, police murder of, 246

Fontaine, Joan, in *Island in the Sun*, 146–47

Fort Huachuca (AZ), 42

Fort Warren (Cheyenne, WY), service of SDJ: overview of the fort and racial prejudice, 50; draft notice, testing, and being sent to, 35–36; entertainment specialist role of SDJ at, 37, 52–54, 59, 176–77; the press repeating the story of his experiences, 49–50; racial bullying of SDJ, xx, 49–52, 174–75, 176, 177; and SDJ's philosophy of talent as anti-racist weapon, 37, 38, 52, 53–54, 59; sexual assault at, SDJ alluding to, 52; white ally and mentor (Sergeant Gene Williams), 59, 175–76. *See also* Jim Crow military in World War II; World War II

Foster, Gloria, 220

Franciosa, Tony, 224

Franklin, Aretha, xxvii, 234; "Respect," 212, 232

Freedom Rides, 199, 215–16

freedom struggle: and faultline between continued commitment to nonviolence and revolutionary self-defense, 193–94, 203, 224–25, 226–27; sit-in era, xxvii, 96, 111, 118, 199, 216. *See also* Black Power; Civil Rights Movement; desegregation; federal government, official anti-racist position of; integration; King, Martin Luther Jr.; NAACP; post-Civil Rights era; race and racism

"Freedom TV Spectacular," 220

Friars Club, 182; celebrity roast of SDJ, 136–38

Gardner, Ava, 149, 154, 184

Garland, Hazel, 170

Garland, Judy, 135

Garland, Robert, 80

Gaston, A. G., 141

Gaston, AL, 224

Gates, Henry Louis Jr., 96

Geisel, Theodore (Dr. Seuss), 41

General Electric Theater (TV), 119–20

Genet, Jean, *The Blacks: A Clown Show*, 90

Georgia: anti-black violence in, 61; white supremacy and regulation of interracial relationships in, 145

Gershwin, George: *Blue Monday*, 78; and *Porgy and Bess* (opera), 78, 79–80, 81–82, 84, 85, 119

Gershwin, Ira, 76, 79

Gershwin, Lee, 76

Gibson, Bob, 177, 234–35

Gibson, Kenneth, 229, 243

Gibson, William, on rewrite team for *Golden Boy*, 154, 155, 156–57, 158, 161, 166

Gielgud, John, 223–24

Gillespie, Dizzy, 216

Giovanni, Nikki, 212

Gitlin, Todd, 282n4

Glazer, Nathan: *Affirmative Discrimination* (1973), 236; *Beyond the Melting Pot* (coauthor Daniel Moynihan, 1963), 202, 236

Glover, Savion, 248

Golden Boy (1937 play by Clifford Odets), 154–56, 158, 161, 165

Golden Boy (1939 film version), 155–56

Golden Boy (1964 Broadway): and the assassination of MLK, 227; and audience baggage of racial politics, 159–61; benefit performances of, 207; branding of the show, 158–59; Civil Rights Movement as context of, 156–57, 159–64, 165–66; Civil Rights Movement, runs interrupted for, 166, 222, 223; critical reception of, 160–61, 162–63, 165, 191; hate mail and threats of physical harm to actors, 160–61, 165, 166, 221; history

hate mail and death threats made to SDJ: after Cantor touched him on *Colgate Comedy Hour,* 104, 105–6, 119, 134, 149, 179; May Britt marriage and, 152; and *Golden Boy,* 160–61, 165, 166, 221; March on Washington (1963), 218; Kim Novak relationship, mob threats against, 149–50, 208; White Citizens Council's "Ten Most Wanted List," 218, 221, 222

Haygood, Wil, *In Black and White,* xxi, 26, 172; on *Porgy and Bess,* 86; on vaudeville childhood, 26, 28–29

Henderson, Finis, 110, 184

Hendrix, Jimi, xxi, 225–26

Here's Lucy (TV), 134

Hess, Cliff, 6

Heston, Charlton, 216, 217

Heyward, Dorothy, 78

Heyward, DuBose, and *Porgy and Bess,* 77–78, 79–80, 81–82, 84–85, 88, 119

Heyward, Janie DuBose, 77

Hill, Lauryn, 235

Hines, Gregory, xxviii, 97; as revering SDJ, 250; in *Tap,* 239, 246–50

Hines, Maurice, 97

Hinton, Elizabeth, 242

hip hop, 248

Hitler, Adolf, 43, 134

Hoffer, Eric, 236

Holder, Geoffrey, 81

Holiday, Billie, 6, 58, 87, 113, 118; "Strange Fruit," 211–12

Holloway, Jonathan, 119

Hollywood in a Suitcase (1980): do-over of his own presentation of his politics, 236–37; on his role in *Porgy and Bess,* 86; on hugging Nixon, 244; on Kennedy's role in the March on Washington, 219, 220

Hollywood. *See* film industry

hooks, bell: on "cool," 113; on patriarchy, 189–90; on sex and black masculinity, 165

Hoover, J. Edgar, 206, 208, 228, 233, 238. *See also* FBI

Hope, Bob, 2121

Horne, Lena, 33, 68, 134, 211; autobiography (*Lena*), 168, 189; and the Civil Rights

Movement, 207, 210, 217, 220; and desegregation of Las Vegas, 110; on the Jim Crow army, 35; "Now," 217; songs of, 33, 81; on white-over-black structure of the industry, 119; as World War II troop entertainer, 58–59

Horton, Willie, 245

House Un-American Activities Committee. *See* McCarthyism

Huggins, John, 228

Hughes, Langston: on Al Jolson, 31; on "cool," 112–13; death of, 226; "Freedom's Road," 40, 212; on postwar film industry, 64

Hurston, Zora Neale, 80

Ice Cube, 251

identity politics: assimilation as claim for inclusion based on "sameness," xxiii–xxiv; "free white persons" as eligible for citizenship, xxii; "individual liberties" in framework of group rights, and white male supremacy, xxii–xxiii; and masculinism, xxiv; pluralism as claim for inclusion based on being "different, but equal," xxiii–xxiv; post-Civil Rights era and, xxii; and "We the People," inclusion and exclusion in the founding of the Republic, xxii–xxiii

I Dream of Jeannie (TV), 99, 134

Immigration Act (1924), eugenics and, 144

Impressions, 210, 212

inclusive hiring. *See* African Americans hired in film and television

Indigenous peoples, xxiii. *See also* Native Americans

individual prejudice as the source of racism, 196, 198, 200, 202–4, 210; *Brown v. Board of Education* decision incorporating, 197–98; Myrdal's *American Dilemma* based on, 194–97; SDJ and, xxvii, 176–77, 186, 194, 203, 209, 229, 231; *To Secure These Rights* (1947 federal report) based on, 197–98. *See also* systemic racism

institutional racism (colonialism), 199, 200. *See also* systemic racism

Jim Crow system of segregation and hierarchy, 18, 19, 103, 106; and black vaudevillians, trouble finding accommodations on the circuit, 27–28; end of, and loss of the black public sphere, 96–98; and group rights, xxiii; Hollywood and, 29–30; Las Vegas as strictly enforced, 107–9; and minstrelsy, 15; New Deal housing and banking policies, 236; sundown town, Miami Beach as, 106–7, 179, 187; unions, 236; the Will Mastin Trio and protection of the young SDJ from, 27, 35, 49–50, 174; in World War I, 39, 43. *See also* freedom struggle; interracial relationships and sexuality; Jim Crow military in World War II; segregation; white supremacy and white supremacists

Jimi Hendrix Experience, and assassination of MLK, 225–26

Johnson, Billy, 20; *A Trip to Coontown* (1898 theater), 17

Johnson, Hall, 6, 79

Johnson, Jack, 159

Johnson, James Weldon, 17, 18

Johnson, John H., 184–85

Johnson, Lyndon B., and administration, 152–53, 208–9

Jolson, Al, xxi, xxvii; black audience disparagement of, 101; interested in *Porgy and Bess,* 79; songs of, 135; tribute of SDJ to, in *Mr. Wonderful,* xxvii, 31, 100, 101

Jones, Chuck, *Spies* (1943), 41

Jones, Clarence, 217, 226

Jones, Jo, 20

Jones, LeRoi (Amiri Baraka), 212; *Blues People* (1963), 33–34, 199

Jones, Tom, 246

Joplin, MO, 27

Josephson, Barney, 33

Judaism, SDJ and, xxiv, 83, 105–6, 138–39, 206, 208, 239

Kansas City, MO, riots following assassination of MLK, 224

Karenga, Maulana, 206, 209, 230, 233, 238

Kaye, Danny, 103

Kelly, Gene, 217

Kennedy, John F.: antidiscrimination position of, 114; assassination of, with no chance to mend fences with SDJ, 219, 220; excluding SDJ and Britt from all photographs at White House event, 219–20; lionized by SDJ as giver of liberation, 219, 220; and the March on Washington (1963), 219, 220; marriage of SDJ and May Britt as cause of concern for, 152–53, 187; SDJ and Britt disinvited from inauguration, 153, 187, 219, 243

Kennedy, Robert: assassination of, 230; endorsed for president by SDJ, 229–30; warning SDJ of death threats at March on Washington, 218, 221, 224

Kerner Commission Report, 193–94, 202, 230

Kern, Jerome, 10, 135

Kersands, Billy, 38

Killian, Lewis, and Charles Grigg, *Racial Crisis in America,* 199

King, A. D., 217

King, Martin Luther Jr., xxvi, xxviii, *221;* assassination of, riots and attempts of celebrities to calm the waters, 224–27; attacked by American Nazi for mentioning SDJ, 141–42, 146, 166; on black restitution, 218; calling on SDJ to contribute to the Movement, 207; the FBI naming as "the most dangerous Negro" in America, 206, 218; funeral of, 38, 166, 229–30; "Get Sammy" as familiar refrain, 213, 221; "I have a dream" speech, 218; and JFK, 219, 220; media strategy of, 199, 211, 217, 222, 235; and the Montgomery Bus Boycott, 213; "The Negro Revolution—Why 1963?," 216; nonviolence philosophy of, 193, 194; *Playboy* interview with Alex Haley, 191; on popular cultural forms, power of, 211, 217; on press coverage of the March, 219; relationship with SDJ, xxi, 166, 193, 211, 224, 233; on rioting as "the language of the unheard," 47, 224; and "safe" black celebrities, power of, 212–13, 215, 222, 223; on willingness to go to jail for integration, 88; *Yes I Can* and epigraph from, 170, 188, 190

Kipling, Rudyard, *Gunga Din,* xix, 125, 127, 128

Kitt, Eartha, xxi, 38, 230; and *Anna Lucasta,* 72, 73, 75, 246; and the Civil Rights Movement, 217; on SDJ, xxviii

Ku Klux Klan (KKK), 111, 134, 137, 144; attacks on *Golden Boy,* 165

Kun, Josh, xxi

Kupcinet, Irv, 86

LaGuardia, Fiorello, 43, 46–47

Lancaster, Burt, 216, 217, 224

Lancaster, Norma, 216

Lane, William Henry (Master Juba), 12, 14, 16, 249

Lansky, Meyer, 107

Lanza, Mario, 104

Last Poets, 212

Las Vegas: overview, 107; black workers brought to, 107–8; desegregation of, 100, 109–11, 182, 184; Jim Crow strictly enforced in, 107–9; SDJ's revue with Jerry Lewis (1988), 239; Westside (all-black area), 97–98, 107–8. *See also* Las Vegas hotels, casinos, and venues

Las Vegas hotels, casinos, and venues: Bally's, 239; Club Alabam, 97; Cove Hotel, 97; Desert Inn, 107, 109, 181–82; Dunes, 107; El Morocco, 97, 182; El Rancho, 107, 108, 110; the Flamingo, 107, 110; Hacienda, 107; Last Frontier, 103, 107, 108–9, 110; Moulin Rouge, 72, 76, 97; New Frontier, 168–69; Old Frontier, 179; Riviera, 107; Royal Nevada, 107; Sahara, 107; Stardust, 107; Town Tavern, 97; Tropicana, 107, 109. *See also* Sands Hotel

Late Night with David Letterman, 1

Laugh-In (TV), "Here Come de Judge" routine, 20, 21, 24, 32

Lawford, Peter, *112;* in *A Man Called Adam,* 65, 92; Civil Rights benefits by, 216; and the John F. Kennedy campaign, 114, 152, 153; liberal politics of, 114; in *Sergeants 3,* xix, 125. *See also* Rat Pack

Lawrence, Steve, 223–24

Lear, Norman, 242, 243

Le Corbusier (Charles-Édouard Jeanneret), 19

Lee, Canada, 70, 212; as blacklisted, 63

Lee, Ruta, 111, 114

Lee, Spike, 235, 242; Black Film Makers Hall of Fame award ceremony (1987), for SDJ and, 250–51; on politicized art, 251; *She's Gotta Have It,* 250

LeGon, Jeni, 13

Lentz-Smith, Adriane, 96

Leslie, Lew, 24

Lewis, Jerry: and the Ciro's splash, 103; Civil Rights benefits and, 217; as friend and mentor to SDJ, 139, 175, 178–79; Las Vegas revue with SDJ (1978), 239; SDJ impression of, 104; songs of, 135; warning SDJ away from Kim Novak, 149–50

Lewis, John, 242

Ligon, Glenn, 251

Lincoln, Evelyn, 153

Lipsitz, George, 100

Little Moon and Jud (1975 film), 130

Little Richard, 210; in *The Girl Can't Help It* (1956), 147–48

Little Rock, AR, integration struggle in, 93, 214

Little Rock Nine (1957), 214

Liuzzo, Viola, 193

Locke, Alain: and the "New Negro," 17; *The Negro and His Music,* 3, 4, 9, 11, 14, 15–16, 17

Lomax, Alan, 80

Lomax, Almena, 83

London: Black Power Movement supported by SDJ, 230; *Golden Boy* in, 230; Pigalle Club and Nazi pickets of SDJ, 151–52; racial climate contrasted with the US, 187–88

Long Island, 214

Lorde, Audre, 242

Los Angeles: Civil Rights benefits in, 215–16; Cocoanut Grove, 135, 230; election of black mayor, 229; Gibson Theater, 26; police response to the Black Panthers, 202; racist slights of SDJ in, 139; SDJ commuting between Las Vegas and, 72; Shrine Auditorium, Sixtieth Anniversary Celebration for SDJ, 250; Slapsy Maxie's, 101. *See also* Ciro's

Louis, Joe, 35; Civil Rights benefits and, 217; Cove Hotel, 97; and entertainment for the World War II troops, 57; Moulin Rouge, 97; and the postwar "official anti-racism," 63

Louisville, Kentucky, *Porgy and Bess* screenings, 88

Loving, Mildred and Richard, xxi

Loving v. Virginia (1967), 142, 145–46, 156, 166

Lowery, Joseph, 141

Lyles, Aubrey, 18

McCarthyism: and danger of racial liberalism, 68; and demise of the Popular Front, 212; and FBI file on SDJ, 207

McCrae, Carmen, 81, 216

McDaniel, Hattie, 58

McDonald, Flash, 24, 107

McKay, Claude, xxiii

MacKay, Claude, "If We Must Die," 39

McKinney, Nina Mae, 6

Mack, Roy, 6

McQueen, Butterfly, 58, 67

Major League Baseball, 177, 234–35

Malcolm, Roger, 61

Malcolm X, 90, 163, 198; *The Autobiography of Malcolm X* (1965, coauthored by Alex Haley), 168, 174, 186, 191, 194, 198, 199, 200–201; quoted by SDJ on black destiny as the destiny of American democracy, 194, 201–2; SDJ on killers of, 232–33

Malone, Jacqui, 16, 30

Maltz, Albert, *The House I Live In* (1945 film short), 109

Mamoulian, Rouben, 82

A Man Called Adam (1966 film): overview, 65, 98; anti-black violence in, 94–95; critical reception of, 89, 95, 191; plot of, 89, 90–95, 186; politics of, as a range of Civil Rights positions, 88–90, 156, 249; SDJ and, 89, 90, 95; SDJ's part in (Adam), 90–95

Mansfield, Jayne, in *The Girl Can't Help It* (1956), 147–48

March on Washington (1941), 36, 44, 49, 111

March on Washington for Jobs and Freedom (1963): Arts Group, 217, 219; celebrity fundraisers and attendance, 216–17; death threats against SDJ, 218; "I have a dream" moment as eclipsing the far more radical positions of King, 218; narratives of, vs. the actual temper of the time, 217–18; organizers of, 89–90, 218; press coverage as respectful and commensurate, 219; SDJ and, 207, 213, 216–17, 218, 219, 220

Markham, Pigmeat, xxi, 20–21; *Here Comes the Judge,* 32

Marshall, George C., 55

Marsh, Henry, 229

Marsh, Sy, 120–21, 122

Martha and the Vandellas, "Dancing in the Street," 232

Martin, Dean, xxiv, *112, 117;* and the Ciro's splash, 103; Civil Rights benefits and, 220; *Dean Martin Celebrity Roast* of SDJ, 136–38; at the Moulin Rouge, Las Vegas, 97; in *Ocean's Eleven,* 115; in *Sergeants 3,* xix, 125, 127; songs of, 135, 187. *See also* Rat Pack

Martin, Pete, 235

masculinism, xxiv, 38–39; and African American participation in US military engagements, 38–39; and dance competition, 13, 14; and racial bullying in the Army, 52; the Western genre and, 122

Master Juba. *See* Lane, William Henry (Master Juba)

Mastin, Will ("uncle"): age of, 1, 3; background of, 4–5; as "pickaninny" in childhood, 10. *See also* black vaudeville; Mastin, Will, vaudeville troupe of; vaudeville; Will Mastin Trio

Mastin, Will, vaudeville troupe of: abandonment of, and formation of Will Mastin Trio, 26; expansion of, 20; *Holiday in Dixieland* show, 4, 26, 118; parents of SDJ meeting while touring with, 4–5. *See also* child performer, SDJ as; Will Mastin Trio

Mathis, Johnny, 216

May, Lary, 262n80

Meeropol, Abel, 109

Memphis, TN, 119
Meredith, James, 207, 224
Miami Beach, FL: Beach Comber, 104, 106; as desegregated by SDJ, 100; Fontainebleau Hotel, xix, 187, 237; as Jim Crow sundown town, 106–7, 179, 187; Lord Calvert Hotel, 106, 107
Michael X (Michael de Freitas), 230
Michigan, and Jim Crow, 27
Midday with Bill Boggs (TV), 244
The Mike Douglas Show, guest hosted by SDJ and interview with Muhammad Ali, 204, 233
military: desegregation of (Executive Order 9981, *To Secure These Rights*) (1947), 36, 60–62, 197–98; segregationists lobbying to stop *Island in the Sun* being shown on bases, 147. *See also* Jim Crow military in World War II; World War I; World War II
Miller, Flournoy, 18
Mills Brothers, 97, 148
Mills, Florence, 13, 18
Mills, Marty, 179
Minneapolis, MN, George Floyd police murder, 246
minstrelsy: black citizenship disparaged by, 143; black masculinity defanged by, 143; and commodification of blackness, 29, 34; as contested terrain of black resistance, 6, 9–10; early nineteenth-century lithographs as model for, xxvii; the film industry as perpetuating, 29–30; Jim Crow excluding black performers from, 15; as mutual black/white mimicry, 14–16; *Porgy and Bess* as, 77, 79–80, 81–82, 86, 88; postwar discrediting of, 63; prescribed by the government for USO entertainments, 54–55, 57; as racial libel, 6; *Rufus Jones for President* (1933 film), *xxv*, 5–10, *7*, 16, 29; SDJ's continued use of vaudeville elements handed down from, 30–32; *Song of the South* (1946) and, 68–69; and talent as anti-racist weapon, 38; tap dance and, 3, 14–16; white-over-black control in, 6, 9–10; by the Will Mastin Trio, as

chafing SDJ, xxvii, 118, 180–81. *See also* blackface; Jolson, Al
miscegenation. *See* interracial relationships and sexuality
Mississippi: anti-black violence in, 88; "Christmas for Mississippi," 207, 220–21; Civil Rights rally with SDJ, 224; killing of Chaney, Schwerner, and Goodman, 193, 245; killing of James Meredith, 207, 224; Ronald Reagan cynical campaign stop in, 245
Monroe, Marilyn, xxi, 149, 184
Monroe Massacre (Georgia), 61
Monterey, CA, Jim Crow military experiences of SDJ, 50
Montgomery, AL: bus boycott, xxviii, 110–11, 213–14, 215; march at, 207
Morgan, Danielle Fuentes, 58
Morial, Ernest, 229
Morrison, Toni, 235, 242; *Love,* 75
Morton, Joe, 247
Moss, Carlton, *The Negro Soldier* (1944 film), 61–62, 67
Moulin Rouge (Las Vegas), 72, 76, 97
Moynihan, Daniel: *Beyond the Melting Pot* (coauthor Nathan Glazer, 1963), 202, 236; *Moynihan Report* (1965), 202–3, 236
Mr. Wonderful (1956 Broadway show), *183*; Civil Rights Movement work by cast of, 213; critical reception of, 31, 63, 101, 171; and desegregation of Broadway, 100–101; *Golden Boy* as the chance to make up for (SDJ), 154; tribute to Al Jolson in, xxvii, 31, 100, 101; vaudeville elements handed down from minstrelsy in, 31
Muhammad, Elijah, 200
multiculturalism: Hollywood, 246, 248; and post-Civil Rights era identity politics, xxii
multiculturalist white supremacy, 241–42
Murphy, George, 55
Murray, Albert, 113
Murray, Jan, 137
Murrow, Edward R., *Person to Person* (TV), 123
Muse, Clarence, 67

music recordings by SDJ: companies owned by SDJ, 215; *If I Ruled the World,* 167; *Porgy and Bess* (with Carmen McRae), 81, 84; *Starring Sammy Davis Jr.* (1955), 33. *See also* songs

Mussolini, Benito, 39

Myles, Meg, 149

Myrdal, Gunnar, *An American Dilemma* (1944): individual prejudice as source of racism, xxviii, 141, 194–97, 202; institutions as the solution to individual prejudice, 196, 200; predicting increased discontent of African Americans following World War II, 45; unconscious white bias in assumptions of, 196–97

NAACP: anti-black violence against leaders of, 88; on anti-black violence in World War II, 45; campaign against miscegenation laws, 146; continuing after the assassination of MLK, 228–29; deal with Hollywood studios to codify changes in hiring and representation, 67, 68; declining to comment on *Porgy and Bess,* 81; and desegregation of Las Vegas, 110–11; FBI file on SDJ and, 206; as giving way to more radical politics, 210; and the "official" anti-racism forged during World War II, 61, 67; and *Porgy and Bess* picketing, 88; protests of *Birth of a Nation* as fight for representation, 67; SDJ as indispensable ally to, 212, 215, 216, 220, 230; Springarn Award (1969) awarded to SDJ, 230

Nadel, Alan, 120

Nash, Diane, xxviii

Nathan, George Jean, 29

National Advisory Council on Economic Opportunity (1972 Nixon appointment of SDJ), 243

National Association for Black Law Enforcement Executives (1976), 229

National Association of Black Journalists (1975), 229

National Association of Blacks in Criminal Justice (1974), 229

Nation of Islam, 193, 200

Native Americans: as effaced through casting of Sicilian Henry Silva in a lead indigenous role, 127–28, 129; group treatment of, vs. "individual liberties," xxiii; intermarriage and dilution of racial identity of, and loosened grip on tribal lands, 142; reference to chants of, in SDJ's arrangement of "Under My Skin," 136; resistance of, as ongoing, 126; and the Western genre, 122, 123, 124–26, 127–28, 129, 131–32

Nazi Germany: and affinity of Jews and the black community, 105–6, 139; anti-Semitic Nuremberg Laws, 36, 38–39, 43; eugenics, 144; fascism as racism, and the Jim Crow military, 39–40; fascism as racism, and the "official anti-racism" of the US federal government, 36

Nazi Party (UK), and marriage of SDJ, 151–52, 187

NBC television network: exclusionary hiring practices, 233; hate mail received following *Colgate Hour* appearance of SDJ, 105; and *Julia,* 209–10; and the *Nat King Cole Show,* 120

Negro dialect, *Porgy and Bess* and, 77, 79–80, 83

Negro League Baseball, 96–97

neo-Nazis, rally in Charlottesville, VA, 245

Newark, NJ: election of black mayor, 229, 243; Jimi Hendrix Experience show after assassination of MLK, 225–26; tanks on the streets of, 202, 225

Newcomb, Don, 211

New Deal, exclusionary housing and banking policies, 236

Newley, Anthony, 135

Newman, Randy, "Sail Away," 229

"New Negro," xxv, 16–17, 17, 29, 39

New Orleans, election of black mayor, 229

New York City: anti-black violence in, 88; Apollo Theater, 20, 215; Capitol Theater, 118, 177; Carnegie Hall, Civil Rights benefits, 212–13, 215–16; Cotton Club, 1, 25; Draft Riots (1863), 144; Hippodrome Theater, 25; Lincoln theater, 24; Lindy's, 177; Madison Square Garden, Civil Rights benefits, 213, 220; Majestic,

119, 222, 223–24; Paramount, 25; Radio City Music Hall, 20; Roxy, 25; Strand Theater, 25, 118; Waldorf-Astoria, xix, 237. *See also* Copacabana (New York City); Harlem

NFL, 234

Nicholas Brothers (Fayard and Harold), 1, 6, 9, 18, 109, 250

Nicholas, Harold, 246, 248

Nichols, Nichelle, 81

nightclub/casino circuit and SDJ: black vaudeville replaced by, 28; SDJ's name up in lights on the Las Vegas Strip, 111, 118; vaudeville material used in, 32–34; Will Mastin Trio and switch to, 101–4, *102*, 106, 108–9, 118, *178*. *See also* Las Vegas; Rat Pack

Nixon, Richard: "Checkers speech" (1952), 244; as despised by progressives and the African American community, 239; "enemies list," 228; "first civil right" speech, 227–28, 240; hugged by SDJ, 239–42, *241*, 243–45; interracial marriage of SDJ used against Kennedy (1960 campaign), 153; "law and order" policing, 133, 227–28, 239, 244; political appointments of SDJ by, xxi, 59, 243; and "post-Civil Rights," 240; "Southern strategy," 245

North: *de facto* segregation in, 163–64, 185–86; and systemic racism, articulation of, 200. *See also* freedom struggle; Great Migration

North Carolina, white supremacy and, 149

Northrop, Solomon, *Twelve years a Slave* (1853), 204

Novak, Kim, 149–50, 184, 208

Oakland, CA, election of black mayor, 229

Obama, Barack, 45, 235, 240, 242, 246

Ocean's Eleven (1960 film), 59, 115

O'Connor, Carroll, *240*, 242–43

O'Connor, Donald, 26, 99, 232

Odets, Clifford: death of (1963), 154; Popular Front author, 154. *See also Golden Boy*

Odetta, 212, 222, 234

Office of War Information (OWI), 61, 67

O'Neal, Pete, 228

O'Neill, Eugene, *Anna Christie,* 70–71

Orleck, Annelise, 98, 108

Orwell, George, 38

Oscar Peterson Trio, 33

Otvos, Dorian, 6

Owens, Jesse, 63

Ozawa, Takeo, xxiv

Paige, Janis, 103–4, 178

Paris, France, Moulin Rouge, 25

Parker, Albert, "Four Freedoms at Home," 42

Parker, Charlie, xxvii

Parker, Pat, xvii–xviii

Pascoe, Peggy, 143

Pattin' Juba, 11, 29

The Patty Duke Show (TV), 134

Penn, Arthur, 159, 160

Perry, Eleanor, 170

"personal responsibility," American conservatism and, 202–3

Person to Person (TV, Edward R. Murrow), 123

Peters, Brock, 81

Petry, Ann, "In Darkness and Confusion," 47–49

Philadelphia, PA: Dunbar theater, 24; Earl, 25; New Standard theater, 24; Pearl, 25; Standard Theater, 5, 25, 26; Uptown, 25

Philippines, wars of 1898–99 in, 39

Philips, Kimberly, 40, 41

photography, and SDJ, xxvi

Pickett, Wilson, 135

Pine, Lester, 88–89, 90, 92, 95. See also *Man Called Adam, A*

Pittsburgh Pirates, 234

Platters, 97

plausible deniability of racism, 100

Playboy interview. See Haley, Alex, interview with SDJ for *Playboy*

pluralism: definition of, xxiii; and misreading of assimilationism, xxiv–xxv

Podell, Jules, 117–18, 188

Poitier, Sidney: and the Civil Rights Movement, 191, 210, 213, 214–15, 220, 222, 224, 234; in *The Defiant Ones,* 75–76, 212; in *Guess Who's Coming to Dinner,*

Poitier, Sidney *(continued)*
147; and *In the Heat of the Night,* 130–
31, 132–33, 212; *Lilies of the Field,* 212; in
Long Ships, 86; MLK commending, 213;
in *Porgy and Bess,* 76–77, 81, 82, 83, 86;
and the postwar "official anti-racism,"
63, 235
police violence, 46, 242, 246
policing, "law and order" (post-Civil Rights
era), 133, 227–28, 239, 244
politics of representation: African American theater and, 17–18; definition of,
xxvii; and interracial relationships,
146–48; and minstrelsy, 34; optimism
of the Great Migration and, 16–17; and
postwar racial liberalism and all-black
films, 65–66; stigmatic blackness, 121.
See also African Americans hired in
film and television; representation of
African Americans in film and
television
politics of SDJ: overview, 233–34, 235–36;
and the black community, critiques by
SDJ, 235–36; black identity, 232; Black
Power Movement, 230; "bootstraps"
ideology trap, 236; do-over of his own
presentation of, 236–37; individual
prejudice as the source of racism, xxvii,
176–77, 186, 194, 203, 209, 229, 231;
media politics and, 235; NAACP Spring-
garn Award (1969), 230; and the Nixon
hug, 239–42, *241,* 243–45; post-Civil
Rights era, 229–34; South Africa's Sun
City center, boycott of, 250–51; and style,
politics of, xxiv, 191, 204, 235, 250; systemic racism, 191, 193–94, 201–2, 203,
204, 229, 233; as a text, 205, 233–34, 235;
violent means, critique of, 226–27, 233.
See also assimilationism of SDJ; Civil
Rights Movement, SDJ's participation in
polygenists, 144
polyrhythms, 11–12, 18, 19
Poplarville, MS, anti-black violence in, 88
Popular Front: as alternate path in culture
industries, 210; fascism as equated with
racism, 39–40; McCarthyism and
demise of, 212; Clifford Odets and, 154,
166; and postwar racial liberalism, 68

Porgy and Bess (1925 Heyward novel),
77–78
Porgy and Bess (1927 Heyward play), 78–79
Porgy and Bess (1935 Gershwin opera), 78,
79–80
Porgy and Bess (1959 film): overview, 65,
76–77, 89, 98; as black space expressive
of an earlier era's social codes, 65, 119,
247–48; counter-interpretation by Bess
actresses, 85; critical reception of, 74;
critical reception of film, 85–87, 95;
critical reception of property, 77–79,
80; history of property, 77–80; as
minstrelsy, 77, 79–80, 81–82, 86, 88;
racial essentialisms in, 77; racial ventriloquism and cultural appropriation
in the music of, 79–80; and scripts of
the black masculine body, 69; SDJ,
critical reception of, 85–86; SDJ's
enthusiasm for his part in, 76, 77, 81, *82,*
83–84; white audiences vs. black audiences and perception of, 76–79, 80,
81–83, 86–88, 95; as white space in
disguise, 119
post-Civil Rights era: 1968 as inflection
point, 227; anti-racist stream in, 245–
46; black leadership, divisions among
and losses of, 228; black political
appointments, 245–46; and Black
Studies, emergence of, 229; "bootstraps"
ideology and disavowal of white privilege, 236, 244; Congressional Black
Caucus, 228, 245; electoral politics and
rise of African American mayors, 229,
245; the FBI's COINTELPRO vigilante efforts to "neutralize" anti-racist
activism, 133, 227, 228, 229; King's
mantle, black clergy vying for, 228; "law
and order" policing, 133, 227–28, 239,
244; loss of the black public sphere,
96–98; new and continued social justice
activism, 228–29, 242; *new phase of an
ongoing struggle* perspective, 242; Nixon's "first civil right" to be free of the
upheavals of the Civil Rights Movement, 227–28, 240; "personal responsibility" ideology, 202–3, 244; pluralistic
ethos of, xxiv–xxv; police violence and,

242, 246; politicized art and, 234–35, 251; professional organizations and, 229; progressive commentary on, 240–42; Republican Party's "Southern Strategy" as stream in, 245; splintering of the movement, 228–29; *Tap* (1989 film) as production of, 247–48; *the black community lost* perspective, 240–42; *we won* perspective, 242, 247–48. *See also* politics of SDJ

Powell, Adam Clayton Jr., 163; on the 1943 Harlem uprising, 47

Powell, Colin, 246

Pratt, Geronimo Ji-Jaga, 228

"Prayer Pilgrimage for Freedom," 206–7, 213, 215

Preminger, Otto, xxi; and *Porgy and Bess*, 82–83, 85, 86, 87, 119

Presley, Elvis, xxi, 231

press: the Ciro's breakthrough and, 104; Civil Rights frame in coverage of SDJ, 213–14, 222; on interracial relationships of SDJ, 149, 150–51, 153; and the Kennedy campaign (1960), 153; March on Washington coverage as respectful and commensurate, 219; and the Nixon hug, 244, 245; World War II experiences of SDJ widely repeated by, 49–50

press, black: on boxer Jack Johnson's prosecution for interracial relationships, 159; Civil Rights Movement coverage of SDJ, 215–17; critical reception of *Yes I Can,* 170, 171; and the Double Victory campaign, 44; harsh judgments of SDJ, and difficulty of SDJ in understanding, 184–85; on interracial relationships of SDJ, 149; on the Jim Crow military in World War II, 42–45; on SDJ and May Britt excluded from photographs at Kennedy event, 220; on urban geography choices of SDJ, 164

Preston, Robert, 223–24

Previn, Andre, 85

Price, Leontyne, 85

Prima, Louis, 99

Prinze, Freddy, 137

Pryor, Richard, 138

Puerto Rico, xxiii; substituted for Cuba in SDJ's lineage, 4, 115

Quinn, Samuel, 88

race and racism: the culture industries and invention of the Negro, xxvi, xxvii, 4; early 1960s best-selling treatments of, 168; and escape of SDJ, 100; exaggerated sensuality narrative of blackness, 86–87; the myth of racial purity, 143, 144–46; plausible deniability of racism, 100; "scientific" justifications of, 143, 144; white/black binary, creation and defense of, 144; white dismissal of the skills required to tap dance, 29; *Yes I Can* as best-selling treatment of, 168–69, 203. *See also* freedom struggle; individual prejudice as the source of racism; racial liberalism in the postwar era; systemic racism; whiteness; white supremacy and white supremacists

"race movies": falling out of favor in postwar racial liberalism, 68; postwar all-black films distinguished from, 65. *See also* Vitaphone, African American shorts

racial liberalism in the postwar era: Cold War imperatives and the geopolitics of decolonization, 63, 68; cycle of race-themed films reflecting, 67–68; fetishizing race as "chic," 162; *Golden Boy* and, 159, 160, 162, 164; the icon of the sacrificing black member of the multiracial platoon, 60; the icon of the wronged black soldier, returned to injustices after fighting to defeat fascism, 60–62; insults in spaces of, SDJ on, 182; and interracial relationships in films, 147; the "official anti-racism" of desegregating the military as the hallmark of, 60–63; plausible deniability of racism, 100; the Rat Pack and, 111, 114, 128; rising power of anti-communism and dangers of, 68; Southern censors' challenge to, 68–69; treatments of anti-Semitism and, 68. *See also* all-black films, postwar racial liberalism and cycle

racial liberalism *(continued)*
 of; federal government, official anti-
 racist position of racial ventriloquism,
 9–10, 79–80
A Raisin in the Sun (Hansberry, 1961 film),
 65, 68, 89, 91, 199, 203
Randolph, A. Phillip, xxviii; threatened
 March on Washington over racist
 hiring practices in war industries (1941),
 36, 44, 111
Rankin, John, 173
rap music, 32
Rat Pack, *112*; overview, 111, 116; assimilationism of SDJ and membership in,
 xxiv; burden of SDJ for caretaking the
 white audience, 115–17; Civil Rights
 benefits and, 215–16, 217, 230; and
 "cool," 111, 112–13; exaggerated silent
 laugh of SDJ, 116–18, *117*; hurtfulness to
 SDJ, 116; Kennedy campaign of 1960
 and, 152–53; and liberalism, 111, 114, 128;
 and masculinism, xxiv; *Ocean's Eleven,*
 59, 115; racial humor of, 111, 113–16, 119,
 136–38, 162, 205, 220, 232; rage of SDJ
 and, 117–18; the Sands "Summit," 111,
 112, 113–16, 118; SDJ as "mascot" of, 111,
 114, 232; SDJ as never equal to the white
 members of, xxiv, 99–100, 115, 129, 232;
 SDJ on being submerged as a human
 being in, 232; *Sergeants 3,* xix–xx, 59, 111,
 125–29, 131; as white allies, 175; white-
 over-black dynamic of, 111
Raymond, Emilie, 214–15
Reagan, Ronald, 55, 202–3; and the "Southern strategy," 245
Reconstruction: concealment of white
 agency implying failure of black governance, 197; crushing of, and stripping of
 black citizenship, 145; Myrdal's *American Dilemma* replicating white
 supremacist trope of, 197; slanders
 about black governance, 10; and white
 panic about black citizenship, 144–45.
 See also Jim Crow system of segregation
 and hierarchy
Redding, Otis, 135, 226
Redwood City, CA, anti-black violence
 in, 36

Reeb, James, 223
representation of African Americans in
 film and television: black activism for,
 67; debates about black identity vs.
 universalist formula, 68, 74; definition
 of, 66; and democracy, 64, 66; as distinct from the inclusive politics of
 hiring, 66, 67; of enslaved or recently
 freed people, disrupting the norm of
 erasure, 129; insistence on dignified
 roles as threat to black employment, 67;
 SDJ on obligation for, 233; and whiteness as norm, creation and policing of,
 119–21. *See also* African Americans
 hired in film and television; all-black
 films, postwar racial liberalism and
 cycle of; politics of representation
Reprise Records, 215
Republican Party: black political appoint-
 ees, 245–46; Civil Rights platform
 planks (1944), 36; "Southern strategy"
 of, 245. *See also* Nixon, Richard; post-
 Civil Rights era
respectability politics, of *Guess Who's
 Coming to Dinner,* 147
Revolutionary War, 38
Rhodes, George, 115–16
rhythm and blues, 210, 248
Rice, Condoleeza, 246
Richmond, VA, election of black mayor,
 229
Rickles, Don, 137
The Rifleman episodes (TV), 100, 123–25,
 131
Riis, Thomas, 15
riots: MLK on rioting as "the language of
 the unheard," 47, 224; SDJ on, 194
Rivera, Chita, 223–24
Robbins, Edward, 175
Robeson, Paul, 70; as blacklisted, 63; on the
 enforced gradualism of the post-*Brown*
 years, 100; as fighting for inclusion, 67;
 and the Popular Front, 210; tutored in
 Negro dialect, 10; "What Is America to
 Me?|," 212
Robinson, Bill, xxi, xxviii, 12, 182; birth of,
 1, 3; and *Black Birds of 1928,* 18, 25, 30;
 Broadway stardom of, 18; compared to

Fred Astaire by SDJ, 185; and conflict between self and stereotype, 15–16; death of, and the death of tap dance, 30; *Harlem Is Heaven,* 30; heckled by black audiences, 5; and limitations on freedom, 17; photo appearing in *Tap,* 246; protest of the Jim Crow military, 43; as "race man," 5; and Shirley Temple, films with, 5, 30, 146; song ("Mr. Bojangles") not a reference to, 250; tap dance style of, 18; tutoring SDJ, 27, 30; in Vitaphone shorts, 6

Robinson, Cedric, *Forging Memory and Meaning,* xxvi, xxvii, 4

Robinson, Edward G., sendup by SDJ, 104

Robinson, Jackie, 63, 211

Robinson, Lavaughn, 24

Robinson, Sugar Ray, 52, 106

rock and roll: and decline of tap dance, 3; and outdated nature of SDJ's songbook, 210; in *Tap,* 247, 248, 249; and white panic about interracial relationships, 145

Rock, Chris, 138

Rockwell, George Lincoln, 124

Rodgers and Hammerstein, *South Pacific* (1958), 147

Rodriguez, Dylan, 241–42

Rooney, Mickey, xxi, 21, 175, 177, 232; Will Mastin Trio opening for, 102

Roosevelt, Franklin Delano, 36, 43, 44, 45, 49

Rowan & Martin's Laugh-In (TV), "Here Come de Judge" routine, 20, 21, 24, 32

Rufus Jones for President (1933 film), *xxv,* 5–10, *7,* 16, 29

Rumsfeld, Donald, xxi

Russell, Nipsey, 137, 180–81, 216

Russell, Richard, 145

Rustin, Bayard, "Black Power and Coalition Politics," 198, 199

Saiger, Morton, 108–9

St. Louis, MO: Booker T. Washington theater, 24; Kiel Theater, 135; World War II troop entertainers Jim Crowed in, 58

Saks, Eva, 150

Sammy and Company (TV), 239

Samoans, xxiii

Sanchez, Elvera (mother of SDJ), 4, 5, 25, 148

Sands Hotel (Las Vegas): desegregation of, xix, xxviii, 110, 237; development of, 107; draining the pool after a swim by SDJ, 109; Jim Crow enforcement at, 109, 110; the Rat Pack "Summit," 111, *112,* 113–16, 118; and white-over-black structures, persistence of, 119

San Francisco: Fairmont Hotel, 182; Geary Theater bomb threats, 152

Santa Monica, CA, Civil Rights benefits, 220

Sawyer, Grant, 111

Schreiber, Belle, 159

Schuyler, George, 171

Schwerner, Michael, 34, 193, 245

SCLC (Southern Christian Leadership Conference): donation by SDJ, 207; FBI file on SDJ and, 206, 207; as giving way to more radical politics, 210; SDJ as indispensable ally to, 212–13, 221, 230

Scott, Hazel, 210; as blacklisted, 63; and desegregation of Las Vegas, 110; as Jim Crowed World War II troop entertainer, 58, 59

Screen Actors' Guild (SAG), 67

Seale, Bobby, 228

Seberg, Jean, 230

segregation: Christianity used to justify, 145–46, 152; *de facto* as long and continuing history, 99; *de facto* in the North, 163–64, 185–86; *de facto* of suburbanization, 164; degradation and hierarchy as the point of, 41–42; prevention of interracial relationships used as defense of, 141, 145–46, 148–49, 157. *See also* Jim Crow military in World War II; Jim Crow system of segregation and hierarchy

Seibert, Brian, 14, 15, 19

Selma, AL: "Broadway Answers Selma" benefit for families of those murdered, *221, 223*; killing of Viola Liuzzo, 193; MLK's media strategy in, 199; Voting Rights march (1965), 166, 221–23, *223,* 237

Sergeants 3 (1962 film), xix–xx, 59, 111, 125–29, 131
Serling, Rod, *Twilight Zone,* 122
settler colonialism: race-as-lineage as organizer of land ownership, 142; racial intermarriage as loosening the indigenous grip on tribal lands, 142
Shakur, Assata Olugbala, 228
Shakur, Zayd, 228
Shamroy, Leon, 83
Sharon, Lee, 149
Siegel, Benjamin "Bugsy," 107, 110
Silber, Arthur Jr., 106, 116, 117, 187; *Captured* (1957 film short with SDJ), 123
Silberman, Charles, *Crisis in Black and White,* 199
Silva, Henry, 127–28, 129
Silva, Michael, 116, 135–36
Silvers, Phil, 10
Simone, Nina, xxvii, 85, 234; "Mississippi Goddam," 212; response to assassination of MLK, 226; "Why? (The King of Love Is Dead)," 226
Sims, Howard "Sandman," 3, 246–47, 248, 249
Sinatra, Frank, xxi, xxiv, xxviii, *112, 117*; as best man at SDJ's wedding, 152, 153; Civil Rights Movement benefits by, 213, 216, 220, 230; and desegregation of Las Vegas, 109, 110; *The House I Live In* (1945 film short), 109; and the John F. Kennedy campaign, 114, 152, 153; lobbying for SDJ to do *Porgy and Bess,* 76; at the Moulin Rouge, Las Vegas, 97; in *Ocean's Eleven,* 115; progressive politics of, 109, 114, 129; at the Sands, 109; SDJ as guest of, 177–78; SDJ opening for, 30, 177; in *Sergeants 3,* xix, 125, 126–27; songs of, 33, 135, 187, 232; standards of, as style of SDJ, xxvii, 53, 135, 136, 210, 231–32; as white ally, 175; Will Mastin Trio opening for, 102, 118. *See also* Rat Pack
Sinatra, Frank Jr., 65, 89
Singleton, John, 251
Sissle, Noble, 6, 18, 78–79
sit-in era, xxvii, 96, 111, 118, 199, 216
slavery: the blues as arising from, 33–34; dance and music and, 12, 14–15, 16; and

group rights, xxiii; kinship disowned for children born of rape in, 142–43; the "one drop" rule of black racial identity encoded into law for, 142; white rape of enslaved women to increase chattel, 142–44. *See also* emancipation; jazz; minstrelsy; tap dance
Slyde, Jimmy, 246, 248
Smith, Alfred, 27
Smith, Bessie, 32
Smith, Ellison "Cotton Ed," 145
Smith, Keely, 83
Smith, Lillian, 143–44
SNCC (Student Nonviolent Coordinating Committee), 201, 210, 212
songs of SDJ: overview, 83–84, 135; "Birth of the Blues," 31, 32–34, 78, 114, 135, 168–69; "The Candy Man," 232; "Colorful," 162; "Don't Forget 127th Street," 97, 162–64, 188; "Hey There," 135, 169; "I'll Be Glad When You're Dead, You Rascal you," 7, 27; "Impossible Dream," 60, 232; "It Ain't Necessarily So," 83, 84; "I've Gotta Be Me," 231–32; "I've Got You under My Skin," 135–36; "The Lady Is a Tramp," 135; "Lucretia MacEvil," 60; "Me and My Shadow" (with Sinatra), 187; "Mr. Bojangles," 93, 232, 246, 250; "My Way," 135, 232; "Night Song," 161, 162; "No More," 161, 162, 165, 167; "Old Black Magic," 31; "Ol' Man River," 135; "Rock-A-Bye Your Baby with a Dixie Melody," 135; "Sail Away," 229; "Sam's Song" (with Dean Martin), 187; "Spinning Wheel," 60; "There's a Boat That's Leavin' Soon for New York," 83, 84–85; "What Kind of Fool Am I?," 135, 187
South: black workers brought to the Las Vegas area from, 107–8; censors cutting black figures from postwar race-themed films, 68–69; Democratic Party voters' reaction to Davis-Britt marriage, 152–53; Las Vegas catering to clientele from, 108, 110, 119; objections to *Anna Lucasta* in, 75; objections to *Island in the Sun,* 147; Republican Party "Southern strategy," 245; SDJ doing Civil Rights events

in, 222–23, 224; SDJ refusing to do
Civil Rights events in, 213, 220–21, 222;
television whiteness maintained for,
119–20. *See also* interracial relationships
and sexuality; Jim Crow system of
segregation and hierarchy; slavery;
white supremacy and white
supremacists
South Africa, SDJ boycotting Sun City,
250–51
South Carolina, white supremacy and
regulation of interracial relationships
in, 145, 147
Southern Poverty Law Center (1971),
228–29
Spanish-American War, 39
Spelling, Aaron, *The Trackers* (1971 pilot),
130–34
Spencer, Prince, 21, 24
Spillers, Hortense, 142–43
Sprigle, Ray, on the unfair treatment of
black soldiers post–World War, II,
60–61
Stampp, Kenneth, 68
Standing Rock, 126
"Stars for Freedom" rallies, 213, 220
Star Trek (TV), 234
Stein, Irving, 231
Stelly, Matthew, *Feets, Don't Fail Me Now:
Sammy Davis, Jr. and the Issue of "Role
Conflict,"* 125, 172–73, 203, 205–6, 209,
227, 231, 238
Step'n Fetchit, 67, 103, 113, 129
Stern, Sol, 202
Steve Allen (TV), 118
Stevens, Morty, 33, 175, 180
Stewart, Jimmy, 103, 104
Stoddard, Lothrop, 144
Stokes, Carl, 229
Stokes, Louis, 228
Stop the World—I Want to Get Off (1978),
239
Storch, Larry, 103
Streisand, Barbra, 223–24
structural racism. *See* systemic racism
Stuart, Joan, 149, 150, 184
Sullivan, Ed, xxi, 178–79; *Ed Sullivan
Show,* 104, 118, 120, 246

Supreme Court: *Dred Scott* (1857), 145;
Loving v. Virginia (1967), 142, 145–46,
156, 166. See also *Brown v. Board of
Education* (1954 school desegregation)
Sweet and Low (1947 film short), 101–2
systemic racism: overview of shift of white
mainstream public discourse to, 198,
202–3; "black power" texts and discourse of, 198–202; general social turn
to, 210; "individual liberties" ideal vs.
group treatment of African Americans,
xxiii, 201; institutions and perpetuation
of, 199, 200; the Kerner Commission
Report (federal) and, 193–94, 202, 230;
as longstanding idea, 198; SDJ on, 191,
193–94, 201–2, 203, 204, 229, 233; white
agency and, 198; "white backlash" in,
201; "white devils" phrase of Malcolm
X, 200–201. *See also* individual prejudice as the source of racism

Tap (1989 film), 13, 239, 246–50
tap dance: African lineage and syncretic
cultural exchanges in, 3, 5, 10–12, 248–
49; and the body itself as an instrument
of liberation, 3; the *break*, improvisational interlude, 13; Broadway commercialization and whitening of, 247; buck
dancing (pre-tap), 12–13, 18; "cool" of,
29, 248; as diasporic form, 248, 249;
early film technology not good for, 29;
evolution of style, 18–19; factors in
decline of, 3; fugitivity of the form, 249;
Hollywood Jim Crow and, 29–30; jazz
ethics, 13; jazzman's academy, and
joyous expression of self-emancipation,
13–14, 16, 249; Le Corbusier on, 19; as
marker of generational conflict in the
African American community, 3–4;
masculinism and, 13; memory within
the tradition, 19; minstrel performance
traditions of, 3, 14–16; and modernity,
references to, 19; polyrhythms and, 12,
18, 19; and racial slanders against black
talent, 29; as singular element in the
grammar of African American culture,
16–17; social relations among the dancing ensemble, 12–13, 16; vaudeville

Whipper, Leigh, 82–83

white audiences: as fascinated by black culture, 18, 34; *Porgy and Bess* and, 76–79, 80, 81–83, 86–88; SDJ as caretaking, 115–17, 135, 169; vaudeville and deference to, xxvii; and "vogue" for all things Harlem, 18. *See also* appropriation

White Citizens Council, 145, 218, 221

white ethnics, "bootstraps" ideology and disavowal of white privilege, 236

White, Josh, 40, 212; as blacklisted, 63

White, Kevin, 225

White League, 144

White, Loray (brief marriage to SDJ), 150, 185

whiteness: of American Jews, at the moment of SDJ's conversion, 138; of minstrelsy scripts in government-issue troop entertainment manual (*Minstrel Shows*), 54–55; Myrdal's *American Dilemma* and unconscious bias toward, 196–97; of the racial humor at the *Dean Martin Celebrity Roast* of SDJ, 137–38; tap dancing commercialization and whitening, 247; television and creation and policing as norm, 119–21; of white women, as property, 150

white-over-black structures of the industry: "Birth of the Blues" song, 32, 34; *A Man Called Adam* (1966 film) and seriousness of parting ways with, 65, 88, 95, 248; oversexualization and de-sexualization, 10; and persistence in patterns of white hostility and black strategy, 118–19; persistence of, 119; and postwar all-black films engaging mixed-race liberal audiences, 65, 70; racial ventriloquism and, 9–10, 79–80; the Rat Pack and, 111; *Rufus Jones* and the African American shorts genre, 6, 9–10; self-abnegating humor, 10; top-rung black talents must have white management and coterie, 119; in *Yes I Can*, 181

White Slave Traffic Act (Mann Act), 159

white supremacy and white supremacists: assigning cerebral qualities to whiteness and bodily ones to blackness, 29; in Charlottesville, VA, and Donald Trump, 245; as code in Westerns, 122; in the Democratic Party, 152–53; multiculturalist white supremacy, 241–42; as "paltry dividend" (Du Bois), xxvi; regulation of interracial relationships as foundationally linked to, 143–46, 152–53, 165; Republican "Southern strategy," 245; *Sergeants 3* as naturalizing, 129; slander of black ability-as-mimicry, 29, 31; trope of Reconstruction as failure of black governance, 197. *See also* interracial relationships and sexuality; Jim Crow system of segregation and hierarchy; race and racism; segregation; slavery; white supremacy and white supremacists, triggered by SDJ; white violence against black people

white supremacy and white supremacists, triggered by SDJ: conversion to Judaism, 208; *Golden Boy,* 165; gunslinging skills, 124; intermarriage (May Britt), 141–42, 146, 152–53, 187, 208, 218, 221

white violence against black people: on black veterans in the postwar era, 60–61; in context of *Porgy and Bess* film release, 88; emancipation and increased white "madness" of, 45, 143–45; increasing in advance of significant gains or of promises fulfilled, 45; lynching, 143, 144; and the myth of the black rapist, 143, 144, 145; police complicity or full participation in, 46; World War I, 45; World War II against black soldiers, 44–45; World War II and, 36, 45–49

White, Walter, 61, 67, 68

Whitman, Alice, 13

Whitman Sisters, 1, 25

Why Me? (1989 autobiography with Jane and Burt Boyar): on being black, 237–38; on Civil Rights issues, 237; on escaping from racism, 100; on the pain of being disinvited from JFK's inauguration, 153, 237; *Yes I Can* stories reiterated in, 237

The Wild, Wild West (TV), 123

Williams, Bert, xxi, 3, 12, 15, 17, 20, 106, 137, 182, 246; *In Dahomey* (1902 theater), 17–18

Williams, Cecil, 250–51
Williams, John, 43; *This Is My Country Too,* 199
Williams, Sergeant Gene, 59, 175–76
Willis, Jan, 120
Will Mastin Trio: black travelers and trouble finding accommodations on the circuit, 27–28; Ciro's breakthrough, 103–4, 118, 178, 181; codeswitching backstage, 181; concern for reputation of SDJ in the black community, 183–84; death of vaudeville and the struggle to survive, 26, 28–29; generational and philosophical differences within, 103, 179–80, 182–84, 191; gun-handling act of SDJ in, 123; impressions of white people by SDJ, 102–3, 104, 180; minstrel moves by, as chafing SDJ, xxvii, 118, 180–81; postwar maturation of SDJ into the "kid in the middle" of, 37, *62, 63,* 180; postwar switch to opening for white headliners in white clubs, 101–4, *102, 106,* 108–9, 118, *178*; and racism, shielding the young SDJ from, 27, 35, 49–50, 174; and racism, the adult SDJ looking back on the experiences of, 174–75; *Sweet and Low* (1947 short film), 101–2; tap dance of, 18, 101–2, 104; triumphs alternating with Jim Crow insults, 177–79. See also *Colgate Comedy Hour, The*
Will Vodery Girls, 6, 9
Wilson, August, 124, 235
Wilson, Eunice, 6
Wilson, Flip, 233
Wilson, Lionel, 229
Wilson, Nancy, 229–30
Wilson, Woodrow, 39
Winfrey, Oprah, 235
Winter, Marian Hannah, 11
Winters, Shelley, 222
Wolfe, Patrick, 126
women: and group right to vote, xxiii; labor of, and the Civil Rights Movement, 44, 218; and the masculinist logic that defines the "voting public" as the "fighting public," 38; whiteness as property and, 150; World War II defense-industry work and, 45

Women's Auxiliary of the Brotherhood of Sleeping Car Porters, 44
Wood, Cyrus, 6
Wooding, Russell, Jubilee Singers, 6
Woolworth sit-ins, 199
World War I: anti-black violence, 45; Jim Crow military and, 39, 43; racial egalitarianism in Europe, 188
World War II: anti-black violence and, 36, 44–49; and individual prejudice as the source of racism, 195; as inflection point in racial history of the USA, 36; initial attempt of SDJ to enlist in, 35; newsreels and documentaries and vision of a desegregated America, 67; "official anti-racism" of the federal government established in, 36, 39–40; the Pacific theater as full-on race war, 36, 40–41; racial egalitarianism in Europe, 188; US military propaganda, 41. *See also* Fort Warren (Cheyenne, WY), service of SDJ; Jim Crow military in World War II; racial liberalism in the postwar era; World War II troop entertainment
World War II troop entertainment: black entertainers as Jim Crowed in, 58–59; entertainment specialist role of SDJ, 37, 52–54, 59, 176–77; minstrelsy prescribed for, 54–59; racial ambivalences and ambiguities embedded in, 55–59; *This Is the Army* (1943 film), 55–58, *57,* 262n80
Wyoming. *See* Fort Warren (Cheyenne, WY), service of SDJ

Yes I Can (1965 autobiography with Jane and Burt Boyar): as assimilationist narrative, 172–74, 190; on attempted suicide, 186–87; on the audience response after "Birth of the Blues," 33, 168–69; authorship involving white journalists, 168, 171–74, 192; on being drafted to to fight, 51; as best-selling treatment of race and racism, 168–69, 203; on bigger stardom as racial hatred's antidote, 169, 176, 179, 182; and the black community, critiques of, 136; on black performance practices and white

Founded in 1893,
UNIVERSITY OF CALIFORNIA PRESS
publishes bold, progressive books and journals
on topics in the arts, humanities, social sciences,
and natural sciences—with a focus on social
justice issues—that inspire thought and action
among readers worldwide.

The UC PRESS FOUNDATION
raises funds to uphold the press's vital role
as an independent, nonprofit publisher, and
receives philanthropic support from a wide
range of individuals and institutions—and from
committed readers like you. To learn more, visit
ucpress.edu/supportus.